ENVIRONMENTAL ISSUES
IN AMERICAN HISTORY

ENVIRONMENTAL ISSUES IN AMERICAN HISTORY

A Reference Guide with Primary Documents

Chris J. Magoc

Major Issues in American History
Randall M. Miller, Series Editor

GREENWOOD PRESS
Westport, Connecticut • London

10-19-2007
LAN
₱ 85

Library of Congress Cataloging-in-Publication Data

Magoc, Chris J., 1960–
  Environmental issues in American history : a reference guide with primary documents /
Chris J. Magoc.
      p.   cm.—(Major issues in American history, ISSN 1535–3192)
  Includes bibliographical references and index.
  ISBN 0–313–32208–2 (alk. paper)
  1. United States—Environmental conditions—History—Sources. 2. Human ecology—United
States—History—Sources. 3. Nature conservation—United States—History—Sources.
  4. Environmental protection—United States—History—Sources. I. Title. II. Series.
  GE150.M338 2006
  333.70973—dc22   2005034852

British Library Cataloguing in Publication Data is available.

Library of Congress Catalog Card Number: 2005034852
ISBN: 0–313–32208–2
ISSN: 1535–3192

First published in 2006

Greenwood Press, 88 Post Road West, Westport, CT 06881
An imprint of Greenwood Publishing Group, Inc.
www.greenwood.com

Printed in the United States of America

The paper used in this book complies with the
Permanent Paper Standard issued by the National
Information Standards Organization (Z39.48–1984).

10 9 8 7 6 5 4 3 2 1

ADVISORY BOARD

For Mary Ellen

Contents

Series Foreword

This series of books presents major issues in American history as they have developed since the republic's inception to their present incarnation. The issues range across the spectrum of American experience and encompass political, economic, social, and cultural concerns. By focusing on the "major issues" in American history, the series emphasizes the importance of an issues-centered approach to teaching and thinking about America's past. *Major Issues in American History* thus reframes historical inquiry in terms of themes and problems rather than as mere chronology. In so doing, the series addresses the current, pressing need among educators and policymakers for case studies charting the development of major issues over time, so as to make it possible to approach such issues intelligently in our time.

The series is premised on the belief that understanding America demands grasping the contentious nature of its past and applying that understanding to current issues in politics, law, government, society, and culture. If "America" was born, and remains, as an idea and an experiment, as so many thinkers and observers have argued, issues inevitably have shaped whatever that America was and is. In 1801, in his presidential inaugural, Thomas Jefferson reminded Americans that the great strength of the new nation resided in the broad consensus citizens shared as to the rightness and necessity of republican government and the Constitution. That consensus, Jefferson continued, made dissent possible and tolerable, and, we might add, encouraged dissent and debate about critical issues thereafter. Every generation of Americans has wrestled with such issues as defining and defending freedom(s), determining America's place in the world, waging war and making peace, receiving and assimilating new peoples, balancing church and state, forming a "more perfect union," and pursuing "happiness." American identity(ies) and interest(s) are not fixed.

A nation of many peoples on the move across space and up and down the socioeconomic ladder cannot have it so. A nation charged with ensuring that, in Lincoln's words, "government of the people, by the people, and for the people shall not perish from the earth" cannot have it so. A nation whose heroes are not only soldiers and statesmen but also ex-slaves, women reformers, inventors, thinkers, and cowboys and Indians cannot have it so. Americans have never rested content locked into set molds in thinking and doing—not so long as dissent and difference are built into the character of a people that dates its birth to an American Revolution and annually celebrates that lineage. As such, Americans have been, and are, by heritage and habit an issues-oriented people.

We are also a political people. Issues as varied as race relations, labor organizing, women's place in the work force, the practice of religious beliefs, immigration, westward movement, and environmental protection have been, and remain, matters of public concern and debate and readily intrude into politics. A people committed to "rights" invariably argues for them, low voter turnout in recent elections notwithstanding. All the major issues in American history have involved political controversies as to their meaning and application. But the extent to which issues assume a political cast varies.

As the public interest spread to virtually every aspect of life during the twentieth century—into boardrooms, ballparks, and even bedrooms—the political compass enlarged with it. In time, every economic, social, and cultural issue of consequence in the United States has entered the public realm of debate and political engagement. Questions of rights—for example, to free speech, to freedom of religion, to equality before the law—and authority are political by nature. So, too, are questions about war and society, foreign policy, law and order, the delivery of public services, the control of the nation's borders, and access to and the uses of public land and resources. The books in *Major Issues in American History* take up just those issues. Thus, all the books in this series build political and public policy concerns into their basic framework.

The format for the series speaks directly to the issues-oriented character of the American people and the democratic polity and to the teaching of issues-centered history. The issues-centered approach to history views the past thematically. Such a history respects chronology but does not attempt to recite a single narrative or simple historical chronology of "facts." Rather, issues-centered history is problem-solving history. It organizes historical inquiry around a series of questions central to understanding the character and functions of American life, culture, ideas, politics, and institutions. Such questions invariably derive from current concerns that demand historical perspective. Whether determining the role of women and minorities and shaping public policy, or considering the "proper" relationship between church and state, or thinking about U.S. military obligations in the global context, to name several persistent issues, the teacher and student—indeed, responsible citizens everywhere—must ask such questions as "how and why did the present circumstance and interests come to be as they are" and "what other choices as to a policy and practice have there been" so as to measure the dimensions and point the direction of the issue. History matters in that regard.

Each book in the series focuses on a particular issue, with an eye to encouraging readers and users to consider how Americans at different times engaged the issue based on the particular values, interests, and political and social structures of the day. As such, each book is also necessarily events-based in that the key event that triggered public concern and debate about a major issue at a particular moment serves as the case study for the issue as it was understood and presented during that historical period. Each book offers a historical narrative overview of a major issue as it evolved; the narrative provides both the context for understanding the issue's place in the larger American experience and the touchstone for considering the ways Americans encountered and engaged the issue at different times. A timeline further establishes the chronology and place of the issue in American history. The core of each book is the series of between ten to fifteen case studies of watershed events that defined the issue, arranged chronologically to make it possible to track the development of the issue closely over time. Each case study stands as a separate chapter. Each case study opens with a historical overview of the event and a discussion of the significant contemporary opposing views of the issue as occasioned by the event. A selection of four to nine critical primary documents (printed whole or in excerpts and introduced with brief headnotes) from the period under review presents differing points of view on the issue. In some volumes, each chapter also includes an annotated research guide of print and non-print sources to guide further research and reflection on the event and the issue. Each volume in the series concludes with a general bibliography that provides ready reference to the key works on the subject at issue.

Such an arrangement ensures that readers and users—students and teachers alike—will approach the major issues within a problem-solving framework. Indeed, the design of the series and each book in it demands that students and teachers understand that the crucial issues of American history have histories and that the significance of those issues might best be discovered and recovered by understanding how Americans at different times addressed them, shaped them, and bequeathed them to the next generation. Such a dialectic for each issue encourages a comparative perspective not only in seeing America's past but also, and perhaps even more so, in thinking about its present. Individually and collectively, the books in *Major Issues in American History* thereby demonstrate anew William Faulkner's dictum that the past is never past.

Randall M. Miller
Series Editor

Preface and Acknowledgments

This book reflects more than a decade of teaching, thinking, and previous writing about one of the passions of my life, U. S. environmental history. Although still in its relative infancy, this multi- and interdisciplinary field encompasses the work of historians, scientists, journalists, geographers, sociologists, economists, public health professionals, and anthropologists. Indeed, only a small portion of the vast body of environmental history generated over the past thirty years or so is represented in the bibliography found at the end of this volume. Obviously, *Environmental Issues in American History* does not aim to represent the totality of the field. Quite daunting enough, its overarching purpose is to distill the American experience with and in the environment through representative pivotal moments in that history. I suspect that a number of the sixteen episodes highlighted here would not make the list of many of my colleagues or students— a reminder that all history is as much art as science, vulnerable to human subjectivity even while it remains grounded in empirical fact.

Given that inherent difficulty, and also the need to sweep over the entire course of American history, I aimed first to pronounce those events that served to ingrain, in the form of government policy, American beliefs about nature. Policies such as the Land Ordinance of 1785 and the Reclamation Act of 1902 reflected the thinking of the political and economic elite of their time certainly, and bore profound environmental, economic, and social consequences for the nation. Other chapters capture enduring cultural and political tensions over the environment, such as the conflict between preservation and conservation forces in the Hetch-Hetchy Valley of Yosemite National Park. Still others, like those focused on Rachel Carson and Lois Gibbs, illustrate the power of environmental history to turn on a dime through the force of personal and intellectual courage or citizen action. I wish I could say that it is "all here." Alas, this is akin to a box of snapshots that cannot fully depict one's life. My hope is that they are representative enough and the interpretation sufficiently cogent that I have satisfied the other key objective of this volume: to reinforce the central importance to American history of the relationship Americans have had with the natural world.

The book begins with a detailed chronology of major events in U.S. environmental history. Each chapter then offers first an overview of the history of the environmental issue, followed by a selection of primary documents that reveal contending perspectives of that history. Just as the chronological scope of topics extends from the Euro-American dispossession of Indian land to the contemporary debate over energy policy, the selection of documents is also wide-ranging. Readers will find court decisions, speeches, magazine and newspaper excerpts, and congressional testimony, to name a few examples. A topical annotated bibliography follows the end of each chapter, with a more comprehensive bibliography following the final chapter.

I am grateful beyond words to my editor, Dr. Randall Miller, who graciously invited me to this task long ago and provided encouraging feedback, insightful comments, and helpful editorial suggestions on earlier drafts of the volume. His generous spirit and the seemingly endless patience of Greenwood Press were indispensable. Many thanks also to Lynn Falk at the interlibrary loan desk of Hammermill Library at Mercyhurst College. Lynn's perseverance in tracking down many of the documents contained in the book was invaluable. I am in debt also to Melissa MacFarland, who served as my student Research Assistant in 2002–2003 and conducted much of the primary source research and preliminary analysis of several chapters. Her work was exceptional. I acknowledge also the generous assistance of the Mercyhurst College Faculty Research program, through which I was able to secure a little more time out of the classroom to advance this project in its early stages. Always, there is my wife, Mary Ellen, without whose love and presence I simply could not be. And to our children, Ethan and Caroline, thank you for reminding me daily why the work of creating a more sustainable future is both sacred and necessary.

Chronology of Events

Sixteenth–Eighteenth Centuries

Early 1500s	European disease begins to ravage Native American populations
1520–1540s	Spanish introduce cattle and horses to North America
Early 1600s	Virginia and Massachusetts colonists learn cultivation of maize and other New World crops from Native American tribes; import livestock, vegetation, and disease; begin fencing lands for livestock
1619	First Virginia tobacco crop shipped to England; first slaves arrive in British North America
1630s	First smallpox epidemic in New England devastates Algonquians
1643	First major iron works established in North America, in Lynn, Massachusetts
Late 1600s	Beaver population in southern New England severely reduced by overhunting
1690	Proprietor William Penn requires Pennsylvania settlers to preserve one acre of trees for every five acres cleared
1691	British Broad Arrow Policy reserves large trees in Massachusetts for ship building
1699	Virginia legislature adopts regulation to limit hunting of white-tailed deer

1743	American Philosophical Society organized, promotes scientific agriculture
1750s	Deforestation in New England reported to be causing regional climate change
1762–1769	Philadelphia committee led by Benjamin Franklin attempts to regulate waste disposal and water pollution
1770s–1782	Inventor Oliver Evans develops the idea for the high-pressure steam engine later used in locomotives and devises the first automatic mill near Newport, Delaware
1785	Land Ordinance passed by Congress established the means by which lands in the Northwest Territory were to be sold, established precedent for lands further west
1787	Northwest Ordinance passed, provided the means by which new states would be created out of western lands and admitted into the Union
1790	First U.S. Census counts nearly 4 million people, 90 percent engaged in agriculture
1793	Eli Whitney develops "gin" for rapid processing of short-staple cotton
1795	Yazoo Land Fraud scandal in Georgia highlights early America's speculative land hunger

Nineteenth Century

1780s–1820	Enormous land cessions from Native American tribes to the United States
1790–1820	Accelerated migration into Ohio and Mississippi river valleys
1801	Creek chieftain Mad Dog complains: "our deer and game is almost gone"
1803–1806	Louisiana Purchase and Lewis and Clark "Corps of Discovery"
1806	Lieutenant Zebulon Pike's expedition into the newly formed Louisiana Territory
1808	John Jacob Astor organizes the American Fur Company
1811	First successful steamboat run down the Ohio and Mississippi rivers
1812–1815	War of 1812 defeats British, cripples Indian resistance in Ohio River valley, and opens Gulf region to settlement
1820	Following Stephen Long expedition to the Rocky Mountains and Great Plains, maps of the region declare land between the Mississippi River and the Rocky Mountains to be an uninhabitable "Great American Desert"

1820s–1830s	Hudson River School of painting helps place nature at center of emerging American culture
1825	Completion of Erie Canal accelerates movement of resources and goods along an east-west axis
1825–1860	Cotton becomes the largest American export
1826	Colonel John Stevens demonstrates feasibility of circular-track steam locomotion
1830	Peter Cooper designs the *Tom Thumb*, the first American-built steam locomotive operated on a common-carrier railroad
1830s	Final Indian removal to "Indian Territory" west of Mississippi River
1830s	Lowell, Massachusetts, textile mill owners reshape water law
1832	Artist George Catlin becomes first to propose "nation's park" in the West; Arkansas Hot Springs established as a "national reserve"
1834	Cyrus McCormick patents grain reaper
1835	Ralph Waldo Emerson publishes his essay, *Nature*
1837	John Deere patents steel plow
1842	Landscape architect Andrew Jackson Downing copublishes *Cottage Residences,* enshrines rural simplicity as an early suburban middle-class romantic ideal
1842	New York City physician John Griscom writes *The Sanitary Condition of the Laboring Population of New York City*, linking poverty and disease
1845	The legendary but very real man, Johnny Appleseed, dies
1846	Mormons begin irrigating Utah territory
1848	Gold discovered at Sutter's Mill on California's American River
1849	Cholera strikes New York City, killing 5,000, mostly poor Irish, leading to the first serious calls for urban environmental reform
1854	Daniel Halladay introduces mechanical windmill for pumping water
1854	Henry David Thoreau publishes *Walden*
1855	First comprehensive city sewer plan in U.S. in Chicago (Baltimore sewer system, begun in 1915, is the last major eastern city to build a comprehensive system)
1856	Bessemer blast furnace developed for steel production
1857	Study on depleted fish populations in Connecticut River completed by George Perkins Marsh

1858	Frederick Law Olmsted designs Central Park in New York City, the first park designed entirely for public use
1859	Colonel Edwin Drake successfully drills for oil in Titusville, Pennsylvania
1860s	Railroads and regional boosters in Great Plains promote former "Great American Desert" as a new "American Garden of Eden"
1861	U.S. Sanitary Commission formed to help prevent disease-related death in the Civil War
1862	Homestead Act and Morrill Land Grant College Act passed
1864	President Abraham Lincoln signs legislation granting the Yosemite Valley to California
1864	George Perkins Marsh publishes *Man and Nature*
1866	American Society for the Prevention of Cruelty to Animals founded
1866	First long "cattle drive" out of Texas
1867	Chicago opens new waterworks system, drawing water from Lake Michigan
1867	Pennsylvania legislature rejects bill to regulate water pollution, despite pollution in Delaware River threatening public health
Late 1860s	Organized hunts of North American bison on the southern Great Plains begin
1869	First transcontinental railroad completed
1870	First coal mine safety law passed in Pennsylvania following a fire that killed 179 men
1871	A result of deforestation, the Peshtigo Fire kills 1,500 in northern Wisconsin
1871	U.S. Fish Commission formed to study decline of coastal fisheries
1872	American Public Health Association established
1872	General Mining Law passed, allows purchase of mining rights for five dollars per acre with minimal environmental cleanup
1872	Yellowstone National Park established
1872	Arbor Day initiated by J. Sterling Morton of Nebraska City
1873	Joseph Glidden invents barbed wire, reshapes the western range
1875	Bonanza (large mechanized) farming begins in Red River valley, Dakota Territory
1875	President Ulysses Grant vetoes a bill protecting buffalo and other wildlife
1876	American Association for the Advancement of Science calls for federal legislation to protect timberlands
1877	Massachusetts passes first factory inspection law in the nation

1878	John Wesley Powell argues for low-density development of the arid West
1879	Thomas Edison develops electric light bulb
1880s	First U.S. municipal smoke abatement laws aimed at reducing air pollution, regulated under local boards of health under common law nuisance statutes
1880s–1894	Preservationists defend Yellowstone National Park from attempts to extend rail line into the park
1881	Interior Department's Division of Forestry established
1882	Massachusetts passes first pure food laws, inspired by investigations of Ellen Swallow Richards, first female graduate of Massachusetts Institute of Technology and first scientist to apply concept of "ecology" to the human environment
1882	World's first hydroelectric power plant starts operation in Appleton, Wisconsin
1883	Last of the northern Great Plains bison herds slaughtered
1884	Judge Lorenzo Sawyer's decision ends hydraulic mining in California
1885	Following the near-demise of the bison, U.S. Biological Survey created
1885	New York state legislature establishes Adirondack Forest Preserve
1887	Boone and Crockett Club founded by Theodore Roosevelt and George Bird Grinnell
Early 1890s	Minnesota's Mesabi region becomes number one producer of iron ore
1890	General Federation of Women's Clubs founded, conservation a major focus
1890s–1910	City Beautiful Movement aims at urban environmental planning and reform
1891	First National Forest Preserves established by President Benjamin Harrison
1892	Department of Agriculture distributes arsenic compounds and lead arsenate as insecticides; frequent reports of illness and death from eating sprayed fruit are dismissed by government and industry officials as "absolutely without foundation"
1892	Sierra Club organized by John Muir
1893	Historian Frederick Jackson Turner delivers lecture on the "Significance of the Frontier in American History"

1893	George Westinghouse demonstrates a system for generating and transmitting alternating electric current, propelling the widespread application of electricity
1894	Col. George Waring takes over and revolutionizes New York City Department of Streets Cleaning
1897	Forest Management Act passed, authorizes managed commercial use of public forests
1898	Gifford Pinchot becomes head of Interior Department's Division of Forestry
1899	Rivers and Harbors Act passed, first federal recognition of water pollution

Twentieth Century

1900	Lacey Act passed, regulates interstate traffic of endangered wild birds, result of lobbying of women's clubs and Audubon Society
1900	Missouri sues Illinois and Chicago for polluting the Mississippi River
1901	*Our National Parks* by John Muir is published, establishes his national reputation
1901–1909	President Theodore Roosevelt greatly expands National Forest and National Park systems, establishes first national Wildlife Refuges and National Monuments; more than 230 million acres placed under federal management during his tenure
1902	Newlands Reclamation Act passed, establishing the Bureau of Reclamation and putting the federal government in the irrigation business
1902	George Washington Carver publishes *How to Build Up Worn Out Soils*
1903	Naturalist John Burroughs attacks popular nature writers as "nature fakers"
1903	Planning for World's Fair sparks smoke abatement movement in St. Louis
1904	Child lead poisoning linked to lead-based paints
1904	Upton Sinclair's *The Jungle* published, exposed horrible conditions of meatpacking houses
1905	Division of Forestry transferred to the Department of Agriculture and becomes the U.S. Forest Service
1906	Congress establishes Yosemite National Park
1906	"Dryland" farming attempted in Great Plains after cyclic series of droughts
1906	Meat Inspection Act, Pure Food and Drug Act passed to regulate slaughterhouses and food processing industries

1906   National Antiquities Act passed, establishing Devils Tower National Monument and paving the way for a system of national monuments

1907–1913   John Muir leads an ultimately failed effort to prevent damming of Hetch-Hetchy Valley in Yosemite National Park

1908   First continuous chlorination system in the U.S. begins operation in Jersey City to purify drinking water

1908   First warning (from a Swedish chemist) that human industrial activity was warming the planet

1908   Progressive reformer Caroline Bartlett Crane begins city and state "sanitary surveys"

1909   Urged by President Roosevelt and Gifford Pinchot, National Conservation Commission Report produced

1910   Alice Hamilton investigates "dangerous trades" in Illinois lead industry, pioneers occupational health reform

1910   U.S. Bureau of Mines established after mine disaster in West Virginia kills 372

1914   Last passenger pigeon dies in captivity in the Cincinnati Zoo

1914–1925   "Great Plow-up" of Great Plains for wheat production helps trigger Dust Bowl

1916   National Park Service established

1916   Margaret Sanger opens first birth control clinic

1920s   Tremendous expansion of auto, oil, gasoline industries, road building

1920s   Electrification of manufacturing accelerates

1920   Water Power Act authorizes federal hydroelectric projects

1921   General Motors researchers recommend tetraethyl lead (TEL) as an antiknock gasoline additive, goes on market despite secret Public Health Service report warning of dangers

1922   Army Corps of Engineers harbor masters issue grim report of coastal pollution and degraded fisheries

1922   Colorado River Compact signed among the states of Arizona, California, Colorado, Nevada, New Mexico, Utah, and Wyoming; calls for massive dam building to advance industrial and agricultural development of the region

1922   National Coast Anti Pollution League formed to stop oil dumping

1924   Teapot Dome oil leasing scandal involving Interior Department secretary Albert Fall

1924   A weak Oil Pollution Act passed, with minimal regulations and penalties

1924–1925	Seventeen oil workers die, some "violently insane" from exposure to leaded gasoline
1926	Amid criticism from Alice Hamilton and other public health experts, the U.S. Surgeon General allows leaded gasoline to continue to be sold
1927	Five New Jersey women, called the Radium Girls, file lawsuits against former employer for negligence in creating dangerous working conditions. All five later die of radiation-induced cancer
1928	Public Health Service begins checking air pollution in eastern U.S. cities, reporting sunlight cut by 20 to 50 percent in New York City
1928	St. Francis Dam, part of controversial and corruption-laced Owens Valley water project in Los Angeles, gives way, killing over 500
1932	First lawsuits filed by workers and families affected by Gauley Bridge/Hawks Nest disaster in West Virginia; 700 die, 2,000 debilitated by silicosis (mostly African American) while working for a hydroelectric tunneling project
1933	Civilian Conservation Corps formed; 2,000 camps opened, trees planted, roads, fire towers, buildings and bridges constructed across the country
1933	Tennessee Valley Authority established under President Franklin Roosevelt's New Deal, with wide-ranging mission: conservation, public utility regulation, agricultural development, and social and economic development of impoverished regions
1934	Dust Bowl storms begin, prompting the establishment of the Soil Conservation Service and the passage of the Taylor Grazing Act, designed to restore and scientifically manage the grasslands of the Great Plains
1935	Wilderness Society founded
Mid-1930s	Franklin Roosevelt's New Deal agricultural policies encourage conservation but also favor large landowners over small and single staple crop farming over poly-cropping
1936	Hoover Dam completed
1936	Rural Electrification Act passed, bringing electricity to the nation's rural farms
1939	Severe smog episode in St. Louis keeps lanterns on during midday for a week
1941	St. Louis adopts first strict smoke control ordinance in the United States
1941–1945	Manhattan Project produces the world's first atomic bomb; bombs dropped at Hiroshima and Nagasaki bring the world into the nuclear age

1945   U.S. President Harry Truman issues Proclamation on the Continental Shelf clearing way for oil drilling offshore

1946–1948   United States conducts nuclear tests at Bikini and Eniwetok atolls, Marshall Islands, South Pacific

1947   Marjory Stoneman Douglas, who spearheaded the campaign for the establishment of Everglades National Park, is honored by President Truman at park's opening

1947   First Levittown development built, spurs nationwide postwar suburban boom

1948   Donora, Pennsylvania, smog incident; twenty people die, 600 are hospitalized

1948   Federal Water Pollution Control Act passed

1949   Aldo Leopold's *A Sand County Almanac* published

1949   First U.S. conference on air pollution, sponsored by Public Health Service

1951   Nature Conservancy formed; by the year 2000, had protected 10 million acres of land from development

1953   New York City smog incident kills more than 150 people

1953   Room air conditioner sales exceed 1 million units, demand exceeds supply

1954   Smog shuts down schools and industry in Los Angeles for much of October

1955   Air Pollution Control Act passed; weak, but paves way for stronger legislation

1955–1956   Sierra Club leads successful opposition to a dam in Dinosaur National Monument

1956   Interstate Highway Act passed

1957   First commercial nuclear power generator opens at Shippingport, Pennsylvania; Price-Anderson Act limits liability for nuclear utilities and contractors in the event of an accident at a nuclear power plant

1960   Wallace Stegner's *The Wilderness Letter* advocates federal wilderness protection

1962   Rachel Carson publishes *Silent Spring*, generating intense controversy over the use of pesticides, which ultimately leads to their regulation and the banning of DDT

1962   Murray Bookchin publishes *Our Synthetic Environment*

1963   Partial Nuclear Test Ban Treaty bans above-ground and underwater testing

1964   Wilderness Act passed

1965	Congress passes Water Quality Act setting standards for states
1965	Congress passes Water Quality Act and Solid Waste Disposal Act
1965	Senate hearings on leaded gasoline expose fraudulent industry research on health effects
1965	Sierra Club sues to protect New York's Storm King Mountain from a power project; case establishes precedent that an organization can have standing in court for a noneconomic interest; also leads to formation of the National Resources Defense Council and the Environmental Defense Fund
1965	*Time* publishes story on the biological "Death of Lake Erie"
1965	U.S. Public Health Service report on unsafe and unhealthy working conditions of working Americans helps lead to establishment of the Occupational Safety and Health Administration (OSHA) in 1970
1967	Clean Air Act passed, authorizing grants to state air pollution control agencies to meet air quality standards
1967	Environmental Defense Fund established, initially to push for a ban on DDT
1968	Edward Abbey publishes *Desert Solitaire*
1968	Paul Erlich publishes *The Population Bomb*
1968	Garrett Hardin publishes "The Tragedy of the Commons" in *Science*
1968	United Farm Workers make pesticide exposure a central organizing issue
1968	Wild and Scenic Rivers Act and National Trails System Act passed
1969	Alaskan oil exploration and development begins on the North Slope
1969	Cuyahoga River bursts into flames five stories high from oil and chemical pollution
1969	National Environmental Policy Act passed, establishing environmental review of federally funded projects
1969	Santa Barbara oil well blowout covers thirty miles of beach with oily tar
1970	Clean Air Act passed, demonstrating strong national commitment on air quality
1970	Environmental Protection Agency established
1970	First Earth Day celebrated
1970	Occupational Health and Safety Act passed
1971	Barry Commoner publishes *The Closing Circle*, articulating "rules of ecology"
1971	Greenpeace founded in response to U.S. nuclear testing in Aleutian Islands
1972	Buffalo Creek, West Virginia, strip mining flood disaster kills 125 people

1972   DDT banned
1972   Donella Meadows publishes *Limits to Growth*
1972   Federal Water Pollution Control Act, Coastal Zone Management
            Act, Toxic Substances Control Act passed
1972   First bottle recycling bill passes in Oregon
1972   United Nations Conference on the Human Environment
            convenes in Sweden

1973   Eighty nations sign Convention on International Trade in
            Endangered Species (CITES), considered the "Magna Carta for
            wildlife"; complementary Endangered Species Act becomes law
            in the U.S.
1973   First "environmental strike" ever (over occupational health)
            waged by Oil, Chemical, and Atomic Workers Union
1973   E. F. Schumacher publishes *Small Is Beautiful: Economics as if
            People Mattered*
1973   U.S. support for Israel in Middle East conflict provokes OPEC oil
            embargo and the energy crisis
1973   Congress approves Alaskan oil pipeline

1973–1974   Tellico Dam controversy, Endangered Species Act blamed for
            temporarily halting massive dam project on Tennessee River

1974   Scientists warn that refrigerant CFCs (chlorofluorocarbons) are
            breaking up the protective ozone layer shielding the earth from
            excessive ultraviolet rays
1974   Karen Silkwood dies suspiciously on way to meet *New York
            Times* reporter with documents concerning safety problems at
            Kerr-McGee nuclear facility

1975   Edward Abbey publishes *The Monkey Wrench Gang*
1975   Atlantic salmon return to Connecticut River after 100-year
            absence

Mid-1970s   First modern warnings from international scientific community
            of global warming caused by buildup of greenhouse gases from
            human activity

1976   Catastrophic failure of Grand Teton Dam in Wyoming kills
            fourteen
1976   EPA and federal courts order final phaseout of leaded gasoline
1976   Resource Conservation and Recovery Act (RCRA) to regulate
            hazardous waste and garbage, Federal Land Policy Management
            Act passed

1977   In *TVA v. Hill*, U.S. Supreme Court upholds the 1973
            Endangered Species Act, stops construction of Tellico Dam
            (decision later reversed by Congress)

Late 1970s Corporate-funded Sagebrush Rebellion in the West challenges
            federal environmental regulation of public lands

1978   Robert Bullard's "Cancer Alley" report exposes DDT contamination in Triana, Alabama, and helps spark "environmental justice" movement

1978   National Energy Act passed, includes tax credit incentives for development of renewable clean energy sources (later eliminated during Reagan administration)

1978–1980   Battle waged by Lois Gibbs and Love Canal Homeowners Association over deadly exposure to toxic waste results in their relocation and ultimately federal Superfund legislation to clean up hazardous waste nationwide

1979   Earth First! organized

1979   Three Mile Island nuclear accident near Harrisburg, Pennsylvania

1980   After intense lobbying by Carter administration and celebrities like John Denver, Congress passes Alaska National Interest Lands Conservation Act, preserving over 100 million acres and 26 rivers

1980   Superfund (CERCLA: The Comprehensive Environmental Response, Compensation and Liability Act) passed to clean up toxic waste

1981   Vice President George Bush's Task Force on Regulatory Relief proposes to relax or eliminate U.S. leaded gas phaseout, despite evidence of serious health problems

1982   PCB-dumping episode in a largely African American community of Warren County, North Carolina, further fuels environmental justice movement

1983   Reagan cabinet members, James Watt of Interior and Anne Gorsuch of EPA, resign under public protest of antienvironmental policies and decisions

1986   In response to Bhopal, India, catastrophic disaster and other incidents in the U.S. involving chemical exposure, Congress passes Emergency Planning and Community Right to Know Act

1987   Montreal Protocol international agreement to phase out ozone-depleting chemicals signed by twenty-four countries, including the United States

1987   U.S. General Accounting Office study shows strong correlation between location of toxic waste dump sites and minority and poor communities

1989   Congress halts logging in Alaska's Tsongass National Forest, the last undisturbed temperate rain forest in the United States.

1989   Department of Energy estimates cost of nuclear weapons production cleanup at $53 billion to $92 billion—an estimate more than doubled later on

1989   *Exxon Valdez* oil tanker runs aground in Prince William Sound, Alaska, spilling 11 million gallons

1990   Clean Air Act strengthened

1990   Thirtieth Anniversary of Earth Day coincides with United Nations call for global reductions in carbon dioxide emissions causing global warming

1990–1991   Persian Gulf War creates environmental disaster through Saddam Hussein's burning of oil wells, U.S. use of depleted uranium bombs; triggers staggeringly high rates of cancers and other diseases among Iraqi children and U.S. veterans

1992   Earth Summit in Rio de Janeiro, Brazil; conference focuses on advancing environmentally sound development of developing nations, an "Earth Charter" to reconcile international conflicts over many resource issues, forest preservation, framework on climate change, began process that led to the Kyoto Protocol, and the Convention on Biological Diversity to conserve biological diversity. United States refuses to sign the Earth Summit convention

1993   President William Clinton signs order restricting logging in old growth forests

1994   United Nations Intergovernmental Panel on Climate Change report (the product of nearly 1,000 scientists from around the globe) warns of severe environmental, human, and economic impacts from global climate change

1995   Jonathan Harr publishes *A Civil Action*

1995   Republicans control U.S. Congress for first time in decades; attack on environmentalism a major priority

1995   Wolves reintroduced to Yellowstone National Park

1997   Julia Butterfly Hill climbs a 180-foot California coast redwood tree in defiance of loggers, spends two years in the tree as a protest against redwood logging

1997   Kyoto Protocol calling for modest reductions in greenhouse gases responsible for global warming signed by the United States, 121 other nations; not ratified by U.S. Senate

1999   Worldwatch Institute reports that seven out of ten scientists believe planet Earth is experiencing the largest mass extinction of species in history

2000   President Clinton protects 58 million acres of national forest from logging, establishes new national monuments covering 8 million acres of land

2001   At Coldwater Creek, Kentucky, over 210 million gallons of toxic
                coal sludge breaks through the dam wall of a slurry sediment
                pond in the town of Inez; slurry contains poisonous heavy
                metals and covers a 60-mile-long area leading to the Ohio River;
                in February 2004, the Bush administration demotes its top
                investigative official for raising questions about the accident

2001   President George W. Bush's energy plan emphasizes oil
                exploration and new construction of coal and nuclear power
                plants, de-emphasizes conservation and renewable clean energy

2001   President Bush denounces Kyoto Protocol on global warming

2001–2005   Bush administration compiles what virtually every environmental
                organization in the United States describes as the worst
                environmental record of any president in history; Bush and
                congressional Republicans target for weakening the Clean Air Act,
                Clean Water Act, Superfund, Right to Know Act, Endangered
                Species Act, Marine Mammal Protection Act, sustainable forest
                management, mine safety, the EPA, and OSHA, to name a few

2005   Kyoto Protocol takes effect, without the United States

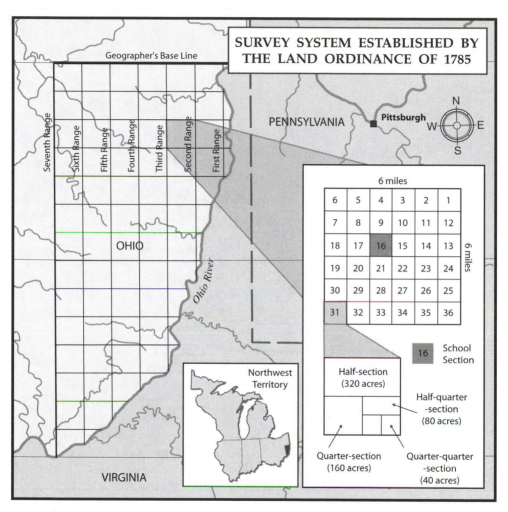

SURVEY SYSTEM ESTABLISHED BY THE LAND ORDINANCE OF 1785

The grid pattern for surveying, selling, and developing western lands reflected both the intellectual rationality of European Americans, as well as their propensity toward abstract commodification of natural resources.

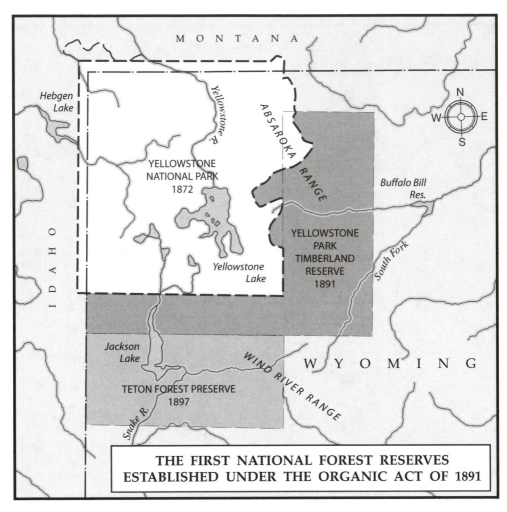

THE FIRST NATIONAL FOREST RESERVES ESTABLISHED UNDER THE ORGANIC ACT OF 1891

The establishment of the forest reserves ultimately brought "multiple use" management to nearly two hundred million square acres of land in the United States. A regime of government regulation of grazing, logging, and mining rights, as well as recreational uses of those lands, was intended to provide for the needs of all Americans in perpetuity.

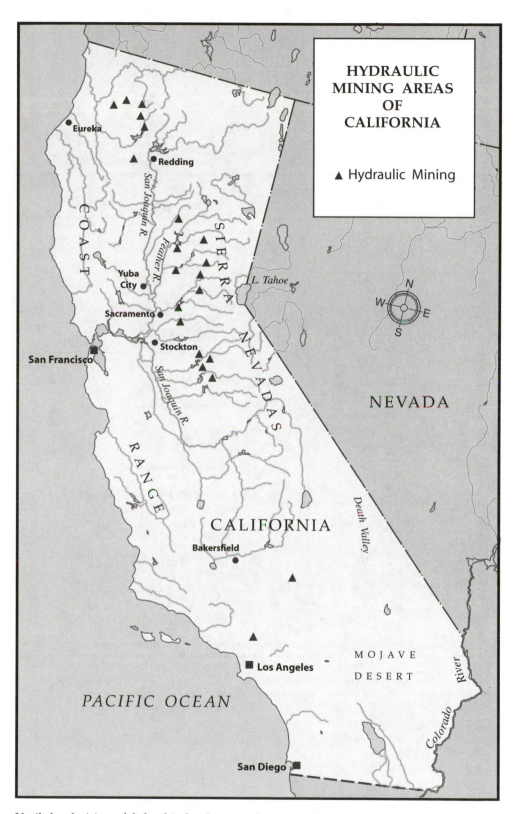

HYDRAULIC MINING AREAS OF CALIFORNIA

▲ Hydraulic Mining

Eureka

Redding

San Joaquin R.

Feather R.

Yuba City

Sacramento

Stockton

San Francisco

San Joaquin R.

L. Tahoe

SIERRA

NEVADAS

RANGE

COAST

N W E S

NEVADA

CALIFORNIA

Death Valley

Bakersfield

Los Angeles

MOJAVE DESERT

Colorado River

PACIFIC OCEAN

San Diego

Until the decision of federal judge Lorenzo Sawyer in 1884 brought an end to hydraulic mining, numerous operations in northern California brought enormous wealth to the state but also environmental devastation.

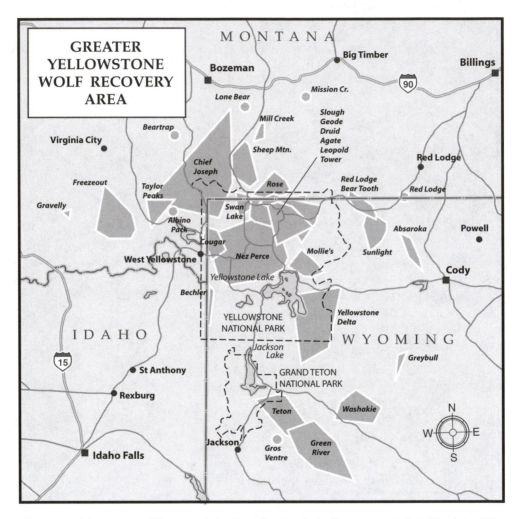

Recovery of the gray wolf began with reintroduction in Yellowstone National Park in 1995 and now extends throughout the greater Yellowstone ecosystem and beyond.

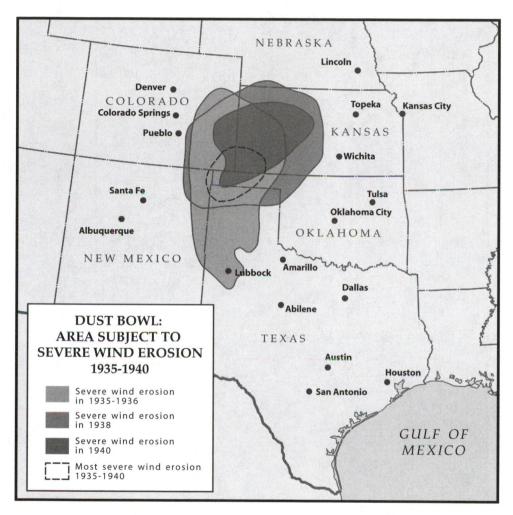

DUST BOWL: AREA SUBJECT TO SEVERE WIND EROSION 1935-1940

- Severe wind erosion in 1935-1936
- Severe wind erosion in 1938
- Severe wind erosion in 1940
- Most severe wind erosion 1935-1940

Although concentrated in that part of the southern Great Plains known as the "Dust Bowl" (shown here), the areas damaged by overproduction and overgrazing extended well into the northern plains.

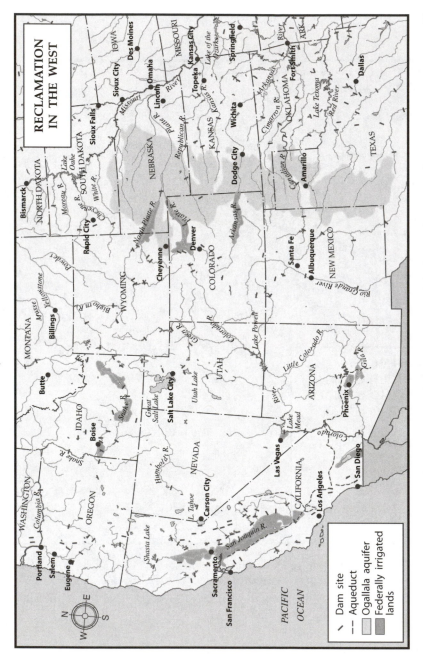

Since the 1950s, the underground Ogallala Aquifer has been tapped far beyond its natural capacity to regenerate itself. Elsewhere beyond the 100th meridian (the approximate dividing line between temperate and arid climates, roughly the eastern edge of the Ogallala), every river in the West has been dammed to serve American agriculture and to power the growth of cities.

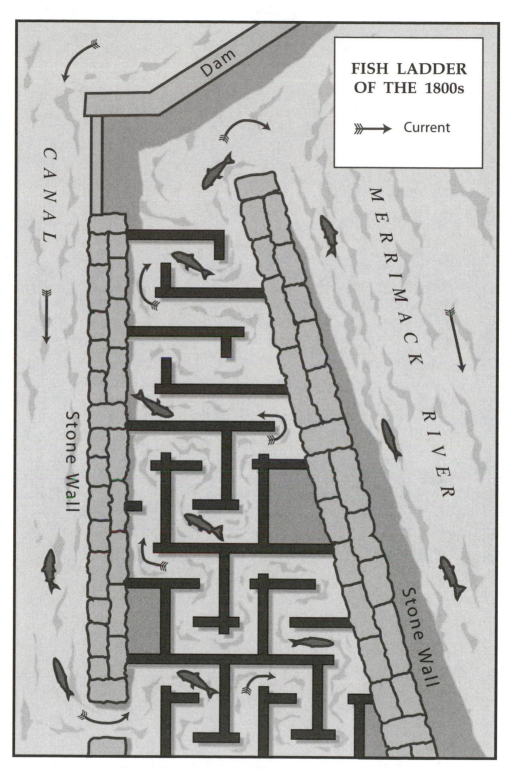

Although they sometimes failed, fish ladders constructed around dams (and imposed on early industrialists by some state legislatures) were supposed to allow important species of fish to reach spawning grounds.

ENVIRONMENTAL ISSUES
IN AMERICAN HISTORY

1

Introduction

> That man is, in fact, only a member of a biotic team is shown by an ecological interpretation of history. Many historical events, hitherto explained solely in terms of human enterprise, were actually biotic interactions between people and land.
> —Aldo Leopold, *A Sand County Almanac*, 1949

From roughly 1900 to 1920 Lake Erie fishermen hauled nearly 25 million tons of fish annually into Erie, Pennsylvania. Just a decade later, according to the official report of the U.S. Bureau of Fisheries, "the impossible, the incredible happened. The herring of Lake Erie, suddenly and without warning, gave out."[1] The legendary blue pike was also disappearing. By the late 1960s Erie's fabled commercial fishing industry had essentially ceased to exist.

The demise of one of the most productive commercial fisheries in human history serves as a telling overture to this anthology of pivotal moments in U.S. environmental history. To enjoy Lake Erie sturgeon in a fine New York restaurant during the heady years of the Erie fishing boom, or to have labored in the booming maritime industry of northwestern Pennsylvania, was to be linked to a magnificent story of, in Aldo Leopold's words, human enterprise. Few understood the ecological balance that had evolved in those waters since the end of the last Ice Age, or the spiritual connection to the lake once held by the region's indigenous peoples. Not until the late 1960s did the Lake Erie fishery begin to appear less a human supermarket and more a damaged natural system. Steam tugboats and mile-long gill nets, as well as the industrial society that lined the shores, had long symbolized the civilization that had made "nature" so stunningly productive here. By the 1960s, human mastery of the lake meant *over*fishing, pollution, and ecologically disruptive invasive species.

What suddenly happened in Lake Erie suggests some of the central themes of American environmental history. Let us begin with a verb-driven definition of this discipline. This is the story of how humans on the mid–North American continent have intellectually understood, spiritually perceived, culturally depicted, and materially shaped, utilized, developed, fought over, exploited, conserved, and preserved the natural resources of the nation. Although over-looked well into Leopold's time, it is now widely understood among historians that the narrative of American environmental change is inextricably entwined with the larger political, social, economic, cultural, and military history of the nation.

The contours of U.S. environmental history begin with the collision of Native American peoples and the land's European colonizers. Commencing in the late fifteenth century, this epic struggle was from the beginning inscribed with deep fault lines over the perception and use of nature. In its most extreme caricature, the image of American Indians as the nation's "first ecologists" suggests that indigenous Americans had virtually no impact on the land. This, of course, is untrue. From coastal regions to the Great Plains, Native Americans feasted on the seasonal abundance of whatever species dominated. The common practice of setting fire to the understory of forests in order to improve hunting, as well as Indian agricultural systems, shaped the landscape that explorers and colonists saw when they first arrived.

Like many stereotypes in history, there is truth in the image of the Indian as ecologist. In hunting the moose, the Abenakis of New England ritually heeded their shamans who urged hunters to propitiate ceremonially the spirit of their fallen prey. Hunters who ignored such rituals, or who hunted beyond need, did so at the tribe's peril. All of nature was imbued with sacred attributes, which, if properly respected, would continue to sustain them. Unlike English colonists, the life-giving force of the deity was not above and beyond but here and now, suffused into rocks and trees and clams.

Prior to European colonization, North American Indians generally lived within nature's limits. Long accustomed to seasons of plenty and times of dep-rivation, they simply expended less energy (to the Puritans a sign of evil sloth-fulness) and survived on fewer resources and moved to wherever they were. To the English, who came from a world of fixed settlements and rights of ownership assured by legal title, seasonal migration was incomprehensible and an invita-tion to take possession. Land "abandoned" was for the taking.

For Puritan leaders like John Winthrop, the pandemic disease that struck Indian people provided further evidence that God had destined the English to seize control. As large majorities of tribes fell to disease against which they had no immunity, Indian shamans, rituals, and medicines seemed powerless to stop it. Consequently, beyond providing further religious justification to colonists for Indian dispossession, disease also weakened the belief systems that bound native people to nature. For example, Indians had long hunted beaver for multiple uses and imbued the animal with sacred attributes. However, shaken spiritually and devastated in numbers by disease, increasingly surrounded by a world of fences and farms, and attracted to European goods that larger numbers of beaver could fetch from English and French traders, Indians traveled farther and farther from home to take ever greater volumes of beaver pelts. These forces compounded the exhaustion of species and worsened intertribal conflict by pitting Indians against one another for a shrinking land and resource base.[2]

What replaced Native American beliefs about the natural world was an equally complex, though very different, view of nature. The book of Genesis urged colonists to fear and "subdue" unruly places in nature that they termed "wilderness." To protect the livestock and crops upon which their survival depended, settlers cut trees, drained swamps, and killed wolves by the score. Biblical dictates placed God above men and men above nature.

As environmental historian Carolyn Merchant has shown, however, most farmers of the colonial era continued to practice "organic" modes of production that fall somewhere in the middle of the continuum between the Indian "animistic" approach, wherein all of nature merits reverence, and the "mechanistic" philosophy that came to dominate fully by the nineteenth century. In the latter worldview, nature was reduced to inanimate parts to be extracted, manipulated, and used for human benefit and ultimately the generation of wealth. Organic ideas harkened back to a polytheistic world in which farmers shared an ideal of symbiotic interdependency with the health of nature. Although Christian theology permeated their consciousness, farmers clung to ancient ideas demanding the propitiation of nature's multiple spirits with a bewildering array of fertility rituals and traditions to bring forth rain, sun, and a bountiful harvest.[3] Though European farmers exacted a heavier toll on the land than Indians, the extent to which they accepted the produce-for-profit paradigm varied greatly.

Inexorably, the forces of market capitalism came, altering agriculture, social relations, and the land itself. Take the beaver for example. Mercantile capitalists certainly did, transforming a pivotal member of a biotic community into an agent of commerce. When beaver hats became the fashion, so many pelts brought so many pounds to traders on the London market; for Indians, however, more beaver returned wampum beads, tools, and other highly valued items. The hunt was on. Ecological consequences followed the beaver's decline that came throughout much of New England by the end of the eighteenth century: their untended dams collapsed, leaving homeless a food web of animals that had depended on those riparian habitats. Where ponds had been, fertile soil gave life to grasses that fed colonists' cattle.

Equally dramatic were the impacts of early deforestation. New England forests absorbed rainfall and snowpack and thus helped regulate stream flow and regional climate. By the early 1800s, however, two centuries of cutting to serve the insatiable lumber needs of both colonists and British ship builders wrought largely denuded mountainsides that not only reduced wildlife habitat, but also increased flooding and drought. In 1691 the British Crown inserted into the Massachusetts charter the Broad Arrow Policy, the first official act of conservation in American environmental history. The act reserved to ship builders all trees larger than twenty-four inches in diameter, but it was flagrantly ignored by colonists. Continual pressure to fell trees came from many sources, not the least of which was the need for new agricultural lands to the west. The failure of farms on New England's rocky soil led subsequent generations into western New York, where trees were cut to establish fields and pasture.

In the Chesapeake region, perennial tobacco cropping exhausted the once-mineral-rich soil of the coastal plain. Yeoman farmers then unsuccessfully tried to raise wheat and corn on the exhausted soil of abandoned plantations. The large tobacco farmers moved beyond the Fall Line to the Piedmont Plateau, where they repeated the process—clearing new lands of timber and Indians and mining the soil of nutrients and minerals. Thomas Jefferson and George Washington were among the few planters who experimented with soil-enrichment fertilization or crop rotation to extend the life of the soil. Most plantations were managed for the immediate future—healthy profits on the next crop.

Cotton production exacted its own toll across an ever-expanding "cotton South" that over time stretched from the Carolinas to Texas. Following Eli Whitney's invention of the cotton gin in 1793, slave-intensive cultivation of short-staple cotton increased dramatically, as did its processing in the textile mills of London and New England. Land planted perpetually in cotton suffered severe soil depletion and degradation. Neither southern soil nor climate was conducive to growing grass that could have fed cattle, whose manure might have been used to fertilize land under cultivation. With the largest planters' capital tied up in slaves, with manure at a premium, and with lands available to the west, there was little incentive to be good stewards.

Tragically, when artificial fertilizers became available after the Civil War, the big planters remained committed to cotton, which became vulnerable to widespread attack by the dreaded boll weevil. Although this scourge did not modify the exploitative nature of King Cotton—now dependent on sharecropping and tenant farming—it pushed the crop further westward where it was less vulnerable to the insect.

More land, more beaver, more cotton. One begins to see that the continuous expansion that has been the overarching central theme of U.S. economic history has had ramifications for the natural world upon which the human economy is built. And as environmental historians and American Studies scholars have argued, the enduring complex of ideas and beliefs we characterize as cultural *myths* have had as much to do with shaping the course of environmental change as political or economic forces. Myths, in this context, mean essentially those enduring ideals or complex of beliefs that Americans have come to hold as truth, from which spring both individual actions and national policies. They are the great stories we need to tell ourselves about ourselves. National myths are not false, though they do take on a power of their own. Economic elites of the late 1800s, for example, used the myth of success—the notion that any virtuous, hardworking citizen can rise to wealth—to argue against government intervention in an economy increasingly controlled by corporations and the privileged few.

A number of myths have shaped U.S. environmental history. We have alluded to the colonists' preexisting fear of wilderness. The flip side of that apprehension was a psychological and emotional preference for wilderness *tamed:* nature given order and made virtuous by the actions of a civilized people. Hence the obsession of Americans for the "middle landscape"—green and bucolic places safely distant from the noise, congestion, and immigrants of city life—and yet retaining the finer elements of civilization and good taste. Indeed, by the 1830s, parks and suburbs, like leisure trips to sublime and picturesque locales, became marks of good taste for the upper classes.

There is also what Laurence Shames calls "the *more* factor."[4] From the moment European explorers set foot on the shores of New England, Americans have assumed the resources of the continent to be without limit. The roots of America's mythology of endless abundance lie in the Old World. By the time of American colonization, European forests had been devastated, the best lands exhausted or controlled by aristocracy, and all the riches of the known world discovered and imperiously claimed by one power or another. Thus did Spanish conquistadors dream dreams of fabulous wealth as they slaughtered their way through the Pueblo villages of New Mexico. Thus could French and English explorers of the sixteenth century write fantastic tales of streams so laden with fish that one could cross them without touching bottom. Early colonists told of squirrels leaping from tree to tree from the white pine forests of the Carolinas all the way to the western prairie. They reported animals that had never been seen before, and others that had long vanished from European woods. Across the Mississippi lush prairie grasses standing more than ten feet tall stretched on for 400 million acres of the mid-American continent.

Thus for good reasons did the resources of the "New World," this "virgin" land, appear endless. And here are two other myths: America was neither new nor untouched, having been shaped by hundreds of Indian nations who had called it home for thousands of years. For Europeans to think of it as *terra nova* invited the dismissal of natives on the land—their history and their very existence—and helped justify European conquest.

Control of the land was wrested by a people who were intent on establishing permanent settlements and transforming chaotic wildness into a cornucopia of market-bound resources. From that bounty they would *produce*—initially for subsistence, increasingly for market. In the process nature itself was rendered an abstract medium of monetary exchange. The rendering of nature, or natural capital, into *commodities* to be bought and traded on distant markets constitutes the single most important outcome of the colonial era of environmental history.

The new paradigm turned swimming beaver into British pounds and living forests into board feet of timber. It allowed a linear grid to be superimposed upon a diverse landscape, from which parcels could be bought and sold by speculators eager for profit and energetic farmers itching for a new start (Chapter 2). In 1837 John Deere made cutting into the deep native prairie grasses much easier with his invention of the steel plow. Thus were millions of acres of an ecologically complex environment—along with the dozens of indigenous peoples that had been part of it—supplanted by fields of wheat and corn. By the 1860s traders on the Chicago Board of Trade could buy grain "futures"—the right to trade grain six months hence at a fixed price, further signaling the abstract commodification of nature.

In New England, iron furnace and textile mill owners turned water into a commodity. Since the early 1700s mills throughout colonial America had been powered by large wooden wheels that captured the energy of water falling rapidly downstream and applied it to grinding grain, cutting timber, and processing wool. Reduced stream flow and spring fish runs resulted from these mostly seasonal operations. Yet these impacts were minimal compared to what followed when the massive operations of blast furnaces and textile mills began requiring increasing volumes of continuously flowing water for nonstop production. By the 1830s, the "reasonable use" doctrine of water law had emerged, allowing large mill and dam operators to engineer water flow through complex systems of dams, locks, canals, and basins extending miles from the mill. Negative consequences resulted, not only for riparian-dwelling species but also for many small farmers who had to buy water allotments from dam owners. Thus the Industrial Revolution in New England not only produced staggering volumes of cloth spun from southern cotton; by redefining water as a marketable, movable commodity, it also transformed the region's hydrology and redistributed both wealth and power upward.

The commodification of animals continued. From Maine to Oregon settlers and bounty hunters hunted the wolf mercilessly—some for money, many out of concern for their herds and flocks, and still others for the pure joy of killing a much-feared and misunderstood animal. The mountain men who followed Lewis and Clark into the West became leading participants in the region's first major extractive industry, the mining of beaver pelts (traders had earlier proven sea otters in the Pacific Northwest lucrative). Trappers, natives, and fur-trading companies brought the beaver to the brink of extinction by 1840. A few decades later came the stunningly sudden extinction of the passenger pigeon. These birds, which had once blackened eastern skies by the thousands, had been forced to their last refuge in the northern Midwest by the 1850s. Rail transportation to distant markets intensified hunting of the bird, and logging brought further habitat loss. Compounded by the limitations of its own reproduction cycle, the bird faced extinction by the end of the century. The disappearance of the passenger pigeon, like the loss of Lake Erie herring, marked the transformation of nature's limitless resources into disappearing marketable commodities.

The North American bison (buffalo) came perilously close to meeting the same fate. Following the introduction of the horse to the southern Great Plains, Indians hunted the bison more efficiently. Although overhunting did occur—particularly after the trade in buffalo robes in the 1840s induced Indians to kill more—natives generally killed for need and used virtually every ounce for dietary or cultural purposes. The chief culprits were white market hunters who, beginning in the late 1860s, could ship heavy buffalo robes by rail to eastern tanners who had devised a method for turning skins into leather belts to run textile and other industrial machinery. Within a generation the bison population was almost depleted, from roughly 30 million to fewer than 200 animals.[5] Those last specimens became a symbol of the vanishing "Old West" and a rallying cry for conservation generally. By the early 1880s, millions of head of cattle—far too many, as it turned out—fed voraciously on the bison's former grassland.

It is difficult to fathom the absolute central importance of trees to Americans who lived before the age of oil, plastics, and steel. From the early colonial era through most of the nineteenth century, Americans fashioned from trees everything from homes and fences to teeth and tools. Wood was burned to make charcoal and potash, the latter vital to making soap at home and a variety of products in the early chemical industry. Americans burned staggering volumes to heat their homes, and to power steamboats and railroads. From 1840 to 1860 the volume of wood consumption increased tenfold, to nearly 13 billion board feet—most of that coming from New England and the South.

Beginning in the 1860s, logging shifted to the vast forests of the upper Great Lakes. As the Erie Canal had accelerated timbering in the Northeast, so did the Illinois-Michigan Canal in the upper Midwest. Balloon-frame structures came to dominate home building and demanded more milled lumber. More significantly, rather than buy locally from small sawmills or cut trees themselves, people increasingly bought wood from large corporate entities that had bought up large tracts of timber in the region. With mammoth-size band saws and steam-powered mills, and heavily subsidized by federal land giveaways, large corporations greatly accelerated timbering—leveling whole forests rather than chopping down individual trees as had been the farmer's custom. Further, the largest operations, epitomized by Frederick Weyerhauser, established vertical control of the entire industry—logging, transporting, and milling the logs into finished lumber. Within thirty years the pine forests of the northern Great Lakes region were gone, followed by the tragic coda: clear-cutting the big trees exposed the underbrush to massive forest fires that ravaged the entire region from 1870 through 1920.

Earlier in the century, deforestation in New England had provoked both a romantic and practical urge to save the trees. Hudson River school landscape painter Thomas Cole mourned the "meager utilitarianism" of Americans that left behind scarred landscapes. James Fenimore Cooper's Leatherstocking novels decried the "wasty ways" of the hardy pioneer who imprudently cleared one forest after another. These were among the voices that inspired the preservation ideal to protect from development select areas of nature for their sublime grandeur and picturesque beauty.

In 1872 preservation interests intersected with those of the Northern Pacific Railroad to bring the establishment of Yellowstone National Park—the world's first such preserve. In this remote corner of the West, explorers saw a vast, spectacular, and unprecedented concentration of nature's wonders, while the railroad saw increased investment and traffic on its line that was to run just north of the park. Although management and control of the park remained matters of contention in the ensuing years, the precedent of nature preservation had been established on a grand scale—soon to be followed by many more parks, national monuments, wildlife refuges, and eventually wilderness areas.

The more utilitarian conservation movement had its roots in the same exploited landscape. George Perkins Marsh's *Man and Nature* received little notice when first published in 1864, but within a generation the book became the seminal work on the emerging conservation movement. Marsh reviewed the history of fallen civilizations and concluded that their demise derived from the exhaustive use and profligate waste of natural resources, particularly forests. Without a sound program aimed at conservation, he warned his fellow countrymen, the same fate awaited them.

With the impacts of deforestation evident in many regions, the government began to respond, establishing the first forest preserves in 1891. Bernard Fernow, the first head of the Department of Agriculture's Division of Forestry, urged a management strategy based on the ecological—and ultimately economic—benefits of forests, specifically their capacity to protect soil, control flooding, and protect the health of watersheds. In 1898 Gifford Pinchot, whose philosophy drew more heavily on the principles of efficiency-for-production then being implemented in American industry, replaced Fernow. Pinchot argued that the National Forests should be managed to serve "the greatest good for the greatest number of people." He and President Theodore Roosevelt would soon make the same argument for federally owned rangelands, water, and game animals. This meant harvesting trees like corn: cutting and replanting in a scientifically sound and sustainable manner that would allow for a continual supply of timber. Forests were not to be managed primarily as ecological entities, but rather with utilitarian goals in mind. Tensions between the preservation and conservation movements would come to a head in the 1907–1913 debate over the proposal to dam Hetch-Hetchy Valley (Chapter 8) in Yosemite National Park in order to supply San Francisco with water.

Environmental protection was even less a consideration in mineral extraction. Beginning in California in 1848, the mining enterprise evolved rapidly from one of romanticized individual opportunity and relatively modest environmental impact to an industry largely controlled by heavily capitalized operations. Corporate mining generated massive wealth, but was also defined by wage labor, the displacement of Native and Mexican American peoples, and horrific ecological consequences for entire watersheds.

How to develop the nation's arid lands west of the ninety-eighth meridian remained a vexing challenge for policymakers. Once dismissed as the "Great American Desert" best suited for Indians, the Great Plains between the western end of the lowland prairie and the Rocky Mountains were redefined following the Civil War and the completion of the first transcontinental railroad in 1869. In 1862 the Homestead Act encouraged settlement on "free" lands in the West and railroads promoted the fantastic concept that "rain follows the plow." So great was the rhetorical force of Manifest Destiny that Americans believed they could make the desert bloom. The Mormons of Utah already had done so—establishing a fruitful civilization in the midst of a salt bed surrounded by alkaline desert and imposing mountains.

The Mormons succeeded largely because they were willing to work in a cooperative spirit, with the overall good of their community first in mind. In 1869 one-armed Civil War general John Wesley Powell explored the arid Southwest, famously journeying down the Colorado River through the Grand Canyon. His report to the U.S. government in 1878 urged that only Mormon-style, communally based, low-density development could succeed in such an arid environment. With enormous pressure from cattle barons and other development interests, Powell's recommendations were largely ignored. Established in 1902, the federal Reclamation Service (later the Bureau of Reclamation) worked closely with business and political leaders in constructing dams throughout the West to control flooding, provide irrigation for capital-intensive agriculture, and generate electric power for the region's expanding urban population.

By then western industrial cities like Butte, Montana, were contending with the same problems of urban waste and industrial pollution that had long plagued cities of the East. Toxic pollutants emanating from the steel and coke-making operations of the Pittsburgh area shortened the lives of workers who made the steel; as recently as 1945 the smog was so thick in Pittsburgh that residents drove with their headlights on at noon. Horse manure and human waste filled urban streets, occasionally invading public water supplies and leading to frequent outbreaks of typhus and cholera. Chicago's Packingtown district near the slaughterhouses was among the vilest places on earth at the turn of the century. Here lived the real-life version of characters that filled the pages of Upton Sinclair's *The Jungle*. Although Sinclair's book sparked public outrage and led to the 1906 Meat Inspection Act, his real goal—to reform the brutal conditions to which slaughterhouse workers were continually exposed—was left unfulfilled.

In general, occupational safety and public environmental health were issues raised not by men but by a generation of women urban reformers. Throughout the Progressive Era, the General Federation of Women's Clubs, along with women such as Caroline Bartlett Crane and Mary McDowell, led wide-ranging efforts to improve public health in urban industrial America. Such "municipal housekeeping" included advocacy for larger budgets and improved scientific methods for managing waste, along with better pay for sanitation engineers and their street crews. Physician Alice Hamilton spearheaded the fledgling occupational health movement. Her pioneering efforts to ensure the safety of workers in the lead industry foreshadowed the later investigative and reform efforts of miners and other workers engaged in hazardous occupations. Crane, meanwhile, hammered away at the weak enforcement of the meatpacking industry by the federal government and led sanitary reforms across much of the nation.

Derived from the Pinchot era, the belief that natural resources could be scientifically managed for efficiency and maximum production was invoked again following the Dust Bowl of the 1930s, arguably the most cataclysmic disaster in U.S. environmental history. In the spring of 1935, a nine-mile-high black cloud of soil arose out of the Great Plains and carried all the way to ships on the Atlantic coast. A government committee investigated and debated the causes of the dust storms. Some concluded that nature had been the sole culprit, while others argued the greater villain to be intensive wheat cultivation that had left the soil vulnerable to a regularly occurring cycle of drought. Ecologists grimly declared that once more an economic system had converted a natural resource—in this case, soil—into an abstract, profit-generating commodity without thought of the complex ecological system to which it was attached. In the end, Franklin Roosevelt's administration advocated relief and regulatory measures designed to assist farmers and manage the resource more scientifically.

Following World War II, natural resource and "environmental" issues virtually disappeared from the national agenda. Confronting the communist threat and keeping the economy booming occupied policymakers and most Americans. And boom it did, as wartime technologies were converted to an array of new civilian products. Synthetics and plastics—in every form imaginable—came to dominate, with little thought given either to the supply of petroleum upon which such products depended, nor to the associated environmental consequences. In the spirit of boundless optimism that ruled that era, the Atomic Energy

Commission promised nuclear energy "too cheap to meter" with few environmental risks. That illusion would not be shattered until the accident at the Three Mile Island plant near Harrisburg, Pennsylvania, in March 1979.

In the same vein of naïve optimism, the U.S. Forest Service cut billions more board feet of timber than the agency's own studies had indicated was sustainable. Much of the timber went to supply the explosion in suburban tract housing. Blue-collar union workers joined the ranks of the middle class and moved to the suburbs, with Americans from 1950 to 1970 plowing up for suburbanization an area larger than the state of Ohio. With housing came an auto-centric culture of drive-through restaurants and strip malls, bringing urban problems of traffic and congestion right behind the suburban emigrants. Less noticed, at least initially, was the problem of diffuse, nonpoint source water and air pollution emitted from exponentially greater numbers of cars, aerosol sprays, and square miles of asphalt. By the 1980s the problems associated with suburban sprawl entered the national debate, as initiatives to promote "smart growth" and preserve green space on the periphery of urban areas proliferated.

More cars, rising incomes, and greater leisure time, along with the Interstate Highway Act of 1956 allowed far greater numbers of Americans to discover the expanded state and national systems of parks, refuges, and forests. That development bore fruit for preservationists as broader public appreciation for western parks allowed the Sierra Club to halt proposed dams on the Colorado River inside Dinosaur National Monument and the Grand Canyon—unprecedented victories and testament to the symbolic value such places had acquired in American culture. Though hotly contested by opponents, environmentalists used widespread public support to help bring final passage of the 1964 Wilderness Act, which established a system of wilderness preserves "untrammeled by man" and worthy of the most stringent form of protection by the federal government.

"Better Things Through Better Living Through Chemistry" went the slogan of one chemical company in the 1950s. And few dared question the mantra of an industry that provided the chrome finish on automobile tail fins and the weed-anol cyanol that killed crabgrass on the front lawn. Yet, by the end of the decade, Americans across the country were beginning to see the negative side effects of indiscriminate use of pesticides and chemicals generally in the environment. With eloquent language and scientific reason, former government wildlife biologist Rachel Carson chronicled that story in *Silent Spring*. Published in 1962, the book sparked a societal and legislative debate that ultimately led to the banning of the pesticide DDT and to government regulation of all chemical pesticides. The book's larger underlying message was to warn of the deleterious consequences that human activity in modern industrial society can have on both the environment and on human health.

Though Carson's book is often credited with launching the modern environmental movement, other forces were at work in raising the nation's consciousness about environmental issues. Pesticide spraying, for example, had been afflicting migrant farm workers for over a decade and few environmentalists said anything about that, nor did large environmental organizations support Navajo uranium miners and Appalachian coal miners who in the 1960s campaigned for stronger occupational health laws. Increasingly, a steady stream of events and studies of the poor environmental conditions afflicting marginalized communities encouraged working people and minorities to raise a cry for what was called by the 1980s "environmental justice." The movement challenged the largely white middle-class environmental movement and raised fundamental questions about *which* places in nature were worthy of protection.

Other deleterious effects of the nation's unfettered economic expansion surfaced. Prior to the 1950s air pollution had been a matter strictly under the purview of state and local governments. However, crises in Donora, Pennsylvania, and Los Angeles, California, in the late 1940s that killed dozens of people, along with the obvious fact that pollutants crossed the arbitrary boundary lines of state and local governments, made clear that this was an issue requiring federal intervention. Despite opposition from industry, a series of increasingly tougher federal laws from the mid-1950s through the early 1970s called for reductions in emissions from industry and power plants. The same was true for water. Artificial fertilizers and pesticides flowing from farmers' fields, sludge, and toxic effluent spewing largely unregulated from industry, compounded by the rising impact of suburban sprawl, all contributed to the crisis afflicting America's waters by the end of the 1960s. The severity of the problem crystallized in the national media when a skein of oil and chemicals on the surface of the Cuyahoga River flowing into Lake Erie ignited in 1968. The event dramatized the "Death of Lake Erie" in a way no biologist's study could have. Then, in the fall of 1969, an oil rig stationed off the coast of Santa Barbara, California, suffered a "blowout" of 200,000 gallons of crude oil that covered 800 square miles of coastline.

A decade of rising consciousness about the deteriorating quality of the environment evidenced by real events, best-selling books, and increased visibility of the environmental movement climaxed in 1969–1970 with the establishment of the federal Environmental Protection Agency (EPA) and the creation and strengthening of other federal and state environmental laws through the decade of the 1970s.

The bureaucratic superstructure of environmental regulations imposed by 1980 provoked a storm of counterprotest from ranchers, farmers, and especially large corporations intent on scaling back the power of what they perceived as an overbearing, intrusive federal government. The tensions between advocates of the "rights of nature" and proponents of largely unfettered economic growth came to a head over the designation of wilderness in the West, giving rise to the antiregulatory "Sagebrush Rebellion" that helped sweep Ronald Reagan into the White House in 1980. Especially controversial was the enforcement of the Endangered Species Act (1973), resulting in conflicts from the Tellico (Tennessee) Dam controversy of the late 1970s to the reintroduction of the wolf in Yellowstone National Park in the 1990s.

There was of course no way to reintroduce the herring to Lake Erie, for there were none. Scientific management of rapidly diminishing natural resources came too late for too many species. Like mining, timber, and agriculture in many ways, the Erie fishing industry was driven by the same economic and cultural desire for *more* that has long fueled the engines of the American economy. James Madison declared during the founding of the nation that "if men were angels there'd be no need for government." Nowhere has that been truer than in the relationship of Americans with their environment. Where natives could rely on a spiritual worldview to curb unsustainable behavior in nature, Americans have been driven from the beginning by the urges of the market. Over time, the loss of species, deforestation, the degradation of air and water, and other crises provoked an increased awareness that "we all live downstream" (who would have thought that what flowed from a farmer's field in western Ohio would impact the fishery in Erie's Presque Isle Bay?), and consequently, a higher level of government protection of what was once called "the commons." And in the true American spirit of resistance to heavy-handed government, coupled with the increasing political dominance of corporate capitalism at the turn of the twenty-first century, we have seen the inevitable counter assault on environmental laws.

Aldo Leopold anticipated this ongoing struggle to reconcile individual economic freedoms with a larger concern for the future and the good of all. He rightly argued that government would never be enough. Americans have always been—for better and for worse—fiercely individualistic people, and as Leopold argued, a "land ethic" based on one's own long-term self-interest in conserving resources is key to restoring the nation's environmental health. To see contemporary America through the prism of environmental history is to understand the folly of disconnecting the human from the natural world, individual gain from the welfare of all, and the past from the future.

NOTES

1. Walter Koelz, "Fisheries of the Great Lakes, General Review," in U.S. Commissioner of Fisheries, *Report*, 1927 (Washington, DC: Government Printing Office, 1927), Appendix 7, 661, quoted in Margaret Beattie Bogue, *Fishing the Great Lakes: An Environmental History, 1783–1933* (Madison: University of Wisconsin Press, 2000), pp. 325–26.

2. William Cronon, *Changes in the Land: Indians, Colonists, and the Ecology of New England* (New York: Hill and Wang, 1983; reprint 2003).

3. Carolyn Merchant, *Ecological Revolutions: Nature, Gender, and Science in New England* (Chapel Hill: University of North Carolina Press, 1989).

4. Laurence Shames, "The More Factor," in Sonia Maasik et al., eds., *Signs of Life in the U.S.A.: Popular Culture for Writers* (New York: Bedford St. Martin's, 1999), pp. 55–61.

5. Richard White, "Animals and Enterprise," in Clyde A. Milner II, Carol A. O'Connor, and Martha A. Sandweiss, eds., *The Oxford History of the American West* (New York: Oxford University Press, 1994), pp. 247–49; Michael S. Sample, *Bison: Symbol of the American West* (Billings, MT: Falcon Press, 1987), pp. 32–34. As these authors make clear, although the numbers are impossible to absolutely determine with precision, most studies now put the number of bison on the Great Plains at no more no thirty million by the 1840s when the herds' precipitous decline began. Their pitiful remnants scattered across the West by the end of the century numbered between 200 and 1,000.

ANNOTATED BIBLIOGRAPHY

Andrews, Richard N. L. *Managing the Environment, Managing Ourselves: A History of American Environmental Policy.* New Haven: Yale University Press, 1999. Locates the environmental laws of the 1970s and 1980s in the context of four centuries of previous efforts both to encourage and restrain the exploitation of the natural world.

Gottlieb, Robert. *Forcing the Spring: The Transformation of the American Environmental Movement.* Rev. ed. Washington, DC: Island Press, 2005. Original analysis of the difficult evolution of the varying, often contested strands of environmentalism in the twentieth century.

Hays, Samuel P. *A History of Environmental Politics since 1945.* Pittsburgh, PA: University of Pittsburgh Press, 2000. Provides a comprehensive view of the shifting attitudes, policies, and politics in the critical postwar era.

Magoc, Chris J., ed. *So Glorious a Landscape: Nature and the Environment in American History and Culture.* Wilmington, DE: Scholarly Resources, 2001. A wide-ranging interdisciplinary anthology of primary source documents and essays with interpretive introductions to each chapter.

Merchant, Carolyn. *The Columbia Guide to American Environmental History.* New York: Columbia University Press, 2002. A fine compendium of the field that features ten chapters that serve as fine introductions to themes and topics.

———, ed. *Major Problems in American Environmental History: Documents and Essays.* Lexington, MA: D. C. Heath, 1993. Compendium of primary documents and interpretive essays on topics and episodes covering the spectrum of American environmental history.

Opie, John. *Nature's Nation: An Environmental History of the United States.* Fort Worth, TX: Harcourt Brace, 1998. Eclipsing somewhat Joseph Petulla's study (see below), this is a fine survey of the centrality of natural resource development, exploitation, and conservation in the development of the nation.

Petulla, Joseph M. *American Environmental History: The Exploitation and Conservation of Natural Resources.* Boston: Boyd and Fraser, 1988. The first bold attempt to locate nature and environment at the center of a broad view of American history.

Price, Jennifer. *Flight Maps: Adventures with Nature in Modern America.* New York: BasicBooks, 2000. Touching on topics ranging from the origins of the American lawn to The Nature Company, contains brilliant insights into the history of the American relationship with nature.

Sale, Kirkpatrick. *The Green Revolution: The American Environmental Movement, 1962–1992.* New York: Hill and Wang, 1993. Captures the evolution of modern environmentalism that began with the 1962 publication of Rachel Carson's *Silent Spring.*

Steinberg, Ted. *Down to Earth: Nature's Role in American History.* New York: Oxford University Press, 2002. Reveals the complex interactions between the natural world and the nation's economic, political, and cultural history. Particularly strong in discussions of the profound impact of resource commodification.

Worster, Donald, ed. *The Ends of the Earth: Perspectives on Modern Environmental History.* New York: Cambridge University Press, 1989. Tackles regional and global themes of environmental history and demonstrates the maturity of the discipline.

2

Nature as a Commodity: Native Americans, White Settlers, and the Land Ordinance of 1785

...[Look] to Frederick, and see what fortunes were made by the Hites and the first takers up of those lands; Nay how the greatest estates we have in this Colony were made. Was it not by taking up and purchasing at very low rates the rich back lands that we possess?
—George Washington, to his friend Captain
John Posey, 1789

The country was made without lines of demarcation and it is no man's business to divide it.
—Hin-mah-too-yah-lat-kekht (Chief Joseph, Nez Perce)

More than perhaps any other single factor, conflicting perceptions of land divided English colonists from the Indian peoples who inhabited the North American continent and set in motion the process of rapid and far-reaching environmental change. Native Americans principally saw the land for its use value. One expression of that came in the form of place names that gave definition to particular locales ("river where the fish come running") and defined their significance in the Indian world. Over time, Indian tribes throughout North America ascribed to themselves the rights to the resources of a particular locale. Claims were linked to actual use of the resource only; absentee ownership of distant property was an alien concept. Instead, land was occupied, often seasonally depending on the resources of a particular locale, for a whole people's sustenance, whether small bands or whole tribes. Indeed, indigenous peoples of the Americas had neither an understanding of nor experience with any of the legal rights of outright ownership as European

Americans understood them. The features of European settlement were all unknown and seemed irrational to Indians: individual rights of possession, deeds of "sale," outright exclusion of others from one's property, seemingly arbitrary grid lines on a map, abstract and capricious values of exchange for beaver, fences that separated fields of corn from domesticated livestock, and year-round settlement even when hunting game provided more abundant sustenance elsewhere. By contrast, Europeans saw lands not fenced and permanently settled by individual Indians as certain evidence of ignorance and sloth. To leave land as wilderness—uncultivated and unsettled—was to surrender it to savagery. God's will ordained that they establish permanent settlements, and that forests become ships and be converted to meadows and fields. Back in London, those funding their enterprise demanded that resources be shipped to market.

These were the intellectual and spiritual fault lines of the conflict between two world views of the human relationship with the natural world, a struggle that did not reach its culmination until the early twentieth century with the final dispossession, sale, and development of native lands in the West. The focus here is on the pivotal period immediately following the Revolutionary War, a time when the first generation of American leaders shaped the future of the nation by inscribing into law the terms by which millions of square acres of former Indian land would be taken and developed by white settlers and developers. This projection of American ownership and power provoked some of the last strains of Indian resistance east of the Mississippi River, as well as an eloquent articulation of the native view of nature that was fading from view. The paradigm shift was profound: from a communal, largely sustainable land use pattern by Indians to the European view shaped by private ownership and the machinations of the marketplace. The transformation bore profound consequences for the natural world and the peoples who had once inhabited it, events that will be traced in the remainder of this volume.

With a belief that occupation of lands only ascribed rights of *use*, it followed that during the early period of European colonization, native people customarily signed treaties believing they were granting farming or hunting rights to settlers, only to realize they had signed away permanent rights of absolute ownership of the land itself. In some deeds, Indians determinedly tried to reserve their fishing and hunting rights by graphically indicating them on maps. As the seventeenth and eighteenth centuries wore on, however, the pressures of conquest overwhelmed them: disease-induced depopulation of Indians, a shrinking resource base exacerbated by market-driven extraction, particularly of beaver into which Indians themselves were tragically drawn, and the sheer numbers of European settlers whose ships kept arriving with more and more free settlers, indentured servants, and slaves, as well as elites to direct the colonies and survey and manage the distribution of lands. All of these forces conspired throughout the colonial era against continued indigenous use and traditional seasonal occupation of lands and resources along the eastern seaboard.

Like the organic farming practices of early colonial farmers (noted in Chapter 1), land use in many areas of early colonial New England resembled that of Indians. The degree of private land ownership varied over time and from town to town, depending on the settlers' place of origin in England and the open or closed-field systems of peasant farming that prevailed there. Even in villages where the buying and selling of real estate commenced early, significant "common" lands were established and, as in Indian villages, their use value designated as pasture, woodlot, or cornfield. Early development was generally a locally managed enterprise. Surveys of agricultural lands often preceded an orderly dispersal of the population from the village center into the hinterlands over the course of a generation or two. Early maps indicated the location of game and other animals; colonial farmers still followed ancient farming practices derived from the Old World that imbued nature with a life force, linked their God with the natural world and themselves, and reinforced ritualistic responsibility to nature.

By the early eighteenth century, however, the new paradigm was beginning to dominate colonial America: land as a commodity to be marked off in arbitrarily fixed parcels and bought and sold at abstract prices dictated by a distant market. Natural features of a landscape became less and less prominent in deeds of sale and in cartographic renderings of place. By the mid-1700s, land in New England and elsewhere in the colonies became valued more as a commodity for the long-term monetary profit it could return to the buyer and less for the immediate subsistence value it held for either retreating Indians or white farmers.

In New England, where the region's rocky soil proved difficult for farming, early compact, subsistence-oriented villages gave way to more diffuse, market-oriented pastoral settlements that bore significant ecological consequences, including greater levels of deforestation. In the upper South, land became chiefly valuable as a place to grow tobacco, far and away the most profitable crop that could yield returns for investors and help poor farmers find their way out of debt. Few crops exhausted the land's nutrient base like tobacco. Several years of tobacco production in one place led tobacco farmers to clear the adjacent forest and plant anew. Invariably, the largest planters promoted the further private capture—through sale or by force—of communally held Indian lands throughout the South.

This underscores the larger fact that throughout the colonies, from the Carolinas to Massachusetts, each enterprise was expected to turn a profit. In a fiercely competitive race to attract new settlers, colonial entrepreneurs who had been granted huge parcels by the king sold "unimproved" wilderness to the west, whether native claims on those lands had been settled or not. Logically, therefore, land and all that stood upon it were reduced to commodities for sale. Even in Pennsylvania, where proprietor William Penn made unequaled efforts to uphold the terms of Indian treaties, a sprawling, highly individualistic form of land ownership commenced, with few constraints on how land was to be cultivated or how much timber was to be cut.

That suited well the often contested interests of both the American pioneer and the land speculator. Aspiring settlers were incensed when, following the French and Indian War in 1763, the British crown issued the Royal Proclamation that prohibited further settlement and land sales west of the Appalachian Mountains. This perfectly rational policy was an effort by the Crown to more firmly consolidate political control over the colonies, protect the speculative interests of English land investors, and save themselves the cost of additional warfare with Indian tribes. For influential investors of land companies like George Washington, as well as for aspiring farmers with an eye on the western frontier, the Proclamation grated, and for some, pushed them toward revolution. This was true whether one saw land as a commodity, in quantified terms of exponentially increasing profit as men of Washington's class did, as a generator of commodities like tobacco and furs, or as an opportunity for a good life as an independent subsistence farmer.

The American Revolution erased the line, but provoked urgent questions for the nation's founders regarding the organization and development of the land they believed they had secured through blood. What to do with 231 million acres of trans-Appalachian undeveloped wilderness, much of it still claimed and seasonally occupied by dozens of Native American tribes? Thinking primarily of local or state interests, some Americans saw in the land opportunity for the payment of government and personal debt accrued prior to and during the war. Others imagined fantastic profits through speculative purchase and lucrative resale. In Georgia just after the Revolution, the Yazoo Land Fraud scandal illustrated the dangers of quick profits alone driving the dispersal of lands. Such events angered not only natives in the region, who had been resisting the sale of their lands, but also men such as Thomas Jefferson who envisioned a West filled with yeoman farmers to serve as the backbone of the republic.

These competing visions for the undeveloped lands in the West—as a source of government revenue, as an instrument of large profits, and as individual landownership—all came to pass to a degree in one region or another as development ensued. All began with the assumption that Indians would lose their lands to the victorious patriots. This position was, with few exceptions, unanimously held through post-Revolutionary America, even by those like Jefferson who occasionally articulated sympathy and admiration for some tribes.

It followed that since the king had granted the land to the colonies, the new states would assume possession of trans-Appalachian lands. Led by Virginia and New York, large and politically influential seaboard states with sea-to-sea charters argued most forcefully for that position in the national debate of the 1780s. The most powerful proponents were land companies and speculators in those states hungering for the opportunity to resell vast acreages of land (granted to them by state legislatures at the end of the war). On the other side of this argument were the six states with no colonial claims to western areas, such as Maryland (and the land companies and speculators within those states). They argued that the federal government should assume possession, giving them purchase rights to the territories. Not surprisingly, Native Americans, their centuries-old traditional claims on the land, and their views of the natural world had little or no voice in the debate.

That was as it should have been, according to men like New York landowner Judge William Cooper (Document 2.1), whose proud portrayal of his taming of the Indians' "melancholy wilderness" typified the views of landed men, large and small. One of the most successful land speculators and developers in the United States during the post–Revolutionary War era, Cooper rightly boasted that he had personally "settled more land than any other man in America." At one point in 1786, he disposed of 40,000 acres (of hundreds of thousands he owned) in a matter of days. By all accounts, Cooper as a landowner (and later as a politician) was generous and fair-dealing in his relations with settlers—unlike many of his fellow land barons who became targets of the bitter, often violent, rebellion of tenant farmers that engulfed much of New York State in the 1840s.

Judge Cooper's legacy as one of the most enlightened agents of the democratic disposal of land to white settlers does not negate his central role in the environmental transformation of his region, which is emblematic of early America. Judge Cooper resigned himself to the disappearance of deer, beaver, and other "useful" species on his lands. He encouraged settlers to rid themselves of predatory animals he deemed "noxious" to their economic interests. Cooper further encouraged them to relentlessly clear forests for planting and to convert burned timber to marketable potash that allowed them to pay their mortgage and stay financially afloat. Thus, the consequences of agricultural development across hundreds of thousands of Cooper's acreage included not only sustained independent farming, but also deforestation and the loss of biological diversity.

The land debate reached a decisive point in 1785 with the passage of the Land Ordinance, which established how the western lands were to be divided, subdivided, and sold. Land was to be surveyed in townships six miles square, divided further into thirty-six 640-acre sections and subsections, and then sold at public auction. A minimum price of one dollar per acre and a minimum purchase of 640 acres favored large landowners, and satisfied the need of the federal government to generate revenue immediately from land sales. The ordinance balanced regional traditions of land dispersal, featuring the New England habit of surveying lands prior to sale, a tradition that promoted relatively orderly settlement and political organization while including the southern practice of selling land to individuals, which tended to foster more ambitious and unregulated capture and development of the land. From the massive checkerboard grid imposed on the land would go parcels to small independent farmers who, in Thomas Jefferson's mind, would constitute the backbone of American democracy. With a landed interest in the future of the country, such freeholding men would guard and provide continued vitality to representative government.

A brilliant stroke of Enlightenment-era rationalism, the Land Ordinance established an orderly, uniform, and theoretically democratic system for land disposition that ultimately extended over one billion acres across the West. Yet, while it systematically assured clear title to the land, the survey, quite tellingly, was oblivious to the features of the land, making no mention of its topographic or biological features. Gone was the convention of describing the lay of the land in deeds of sale; in its place were township, section, and range numbers to identify a farmer's field. And missing was any more than a pretense of Jefferson's belief that the land should go primarily to small farmers. That was clear from the first round of sales to the Ohio Company and Scioto Company speculators, who together bought more than two and one-half million acres using grossly deflated Continental certificates.

Unfortunately, the Ohio River country that was the focus of white men's land hunger following the Revolutionary War and the locus of lands to be settled under the ordinance was also still home to dozens of Native American peoples. Following the Land Ordinance were the Northwest Ordinance of 1787, and the

Indian Intercourse Act of 1790, which established the means by which new territories and states would be organized and welcomed into the Union and ostensibly promised that the federal government would respect Indian rights in the territory. The contradictions abound: the government would somehow respect the indigenous people of the region even as it claimed the land rights that in the European tradition came with conquest. As historian Elliott West has put it, early American Indian policy at this point had "moved beyond contradiction to schizophrenia."[1]

Thomas Jefferson's role in promulgating early Indian policy has only recently become the subject of serious historical inquiry. It was Jefferson who, more than any other single figure, articulated the centrality of land in the future of the republic and at the same time had to resolve, within himself and for the country, the "Indian problem." He was long enamored with the idea that natives who lived close to a virtuous nature were inherently noble. Accordingly, he had clung to the belief that they could survive, albeit in diminished numbers on a smaller land base, in contact with whites. Continued white-Indian conflict on the frontier largely dispelled those notions, although the language survived in the land ordinances and in Jefferson's statements acknowledging "Indian rights." The reality of land hunger made westward movement inexorable. Land laws organized the process and stamped it with authority. In the end, it was Jefferson, driven by his attachment to land and the farmer as the cornerstone of democracy, who rationalized the tragic fate of Indians and laid the groundwork for the Indian removal policies undertaken by his successors.

In three successive Supreme Court decisions in the 1820s and 1830s, Chief Justice John Marshall more explicitly affirmed and authoritatively justified the conquest of Indian lands. The cases collectively delimited Indian sovereignty and helped to shape U.S.-tribal relations for more than a century. Included here (Document 2.7) is his opinion in an 1823 case involving the contested sale of Illinois lands formerly belonging to the Piankeshaw Indians. Marshall's ruling in *Johnson v. M'Intosh* serves as a classic expression of the rights of conquest that Americans had won. It further articulates the long-standing belief that prior Indian use of the land was a profound waste and an abomination. Thus, in 1830, President Andrew Jackson's Indian Removal Act ensured the final outcome of the process that had begun two centuries before, as the "civilized tribes" of the Southeast trekked west on the infamous Trail of Tears. The chief result environmentally was the commandeering of vacated Indian lands by cotton planters who spread the land-intensive (and later, fertilizer- and pesticide-intensive) kingdom of cotton westward.

Indian resistance in the Old Northwest was fierce, though not universal. In the 1780s and 1790s, a number of tribes signed treaties ceding lands away, though most Indian leaders then believed that whites would stay to the south, near the Ohio River. They did not. Throughout the period, Americans by the thousands came pouring down the Ohio River, seeking free and fruitful lands. As the lands of the river valley itself became absorbed, frontiersmen either squatted illegally or settled legally on plots of land further and further north. Military forts provocatively positioned along the northern frontier near Indian lands helped to provoke a confederacy of tribes in the Ohio country centered on the idea that Indian lands were held in common and thus could not be sold off by individual tribal leaders without the consent of all. Supported by traditionalist Indian leaders like Joseph Brant and Little Turtle, the concept was anathema to Americans, to the primacy of the individual in American culture, and seemed to threaten the disposition of lands. Communally held Indian lands stood in opposition to the legal infrastructure of land commodification that worked to satisfy both the hunger of market forces and American desires for ever greater expanses of territory and resources. Expansion depended on the ability of the government to deal, as the market did best, in the currency of one-to-one exchange. That pattern had been weakening Indian resistance for nearly 200 years.

In the second phase of pan-tribal Indian resistance in the Ohio country, Tecumseh, the brilliant Shawnee leader and orator, eloquently rejected the very idea of land-as-commodity. Tecumseh's vision of a united confederacy of all tribes was shattered, however, beginning with William H. Harrison's successful assault on Prophetstown (the Battle of Tippecanoe), and ending with the Battle of the Thames during the War of 1812, a conflict in which some Indian tribes of the Old Northwest, desperately trying to maintain their land base, fought alongside the British against the Americans. That doomed effort signaled the end of effective pan-Indian resistance to white encroachment east of the Mississippi River.

The deluge of settlers who filled the space of former Indian lands would build themselves a prosperous and arguably more democratic civilization than the world had ever seen. Samuel Crabtree (Document 2.6) speaks for countless more Americans who would continue to tame the land and find a home in the West, transforming an unruly wilderness into a domesticated landscape and taking its resources to market. As Doublehead and Tecumseh remind us, however (Documents 2.3 and 2.5), the entire enterprise was predicated on the conquest and resultant dispossession of hundreds of thousands of Native Americans from the Great Lakes to the Gulf Coast, with profound consequences for the land and the natural resources. Abstract lines on a map reduced land and its living biotic systems to commodities for market which were both expressions of progress and symbols of a vanished world.

DOCUMENTS

**Document 2.1   Judge William Cooper on the Sale and Settlement
of Frontier Land**

*Father of James Fenimore Cooper, author of the Leatherstocking
frontier novels, William Cooper was one of many large landowners
who came to dominate the sale and settlement of western lands in the
period before and after the American Revolution—and outside of the
provisions and geographical jurisdiction of the Land Ordinance.
Cooper glowingly describes how these lands in western New York—
once a "waste of Creation" when the domain of Native Americans—
now are "large and fruitful tracts" producing large quantities of
commodities.*

I began with the disadvantage of a small capital and the encumbrance of
a large family, and yet I have already settled more acres than any man in
America. There are forty thousand souls now holding directly or indirectly
under me. . . . I must acknowledge that I look back with self-complacency upon
what I have done, and am proud of having been an instrument in reclaiming
such large and fruitful tracts from the waste of Creation. . . .

In 1785 I visited the rough and hilly country of Otsego, where there existed
not an inhabitant, nor any trace of a road; I was alone three hundred miles from
home, without bread, meat, or food of any kind; fire and fishing tackle were my
only means of subsistence. I caught trout in the brook, and roasted them on the
ashes. My horse fed on the grass that grew by the edge of the waters. I laid me
down to sleep in my watch coat, nothing but the melancholy wilderness around
me. . . .

In May, 1786, I opened the sales of forty thousand acres, which, in sixteen
days, were all taken up by the poorest order of men. . . . This was the first
settlement I made, and the first attempted after the Revolution; it was, of
course, attended with the greatest difficulties; nevertheless, to its success many
others have owed their origin. It was besides the roughest land in all the state,
and the most difficult of cultivation of all that had been settled; but for many
years past it has produced everything necessary to the support and comfort of
man. It maintains at present eight thousand souls, with schools, academies,
churches, meetinghouses, turnpike roads, and a market town. It annually yields
to commerce large droves of fine oxen, great quantities of wheat and other
grain, abundance of pork, potash in barrels, and other provisions; merchants
with large capital and all kinds of useful mechanics reside upon it; the waters
are stocked with fish, the air is salubrious, and the country thriving and
happy. . . .

*Source: William Cooper, A Guide in the Wilderness: A Series of Letters Addressed by Judge
Cooper of Coopers-town to William Sampson, Barrister (Rochester, NY, 1897), pp. 26–28.*

Document 2.2   The Land Ordinance of 1785

By dividing and subdividing western lands into townships, sections, and subsections, the Land Ordinance accelerated the sale and development of ultimately 1 billion acres of land extending into the far West. The law imposed a linear grid on an ecologically diverse landscape. It also crystallized the differences between the worldview of Native Americans that held nature to be alive and its resources used in common, and a Euro-American culture that urged private individuals to transform the natural world into saleable commodities. Further, its follow-up law, the Northwest Ordinance of 1787, disingenuously pledged to protect Indian land rights while it simultaneously charted a course for the political organization of new states from those very lands.

An Ordinance for ascertaining the mode of disposing of Lands in the Western Territory.

Be it ordained by the United States in Congress assembled, that the territory ceded by individual States to the United States, which has been purchased of the Indian inhabitants, shall be disposed of in the following manner:

A surveyor from each state shall be appointed by Congress, or a committee of the States, who shall take an Oath for the faithful discharge of his duty, before the Geographer of the United States, who is hereby empowered and directed to administer the same; and the like oath shall be administered to each chain carrier, by the surveyor under whom he acts.

The Geographer, under whose direction the surveyors shall act, shall occasionally form such regulations for their conduct, as he shall deem necessary; and shall have authority to suspend them for misconduct in Office, and shall make report of the same to Congress or to the Committee of the States; and he shall make report in case of sickness, death, or resignation of any surveyor.

The Surveyors, as they are respectively qualified, shall proceed to divide the said territory into townships of six miles square, by lines running due north and south, and others crossing these at right angles, as near as may be, unless where the boundaries of the late Indian purchases may render the same impracticable, and then they shall depart from this rule no farther than such particular circumstances may require; and each surveyor shall be allowed and paid at the rate of two dollars for every mile, in length, he shall run, including the wages of chain carriers, markers, and every other expense attending the same.

The first line, running north and south as aforesaid, shall begin on the river Ohio, at a point that shall be found to be due north from the western termination of a line, which has been run as the southern boundary of the state of Pennsylvania; and the first line, running east and west, shall begin at the same point, and shall extend throughout the whole territory. Provided, that nothing herein shall be construed, as fixing the western boundary of the state of Pennsylvania. The geographer shall designate the townships, or fractional parts of townships, by numbers progressively from south to north; always beginning each range with number one; and the ranges shall be distinguished by their progressive numbers to the westward. The first range, extending from the Ohio to the lake Erie, being marked number one. The geographer shall personally attend to the running of the first east and west line; and shall take the latitude of the extremes of the first north and south line, and of the mouths of the principal rivers.

The lines shall be measured with a chain; shall be plainly marked by chaps on the trees and exactly described on a plat; whereon shall be noted by the surveyor, at their proper distances, all mines, salt springs, salt licks and mill seats, that shall come to his knowledge, and all water courses, mountains and other remarkable and permanent things, over and near which such lines shall pass, and also the quality of the lands.

The plats of the townships respectively, shall be marked by subdivisions into lots of one mile square, or 640 acres, in the same direction as the external lines, and numbered from 1 to 36; always beginning the succeeding range of the lots with the number next to that with which the preceding one concluded. And where, from the causes before mentioned, only a fractional part of a township shall be surveyed, the lots protracted thereon, shall bear the same numbers as if the township had been entire. And the surveyors, in running the external lines of the townships, shall, at the interval of every mile, mark corners for the lots which are adjacent, always designating the same in a different manner from those of the townships.

The geographer and surveyors shall pay the utmost attention to the variation of the magnetic needle; and shall run and note all lines by the true meridian, certifying, with every plat, what was the variation at the times of running the lines thereon noted.

As soon as seven ranges of townships, and fractional parts of townships, in the direction from south to north, shall have been surveyed, the geographer shall transmit plats thereof to the board of treasury, who shall record the same with the report, in well bound books to be kept for that purpose. . . .

Adopted by the Congress formed by the Articles of Confederation, May 20, 1785. Charles Thomson, Secretary. Richard H. Lee, President.

Source: Library of Congress, Rare Book and Special Collections Division, Continental Congress & Constitutional Convention Broadsides Collection, http://memory.loc.gov/cgi-bin/query/D?bdsdcc:5:./temp/~ammem_XOZ9 (accessed June 5, 2004).

**Document 2.3   Creek Chief Doublehead to U.S. Commissioner
                    Benjamin Hawkins, 1796**

On June 29, 1796, a Creek chief named Doublehead addressed Benjamin Hawkins, agent for the U.S. government, on the occasion of the signing of the Treaty of Colerain on the St. Mary's River in Georgia. Doublehead incisively summarizes the contending Indian-white perceptions of the land and its resources that prevailed throughout North America: for use and market value, respectively.

On this land there is a great deal of timber, pine and oak, which are of much use to the white man. They send it to foreign countries, and it brings them a great deal of money. On the land there is much grass for cattle and horses, and much good food for hogs. On this land there is a great deal of tobacco raised, which likewise brings much money. Even the streams are valuable to the white man, to grind the wheat and corn that grows on this land. The pine trees which are dead are valuable for tar.

All these things are lasting benefits; but if the Indians have a little goods for their lands, in one or two seasons they are all rotted and good for nothing. We are told that our lands are of no service to us, but still, if we hold our lands, there will always be a turkey, or deer, or a fish in the streams, for those young who will come after us. We are afraid if we part with any more of our lands the white people will not suffer us to keep as much as will be sufficient to bury our dead.

Source: John P. Brown, *Old Frontiers* (Kingsport, TN: Southern Publishers, 1938), pp. 442–43.

Document 2.4 **President Thomas Jefferson to Chiefs of the Chickasaw Nation, 1805**

Thomas Jefferson held contradictory, though widely accepted, attitudes toward the Indians and their lands: natives held "possessory" or "aboriginal" rights to the use of their lands, and the U.S. government, by right of conquest, had both right and need to buy Indian lands. Those views are evident in this address delivered to the Chickasaw, as he implores them to sign what would become the second of four treaties ultimately made between the tribe and the U.S. government. With condescending sympathy for their interests, Jefferson instructs them as to the best means of drawing a living from the earth while also suggesting they sell their lands and move beyond the Mississippi.

WASHINGTON, March 7, 1805.

My Children, Chiefs of the Chickasaw nation, Minghey, Mataha, and Tishohotana:

I am happy to receive you at the seat of the government of the twenty-two nations, and to take you by the hand. Your friendship to the Americans has long been known to me. . . .

Your country, like all those on this side the Mississippi, has no longer game sufficient to maintain yourselves, your women and children, comfortably, by hunting. We, therefore, wish to see you undertake the cultivation of the earth, to raise cattle, corn, and cotton, to feed and clothe your people. A little labor in the earth will produce more food than the best hunts you can now make, and the women will spin and weave more clothing than the men can procure by hunting. We shall very willingly assist you in this course by furnishing you with the necessary tools and implements, and with persons to instruct you in the use of them. We have been told that you have contracted a great debt to some British traders, which gives you uneasiness, and which you honestly wish to pay by the sale of some of your lands. Whenever you raise food from the earth, and make your own clothing, you will find that you have a great deal of land more than you can cultivate or make useful, and that it will be better for you to sell some of that, to pay your debts, and to have something over to be paid to you annually to aid you in feeding and clothing yourselves. Your lands are your own, my children, they shall never be taken from you by our people or any others. You will be free to keep or to sell as yourselves shall think most for your own good. If at this time you think it will be better for you to dispose of some of them to pay your debts, and to help your people to improve the rest, we are willing to buy on reasonable terms. Our people multiply so fast that it will suit us to buy as much as you wish to sell, but only according to your good will. We have lately obtained from the French and Spaniards all the country beyond the Mississippi called Louisiana, in which there is a great deal of land unoccupied by any red men. But it is very far off, and we would prefer giving you lands there, or money and goods as you like best, for such parts of your land on this side [of] the Mississippi as you are disposed to part with. Should you have anything to say on this subject now, or at any future time, we shall be always ready to listen to you. . . .

Source: Albert Ellery Bergh, ed., *The Writings of Thomas Jefferson*, vol. 16 (Washington, DC: Thomas Jefferson Memorial Association, 1905), pp. 410–11.

Document 2.5   Shawnee Chief Tecumseh Addresses Governor William H. Harrison, 1810

William Henry Harrison, Governor of the Northwest Territory, aggressively pursued land purchases with native tribes as the federal government directed him. After the signing of the Treaty of Fort Wayne in which tribal leaders ceded three million acres in exchange for $7,000 in goods and a small annual subsidy, Tecumseh, the great Shawnee orator and leader of a pan-Indian confederacy, came to Vincennes to challenge the legitimacy of the deal. In addressing what he believes to be obligations made but broken by the Americans, Tecumseh's address also goes to the heart of native and white conceptions of land.

Brother, I wish you to give me close attention, because I think you do not clearly understand. I want to speak to you about promises that the Americans have made.

You recall the time when the Jesus Indians of the Delawares lived near the Americans, and had confidence in their promises of friendship, and thought they were secure, yet the Americans murdered all the men, women, and children, even as they prayed to Jesus?

The same promises were given to the Shawnee one time. It was at Fort Finney, where some of my people were forced to make a treaty. Flags were given to my people, and they were told they were now the children of the Americans. We were told, if any white people mean to harm you, hold up these flags and you will then be safe from all danger. We did this in good faith. But what happened? Our beloved chief Moluntha stood with the American flag in front of him and that very peace treaty in his hand, but his head was chopped by an American officer, and that American [O]fficer was never punished.

Brother, after such bitter events, can you blame me for placing little confidence in the promises of Americans? That happened before the Treaty of Greenville. When they buried the tomahawk at Greenville, the Americans said they were our new fathers, not the British anymore, and would treat us well. Since that treaty, here is how the Americans have treated us well: They have killed many Shawnee, many Winnebagoes, many Miamis, many Delawares, and have taken land from them. When they killed them, no American ever was punished, not one.

It is you, the Americans, by such bad deeds, who push the men to do mischief. . . . You do not want unity among tribes, and you destroy it. You try to make differences between them. We, their leaders, wish them to unite and consider their land the common property of all, but you try to keep them from this. You separate the tribes and deal with them that way, one by one, and advise them not to come into this union. Your states have set an example of forming a union among all the Fires, why should you censure the Indians for following that example?

But, Brother, I mean to bring all the tribes together, in spite of you, and until I have finished, I will not go to visit your President. Maybe I will when I have finished, maybe. The reason I tell you this, you want, by making your distinctions of Indian tribes and allotting to each particular tract of land, to set them against each other, and thus to weaken us. . . .

Brother, you ought to know what you are doing to the Indians. Is it by direction of the president you make these distinctions? It is a very bad thing, and we do not like it. Since my residence at Tippecanoe, we have tried to level all distinctions, to destroy village chiefs, by whom all such mischief is done. It is they who sell our lands to the Americans. Brother, these lands that were sold and the goods that were given for them were done by only a few. The Treaty of Fort Wayne was made through the threats of Winnemac, but in the future we are going to punish those chiefs who propose to sell the land.

The only way to stop this evil is for all the red men to unite in claiming an equal right in the land. That is how it was at first, and should be still, for the land never was divided, but was for the use of everyone. Any tribe could go to an empty land and make a home there. No groups among us have a right to sell, even to one another, and surely not to outsiders who want all, and will not do with less.

Sell a country! Why not sell the air, the clouds, and the Great Sea, as well as the earth? Did not the Great Spirit make them all for the use of his children?

Brother, I was glad to hear what you told us. You said that if we could prove that the land was sold by people who had no right to sell it, you would restore it. I will prove that those who did sell did not own it. Did they have a deed? A title? NO! You say those proves [*sic*] someone owns land. Those chiefs only spoke a claim, and so you pretended to believe their claim, only because you wanted the land. But the many tribes with me will not agree with those claims. They have never had a title to sell, and we agree this proves you could not buy it from them. If the land is not given back to us, you will see, when we return to our home from here, how it will be settled. It will be like this:

We shall have a great council, at which all tribes will be present. We shall show to those who sold that they had no rights to the claims they set up, and we shall see what will be done to those chiefs who did sell the land to you. I am not alone in this determination, it is the determination of all the warriors and red people who listen to me. Brother, I now wish you to listen to me. If you do not wipe out that treaty, it will seem that you wish to kill all the chiefs who sold the land! I tell you so because I am authorized by all tribes to do so! I am the head of them all! All my warriors will meet together with me in two or three moons from now. Then I will call for those chiefs who sold you this land, and we shall know what to do with them. If you do not restore the land, you will have had a hand in killing them!

I am Shawnee! I am a warrior! My forefathers were warriors. From them I took my birth into this world. From my tribe I take nothing. I am the master of my own destiny! And of that I might make the destiny of my red people, of our nation, as great as I conceive to in my mind, when I think of Washemoneto, who rules this universe! The being within me hears the voice of the ages, which tells me that once, always, and until lately, there were no white men on all this island, that it then belonged to the red man, children of the same parents, placed on it by the Great Spirit who made them, to keep it, to traverse it, to enjoy its yield, and to people it with the same race. Once they were a happy race! Now they are made miserable by the white people, who are never contented but are always coming in! You do this always, after promising not to anyone, yet you ask us to have confidence in your promises. How can we have confidence in the white people? When Jesus Christ came upon the earth, you killed him, the son of your own God, you nailed him up!! You thought he was dead, but you were mistaken. And only after you thought you killed him did you worship him, and start killing those who would not worship him. What kind of people is this for us to trust?

Now, Brother, everything I have said to you is the truth, as Washemoneto has inspired me to speak only truth to you. I have declared myself freely to you about my intentions. And I want to know your intentions. I want to know what you are going to do about taking our land. I want to hear you say that you understand now, and you will wipe out that pretended treaty, so that the tribes can be at peace with each other, as you pretend you want them to be. Tell me, Brother. I want to know.

Source: Samuel G. Drake, *The Book of the Indians of North America* (Boston: Josiah Drake at Antiquarian Bookstore, 1833), pp. 121–22.

Document 2.6   Englishman Samuel Crabtree to His Brother, 1818

In 1813, Tecumseh was killed at the Battle of the Thames, ending all hope that the tenuous pan-Indian confederacy would be able to stem the tide of white western migration. The only real losers in the War of 1812 were the native Indian tribes who had sided with the British in the hopes that they could halt further American expansion. It was not to be, as is made clear in this 1818 letter from English immigrant Samuel Crabtree to his brother in which he revels in the wonders of Tecumseh's country, now home to a flood of white settlers. The letter also illustrates the American myth of endless abundance, often given in statistic-laden testimonials.

This is the country for a man to enjoy himself: Ohio, Indiana, and the Missouri Territory; where you may see prairie sixty miles long and ten broad, not a stick nor a stone in them, at two dollars an acre, that will produce from seventy to one hundred bushels of Indian corn per acre: too rich for wheat or any other kind of grain. I measured Indian corn in Ohio state last September more than fifteen feet high, and some of the ears had from four to seven hundred grains. . . . I was at many plantations in Ohio where they no more knew the number of their hogs than myself. And they have such flocks of turkeys, geese, ducks, and hens as would surprise you; they live principally upon fowls and eggs, and in summer upon apple and peach pies. The poorest family has a cow or two and some sheep and in the fall can gather as many apples and peaches as serve the year round. Good rye whiskey; apple and peach brandy, at forty cents per gallon, which I think equal to rum. Excellent cider at three dollars per barrel of thirty-three gallons, barrel included. . . .

The poorest families adorn the table three times a day like a wedding dinner— tea, coffee, beef, fowls, pies, eggs, pickles, good bread; and their favorite beverage is whiskey or peach brandy. Say, is it so in England?

If you knew the difference between this country and England you would need no persuading to leave it and come hither. It abounds with game and deer; I often see ten or fifteen together; turkeys in abundance, weighing from eighteen to twenty-four pounds. The rivers abound with ducks and fish. There are some elk and bears. We have no hares, but swarms of rabbits: the woods are full of turtledoves, and eight or nine kinds of woodpeckers. Robin redbreast about the size of your pigeon.

Source: John Knight, *Important Extracts from Original and Recent Letters Written by Englishmen, in the United States of America, to Their Friends in England*, Second Series (Manchester, England, 1818), pp. 111–12.

**Document 2.7   Chief Justice John Marshall, *Johnson v. M'Intosh,*
                    Supreme Court of the United States, 1823**

> *The case involved the sale of the same Illinois lands twice—the first
> time by Piankeshaw Indians, and subsequently by the U.S. govern-
> ment to the defendant. In deciding for the defendant, Justice Marshall
> established firmly, the important legal principle that Indians had only
> "aboriginal" title to the land—that is, the right to use and occupy it—
> until such time as the nation holding rights of conquest, the United
> States, opted for the sale and disposition of the land. As the sovereign
> power, the United States held absolute title over Indian lands and had
> no legal obligation to protect Indian land rights.*

...On the discovery of this immense continent, the great nations of Europe
were eager to appropriate to themselves so much of it as they could respectively
acquire. Its vast extent offered an ample field to the ambition and enterprise of all;
and the character and religion of its inhabitants afforded an apology for considering them as a people over whom the superior genius of Europe might claim
an ascendancy. The potentates of the old world found no difficulty in convincing
themselves that they made ample compensation to the inhabitants of the new, by
bestowing on them civilization and Christianity, in exchange for unlimited independence. But, as they were all in pursuit of nearly the same object, it was
necessary, in order to avoid conflicting settlements, and consequent war with
each other, to establish a principle, which all should acknowledge as the law by
which the right of acquisition, which they all asserted, should be regulated as
between themselves. This principle was, that discovery gave title to the government by whose subjects, or by whose authority, it was made, against all other
European governments, which title might be consummated by possession.

The exclusion of all other Europeans, necessarily gave to the nation making
the discovery the sole right of acquiring the soil from the natives, and establishing settlements upon it. It was a right with which no Europeans could
interfere. It was a right which all asserted for themselves, and to the assertion of
which, by others, all assented....

While the different nations of Europe respected the right of the natives, as
occupants, they asserted the ultimate dominion to be in themselves; and
claimed and exercised, as a consequence of this ultimate dominion, a power to
grant the soil, while yet in possession of the natives. These grants have been
understood by all, to convey a title to the grantees, subject only to the Indian
right of occupancy....

The ceded territory was occupied by numerous and warlike tribes of Indians;
but the exclusive right of the United States to extinguish their title, and to grant
the soil, has never, we believe, been doubted....

The United States, then, have unequivocally acceded to that great and broad
rule by which its civilized inhabitants now hold this country. They hold, and
assert in themselves, the title by which it was acquired. They maintain, as all
others have maintained that discovery gave an exclusive right to extinguish the

Indian title of occupancy, either by purchase or by conquest; and gave also a right to such a degree of sovereignty, as the circumstances of the people would allow them to exercise....

The title by conquest is acquired and maintained by force. The conqueror prescribes its limits. Humanity, however, acting on public opinion, has established, as a general rule, that the conquered shall not be wantonly oppressed, and that their condition shall remain as eligible as is compatible with the objects of the conquest. Most usually, they are incorporated with the victorious nation, and become subjects or citizens of the government with which they are connected. The new and old members of the society mingle with each other; the distinction between them is gradually lost, and they make one people. Where this incorporation is practicable, humanity demands, and a wise policy requires, that the rights of the conquered to property should remain unimpaired; that the new subjects should be governed as equitably as the old, and that confidence in their security should gradually banish the painful sense of being separated from their ancient connexions, and united by force to strangers.

When the conquest is complete, and the conquered inhabitants can be blended with the conquerors, or safely governed as a distinct people, public opinion, which not even the conqueror can disregard, imposes these restraints upon him; and he cannot neglect them without injury to his fame, and hazard to his power.

But the tribes of Indians inhabiting this country were fierce savages, whose occupation was war, and whose subsistence was drawn chiefly from the forest. To leave them in possession of their country, was to leave the country a wilderness; to govern them as a distinct people, was impossible, because they were as brave and as high spirited as they were fierce, and were ready to repel by arms every attempt on their independence....

Frequent and bloody wars, in which the whites were not always the aggressors, unavoidably ensued. European policy, numbers, and skill prevailed. As the white population advanced, that of the Indians necessarily receded. The country in the immediate neighbourhood of agriculturists became unfit for them. The game fled into thicker and more unbroken forests, and the Indians followed. The soil, to which the crown originally claimed title, being no longer occupied by its ancient inhabitants, was parcelled out according to the will of the sovereign power, and taken possession of by persons who claimed immediately from the crown, or immediately, through its grantees or deputies....

Source: Johnson v. M'Intosh, 21 U.S. 543, 5 L.Ed. 681, 8 Wheat. 543 (1823).

NOTE

1. Elliott West, "American Frontier," in Clyde A. Milner II, Carol A. O'Connor, and Martha A. Sandweiss, eds., *The Oxford History of the American West* (New York: Oxford University Press, 1994), pp. 26–27.

ANNOTATED BIBLIOGRAPHY

Cronon, William. *Changes in the Land: Indians, Colonists, and the Ecology of New England.* Anniversary edition. New York: Hill and Wang, 2003. Pathbreaking work, essential to understanding the environmental changes that ensued from the clash of two fundamentally different civilizations.

———. *Nature's Metropolis: Chicago and the Great West.* New York: W. W. Norton, 1992. Superb environmental history that illustrates the profound and far-reaching environmental consequences that ensued from the taking of the Old Northwest.

Gilbert, Bil. *God Gave Us This Country: Tekamthi and the First American Civil War.* New York: Scribner, 1989. The most authoritative history of the life of Tecumseh, the book also offers a vivid chronicle of the decades-long bloody warfare that determined the fate of the Ohio River Valley.

Grinde, Donald A. *Ecocide of Native America: Environmental Destruction of Indian Lands and Peoples.* Santa Fe, NM: Clear Light Books, 1998. Passionate and thoughtful interpretation of the environmental degradation of native lands in various regions of the country; includes both historical episodes and contemporary struggles.

Hallock, Thomas. *From the Fallen Tree: Frontier Narratives, Environmental Politics, and the Roots of a National Pastoral, 1749–1826.* Chapel Hill: University of North Carolina Press, 2003. Chronicles the ways in which Anglo-Americans, from the era of territorial expansion through the period of Indian dispossession, deployed Edenic pastoral imagery to craft a national psyche of righteous, natural possession of the continent. Deconstructs the myth of a vacant eastern wilderness, telling us much about how yeoman farmers—the vanguard of Jefferson's "Empire of Liberty"—played a central if unconscious role in the conquest of what was most certainly not virgin wilderness.

Jennings, Francis. *The Invasion of America: Indians, Colonialism, and the Cant of Conquest.* New York: W. W. Norton, 1976. Broke new ground and remains a vital study of the ideology that buttressed European American conquest of Native America.

Linklater, Andro. *Measuring America: How an Untamed Wilderness Shaped the United States and Fulfilled the Promise of Democracy.* New York: Walker, 2002. Explains how land ownership proved central to solidifying the cornerstone American myth of individualism and the sacredness of private property in the development of the republic.

Onuf, Peter S. *Jefferson's Empire: The Language of American Nationhood.* Charlottesville: University of Virginia Press, 2000. Develops the transformation of Jefferson's thinking about Indians as they came to pose a greater threat to the expansion of a white man's republican "Empire of Liberty."

Richter, Daniel K. *Facing East from Indian Country: A Native History of Early America.* Cambridge, MA: Harvard University Press, 2003. Interprets the story as one of tenacious, enduring Indian presence in the East—even after the critical decade of the 1780s when Americans set out to measure and take Indian land.

Saunt, Claudio. *A New Order of Things: Property, Power, and the Transformation of the Creek Indians, 1733–1816.* New York: Cambridge University Press, 1999. Describes the profound transformation experienced by one tribe as the cultural values and market forces of Anglo-American society penetrated into the deep South and overwhelmed native peoples.

Wallace, Anthony F. C. *Jefferson and the Indians: The Tragic Fate of the First Americans.* Cambridge, MA: Belknap Press, 2001. Probes the tragically contradictory views of Indians held by Jefferson, demonstrating how his ostensibly shifting ideas about and attitudes toward native tribes reflected romantic ideals about nature and republican virtue as well as the nationalistic impulse of conquest.

White, Richard. *The Middle Ground: Indians, Empires, and Republics in the Great Lakes Region: 1650–1815.* New York: Cambridge University Press, 1991. Makes clear that the history of white-Indian relations cannot be reduced simply to one of conquest.

3

Controlling Water in the Early Industrialization of New England

> ...inland streams which had initially been dammed for rural sawmills and gristmills are by and by turned to other uses. Wherever a good water privilege exists there soon spring up various manufacturers, requiring many laborers and the greatest economy of the power of the stream, The village becomes a factory town,...the dam is soon raised, and where instead of a free movement of the water, tumbling over the fall in its superabundance as in former days, we find a great reservoir.
> —Massachusetts State Board of Health, 1871[1]

An old Chinese proverb holds that "he who controls the water controls the people." There was much truth in that adage in the early industrial history of the United States. The story of water in the nineteenth century—how it was used and developed, by whom, and for what purposes—suggests, first, the intensifying pace and degree of environmental change that transpired as the nation applied its resources to industrialization. It also illustrates the shifting legal and legislative terrain that increasingly gave advantages to large corporate industrial development over the interests of both individual Americans and their environment.

This chapter, the first of three to grapple with this pivotal history, centers on the massive engineering projects that in the 1830s and 1840s transformed New England lakes and flowing rivers into the energy force that drove American textile mills and gave life to celebrated industrial towns like Lowell and Lawrence, Massachusetts. Extending over hundreds of square miles, elaborate systems of dams, locks, canals, and impoundment reservoirs changed the natural and human ecology of the entire region. Corn fields flooded, fish spawning runs came to an end, and human population density increased, bringing associated problems of sanitation and disease. Moreover, the environmental dimensions of this history are closely intertwined with—indeed are *agents of*—the more familiar aspects of social and economic change of this first phase of America's industrial revolution. Beyond drawing farmers' daughters to labor as mill hands in the factories made possible by dams and locks, the engineering of New England's hydrology foreshadowed the broader upward shift of economic and political power that became severe by the last quarter of the century. Large industrial interests broadly exercised the power of eminent domain that displaced farmers and village mill operators, a harbinger of future events in other parts of the nation. In building river and lake impoundments, large companies also terminated traditional fishing rights of those living upstream. Those affected lost customary avenues of redress of grievances against those who obstructed the flow of the river.[2] All of this signaled a national trend that would extend far into the future: local, relatively low-impact use of natural resources by individual citizens would yield to large-scale economic development directed from a distance. Increasingly the powers of both state and nation would deem this incorporated taking of nature more compelling to the public interest.

The broad application of waterpower to America's industrialization exemplified in the New England story marked a turning point in one other profound way. Marking off and selling land in parcels had been going on for more than two centuries, and was legislatively and methodically inscribed in the Land Ordinance, but water was another matter. Fluid and in motion, the water of rivers and streams was not easily captured or sold. In the 1830s, the Proprietors of Locks and Canals (PLC) on the Merrimack River changed all that when it sold water in units of "mill powers" to textile mill owners downstream of their power canals. Separating the sale of water rights from the land itself, the PLC severed the inseparable. When the most vital elements of the natural world could be sundered and sold, when the relentlessly moving source of all life on the planet could be commandeered and commodified, a pivotal moment in environmental history had occurred.

Much of the history of water swirls around the law. American water jurisprudence derived from centuries of British common law, which held that persons had the right to use the stream or river adjoining their riparian land so long as they did not diminish the flow or degrade the quality of the water for others. Common law tradition also protected one's land from damages that might accrue from the impoundment of water by one's neighbor. And in a society that was still largely agricultural, little different from the British world of the Magna Carta in which the doctrine was established, citizens had the right to expect the great annual migrations of fish upstream to spawning grounds. Thus, no person had the right to obstruct the passage of anadromous (migratory) fish. Transplanted from Britain, common law, or "natural flow" tradition allowed persons physically to remove obstructions that flooded one's fields, prevented the passage of fish upstream, or in other ways diminished the quality of water adjacent to one's property. Deemed by individuals to be a "public nuisance," such dams were vulnerable to common law-sanctioned destruction. More than a few aggrieved farmers in the 1700s deployed hammers and crowbars against the sides of wooden dams that had impounded streams and flooded their land. Court action came *after* such destruction. Only "prescription" rights—attained when a landowner used water over a long period of time without objection—afforded legal protection to the landowner when his use brought deleterious impacts to others. These pillars of water law, deeply embedded in an agrarian Old World and still a familiar part of colonial America, began to crumble as the new nation aggressively developed its manufacturing capacity in the early 1800s. Thus Henry David Thoreau's mischievous musing (Document 3.2) about what a "crow-bar [would do] against the Billerica dam" on the Concord River suggests a familiar—but by 1839 increasingly anachronistic and unacceptable—tradition.

To be sure, most dams were never harmed, for in this early period they were too important to farmers' livelihood and posed no threat to most. Indeed, the impoundment of streams in early America to erect sawmills, gristmills, and woolen mills was absolutely essential to the processing of the farmers' subsistence needs. Mills served a vital public purpose, and legislatures and local governments throughout the colonies thus encouraged their establishment by passing "Mill Acts," laws designed to encourage the building of mills even as they effectively curtailed the common law water rights described above. Though they varied, most such statutes required the builder of the milldam to pay a fee to the aggrieved landowner, either as annual rent or increasingly as a onetime payment, for the privilege of flooding that land. Still, the assumption throughout the early period was that mills were to serve and benefit agriculture; they were not to function as separate, commercially driven enterprises. The dams themselves were small in scale and the flooding relatively modest and sporadic.

Most milldam owners accepted the Mill Acts as a reasonable compromise between private and public interests. They resigned themselves as well to the Fish Acts, also imposed by colonial legislatures that sought to protect fishing rights on all navigable waterways. The laws prevented anyone from building a dam on navigable portions of waterways that obstructed the passage of fish during the spring spawning season. Fishing rights above the point of navigation belonged to the riparian landowner—subject to regulation by legislature so as to prevent the obstruction of the passage of fish. The Fish Acts required mill owners to construct for the spring fish runs a "fishway"—a kind of inclined sluice ladder over the dam that would allow fish to pass over the dam. Though mill owners saw water as an energy resource and farmers saw those same streams as a means of sustenance through fishing, conflicts were relatively rare—again owing to the importance of the mills, the minimal threat posed by their dams, and the seasonal running of their mills. Even the first canals built by the PLC on the Merrimack River in 1792, though they diverted the water's course and obstructed its flow in places around waterfalls, provoked relatively little conflict, as those canals helped carry the farmers' produce downstream to market and thus were generally perceived as an instrument of the public good.

This generally tranquil scene was disrupted by the full-blown emergence of industrial capitalism. Dependent on both wage labor and a continuous flow of great volumes of water, iron-making blast furnaces from Pennsylvania to Rhode Island, unlike sawmills and gristmills, produced for the market, not to satisfy local need. Conflicts between farming and industrial interests erupted, in part because the furnaces were often fired up in the spring, when shad and alewives began migrating upstream. Although fishways were required of such furnace operators, they often failed, giving rise to opposition from farmers and petitions to legislative bodies for redress.

Though farmers in the early 1800s still won more battles than they lost, the allure of the market economy strengthened the desire of the states to establish manufacturing operations. Individual state legislatures and judges began reconsidering the core principle of common water law: that is, the public benefits accruing from clean, free-flowing water. Most famously, Samuel Slater, who built the first water-powered cotton mill in America at Pawtucket Falls, Rhode Island, in 1792, never was forced to construct a fishway on his dam, despite vigorous protests and petitioning from farmers who had lost the ability to fish the river and small mill operators whose waterwheels were obstructed by Slater's diversion of water. As the economic wealth generated from the cotton mills continued to grow, owners of such enterprises like Slater continually—and increasingly successfully—made the argument that their ventures were central to the rising prosperity of the state and thus served a much greater public purpose than either a healthy unimpeded fishery or small-time local millers. Property-owning farmers and citizens feared being overwhelmed by the alien interests of manufacturing capital that Jeffersonians had long warned posed a threat to republican liberty.

Yet, the conflict continued as the growth of market-based agriculture and manufacturing depended on the improvement of navigation and necessarily the enlargement of the dam-building enterprise. Manufacturers could scarcely hope to transport their products to new and distant markets without rapid and inexpensive transportation. That required "improving" the rivers—in particular, constructing locks and canals that would facilitate passage of vessels around waterfalls up and down the river. State governments throughout New England anxious to develop their respective economies soon obliged. They employed the language of the Mill Acts to attract the capital and expertise that could engineer elaborate and expensive projects. Dams grew larger, the canal systems longer, the water impoundments deeper and wider. Acts of incorporation granted to the canal and dam builders allowed the companies the right to flood property by eminent domain and gave inundated property owners the right to claim monetary damages in court.

In 1801 Timothy Dwight marveled at the growing number of manufacturing works throughout the Connecticut River Valley. Thirty years later, his younger brother Theodore would see an even more industrialized, thriving, and dramatically transformed landscape (Document 3.1). The impoundment of the Merrimack River at Lawrence and the stunningly productive and orderly textile mills that flourished there epitomized the regional trend: manufacturers of textiles, chemicals, paper, and other goods located their operations near the falls of major river systems throughout New England, as well as the populated upper eastern seaboard of the United States. There, larger amounts of capital combined technology and engineering expertise to capture and channel waterpower into manufacturing enterprises that put tens of thousands of men and women to work in burgeoning industrial towns and cities. By the middle of the nineteenth century, the Essex Company and the PLC, subsidiaries of Boston Associates, a powerful group of Boston entrepreneurs, had completely reshaped New England waters. Their dams powered factories at Lowell and Lawrence, Massachusetts, and Manchester, New Hampshire. They controlled forty-five miles of the Merrimack River, producing millions of dollars' worth of cotton textiles annually, and selling water in "mill power" units to smaller mills along the river corridor. The well-regulated wage-labor workforce employed in these enormously profitable factories that launched the American Industrial Revolution was paralleled and made possible by the command and commodification of the waters outside.

For forty years, New England state courts had been grappling with the issue of how to encourage the industrial development of their states—necessarily driven by the engineering of their waterways—while maintaining the public's right to fish those same waters. By virtue of its charter, the Essex Company had been obliged to build a "fishway" to allow for the passage of fish whose survival depended on upstream spawning beds. Because the fishway failed, the legislature subsequently required them to compensate upstream fishers for that loss. Yet, responding to public pressure, in 1856 the legislature passed a law requiring the company to construct a new passageway for fish. In the 1859 decision in *Commonwealth v. Essex Company*, the Massachusetts Supreme Court ruled that the state had gone too far and had impinged on the rights of the company that had been granted to advance the public interest. Beyond exacerbating the ongoing ecological devastation of the Merrimack fishery, the decision illustrated the degree to which well-inscribed assumptions and legal definitions of natural resources as "public" and protected for all were giving way to corporate capture that suggested a new definition of how nature should serve the public interest.

From the logging of forests to feed factory towns to the flooding of fields, the surrounding rural countryside felt the impact of the Industrial Revolution. But as the companies were quick to remind judges when farmers took them to court seeking damages from flooding, farmers had benefited enormously from the markets and general prosperity brought by dams, canals, and the factory towns they spawned. In 1835 the Palmer (textile) Company successfully argued that the improvements they had brought to the region had rendered the farmers' land more valuable than if they had not located there or if the dam in question were to be removed.[3]

The general trend was a move away from the common law era in which water could neither be owned nor diminished or degraded for the neighbor downstream. Courts increasingly redefined water as a commodity whose most important value was its capacity to advance economic development. From 1850 to 1870, numerous state court decisions in favor of the sprawling waterpower infrastructure and against small farmers and mill operators justified degradation of clean, free-flowing waterways in service to that larger societal goal. In determining water's value toward maximum production, the law accepted that certain costs would have to be borne by the society with such "reasonable use" of waterways, as it came to be called. In effect, men in black robes arbitrated contested views of how water could be used, by whom, and to what extent it could be fouled.

The environmental impacts of industrialized development of rivers and streams sanctioned by the courts as an acceptable trade-off were indeed pervasive. Beyond flooding and the damage to the fishery resulting from dams, there was also massive human and animal waste that came with factory towns and industrial effluent that poured into the natural sewers that rivers everywhere became. By 1880 the Connecticut River, whose "purity, salubrity, and sweetness" had been praised by Timothy Dwight in 1803, was largely unfit for all but industrial uses. Fish populations shrank to mere remnants of what Thoreau had seen two generations before; efforts to restore certain species through the new science of "fish culture" largely failed. The ruination of the rivers prompted both Massachusetts and Connecticut to devise ways to minimize the damage while at the same time not hampering industrial development of the river valleys. Most notably, a water purification system developed by the Boston Associates became a model for the nation by the end of the century. The Essex Company's chief engineer assumed a leadership role on the Massachusetts Board of Health, which led to the establishment of an Essex Company facility in Lawrence to conduct intensive studies on sewage treatment and water purification. Out of this development emerged the nation's first slow sand filter to combat the pervasive problem of typhoid in drinking water.

Thus, after nearly a century, the corporate industrialization of New England waters pointed the way toward the remedies necessary to counter and correct the abuses inflicted on local and regional waterscapes. By then few could recall the profound transformation that had taken place. The engineered control, marketplace commodification, and incidental despoliation of once free-flowing public waters illustrated the degree to which society had come to value maximum industrialized production.

DOCUMENTS

Document 3.1   Theodore Dwight Reports on the Commercial Progress of New England River Valleys, 1833

In 1821 and 1822, Timothy Dwight's Travels in New England and New York *became one of the leading travel accounts of the young nation. Like his more famous brother Timothy, in the 1830s Theodore Dwight trumpeted the development of New England. Writing in 1833, Dwight chronicled the natural features of the Connecticut and Merrimack River valleys that had attracted phenomenal economic investment. Although the book was written in matter-of-fact encyclopedic style, the reader can sense Dwight's enthusiasm for the region's prosperity as the rivers themselves were channeled and developed for industrial production through the elaborate engineering system of dams, locks, and canals—developments that had led to the establishment of Lowell, Massachusetts, as the "American Manchester [England]."*

CONNECTICUT r[iver]. The principal and most important stream of New England, rises in the highlands,... the headwaters of which, forming Lake Connecticut, are 16 hundred feet above the level of L[ong] I[sland] Sound. Within the first 25 ms. Of its course, which is s.w., it falls about 600 ft; afterwards pursuing a more southerly course to the head of Fifteen Mile falls, it has a farther descent of 250 ft. in 20 ms. Between the latter, and the foot of Enfield falls, where it meets the tide water, are several other descents and rapids.... Numerous bridges are thrown across the river, the lowest of which is at Hartford, At the N. boundary of Vt. The Conn. Is 150 ft. wide; 60 ms. Below, 390 ftl; and in Mass. and Conn. It varies from 450 to 1,050 ft. in width. Salmon, which formerly were abundant in the Conn. have entirely disappeared; the principal fishery is shad, which is very valuable. Large quantities of other fine fish also abound in it. The Connecticut is navigable to Hartford, 50 ms. from its mouth, for vessels of 8 ft. draft, and to Middletown, for those drawing 10 ft. of water. Large steam boats ply daily between the former place and the city of N. York, touching at the intermediate places on the r. above Hartford numerous flat bottom boats of 15 to 30 tons burthen ascend 220 ms. above Hartford, to Wells r. by aid of locks and canals around the falls. These are principally towed by small steam boats, six in number, placed on the different sections between Springfield, Mass., and Wells river. Two steam boats, for passengers, also ply daily between Hartford and Springfield. The improvements recently made, and others contemplated in the navigation of the river, have already given a fresh impulse to business, as is evident from the great increase of merchandise and produce transported upon its waters, and the increasing intercourse between the towns and villages in its vicinity.

LOWELL, the American Manchester, situated at the confluence of Merrimack and Concord rs. Middlesex co. Mass. This place is undoubtedly destined to be a manufacturing city. Its growth for a few years has been almost unparalleled. The foundation of the second factory was laid here in 1822, at which time, the territory now included in the town, exclusive of one factory establishment, contained less than 100 inhabitants. There are now [1832] 8 manufacturing cos. Viz. the Merrimack manufacturing company, having a capital of $1,500,000, 5 large brick factories, containing 26,000 spindles, and about 1,000 looms. These employ from 3 to 400 males, and 8 to 900 females, using 5,000 bales of cotton, or about 1,500,000 lbs. annually, and manufacturing, bleaching and printing 6,500,000 yards yearly.... There are in the place 200 machinists, who work up 600 tons of iron, annually, into machinery. It is computed that upwards of 5,000 tons of anthracite coal are annually consumed.... The Lock and Canal company, who own and dispose of the water privileges, have a capital invested of $600,000. This company owns a machine shop 150 ft. by 40, and 4 stories high, in which are employed about 200 hands. The stock of this co. is 160 per cent. Advance. The great water power is produced by a canal a mile and half long, 60 ft. wide, and 8 ft. deep, from its commencement above the head of Pawtucket falls on the Merrimack, to its termination in Concord r. The water is taken from this canal by smaller canals, and conveyed to the factories, and thence into the Merrimack. There are room and water power sufficient for 50 huge additional factories!...

MERRIMACK r. N.H., the largest in that state and one of the principal rs. Of New England, ... There are many falls, the principal of which are dammed, and supply water to important manufactories. Canals have been made round them all, with locks, by which the r. has been navigated in boats for some years, up to Concord....

Source: William Darby and Theodore Dwight, Jr., *Gazetteer of the United States of America* (Hartford, CT: Edward Hopkins, 1833), pp. 110–11.

Document 3.2   Henry David Thoreau Bemoans the Taming of New England Rivers, 1839

> *In this excerpt from* A Week on the Concord and Merrimack Rivers, *Henry David Thoreau muses on the natural history and beauty of the same waterscape whose economic development Dwight had championed. This contrast signaled the intellectual debate that emerged later in the century between those who stood for unfettered development of natural resources and those in the Thoreau tradition who began to "speak for the fishes."*

Whether we live by the seaside, or by the lakes and rivers, or on the prairie, it concerns us to attend to the nature of fishes, since they are not phenomena confined to certain localities only, but forms and phases of the life in nature universally dispersed. The countless shoals which annually coast the shores of Europe and America are not so interesting to the student of nature, as the more fertile law itself, which deposit their spawn on the tops of mountains, and on the interior plains; the fish principle in nature, from which it results that they may be found in water in so many places, in greater or less numbers. The natural historian is not a fisherman, who prays for cloudy days and good luck merely, but as fishing has been styled, "a contemplative man's recreation," introducing him profitably to woods and water, so the fruit of the naturalist's observations is not in new genera or species, but in new contemplations still, and science is only a more contemplative man's recreation. The seeds of the life of fishes are everywhere disseminated, whether the winds waft them, or the waters float them, or the deep earth holds them; wherever a pond is dug, straightway it is stocked with this vivacious race. They have a lease of nature, and it is not yet out. The Chinese are bribed to carry their ova from province to province in jars or in hollow reeds, or the water-birds to transport them to the mountain tarns and interior lakes. There are fishes wherever there is a fluid medium, and even in clouds and in melted metals we detect their semblance. Think how in winter you can sink a line down straight in a pasture through snow and through ice, and pull up a bright, slippery, dumb, subterranean silver or golden fish! It is curious, also, to reflect how they make one family, from the largest to the smallest. The least minnow that lies on the ice as bait for pickerel, looks like a huge sea-fish cast up on the shore. In the waters of this town there are about a dozen distinct species, though the inexperienced would expect many more.

It enhances our sense of the grand security and serenity of nature, to observe the still undisturbed economy and content of the fishes of this century, their happiness a regular fruit of the summer. The Fresh-Water Sun-Fish, Bream, or Ruff (*Pomotis vulgaris*), as it were, without ancestry, without posterity, still represents the fresh-water sun-fish in nature. It is the most common of all, and seen on every urchin's string; a simple and inoffensive fish, whose nests are visible all along the shore, hollowed in the sand, over which it is steadily poised through the summer hours on waving fin. . . .

The Common Perch, . . . is one of the handsomest and most regularly formed of our fishes, and at such a moment as this reminds us of the fish in the picture which wished to be restored to its native element until it had grown larger; . . .

The chivin, dace, roach, cousin trout, or whatever else it is called (*Leuciscus pulchellus*), white and red, always an unexpected prize, which, however, any angler is glad to hook for its rarity. A name that reminds us of many an unsuccessful ramble by swift streams, when the wind rose to disappoint the fisher. . . .

The shiner (*Leuciscus crysoleucas*) is a soft-scaled and tender fish, the victim of its stronger neighbors, found in all places, deep and shallow, clear and turbid; generally the first nibbler at the bait, but, with its small mouth and nibbling propensities, not easily caught. It is a gold or silver bit that passes current in the river, its limber tail dimpling the surface in sport or flight. . . .

The pickerel (*Esox reticulatus*), the swiftest, wariest, and most ravenous of fishes, which Josselyn calls the Fresh-Water or River Wolf, is very common in the shallow and weedy lagoons along the sides of the stream. It is a solemn, stately, ruminant fish, lurking under the shadow of a pad at noon, with still, circumspect, voracious eye, motionless as a jewel set in water, or moving slowly along to take up its position, darting from time to time at such unlucky fish or frog or insect as comes within its range, and swallowing it at a gulp. . . .

The suckers (*Catostomi Bostonienses* and *tuberculati*), common and horned, perhaps on an average the largest of our fishes, may be seen in shoals of a hundred or more, stemming the current in the sun, on their mysterious migrations, and sometimes sucking in the bait which the fisherman suffers to float toward them. . . .

The common eel, too (*Muræna Bostoniensis*), the only species of eel known in the State, a slimy, squirming creature, informed of mud, still squirming in the pan, is speared and hooked up with various success. . . .

In the shallow parts of the river, where the current is rapid, and the bottom pebbly, you may sometimes see the curious circular nests of the lamprey eel (*Petromyzon Americanus*), the American stone-sucker, as large as a cart-wheel, a foot or two in height, and sometimes rising half a foot above the surface of the water. They collect these stones, of the size of a hen's egg, with their mouths, as their name implies, and are said to fashion them into circles with their tails. They ascend falls by clinging to the stones, which may sometimes be raised, by lifting the fish by the tail. As they are not seen on their way down the streams, it is thought by fishermen that they never return, but waste away and die, clinging to rocks and stumps of trees for an indefinite period; a tragic feature in the scenery of the river bottoms worthy to be remembered with Shakespeare's description of the sea-floor. They are rarely seen in our waters at present, on account of the dams, though they are taken in great quantities at the mouth of the river in Lowell. Their nests, which are very conspicuous, look more like art than anything in the river. . . .

Salmon, shad, and alewives were formerly abundant here, and taken in weirs by the Indians, who taught this method to the whites, by whom they were used as food and as manure, until the dam, and afterward the canal at Billerica, and the factories at Lowell, put an end to their migrations hitherward; though it is thought that a few more enterprising shad may still occasionally be seen in this part of the river. It is said, to account for the destruction of the fishery, that those who at that time represented the interests of the fishermen and the fishes, remembering between what dates they were accustomed to take the grown shad, stipulated, that the dams should be left open for that season only, and the fry, which go down a month later, were consequently stopped and destroyed by myriads. Others say that the fish-ways were not properly constructed. Perchance, after a few thousands of years, if the fishes will be patient, and pass their summers elsewhere, meanwhile, nature will have levelled the Billerica dam, and the Lowell factories, and the Grass-ground River run clear again, to be explored by new migratory shoals, even as far as the Hopkinton pond and Westborough swamp.

One would like to know more of that race, now extinct, whose seines lie rotting in the garrets of their children, who openly professed the trade of fishermen, and even fed their townsmen creditably, not skulking through the meadows to a rainy afternoon sport. Dim visions we still get of miraculous draughts of fishes, and heaps uncountable by the river-side, from the tales of our seniors sent on horseback in their childhood from the neighboring towns, perched on saddle-bags, with instructions to get the one bag filled with shad, the other with alewives. . . .

Shad are still taken in the basin of Concord River at Lowell, where they are said to be a month earlier than the Merrimack shad, on account of the warmth of the water. Still patiently, almost pathetically, with instinct not to be discouraged, not to be *reasoned* with, revisiting their old haunts, as if their stern fates would relent, and still met by the Corporation with its dam. Poor shad! where is thy redress? When Nature gave thee instinct, gave she thee the heart to bear thy fate? Still wandering the sea in thy scaly armor to inquire humbly at the mouths of rivers if man has perchance left them free for thee to enter. By countless shoals loitering uncertain meanwhile, merely stemming the tide there, in danger from sea foes in spite of thy bright armor, awaiting new instructions, until the sands, until the water itself, tell thee if it be so or not. Thus by whole migrating nations, full of instinct, which is thy faith, in this backward spring, turned adrift, and perchance knowest not where men do *not* dwell, where there are *not* factories, in these days. Armed with no sword, no electric shock, but mere Shad, armed only with innocence and a just cause, with tender dumb mouth only forward, and scales easy to be detached. I for one am with thee, and who knows what may avail a crow-bar against that Billerica dam?—Not despairing when whole myriads have gone to feed those sea monsters during thy suspense, but still brave, indifferent, on easy fin there, like shad reserved for higher destinies. Willing to be decimated for man's behoof after the spawning season. Away with the superficial and selfish phil-*anthropy* of men,—who knows what admirable virtue of fishes may be below low-water-mark, bearing up against a hard destiny, not admired by that fellow-creature who alone can appreciate it! Who hears the fishes when they cry? It will not be forgotten by some memory that we were contemporaries. Thou shalt erelong have thy way up the rivers, up all the rivers of the globe, if I am not mistaken. Yea, even thy dull watery dream shall be more than realized. If it were not so, but thou wert to be overlooked at first and at last, then would not I take their heaven. Yes, I say so, who think I know better than thou canst. Keep a stiff fin then, and stem all the tides thou mayst meet.

At length it would seem that the interests, not of the fishes only, but of the men of Wayland, of Sudbury, of Concord, demand the levelling of that dam. Innumerable acres of meadow are waiting to be made dry land, wild native grass to give place to English. The farmers stand with scythes whet, waiting the subsiding of the waters, by gravitation, by evaporation or otherwise, but sometimes their eyes do not rest, their wheels do not roll, on the quaking meadow ground during the haying season at all. So many sources of wealth inaccessible. They rate the loss hereby incurred in the single town of Wayland alone as equal to the expense of keeping a hundred yoke of oxen the year round. One year, as I learn, not long ago, the farmers standing ready to drive their teams afield as usual, the water gave no signs of falling; without new attraction in the heavens, without freshet or visible cause, still standing stagnant at an unprecedented height. All hydrometers were at fault; some trembled for their English even. But speedy emissaries revealed the unnatural secret, in the new float-board, wholly a foot in width, added to their already too high privileges by the dam proprietors. The hundred yoke of oxen, meanwhile, standing patient, gazing wishfully meadow-ward, at that inaccessible waving native grass, uncut but by the great mower Time, who cuts so broad a swathe, without so much as a wisp to wind about their horns. . . .

Source: Henry David Thoreau, *A Week on the Concord and Merrimack Rivers* (Boston: Houghton Mifflin, 1906), pp. 30–43.

Document 3.3   Naturalist Jerome Van Crowninshield Smith Argues for Progress

---

One of the leading naturalists of his time, Jerome Van Crowninshield Smith did not share Henry David Thoreau's skeptical view toward progress represented by dams and manufacturing interests. Van Crown-inshield Smith, who later went on to serve as the mayor of Boston, admired nature but believed in the virtues of commerce and the social progress brought by men of capital. Although he acknowledged the damage done to some of the fisheries by dams and manufacturing, he (like industrialists and increasingly most judges as well) declared that laws protecting fish struck against the natural laws of individual enterprise and were futile; better, he argued, that anglers impeded in their fishing rights on one stream should go seek out another.

. . . The remaining fisheries of the Commonwealth, as subjects of general interest, are in a great measure losing, and in some instances have lost their importance. The beautiful *salmon,* which Isaac Walton accounted the king of fish, is a rare visitor to our waters, although we find them occasionally exhibited by those who cater for the public taste. . . .

It is needless to advert to the many laws enacted by the Legislature of this Commonwealth, for the protection of the *alewives* in Taunton Great River; as well as other species of edible fish, peculiar to the rivers directly communicating with the sea-board.

Such laws have never been, nor can they be, of the least possible advantage; the combined forces of the United States, in battle array, could not lessen their numbers,—and it would be utterly impossible to exterminate the species.

Therefore, all such protecting laws are perfectly useless, unphilosophical, and at variance with that grand scheme of nature which provides for the necessities of all organized beings, and sustains the existence of their species, under all changes, incidents and circumstances. . . .

Dams, break-waters, &c. across rivers, are the result of civilization, and fishes may forsake the streams where they once instinctively deposited their roes:— but their loss if trifling, at any particular locality, when compared with the advantages arising from the improvements of their solitary haunts. As animals recede before the inroads of civil life, so do the fishes, and no human laws can restrain them. . . .

Alas! That the manufacturing interest should clash with the success of the *fisheries!* It is not that we complain of these obstructions as preventing the fish from going down to the sea; we should be content to find them *still* where nature placed them. But now, they are dispersed and degenerated in quality, the waters are poisoned, and the legitimate current of the rivers, like the present course of politics, is forced into new and *untried* channels; so that in the anguish of our hearts, adopting a distich to the teeming times, and blending the patriot's apprehension with the angler's regret, the thought occurs to us that

> *"Nullification* is vexation,
> *Division* is as bad—"

For such is the creed of him who is both a lover of his country and its enjoyments. But if fortunately chance should have directed his thoughts and steps to a more favored scene—

> "—Where purple violets lurk
> With all the lowly children of the shade—"

there, having passed a day of temperate pleasure, far from the world of strife, having tried conclusions with none but the companion of his toil, or the victims of his skill, he lingers till "the evening shades prevail," then homeward-bound returns, his basket heavy as his heart is light. . . .

Factories and saw-mills have done their part towards the work of extermination, and the destructive [fishing industry] *net* bids fair to do the rest. But though much diminished from these causes, there are more or less waters all over this state, . . . where the fish live and thrive in the undisturbed possession of their element. . . .

Source: Jerome Van Crowninshield Smith, *Natural History of the Fishes of Massachusetts, Embracing a Practical Essay on Angling* (Boston: Allen and Ticknor, 1833), pp. 20, 157–58, 344–45.

**Document 3.4   Massachusetts Supreme Court Justice Lemuel Shaw,
Nathan W. Hazen v. Essex Company, 1853**

When it was completed in 1848, the Lawrence Dam over the Merrimack River was the largest in the world and an engineering wonder. Built to form a reservoir and divert water into two canals that ran through textile factories (the water flow activating turbines that powered the machinery), the dam drove the development of Lawrence, the archetypal city in America's industrial development. Almost immediately, however, the capture of the Merrimack (and other New England waters) by the Essex Company triggered conflict, as small mill owners and farmers living upstream found their waterwheels obstructed and lands flooded with back-flowing, impounded water. In this important case, the Massachusetts Supreme Court weighed the issue of the company's right to flood the land by eminent domain to serve a public purpose—granted to them by the state legislature— versus the rights of small mill owners such as Nathan Hazen. The decision in favor of the Essex Company reflected the direction American law had been headed since industrialization began to accelerate in the 1830s. Jurisprudence increasingly determined that the large industrial enterprises then driving the nation's development were indeed in the public interest; farmers and grain and sawmill operators like Hazen would have to give way.

... The plaintiff states in his declaration that he owns a mill situated in Andover, on a small stream flowing into the river on the south side, half a mile above the place of the defendants' dam, and that he had a right to the use of this stream at the level, at which it naturally flowed, but that the defendants, ... by means of [their Lawrence] dam, ... flowed back the waters on the wheel of the plaintiff's mill, prevented said stream from passing into Merrimack River at its natural height, &c.

As the owner of land through which a watercourse passes, has a right to the reasonable use of such current as it passes through his land, the plaintiff would have a good right of action, were not the erection of the dam justified by their act of incorporation. The defendants maintain that they are so justified, by an act of the legislature, exercising, as they may, the sovereign power of the state, in the right of eminent domain, to take and appropriate private property for public use; that the plaintiff's property in the mill and mill privilege was so taken, ...

It is then contended [by Hazen] that if this act [of incorporation] was intended to authorize the defendant company to take the mill-power and mill of the plaintiff, it was void, because it was not taken for public use, and it was not within the power of the government, in the exercise of the right of eminent domain.

This is the main question. In determining it, we must look to the declared purposes of the act, and if a public use is declared, it will be so held, unless it manifestly appears by the provisions of the act, that they can have no tendency to advance and promote such public use. The declared purposes are, to improve the navigation of Merrimack River, and to create a large mill-power for mechanical and manufacturing purposes. In general, whether a particular structure, as a bridge, or a lock, or canal or road, is for the public use, is a question for the legislature, and which may be presumed to have been correctly decided by them.... That the improvement of the navigation of a river is done for the public use, has been too frequently decided and acted upon, to require authorities. And so to create a wholly artificial navigation by canals. The establishment of a great mill-power for manufacturing purposes, as an object of great public interest, especially since manufacturing has come to be one of the great public industrial pursuits of the commonwealth, seems to have been regarded by the legislature and sanctioned by the jurisprudence of the commonwealth, and, in our judgment, rightly so, in determining what is a public use, justifying the exercise of the right of eminent domain....

Source: Nathan W. Hazen v. Essex Company, Supreme Court of Massachusetts, Essex (66 Mass. 475; November 1853 decided).

Document 3.5   **A Farmer Challenges the Rising Power of the Dam Builders, 1859**

A few months after the Hazen v. Essex Company *decision, George Young led a group of men in attempting to destroy the top of the Lake Village Dam, an impoundment of Paugus Bay that had repeatedly flooded their land. Left behind in the economic and environmental transformation of the region that had produced great but unevenly distributed wealth, these men directed their frustrations at a wall of stone and concrete that had become a symbol of those changes. Although once a customary, legally sanctioned remedy in such instances, by 1859 their attempt to destroy the dam was futile. The powerful Lake Company controlled over 103 square miles of surface water in New Hampshire's four largest lakes, sending and selling the water to factories downstream. Legislative and judicial attempts to rein in their power in the 1850s had failed. Young acknowledges their enormous power in this letter to the editor of the local newspaper, but clearly he had not yet fully accepted the fact that traditional "public" rights to the water and land were yielding to the rights of corporations.*

... [If by destroying the dam] the Company would arrest me and thereby bring the matter before a proper tribunal for discussion.

But no—Mr. French (manager of the dam), in behalf of the Company, would risk no such experiment. Then I offered them the privilege of sending a man to interfere with me, so that I could arrest him, thereby becoming plaintiff myself. But this was no more an effectual inducement than the other. Again, I offered to submit the matter to two of the justices of the Supreme Court, but this offer also was without avail; the truth being that neither Mr. French nor the Company whom he represents, are willing to have a judicial decision upon the question of rights of individuals, for the Company in this matter have no rights but might.

Source: Letter to the Editor, *Winnipisaukee Gazette,* October 8, 1859; quoted in Theodore Steinberg, *Nature Incorporated: Industrialization and the Waters of New England* (New York: Cambridge University Press, 1991), p. 135.

Document 3.6   **New Hampshire Supreme Court, *Hayes v. Waldron, 1863***

The clearest expression of the "reasonable use" doctrine that sanctioned degradation of waterways in service to the greater good of economic growth came in this important case. The New Hampshire Supreme Court concluded that the right to discharge sawdust and other lumber mill shavings into the Cocheco River stemmed from a "reasonable use" of the waterway that served a vital public purpose. The decision encouraged a pliable flexibility of the "reasonable use" doctrine that manufacturers readily applied as industrialization continued.

. . . [The] plaintiff urges that . . . the defendant had no right to conduct his sawdust and shavings into the river, if they did *any* injury to the plaintiff's lands below, and also, that he had no right to discharge them into the river, unless such discharge was necessary to the running of his mill; and it appears that the court declined to charge the jury in these terms, but did instruct them that each proprietor might use and apply the water, as it runs over his land, to domestic, agricultural, or manufacturing purposes, provided he uses it in a reasonable manner, and so as to work no actual or material injury to the others; and by actual or material injury is meant infringement of the right of others; and again, that the test is, not whether it produces some inconvenience or detriment to him, but whether it impairs the full and reasonable enjoyment of the stream that he is entitled to equally with the proprietor above. . . .

The general principles that govern the use of running streams . . . must also govern in respect to the deposit in the stream of waste matter and foreign substances resulting from the process of manufacture; namely, that a reasonable use may be made, and nothing more. What is such reasonable use in both cases is a question not of law, but of fact, depending upon the circumstances of each particular case. In respect to the former class of cases, it may be considered as well settled that in the use of a stream for domestic, agricultural and manufacturing purposes, to which every riparian owner is entitled, there may of right be some diminution, retardation, or acceleration of the natural current, that is perfectly consistent with the common right, and which is necessarily implied in the right to use it at all. . . . Such owner may even abstract and consume a portion of the water, for domestic purposes, for watering his cattle, and in some cases for irrigating his land, taking care not to interfere materially with a similar right in his neighbor. So, where the nature of the stream requires it, he may detain the water by his dam, to enable him to apply it usefully to manufacturing purposes, and then discharge it in the working of his mills, in quantities greater than the natural flow of the stream; but such use must be reasonable, and so as not to cause material injury or annoyance to his neighbor. What is a reasonable use must depend upon a variety of conditions, such as the size and character of the stream, and the uses to which it can be or is applied; and, from the nature of the case, it is incapable of being defined to suit the vast variety of circumstances that exist; but the rule is flexible, and suited to the growing and changing wants of communities.

As it is in respect to the abstraction, detention, and diversion of the water, so it is and must be in respect to the deposit of waste, or other substances in the stream, . . . In many or most of these modes of use such deposits are to some extent necessarily made. In the construction and repair of mills and dams, in the excavations required for their foundations, and in the frequent removal of the gravel used for tightening such dams, the water must for a time, and necessarily, be rendered so impure as to cause inconvenience occasionally to persons engaged in a kind of manufacture requiring pure water.... So in the use of a stream for purposes of agriculture, such as washing sheep, crossing it with teams, allowing cattle and swine to traverse it,—the same principles will apply. So in the use of many kinds of mills, such as saw-mills, fulling-mills, cotton and woolen factories,—there must be thrown into the stream more or less of the waste....

... [In] determining the reasonableness of suffering the manufacturer's waste to pass off in the current, much must depend upon the use to which the stream below can be or is applied; whether as a mere highway alone, or for purposes of manufacture, requiring pure water, or for the supply of an aqueduct to a large city, as in the case of the Croton river; and in respect to the lands below adjacent to the river, the character of the banks, whether they are usually overflowed or not in high water, should be considered....

Source: Hayes v. Waldron, Supreme Court of New Hampshire (44 N.H. 580, June 1863).

NOTES

1. Massachusetts State Board of Health, *Third Annual Report of the State Board of Health, 1871* (Boston, 1872), pp. 60–61; quoted in John T. Cumbler, *Reasonable Use: The People, the Environment, and the State, New England, 1790–1930* (New York: Oxford University Press, 2001), p. 46.

2. Ted Steinberg, *Down to Earth: Nature's Role in American History* (New York: Oxford University Press, 2002), pp. 55–59.

3. *Palmer Company, Petitioners v. Isaac Ferrill* (34 Mass. 58, 1835).

ANNOTATED BIBLIOGRAPHY

Cumbler, John T. *Reasonable Use: The People, the Environment, and the State, New England 1790–1930.* New York: Oxford University Press, 2001. Centered on nineteenth-century industrialization, the book traces the ecological impacts of factory and dam development, market-driven (over)fishing, and deforestation. Cumbler's discussion of early regional conservationists such as Thoreau and Marsh reminds readers of how prescient they were and how enduringly relevant their ideas still are.

Donahue, Brian. *The Great Meadow: Farmers and the Land in Colonial Concord.* New Haven: Yale University Press, 2004. Innovatively using Geographical Informational Systems data in his analysis of several farm settlements over time, Donahue challenges the idea that colonial New England farmers repeatedly and thoughtlessly exhausted soils before moving on. What brought severe ecological degradation to Concord were the same forces of large-scale corporate capitalism that dammed the waters of the Merrimack and Connecticut rivers.

Evenden, Matthew D. *Fish Versus Power: An Environmental History of the Fraser River.* New York: Cambridge University Press, 2004. Takes the story of contending interests in a river's fate into the late twentieth century and a river in British Columbia. Here, the maturation of environmental science, shifting thinking about the economic value of undammed rivers, and the lessons of environmental history all weighed in to prevent the damming of the river.

Hahn, Steven, and Jonathan Prude, eds. *The Countryside in the Age of Capitalist Transformation.* Chapel Hill: University of North Carolina Press, 1985. Gary Kulik's chapter, "Dams, Fish, and Farmers: Defense of Public Rights in

Eighteenth-Century Rhode Island," provides a thorough treatment of how New England farmers viewed the streams and the fish in them as part of the commons. Extending beyond New England, other essays in this volume recount the fate of small farmers and their farming and husbandry practices as the forces of the market economy penetrated further and further into the backwoods.

Judd, Richard W. *Common Lands, Common People: The Origins of Conservation in Northern New England.* Cambridge: Harvard University Press, 2000. Argues persuasively that the deeply rooted communitarian ethic of rural New England farmers deserves a place in the lineage of American conservation. While the highbrow literati were shaping a modern environmental aesthetic, farmers and small town people fought to defend their well-ordered landscapes, centuries-old traditions of stewardship, and utilitarian rights to the public commons of forest and waters.

Merchant, Carolyn. *Ecological Revolutions: Nature, Gender, and Science in New England.* Chapel Hill: University of North Carolina Press, 1989. Shatters the notion that the first generations of white farmers were rapacious capitalists. Teases out the nuances in worldview and economic interests that separated the native Abenaki from colonial farmers, and them, in turn, from industrial capitalists.

Prude, Jonathan. *The Coming of Industrial Order: Town and Factory Life in Rural Massachusetts, 1810–1860.* Amherst: University of Massachusetts Press, 1985. Analyzes the impacts of New England industrialization upon rural communities, thereby placing the increased control of rivers and streams by large-scale textile manufacturing facilities in the context of a range of other conflicts that ensued between urban men of capital and inhabitants of rural communities.

Steinberg, Theodore. *Nature Incorporated: Industrialization and the Waters of New England.* New York: Oxford University Press, 1994. A layered environmental history of the Industrial Revolution in New England. Makes clear that this momentous development in the history of industrial capitalism in the United States bore major consequences for the regional environment and established the legal precedent that privileged major industrial developers over the interests of small, local users of this vital public resource.

4

Scientific Forestry and the Emergence of Conservation

The rapidity with which this country is being stripped of its forests must alarm every thinking man.

—Carl Schurz, Secretary of the Interior, 1877[1]

The great American nation, which individually never shuts the door behind its noble-self, very seldom attempts to put back anything it has taken from Nature's shelves. It grabs all it can and moves on. But the moving on is nearly finished and the grabbing must stop; and then the Federal Government will have to establish a Woods and Forest Department the like of which was never seen in the world before.

—Rudyard Kipling, 1899[2]

In the enlightened twenty-first century, the undeniable mathematics of deforestation in America provokes an emotional "how could they?" rhetorical outrage: less than 4 percent of the 820 million acres of virgin old-growth forest that once blanketed the United States remains. How and why Americans consumed timber voraciously is answered easily enough. As noted in Chapter 1, cultural fears of a dark and savage "wilderness" inhabited by fearsome creatures reinforced the practical impulse to tame the forest. More pragmatically, colonial Americans cut trees to build ships, clear land for farming, to construct and heat their homes and barns, to fuel cooking fires, to make potash, and to fashion furniture, fences, barrels, tools, and sundry other items. In the nineteenth century, the burgeoning needs of an ever-expanding, urbanizing, industrial civilization compelled men into the forest to take down the trees.

And yet it was indeed the cold fact of disappearing forests that first challenged the American myth of the inexhaustibility of natural resources. More than water, more than the loss of certain species, and more than the public nuisances of smoke and water pollution, the ramifications of turning once-forested regions into barren, damaged, and damaging treeless landscapes served as the catalyst for the conservation movement in America by the late nineteenth century.

The connections between the supply of free-flowing clean water and the quickening pace at which Americans cut their way through the wilderness became clear by the early nineteenth century. As early as 1750, both scientists and farmers began to suspect that deforestation was disrupting the hydrological cycle, causing regional changes in climate. Experience taught growing numbers of Americans that a standing forest held soil in place, thereby preventing its erosion and loss into streams and rivers. The capacity of the forest to serve as a natural sponge, absorbing water and then gradually releasing it through replenished bodies of water as humans needed it, became most evident in region after region after the trees were gone and a region's now sun-baked soil could not hold the water. Deforestation led to reduced regular stream flow, dried up groundwater sources, led to more frequent floods, and caused climatic change.

Still the cutting continued. In the first half of the nineteenth century, thousands of small logging operations and sawmills, vital elements of community building, dotted every region of the American landscape. Forested land was of little value to the American farmer who was anxious to put the first crop in the ground and provide a grassy meadow for livestock. From the westward movement of tobacco and cotton planters in the South to the migration of bedraggled New England farmers into western New York, farmers cleared wooded land at a rapidly accelerating pace. While approximately 114 million acres of woodland had been cut for agrarian development prior to 1850, nearly 40 million acres were cleared in the next decade alone.

Few mourned the "agricultural improvement" of wild America. The Jeffersonian vision of America held farmers as the backbone of democracy, the brave vanguard of civilization into the frontier West. A few voices, however, did protest the rapacious and often recklessly wasteful felling of the wilderness. Addressing the Albemarle Agricultural Society in 1818, President James Madison regretted that of all the costs associated with the nation's agrarian development, "none [was] so much to be regretted, perhaps because none is so difficult to repair, as the injurious and excessive destruction of woodlands." More famously, novelist James Fenimore Cooper's "Leatherstocking" novels of the 1820s bitterly criticized the profligate consumption of passenger pigeons and their forest habitat. In *The Pioneers* (1823), Judge Temple admonished his backwoods neighbors who "[felled] the forests, as if no end could be found to their treasures, nor any limits to their extent. If we go on in this way, twenty years hence, we shall want fuel."[3] Artist Thomas Cole of the Hudson River School decried the "meager utilitarianism" of Americans made manifest in thoughtless cutting of timber. Cole, poet William Cullen Bryant, Susan Fenimore Cooper, and others of the literati were more concerned with the destruction of spiritual and moral attributes imparted by the forest than their material value. Their calls for forest *preservation*, articulated most eloquently by Henry David Thoreau, would be realized in the national and state parks movement at the turn of the century, and in the century to follow, in the designation of wilderness areas.

The concern of most Americans in the 1850s was more pragmatic. As the population of the country grew, demand for lumber soared accordingly—and exponentially. Agricultural clearing of the forest between 1860 and 1910 exceeded the wooded acreage that had been axed during the preceding 250 years. By the time of the Civil War, warnings about timber shortages and deforestation impacts became more prevalent and scientifically grounded, and eventually, too conspicuous to ignore.

In 1847 George Perkins Marsh, then serving Vermont as a U.S. congressman, provided the first full exposition of the connections between deforestation and the deteriorating state of rural land. A little over a decade following his address that year to the Rutland County, Vermont, Agricultural Society (Document 4.1), Marsh was appointed by President Abraham Lincoln to serve as the first American ambassador to the new kingdom of Italy. The position (which he held until his death in 1882) allowed Marsh to deepen his understanding of the historical relationship between profligate resource exploitation and the decline of ancient civilizations. In 1864 he published *Man and Nature*, arguably *the* seminal work of environmental history in the United States that called on Americans to learn the historic lessons of worldwide environmental degradation. He made the case that deforestation, with its associated impacts on climate, the hydrological cycle, and the long-term health of the land, had contributed to the fall of once-mighty nations.

Although the magnitude of the book's message would not be fully appreciated for another century, excerpts of *Man and Nature* were reproduced in national magazines. Further, the book spawned a host of other articles and official investigations into the effects of massive timber cutting that by 1864 had moved from Marsh's New England to the great pine forests of the Great Lakes region. There, technological advances and the concentration of capital into large timber enterprises, led by that of Frederick Weyerhauser, allowed men to take down whole forests in a fraction of the time it had taken the previous generation of lumbermen. The massive steam donkey engine with its high-powered winch enabled men to take much larger trees from the forest, but, because more room was needed to maneuver the big machines, it required that smaller trees, which in an earlier era would have been left standing, be clear-cut along with the big timbers. Powerful circular blade and band saws took half-inch wide cuts and left piles of sawdust on the floor. Railroads penetrated deeper into the woods, leaving their own scars. The combination of thousands of hardworking lumberjacks and modern technology produced breathtaking results. By 1900, in less than half a century, well over half of the original great northern forest was gone. Much of what was not logged burned in massive fires for the next thirty years. Loggers left behind the slash undergrowth that is most vulnerable to such uncontrollable conflagrations. The worst of them, the Peshtigo Fire of 1871 in northern Wisconsin, burned 1 million acres and killed 1,500 people.

Although industrial logging raised greater concerns about deforestation than had agricultural clearing, for most Americans it was one of the marvels of a mechanized age. Prairie farmers and eastern urbanites enjoyed the benefits of the modern timber industry in the form of balloon-frame housing and cheap wood products. An 1867 report commissioned by the Wisconsin legislature on the impact of deforestation on the state's agricultural health was ignored and the cutting continued.

Less easily dismissed were calls to protect the forested watershed that protected the navigation of the Hudson River and the Erie Canal and the drinking water supply of New York City. Beginning in the 1840s, the Adirondack region had become a magnet for growing numbers of genteel sportsmen and summer vacationers from New York City and other urban areas. A mountain of romantic travel literature described the area as a refuge of wilderness from which weary (and well-to-do) urbanites could seek respite and recreation. That was especially true after the publication in 1869 of William H. H. Murray's *Adventures in the Wilderness: or, Camp-Life in the Adirondacks*, which drove urbane men northward into the Adirondack wilderness seeking, as Murray put it, "that perfect relaxation which all jaded minds require."[4] Murray was only the latest to call for preservation of a tract of Adirondack wilderness to serve the spiritual needs of a rapidly urbanizing society.

Yet, these woods would be preserved not to serve such idle pursuits but more practical ends. In holding the water like a sponge and slowly releasing it into lakes, rivers, and streams throughout the drainage area, the heavily forested Adirondack Mountains of upstate New York acted as the great regulator of the hydrological and climatic systems upon which the commerce and urban population of New York City depended. Due to their mountainous terrain and difficulty of access, the Adirondack forests had largely been left untouched to this point. They became vulnerable to logging when demand for timber increased again in the late 1860s and technology improved. In 1872 a newly established New York State Park Commission urged the state to take initial steps in designating a "forest park." Although referring to the pleasure-seeking characteristics of the region, the greater thrust of the commission's subsequent 1874 report (Document 4.3) relied on its utilitarian value.

Gaining influential support from New York City businessmen and newspapers, the economic argument for watershed protection ultimately prevailed when, in 1885, the state established an unprecedented forest preserve of 715,000 acres (Document 4.4). Advocates for stronger protection warned that the law's allowance for limited logging would invite abusive exploitation by rapacious lumbermen. They championed the cause of absolute, "forever wild" preservation. In 1894 New York voters overrode vehement protests from longtime residents and local boosters of the timber industry (Document 4.5) to inscribe the "forever wild" principle into their state constitution.

Following the clear-cutting operations in New York and the Great Lake states, the timber industry in the 1890s set its sights on the vast virgin pines of the South. The federal government estimated in 1880 that the Gulf Coast states held more than 107 billion board feet of longleaf Georgia pine (among other purposes longleaf was essential in the production of turpentine). That figure conjures an image today of an unfathomably thick and vast forest. For the timber industry in 1885, the numbers beckoned and predictably, massive timbering operations commenced in the 1890s. Proposals from scientific foresters and legislative bodies to establish an Adirondack-style preserve in the southern Appalachians failed largely because of concerns about the constitutionality of the federal government purchasing land that was in the South mostly privately held. That obstacle would not be solved until passage of the Weeks Act of 1911—by which time 40 percent of the southern forest would be gone.

In the vast public domain of the West, however, forest preservationists faced no such challenge. Though much of the region between the coast and the Rocky Mountains was arid and inhospitable for timber growth, millions of acres were heavily forested. With much of the region still in the federal public domain, western forests became the target of most of the more than 200 bills that came before the Congress between 1873, when Franklin Hough called for government action (Document 4.2), and the end of the century. First among them, the Timber Culture Act of 1873, was designed to get homesteaders to plant trees on the prairies where a lack of timber had hindered settlement. The scientific theory behind the law—popularized by the railroads and which *seemed* to be grounded in the writings of Marsh and others—was that planting trees (and crops) would alter the climate and increase rainfall. That proved more myth than fact, and the law itself became a dismal failure, noted for its exploitation by large landowners who used it to expand the size of their holdings (based on fraudulent tree-planting claims).

Calls among the nation's small but increasingly influential cadre of forestry experts for more effective and aggressive congressional action eventually culminated in the passage of the Forest Reserve Clause of 1891, which granted the president authority to establish forest preserves. Enacted with little fanfare, the 1891 bill quietly passed following nearly three decades of education by protégés of Marsh and a plea in 1890 for legislative action from President Benjamin Harrison to end "the rapid and needless destruction of our great forest areas." Harrison immediately created 13 million acres of "forest reserves" (later national forests); his successor, Grover Cleveland, added another 4.5 million acres to the young system.

From that point, it fell to stewards trained in the new science of forestry (new in America, that is) to determine how they were to be managed. Gifford Pinchot led the first generation of foresters who were trained in Europe, where they learned that forests could be cut and replanted so as to provide a sustained yield of timber, much like a crop of corn. The 1897 Forest Management Act inscribed that philosophy in law, declaring that the primary purpose of the national forests was to "furnish a continuous supply of timber for the use and necessities of [our] citizens." In 1905 Pinchot successfully lobbied for the relocation of the forestry division into the Department of Agriculture, symbolizing the utilitarian approach to forestry in the United States. His 1905 primer on "practical forestry," sections of which are excerpted here (Document 4.6), makes clear the approach that has largely dominated the U.S. Forest Service since the beginning.

Multiple interests outside of Washington, from western state governments (Document 4.8) to sportsmen's magazines like *Forest and Stream* to wilderness preservationists led by John Muir, all had an avid interest in the direction of forest management. Then, as now, debate was fierce. Virtually all agreed that the national forests would provide for "multiple use" (as the administrative phrase would later put it), including logging and grazing. Initially, even wilderness advocates like Muir had agreed on that point. Muir soon parted with Pinchot and the utilitarian-minded conservationists over the management of the forests, parks, and other resources (Chapter 8). Moderating the dispute was President Theodore Roosevelt, whose administration's conservation *and preservation* legacy is unequaled in American history. Like Muir, Roosevelt believed in the moral regenerative power of wilderness, and moved aggressively to preserve, unspoiled and inviolable to extractive economic activity, large portions of the most treasured American landscapes in national parks, wildlife refuges, and monuments.

But sentimentalist he certainly was not. Roosevelt leaned heavily on Pinchot's scientifically grounded knowledge in pursuing a more practical, utilitarian management approach in the national forests and the majority of other federally owned western lands—even as he continually castigated the selfish motives and shortsightedness of private interests and western governors for their opposition to his policies that he believed were in the best interest of the nation (Document 4.7). A hallmark of the republic in the modern era, the ideological and administrative struggle that ensued in the Roosevelt-Pinchot era among conservationists, preservationists, and advocates of unfettered industrial capitalism would continue to resurface periodically for the remainder of the century and beyond. All three contending factions would achieve some measure of victory, not the least of which were conservationists who at last had translated decades of scientific warning about diminishing forests into national policy.

DOCUMENTS

Document 4.1   **George Perkins Marsh Addresses the Rutland, Vermont, Agricultural Society on the Effects of Deforestation, Rutland, Vermont, September 30, 1847**

When George Perkins Marsh, then a U.S. Congressman from Vermont, addressed the farmers of Rutland, Vermont, in 1847, he offered one of the first accounts of the value of trees to farmers and the effects of deforestation on the health and productivity of the land. He further developed his argument for a prudent strategy of managing the state's remaining forested lands in his seminal 1864 work, Man and Nature. *Marsh's argument crystallized as national conservation policy by the end of the century.*

There are certain other improvements connected with agriculture, to which I desire to draw your special attention. One of these is the introduction of a better economy in the management of our forest lands. The increasing value of timber and fuel ought to teach us, that trees are no longer what they were in our fathers' time, an incumbrance. We have undoubtedly already a larger proportion of cleared land in Vermont than would be required, with proper culture, for the support of a much greater population than we now possess, and every additional acre both lessens our means for thorough husbandry, by disproportionately extending its area, and deprives succeeding generations of what, though comparatively worthless to us, would be of great value to them. The functions of the forest, besides supplying timber and fuel, are very various.... they are of great value in sheltering and protecting more tender vegetables against the destructive effects of bleak or parching winds, and the annual deposit of the foliage of deciduous trees, and the decomposition of their decaying trunks, form an accumulation of vegetable mould, which gives the greatest fertility to the often originally barren soils on which they grow, and enriches lower grounds by the wash from rains and the melting snows. The inconveniences resulting from a want of foresight in the economy of the forest are already severely felt in many parts of New England, and even in some of the older towns in Vermont. Steep hill-sides and rocky ledges are well suited to the permanent growth of wood, but when in the rage for improvement they are improvidently stripped of this protection, the action of sun and wind and rain soon deprives them of their thin coating of vegetable mould, and this, when exhausted, cannot be restored by ordinary husbandry. They remain therefore barren and unsightly blots,... But this is by no means the only evil resulting from the injudicious destruction of the woods. Forests serve as reservoirs and equalizers of humidity. In wet seasons, the decayed leaves and spongy soil of woodlands retain a large proportion of the falling rains, and give back the moisture in time of drought, by evaporation or through the medium of springs. They thus both check the sudden flow of water from the surface into the streams and low grounds, and prevent the droughts of summer from parching our pastures and drying up the rivulets which water them. On the other hand, where too large a proportion of the surface is bared of wood, the action of the summer sun and wind scorches the hills which are no longer shaded or sheltered by trees, the springs and rivulets that found their supply in the bibulous soil of the forest disappear, and the farmer is obliged to surrender his meadows to his cattle,... Again, the vernal and autumnal rains, and the melting snows of winter, no longer intercepted and absorbed by the leaves or the open soil of the woods, falling everywhere upon a comparatively hard and even surface, flow swiftly over the smooth ground,... The suddenness and violence of our freshets increases in proportion as the soil is cleared; bridges are washed away, meadows swept of their crops and fences, and covered with barren sand, or themselves abraded by the fury of the current, and there is reason to fear that the valleys of many of our streams will soon be converted from smiling meadows into broad wastes of shingle and gravel and pebbles, deserts in summer, and seas in autumn and spring. The changes,... are too striking to have escaped the attention of any observing person, and every middle-aged man, who revisits his birth-place after a few years of absence, looks upon another landscape than that which formed the theatre of his youthful toils and pleasures. The signs of artificial improvement are mingled with the tokens of improvident waste, and the bald and barren hills, the dry beds of the smaller streams, the ravines furrowed out by the torrents of spring, and the diminished thread of interval that skirts the widened channel of the rivers, seem sad substitutes for the pleasant groves and brooks and broad meadows of his ancient paternal domain.... It has long been a practice in many parts of Europe, as well as in our older settlements, to cut the forest reserved for timber and fuel, at stated intervals. It is quite time that this practice should be introduced among us.... [There], the economy of the forest is regulated by law; but here, where public opinion determines, or rather in practice constitutes law, we can only appeal to an enlightened self-interest to introduce the reforms, check the abuses, and preserve us from an increase of the evils I have mentioned.

Source: George Perkins Marsh, *Address Delivered before the Agricultural Society of Rutland County, Sept. 30, 1847* (Rutland, VT: Herald Office, 1848).

Document 4.2   **Franklin Hough Addresses the American Association for the Advancement of Science on the Need for Government-Sponsored Forest Conservation, 1873**

Based on his work for the federal census in New York, Franklin B. Hough here echoes the arguments Marsh had made about the deleterious impact of deforestation and the economic value of forests.

> *He calls for government-initiated forest management that would arise from the democratic education of citizens. So impressed with the speech was the American Association for the Advancement of Science that it appointed a committee (headed by Hough) to urge the U.S. Congress to investigate the subject. The result was congressional funding for a federal forest agent (Hough himself) who reported to the Congress on the condition of the nation's forests. Here was the embryonic seed of the government forest conservation that would ultimately be overseen by the U.S. Forest Service.*

The economical value of timber, and our absolute dependence . . . upon it for innumerable uses . . . and the positive necessity for its use in the affairs of common life, even were its use as fuel largely supplanted by the introduction of mineral coal, are too obvious for suggestion. It is this necessity, rather than considerations of climate or of water supply, that has led in several countries of Europe to systems of management and regulation of national forests, as a measure of governmental policy and public economy. . . . [by contrast] our states, as a general rule, own no large forests, and we have no strong central organizations or means of enforcing the stringent regulations which make their system a success. The title to the lands in our older states (where the evils resulting from the loss of forests are liable to be first and most severely felt) has already passed into the hands of individuals, and from the theory of our system of government, the power that must regulate and remedy these evils must begin with the people, and not emanate from a central source. . . .

These considerations present a problem difficult, it may be, of solution, but I have confidence in the ability of our American people to work out a practical system, adapted to our social organization, and our general theory of laws. We must begin at the centre of power, and that centre is the circumference. We must make the people themselves familiar with the facts and the necessities of the case. It must come to be understood that a tree or a forest, planted, is an investment of capital, increasing annually in value as it grows, like money at interest, and worth at any time what it has cost—including the expense of planting, and the interest which this money would have earned at the given date. The great masses of our rural population and land owners, should be inspired with correct ideas as to the importance of planting and preserving trees, and taught the profits that may be derived from planting waste spots with timber, where nothing else would grow to advantage. . . .

However much the public may favor, there will still arise the need of laws to regulate, promote and protect the growth of wood; as we find laws necessary in the management of roads and bridges, or of any other great object of public utility. . . .

Source: Franklin B. Hough, "On the Duty of Governments in the Preservation of Forests," Proceedings of the American Association for the Advancement of Science, Portland Meeting, August 1873.

Document 4.3   Commissioners of State Parks, State of New York, 1874

The mountainous, heavily forested Adirondack region of upstate New York became a focal point for those advocating both the preservation of wilderness for recreation, big game hunting, and "pleasure seeking" and the conservation of forest lands to serve more practical interests. Franklin B. Hough served on the State Parks Commission, whose first report, excerpted here, advocated a utilitarian rationale for creating a "forest park" in the Adirondacks. In discussing the supply of water from Adirondack lakes that was integral to the success of downstate manufacturing enterprise and New York City's water supply, the commissioners clearly appealed to powerful economic interests who could ensure passage of legislation to create the park. They also called for continued, but prudent, and government-supervised, timber cutting in such a reserve.

... We do not favor the creation of an expensive and exclusive park for mere purposes of recreation, but condemning such suggestions, recommend the simple preservation of the timber as a measure of political economy....

Vast portions of the wilderness are owned and controlled by the lumber interests, which, with that of the tanneries, is likely to be most immediately and radically affected by the creation of a state forest park or timber preserve. These lands are generally purchased, held, and valued solely for the timber growing on them. As soon as the pine, spruce and hemlock trees have been taken off, the lands are often abandoned and revert to the State for unpaid taxes. The common and wasteful method among lumbermen, therefore, is to cut all the available timber from a given section at once. This enables them to escape further taxes.... The small trees, even under ten inches in diameter, are cut, and thus the natural process of replacement by a second growth of the valuable varieties of timber, becomes very slow, if not impossible....

... and it is to this [Adirondack] system of lakes, of natural reservoirs, bosomed in the cool primeval forests, that our State is indebted for that water supply that has *created* [emphasis original] our canals, and that steady water power which is the wealth of so many manufactories.

Without a *steady, constant* [emphasis original] supply of water from these streams of wilderness, our canals would be dry, and a great portion of the grain and other produce of the western part of the State would be unable to find cheap transportation to the markets of the Hudson river valley. In Erie, and the neighboring western counties, grain would decrease in value, and the farmers would be in the power of the great railroad companies. The merchants at Albany would also suffer, their summer trade ruined,...

We believe that the great Adirondack forest has a powerful influence upon the general climatology of the State; upon the rainfall, winds, and temperature, moderating storms and equalizing throughout the year the amount of moisture carried by the atmosphere; controlling, and in a measure subduing, the powerful northerly winds, modifying their coldness and equalizing the temperature of the whole State.

It is now generally conceded that forests do not increase the amount of *annual* [emphasis original] rain-fall. Their influence is to cause a distribution of the rain at short intervals throughout the year, while their absence induces droughts, followed by sudden and tremendous storms which are the origin of disastrous floods....

The supply of timber which a State possesses within its own limits is one of the measures of its wealth.... At first sight it may appear that the absorption of all this vast forest (practically the only lumber region now remaining in the State) into a State park would amount to the immediate annihilation of that trade. The idea of such an unproductive and useless park we utterly and entirely repudiate.... The careful protected forests of Europe afford their states large annual incomes; the timber is cut under the direction of officers charged with the care of the forests, who mark the old and mature trees for cutting, and see that as little injury as possible is done to the growing timber.... Should an Adirondack park be created, careful consideration should be given to the utilization of the forest....

Source: Commissioners of State Parks of the State of New York, *First Annual Report*, transmitted to the Legislature May 15, 1873 (Albany: Weed, Parsons and Company, 1874), pp. 5, 9, 14–15, 19–20.

Document 4.4   Act Establishing the Adirondack Forest Preserve, 1885

With increasing pressure from the New York Chamber of Commerce and business interests generally, and with long-standing support from the growing class of genteel sportsmen and vacationers who enjoyed the Adirondacks, the New York legislature in 1885 passed the law creating the Adirondack Forest Preserve. The "lawful business" still allowed exploitive extraction of the forest to take place, prompting a movement for stronger protection that would succeed a decade later.

Sec. 8 The lands now or hereafter constituting the forest preserve shall be forever kept as wild forest lands. They shall not be sold, nor shall they be leased or taken by any person or corporation, public or private.

Sec. 9 The forest commission shall have the care, custody, control, and superintendence of the forest preserve. It shall be the duty of the commission to maintain and protect the forests now on the forest preserve, and to promote as fast as practicable the further growth of forests thereon. It shall also have charge of the public interests of the state, with regard to forests and tree planting, and especially with reference to forest fires in every part of the state.... The forest commission may, from time to time, prescribe rules or regulations ... affecting the whole or any part of the forest preserve, ... but neither such rules and regulations, nor anything herein contained shall prevent or operate to prevent the free use of any road, stream or water as the same may have been heretofore used or as may be reasonably required in the prosecution of any lawful business.

Source: Laws of New York, chap. 283, May 15, 1885, pp. 482–83.

Document 4.5   *Warrensburg* (New York) *News* Decries Economic
                     "Injustice" of Adirondack Forest Park Proposal, 1890

Though most downstate New Yorkers supported the park proposal, many residents of the Adirondack region itself, some of whose families had been eking a living from the land for over a century, opposed the proposal. Many feared the prospect of government ownership and interference in their customary hunting and fishing practices. Others resented the notion of wealthy sportsmen and pleasure-seeking vacationers from the city further entrenching themselves in their woods. Most frightening was the economic threat posed by the loss of jobs associated with timbering. This brief editorial excerpt from a local newspaper, cast in bitingly populist language, embraces the latter two themes of opposition. The opposition ultimately failed, as New Yorkers voted in 1894 to make the Adirondacks "forever wild"—putting an end to extractive uses of the Adirondack Forest Preserve.

When we consider the amount of employment afforded by the lumber industry, the thousands of saw mills, tanneries, pulp and paper mills and factories of all kinds giving labor to hundreds of thousands of poor people and that all of this is to be stopped to afford a deer park and fishing ground for a few wealthy pleasure-seekers to air their smoke-dried anatomies is an injustice, the boldness of which is astonishing.

Source: Warrensburg News, February 27, 1890.

Document 4.6   **Gifford Pinchot Describes the Principles
                     of "Practical Forestry," 1905**

Gifford Pinchot served as the head of the division of forestry (later the U.S. Forest Service) from 1898 until 1910. Trained in Germany, Pinchot adapted European theory and practice of scientific forest management to America's wooded landscape, in particular to the system of forest preserves (later National Forests) that expanded enormously in size and number during his tenure. Throughout his administration, President Theodore Roosevelt transformed Pinchot's ideas about the conservation and "wise use" of all natural resources into national policy.

THE SERVICE OF THE FOREST

Next to the earth itself the forest is the most useful servant of man. Not only does it sustain and regulate the streams, moderate the winds, and beautify the land, but it also supplies wood, the most widely used of all materials. Its uses are numberless, and the demands which are made upon it by mankind are numberless also. It is essential to the well-being of mankind that these demands should be met. They must be met steadily, fully, and at the right time if the forest is to give its best service. The object of practical forestry is precisely to make the forest render its best service to man in such a way as to increase rather than to diminish its usefulness in the future. Forest management and conservative lumbering are other names for practical forestry. Under whatever name it may be known, practical forestry means both the use and preservation of the forest.

THE USES OF THE FOREST

A forest, large or small, may render its service in many ways. It may reach its highest usefulness by standing as a safeguard against floods, winds, snow slides, moving sands, or especially against the dearth of water in the streams. A forest used in this way is called a protection forest, and is usually found in the mountains, or on bleak, open plains, or by the sea. Forests which protect the headwaters of streams used for irrigation, and many of the larger windbreaks of the Western plains, are protection forests. The Adirondack and Catskill woodlands were regarded as protection forests by the people of the State of New York when they forbade, in the constitution of 1895, the felling, destruction, or removal of any trees from the State Forest Preserve.

A farmer living directly on the produce of his land would find his woodlot most useful to him when it supplied the largest amount of wood for his peculiar needs, or the best grazing for his cattle. A railroad holding land which it did not wish to sell would perhaps find it most useful when it produced the greatest number of ties and bridge timbers. In both cases the forest would render its best service by producing the greatest quantity of valuable material. . . .

The greatest return in money may be the service most desired of the forest. If a farmer wished to sell the product of his woodlot instead of consuming it himself, his woodland would be useful to him just in proportion to its net yield in money. This is true also in the case of any owner of a forest who wishes to dispose of its product, but who can not, or will not, sell the forest itself. State forests, like those in the Adirondacks, often render their best service, in addition to their usefulness as protection forests, by producing the greatest net money return.

Regarded as an investment of capital, a forest is most useful when it yields the highest rate of interest. A forest whose owner could sell it if he chose, but prefers to hold it as productive capital, is useful in proportion to the interest it yields on the money invested in it. Thus, an acre of spout land may be worth only $5, while the investment in adjoining land stocked with old trees may be $50 an acre. This is the view which controls the management of State forests in Germany. Lumbermen also regard timberland as an investment, but usually they take no care except for the yield at the moment. They disregard the future yield altogether, and in consequence the forest loses its capital value, or may even be totally destroyed. Well managed forests, on the other hand, are made to yield their service always without endangering the future yield, and usually to its great advantage. Like the plant of a successful manufacturer, a forest should increase in productiveness and value year by year.

Under various circumstances, then, a forest may yield its best return in protection, in wood, grass, or other forest products, in money, or in interest on the capital it represents. But whichever of these ways of using the forest may be chosen in any given case, the fundamental idea in forestry is that of perpetuation by wise use; that is, of making the forest yield the best service possible at the present in such a way that its usefulness in the future will not be diminished, but rather increased.

Source: Gifford Pinchot, *A Primer of Forestry: Part II—Practical Forestry*, Bulletin 24, Part II, Bureau of Forestry, U.S. Dept. of Agriculture (Washington, DC: Government Printing Office, 1905), pp. 1–3.

Document 4.7   President Theodore Roosevelt Affirms the Need for Forest Conservation, 1907

In one of Theodore Roosevelt's most forceful and eloquent calls for conserving the nation's resources, the president castigated those who opposed his energetic conservation-minded administration as standing for the immediate "self-interests of a very few" at the expense of the nation's future. Roosevelt's posture was more complex than it might appear. His conservation policies often favored the interests of well-heeled businessmen over those of small landowners—a course that often belied his populist rhetoric.

Optimism is a good characteristic, but if carried to an excess it becomes foolishness. We are prone to speak of the resources of this country as inexhaustible; this is not so. The mineral wealth of the country, the coal, iron, oil, gas, and the like, does not reproduce itself, and therefore is certain to be exhausted ultimately; and wastefulness in dealing with it today means that our descendants will feel the exhaustion a generation or two before they otherwise would. But there are certain other forms of waste which could be entirely stopped—the waste of soil by washing, for instance, which is among the most dangerous of all wastes now in progress in the United States, is easily preventable, so that this present enormous loss of fertility is entirely unnecessary. The preservation or replacement of the forests is one of the most important means of preventing this loss. We have made a beginning in forest preservation, but it is only a beginning. . . . so rapid has been the rate of exhaustion of timber in the United States in the past, and so rapidly is the remainder being exhausted, that the country is unquestionably on the verge of a timber famine which will be felt in every household in the land. . . . Every business man in the land, every writer in the newspapers, every man or woman of an ordinary school education, ought to be able to see that immense quantities of timber are used in the country, that the forests which supply this timber are rapidly being exhausted, and that, if no change takes place, exhaustion will come comparatively soon, and that the effects of it will be felt severely in the every-day life of our people. Surely, when these facts are so obvious, there should be no delay in taking preventive measures. Yet we seem as a nation to be willing to proceed in this matter with happy-go-lucky indifference even to the immediate future. It is this attitude which permits the self-interest of a very few persons to weigh for more than the ultimate interest of all our people. There are persons who find it to their immense pecuniary benefit to destroy the forests by lumbering. They are to be blamed for thus sacrificing the future of the Nation as a whole to their own self-interest of the moment; but heavier blame attaches to the people at large for permitting such action, whether in the White Mountains, in the southern Alleghenies, or in the Rockies and Sierras. A big lumbering company, impatient for immediate returns and not caring to look far enough ahead, will often de-liberately destroy all the good timber in a region, hoping afterwards to move on to some new country. The shiftless man of small means, who does not care to become an actual home-maker but would like immediate profit, will find it to his advantage to take up timber land simply to turn it over to such a big company, and leave it valueless for future settlers. A big mine owner, anxious only to develop his mine at the moment, will care only to cut all the timber that he wishes without regard to the future—probably not looking ahead to the condition of the country when the forests are exhausted, any more than he does to the condition when the mine is worked out. I do not blame these men nearly as much as I blame the supine public opinion, the indifferent public opinion, which permits their action to go unchecked. . . . There are plenty of men in public and private life who actually advocate the continuance of the present system of unchecked and wasteful extravagance, using as an argument the fact that to check it will of course mean interference with the ease and comfort of certain people who now get lumber at less cost than they ought to pay, at the expense of the future genera-tions. Some of these persons actually demand that the present forest reserves be thrown open to destruction, because, forsooth, they think that thereby the price of lumber could be put down again for two or three or more years. Their attitude is precisely like that of an agitator protesting against the outlay of money by farmers on manure and in taking care of their farms generally. Undoubtedly, if the av-erage farmer were content absolutely to ruin his farm, he could for two or three years avoid spending any money on it, and yet make a good deal of money out of it. But only a savage would, in his private affairs, show such reckless disregard of the future; yet it is precisely this reckless disregard of the future which the op-ponents of the forestry system are now endeavoring to get the people of the United States to show. . . .

Source: President Theodore Roosevelt, Annual Message to the Congress, December 3, 1907; from *State Papers as Governor and President, 1899–1909* (Herman Hagedorn, *The Works of Theodore Roosevelt*, National ed., New York: Charles Scribner's Sons, 1926), vol. 17, pp. 460–63.

Document 4.8   U.S. Senator Henry Teller of Colorado Denounces Federal Conservation

The Denver Public Land Convention of 1907 represented the first large-scale organized opposition to federal conservation policy in the West. Attended by western politicians and representatives of western grazing, agricultural, and mining interests, the convention revealed the deep well of resistance in the West toward Roosevelt's conservation policy. The convention called on the federal government to cede public lands to the states and to restrict the further establishment and regulation of national forests. These lines of conflict between conservationists and western interests still prevail a century later. Senator Henry Teller of Colorado captures the views of many at convention.

. . . It was said by a great English orator that the tenant was but a half-slave, and so I say today I object to landlordism by the rich and by the government alike. (Applause.) And I do not see any difference, except that I believe the individual landlord would be more endurable than a government landlord, and if those of you who have lived in the neighborhood of forest reserves do not support me in that view it is because you have not been observing. (Applause.) . . .

. . . I am intensely interested in maintaining for this state what belongs to it as a sovereign state. (Applause.) I commenced my public life many years ago, but long anterior to that time the question of states' rights was a live question. People contended for it and people fought against it. The first proclamation or declaration in favor of states' rights was made in New England, and secondly it was made in the South for the purpose of protecting their peculiar institution, . . . They asserted that they had a right to go out. Now, that has made the states' rights doctrine odious, . . . The question is: Has the state any rights that the general government is bound to respect? (Applause.) What are our rights here? The Supreme Court of the United States has declared in the most emphatic manner that the natural wealth of this state belongs not to the general government but to us, to our people. (Applause.) The Supreme Court of the United States has declared that the waters of this state belong to the state. (Applause.) All that nature has done for this state it has done for us, and we are entitled—if we want to use all of the water of the state we are entitled to use it. If we want to use all the mineral wealth and we can get it out we are entitled to use it. It is said that we have depleted the forests and that we have done various other things. That may be true to some extent. I can remember, myself, when there were great pine forests in the states of Pennsylvania and New York, and they have disappeared. What became of them? The great, lofty pines were cut down and put into lumber and went to build houses, to build cities and to build towns. Did they cut any more of that timber than was demanded by the needs and wants of the people? And in place of the unbroken forest which the Pilgrim Fathers found when they landed on the New England coast, in place of that you have smiling farms and thriving towns and cities. Which is the better? Which would you rather have today? Take central New York, with its unbroken farms from New York City to Buffalo, with houses such as no other portion of the United States has ever built for the farmer, and with all the conveniences of civilization possessed by any country in the world. Is it not better than an unbroken forest? Are not men better than trees, valuable as they are? (Great applause.) I thank God that the trees are gone and that in their place have come men and women, Christian men and Christian women, liberty-loving men and liberty-loving women; and I assert here today that I do not believe there is an acre of public land where the public timber has ever been cut off that has not gone into beneficial use for the people of this country. (Applause.)

Source: Proceedings of the Public Land Convention. Held in Denver, Colorado, June 18, 19, 20, 1907. By the states and territories containing public lands of the United States and lying west of the Missouri River (Denver, CO: Compiled and published by authority of the convention, Fred P. Johnson, Secretary, 1907), pp. 45–47.

Document 4.9 Richard Ballinger Dismisses the Need for Conservation, 1909

> *When William Howard Taft succeeded Theodore Roosevelt as president in 1909, he slowed the course of conservation and embarked on a program of aggressive resource development on the public lands. Embodying that direction was the appointment of a westerner and friend of regional development interests, Richard Ballinger, as Secretary of the Interior. Ballinger opened public lands and forests in the West to increased extraction and development by corporate interests. Decades later, the administrations of Ronald Reagan and George W. Bush gave new life to Ballinger's basic philosophy.*

. . . You chaps who are in favor of this Conservation program are all wrong. You are hindering the development of the West. These railroads are necessary to the country. And more than that, this whole big [public] domain is a blanket—it is oppressing the people. The thing to do with it—In my opinion, the proper course to take with regard to this domain is to divide it up among the big corporations and the people who know how to make money out of it and let the people at large get the benefits of the circulation of the money.

Source: Richard Ballinger, interview with John L. Matthews, Washington, D.C., quoted in John L. Matthews, "Mr. Ballinger and the National Grab-Bag," *Hampton's Magazine*, December 1909.

NOTES

1. Carl Schurz, United States Department of the Interior, *Annual Report* (Washington, DC: Government Printing Office, 1877), p. xvi.

2. Rudyard Kipling, *From Sea to Sea* (New York: Doubleday and McClure, 1899), vol. 2: 155.

3. James Madison, quoted in Michael Williams, *Americans and Their Forests: A Historical Geography* (New York: Cambridge University Press, 1992), p. 144; James Fenimore Cooper, *The Pioneers*, Mohawk ed. (New York: G. P. Putnam, 1912), p. 105.

4. William H. H. Murray, *Adventures in the Wilderness; or, Camp-Life in the Adirondacks* (Boston: Fields, Osgood, and Company, 1869), p. 22.

ANNOTATED BIBLIOGRAPHY

Hays, Samuel P. *Conservation and the Gospel of Efficiency: The Progressive Conservation Movement, 1890–1920.* Cambridge, MA: Harvard University Press, 1959. A venerable classic. Still appreciated for the way the author unraveled the structures of political power and economic interests that provide the context for the rise of the conservation movement.

Lowenthal, David. *George Perkins Marsh: Prophet of Conservation.* Seattle: University of Washington Press, 2000. Stellar biography of one of the essential figures in U.S. environmental history. Eclipses Lowenthal's own 1958 biography of Marsh.

Marsh, George Perkins. *Man and Nature.* Edited by David Lowenthal. Foreword by William Cronon. Seattle: University of Washington Press, 2003. First published 1864. Seminal work of conservation, a warning to his countrymen of the fate of prodigal resource exploitation.

Miller, Char. *Gifford Pinchot and the Making of Modern Environmentalism.* Washington, DC: Shearwater Books/Island Press, 2004. Argues successfully that Pinchot has been unjustly indicted by environmentalists and historians for his utilitarian approach to conservation. Reestablishes Pinchot as a man truly committed to reining in destructive and unsustainable exploitation of natural resources.

Pinchot, Gifford. *Breaking New Ground.* Commemorative edition. Washington, DC: Island Press, 1998. First published 1947 by Harcourt, Brace. The first chief forester colorfully narrates the story of the birth of forestry in the United States and his role in it.

Steen, Harold K. *The U.S. Forest Service: A History.* Centennial edition. Seattle: University of Washington Press, 2004. First published 1976. The definitive treatment of the agency includes extensive discussions of contested U.S.F.S. policies throughout its history, including recent conflicts over wilderness, below-cost timber sales, and the entangled fates of endangered species and logging communities.

Stradling, David, ed. *Conservation in the Progressive Era: Classic Texts.* Seattle: University of Washington Press, 2004. This fine anthology contextualizes and reproduces the words of not only leading lights of the movement such as Pinchot and Roosevelt, but also obscure but critically important voices of women, farmers, and the industrial working class.

Terrie, Philip G. *Contested Terrain: A New History of Nature and People in the Adirondacks.* Syracuse, NY: Syracuse University Press, 1999. The finest environmental history of the Adirondacks and one of the premier environmental histories of any region. Chronicles the history of conflicts related to the ownership, stewardship, and management of this region, critically important to the history of American conservation and preservation.

———. *Forever Wild: Environmental Aesthetics and the Adirondack Forest Preserve.* Fleischmanns, NY: Harbor Hill Books, 1985. Centered on the shifting cultural attitudes and politics surrounding the establishment of the nation's first wilderness preserve.

Williams, Michael. *Americans and Their Forests: A Historical Geography.* New York: Cambridge University Press, 1992. Chronicles and analyzes in depth the devastating impacts of frontiering agricultural settlement and rapacious logging operations on the Appalachian forests of the East. American attitudes toward their woodlands and the enormously destructive demands they made of them are well covered here.

5

Property Rights, Technology, and Environmental Protection: *Hydraulic Gold Miners v. Farmers in California*

> If gold is the only needful thing, then let the Supreme Court tell us so and let every man alike be at liberty to secure it in the speediest possible manner, even should he be obliged to trespass on his neighbor.
> —*Pacific Rural Press*, March 25, 1882

The story of the California gold rush is not remembered as part of American environmental history. In popular American memory, California gold mining conjures romantic images of grizzled prospectors sifting pans over streambeds in search of nuggets or picking patiently at majestic Sierra Nevada mountainsides. The sheer wealth associated with the story—nearly $600 million in the 1850s alone (equal to $10 billion in today's dollars)—still staggers the imagination. Historians, too, have interpreted California gold mining primarily for the economic thrust it gave to California's development and for its role in helping to power financially the nation's Industrial Revolution in the last third of the nineteenth century.

Yet, this tale of fortunes made and gambled away is also a powerful one of environmental change that bore dramatic consequences for both land and people. Generating enormous wealth from gold-bearing ore was accompanied by the displacement and destruction of California's native populations, the confiscation of vast acreages of lands once held by Mexican families, and the transmogrification beyond recognition of the earth in which those precious metals had been buried by geologic forces. When Judge Lorenzo Sawyer's gavel put an end to hydraulic gold mining in California in January 1884, he struck an important legal blow for individual property rights and against the forces of corporate capital that in just one generation had wrought horrific destruction on small farmers, townspeople, and the natural environment.

Soon after James Marshall discovered gold near Sutter's Mill on California's American River in January 1848, tens of thousands of people from around the world arrived in the region seeking their fortune. But just as quickly as the gold rush began, it seemed to be over. By 1852, the gold lying near the surface of mountainsides, streams, and riverbeds had been "panned out," taken by the fortunate few. Though negligible compared to what followed, early "placer" (surface) mining did bring environmental problems, not the least of which was the human and animal waste and air pollution emitted by a booming population. In addition, timber was cut for cooking, heating, and for building the hundreds of miles of wooden flumes and sluice boxes that allowed miners to sift flecks of gold from watery earthen ore.

With the surface gold all but gone, men turned to their ingenuity to extract the gold that lay buried deeper within the earth. It began innocently enough in March 1853 as Edward E. Matteson, laboriously mining his Nevada City claim with pick and shovel, worked with his partners—fortuitously enough, a sail maker and a tinsmith—to devise the archetypal hydraulic mining device. Believing that the force of water blasted against the hill would crumble the compacted gold-bearing earth, the men constructed a canvas hose with a sheet iron nozzle. This they connected to a fifty-foot column of water and turned their hose upon the vein of gold they had exposed. They watched in delight as the hillside melted away in a mass of mud and gravel that they steered through their sluice channels. Weighing much more than the gravel and dirt, the gold fell and collected behind riffle boards at the bottom of the sluice. With more hose, access to water, and the proper terrain, two or three men could extract as much gold in a day as it formerly took months for scores of men to accomplish with pick and shovel.[1]

Matteson's invention gave birth to a whole new industry. Miners throughout the Sierra Nevada suddenly turned hose and nozzle upon their claims, filling the air with thunderous jets of water that obliterated whole mountainsides and channeled gold nuggets and dust into sluice boxes, where "quicksilver" (mercury) worked like a magnet to draw the precious particles together in an amalgam. In the early 1860s, the "crinoline hose"—made of thicker canvas and bound with iron—allowed miners to triple their water pressure. Two subsequent innovations, the steam-powered Blatchley diamond rock drill and the "Little Giant" hydraulic monitor, allowed water cannons to shoot 16,000 gallons of water every minute, shredding 4,000 cubic yards of earth every day. By 1870, hydraulic mining was producing 90 percent of California's gold.

Pulverizing the Sierra Nevada was not cheap. Not surprisingly, the most successful ventures were the best financed, particularly after the first years of "hydraulicking" extracted the gold nearest the surface, forcing small-timers to sell off and abandon their claims. Those that could control and direct the largest volume of water with more hydraulic derricks, hoses, and men produced the greatest stream of gold-bearing debris. Wealthy capitalists from San Francisco, such as silver king William Ralston and railroad baron Lester Robinson, financed the industry. Their $3.5 million investment in the North Bloomfield Gravel Mining Company netted a $3 million profit before Judge Sawyer's historic court decision in 1884 shut them down.

They were not alone. Other men of capital financed the nearly 500 quartz mills that were scattered around the gold country. John Todd's description of quartz mining sheds light on the massive capital investment these operations required:

> In the quartz mines, a very huge water-wheel...pumps the water from the mine as fast as it accumulates; the ore is then dug or blasted out, broken into pieces about as large as the fist, then put into an iron mortar, and stamped with iron pestles, till it is so reduced to powder, that water will wash it out in the trough, where the quicksilver lies in wait to catch the gold. This amalgam, quicksilver and gold, is next put into a covered retort of iron, with a pipe allowing the fumes of quicksilver to escape, which pipe is cooled by passing through cold water, till the quicksilver fumes are condensed, and it drops down, the pure metal it was, leaving the gold in the retort.[2]

In addition, capital-intensive logging operations cut millions of board feet of timber to feed the insatiable timber appetite of corporate mining. San Francisco–financed water companies built not only impoundment reservoirs in the mountains but also more than 5,000 miles of wooden flumes, canals, and ditches to deliver the water to the operations below. As in New England, water was commodified here, sold by the "miner's inch." Reservoir capacity in hydraulic country reached a staggering 6.4 billion cubic feet. The North Bloomfield Gravel Mining Company's dam delivered 40 million gallons of water every day to its operation—equivalent to 69,000 gallons of water for every dollar in gold yielded by the mine.

Thus, from its mythical origins when thousands of rugged individuals risked all and a few actually made fortunes, gold mining had quickly become a capital-intensive, wage-paying, incorporated industrial enterprise that left deep scars on the land. Yet, at least early on, few dared question it. Employing tens of thousands of men, hydraulic mining brought to life new towns like Marysville, which by 1870 had become the third largest town in California. By supplying miners and residents with food, farmers enjoyed the prosperity as well.

Yet, it was not long before the deleterious effects of corporate mining became apparent. Although quartz mining, with its profligate use of water and mercury and its toxic waste, left its own path of environmental wreckage, it was the impact of hydraulicking that most astonished observers. Only the gold, a minuscule fraction of the gouged-out earth, was actually saved in the sluices. Nearly all of it—now in the form of masses of muddy, gravelly debris—slid down the mountains and into the waterways. The enormous pressure of the powerful jets collapsed centuries-old trees into splinters. Boulders larger than men tumbled down in the cascade of tailings that raised the beds of streams and rivers and smothered farmers' fields and orchards. Once-clear mountain streams that had been salmon spawning grounds became sprawling mud-choked torrents. The bed of the Yuba River rose an astonishing twenty-five feet within a decade. The Sacramento River swelled to a turbid sea fifty miles wide at one point. As debris accumulated in the beds of rivers and their tributaries, steamboats and other large vessels began scraping bottom on loads of silt. Navigation became problematic.

More ominous was the fact that with waterways filling up, there was nowhere for the water to go but over the banks. Situated near the confluence of the Feather and Yuba Rivers, the towns of Marysville and Yuba City were particularly vulnerable. In January 1862, a torrent of water swept over top defensive levees and filled the streets of Marysville with six feet of water.

Yet, with mining the economic lifeblood of the town, Marysville residents remained hesitant to challenge the industry. Instead, they strengthened and raised the height of their protective levees. Through the 1860s the operations expanded, the hydraulic derricks growing ever larger, the number and force of the hoses growing, blasting away more and more massive swaths of earth.

The winter floods of 1872 that pushed debris-filled Dry Creek over its banks destroyed A. J. Crum's peach orchards, prompting him to file suit against the Spring Valley Mining Company—the first volley in the legal war. The company presented a compelling defense, arguing, first, that there was no way to be certain of the source of the mud that killed the fruit trees, since many companies had worked that area. Second, they contended that shutting down the mine would not alleviate the threat posed by existing debris nor prevent further debris from other companies from spilling down. Perhaps most convincing was the cold fact that the value of one day's mining profits exceeded the combined value of all farms damaged by the flood. A jury of farmers and miners exonerated the company.

Despite continued flooding, public opinion remained divided, as both rural and town folk continued to fear the economic ramifications of a shutdown. Rather than challenge the companies, Marysville residents voted in 1873 to raise taxes in order to elevate their fortress of levees.

Sentiment took a turn against mining interests with the catastrophic flood of January 20, 1875, as the debris-filled Yuba River breeched the levee and flooded Yuba City and Marysville. A boy drowned, outhouses floated in the streets, and farmers had to contend with a thick new layer of mud, sand, and gravel. While some farmers resigned themselves to abandoning their land, when more flooding arrived that fall, businessmen and lawyers joined angry farmers in a call for action against the miners. One farmer, James Keyes, distilled the plain wisdom and American legal principle that would eventually triumph:

> I have no objection to the miners digging out all the gold they can find, but I don't want them to send the whole side of a hill down on my ranch and bury me and all I have. And that is just what they have done and are doing. I want to be left alone. I don't know much about law and don't want to. If it is the law that one man shall use his property so as not to injure his neighbor, I should like to see that law put into force.

Daily rejoinders like this one could be found in the *Nevada City Daily Transcript*:

> Supposing someone out of a dozen ranchers in Yuba County do have a half dozen acres of land covered with a coat of good mountain soil once in a while. Suppose a few sloughs are filled up . . . it won't hurt much. . . . Those ranchers depend upon the mountains to consume their produce and furnish them with coin, and we think they don't treat their customers well to try to kick up such a muss about a little matter.[3]

To this very real economic threat the miners added the argument that by virtue of their property rights they held the "reasonable use" right to the water—to which they held first claim—any way they saw fit.

James Keyes would not go away. In July 1876, he sued nineteen hydraulic mining companies, charging collective liability for the hardened mass of muck and rocks that covered the Bear River valley. The companies formed the Hydraulic Miners Association to defend their collective interests and to forestall any state or federal legislative action that might "interfere with or embarrass the operations of hydraulic mining in California." A change in venue to state court helped stall the movement of the case, but in the meantime, more flooding continued to move public opinion against the miners. From the deck of a steamer on the Sacramento River, one reporter saw a "wild waste of waters, broken levees . . . and houses in the water. . . . The beautiful orchards were either in the water or covered with slime."[4] It had become starkly clear that either farming or hydraulic mining—not both—would survive.

Keyes's case rested on the testimony of farmers whose livelihoods had been buried by two decades of gravelly mud. A vigorous defense claimed the right to dump debris by "prescription," arguing essentially that miners had established the accepted practice of waste disposal long before farmers began to complain. They redeployed previous arguments that a shutdown would not prevent the further flow of debris already accumulated but would prohibit the taking of the estimated 90 percent of the region's gold that still lay buried on the mountain. Then came reminders of the mining industry's importance to the area's economy. By 1878 this argument held less weight, however, as agriculture in California had established itself as a major economic engine. Four million acres of wheat in 1881 alone sold on the world market for $34 million— nearly twice the value of quartz and hydraulic mining. As agriculture assumed greater economic value, mining's hold on the state's political power loosened.

In his March 1879 decision, the presiding judge reflected that shifting sentiment in ruling for the farmers. He declared that company privileges did not include the right "to choke and fill . . . the channels of Bear River nor to flow or overflow plaintiff's lands with . . . tailings."[5] The farmers' euphoria was short-lived, as an appeal to the state Supreme Court reversed the decision. The court reasoned, as before, that liability for the disaster could not be attributed to any single mining company, and therefore it was unfair to find them collectively responsible.

As the conflict intensified, state political leaders struggled to find a compromise that could balance the seemingly irreconcilable interests of miners and farmers. The only possible path to a solution lay in a report from state engineer William H. Hall in 1880. In his report, Hall recommended that the state take command of the rivers. In place of the hodgepodge system of levees and dams, the state, said Hall, should construct an elaborate dam and levee system that could control the waterways. Desperate for a solution, state legislators passed the Drainage Act in 1880 centered on Hall's plan for a technological fix.

With twenty years' experience of failed levees, farmers and townspeople remained skeptical. Their doubts seemed validated in January 1881 when the worst flood ever struck the region, leaving fields and towns covered with yet another thick layer of hardened mud and rock. As farmers promised further legal action, miners remained angrily defiant.

When the state Supreme Court ruled the Drainage Act unconstitutional, the San Francisco Board of Trade picked up the mantle of engineering a solution to the problem, urging the city to construct a fortress of protective dams and levees that would allow hydraulic mining to continue. The hope for an engineering fix was echoed in an 1882 decision settling another farmer's claim, this time shutting down a mining company, but allowing it to resume operations once the company built larger impoundment dams to hold back the heaviest debris.

In the fall of 1882, antidebris forces filed what proved to be the climactic lawsuit. The plaintiff, Colonel Edwards Woodruff, owned one square block of the Marysville business district (flooded three times), as well as two parcels of ruined farmland. Filed in the federal courtroom of Lorenzo Sawyer, a 49'er from the gold rush days, the case sought a permanent injunction against the North Bloomfield Company—the largest and most powerful operation of them all. During the course of the trial, Sawyer personally visited hydraulic sites and farmers' fields. That was not a good omen for mining interests. More foreboding was the judge's ruling against a company motion to dismiss on the familiar ground of unclear liability stemming from multiple defendants. Most devastating to the hydraulickers' case was the bursting of the North Bloomfield Company's massive dam in June 1883. That event dramatically punctured one of the company's main lines of defense, that dams could protect farms and towns from further destruction. In January 1884, Sawyer ruled for the plaintiff. The decision effectively shut down the North Bloomfield Company.

Although the companies fought on, Sawyer's ruling was the death knell for hydraulic mining in California and the beginning of the end to it in the United States. The Sawyer decision was one of the few rulings from America's "Age of Robber Barons" in which ordinary Americans—small property owners in this case—emerged victorious over well-heeled capitalists. More important, it was the first significant legal decision in the United States that implicitly argued for environmental protection. Still, the ruling did not settle the issues that dominated the thirty-year conflict—property rights, jobs versus the environment, and how to wrest a living from the earth without compromising the ability of future generations to do likewise. They are still very much with us.

DOCUMENTS

Document 5.1   John Todd Describes the Promise of Hydraulic Gold Mining, 1870

In an excerpt from his promotional travel book, New England minister John Todd writes glowingly of the processes and prosperous results of California gold mining. Like many similar accounts from the period, Todd's passing observations of the grim mined-out landscape seem to be more than outweighed by the wealth generated by the enterprise of hydraulic mining. For most Americans of the period, such industrialized landscapes were telling signs of the technological and industrial progress of the nation.

In mining, the first requisite and essential, after finding evidences of gold, is water—water to wash out the soil and sand, leaving the gold behind. When they first began, they carried the earth on their backs, or on pack-horses, two or three miles to the nearest water.

You are a miner, we will suppose, of the poorest and simplest working power. In that case, you have a pan in which you shovel the earth, and then wash it till the soil is out, and the gold left on the bottom. But the gold, for the most part, is very fine. It is mere dust. Then you put quicksilver [mercury] in the bottom of your pan; that attracts the gold, and forms what is called an amalgam. If you have got beyond the simple pan, you have the rocker,—a larger vessel, round on the bottom, and long, like a hollow log split lengthwise; this you put under running water, and while one shovels in the earth, you rock and wash it. Or, you make a trough, with little slats nailed across the bottom inside. Here, above the slats, you put your quicksilver, and let in a stream of running water, while you shovel in the earth. All the day long you do this, and at night gather out your amalgam. Now, the gold is scattered through all the gulches of the foothills, and the necessity of running water has created Water Companies, who bring it along on the sides of the mountains in ditches, and across ravines in troughs held up on trestle-work. Sometimes this water is brought one hundred and forty miles, and the right to use it is sold to the miner by the square inch. A more productive way is what is called the hydraulic method. This is now the most expensive, and for the placer mining the most profitable.

Suppose you are to get the gold out of a hill or flat where the soil is sixteen or twenty feet deep before you come to the bed-rock, which underlies all the hills. You bring water from any distance, however great, and let it fall, say fifty feet, through a hose six inches in diameter. The hose must be encased in iron rings,—rings, so that you can bend it,—and very near to each other, to prevent its bursting. Or, better still, in place of the hose, you have iron pipes, through which the water rushes, and which is safer than the hose, which is apt to ''buck,'' as they call it; i.e., twitch and jerk as would a live buck, if held by the hind leg. Let in a stream through your pipe, as big as your wrist, upon the bank, and it washes down with amazing rapidity. Being dissolved, it flows through the long trough, where the quicksilver lies in wait to court and embrace, and retain it. The more soil you can thoroughly dissolve, the more gold you get....

Nothing can be more dreary than a territory where the soil has been washed out as low as the water will run off. Ten thousand rocks of all shapes, and forms, and sizes are left; acres and acres, and even miles, of the skeletons of beauty, with the flesh all gone, and nothing but hideousness remaining....

The discovery of gold, and the amount obtained, have given a stimulus to commerce, to agriculture, to every department of life. They have created impulses that have advanced civilization, and shaken up nations, and poured one country into another, till we hardly know what will be next. The arts have advanced, architecture has made new discoveries in applying its skill, manufactures have been called upon to supply more people, and with better garments; and if a few have played the fool by sudden riches, the great mass of the people have been greatly benefited....

Since this outpouring of the silver and the gold from the mines, we are every way improved; we have better clothing, better houses, better carriages, better school-houses and churches, and schools and colleges, better books and libraries, better ships and steamboats, better goods manufactured, and everything better. Not only so, but where one used to have these good things, ten have them now. The whole plane of human comforts and enjoyments has been raised up many degrees.

Source: John Todd, *The Sunset Land; or the Great Pacific Slope* (Boston: Lee and Shepard, 1870), pp. 38–58, 73–75.

Document 5.2   **The *Mining and Scientific Press* Objects to Suggestion of Hydraulic Mining Regulations, 1860**

This brief excerpt from a mining publication in 1860 reflects the industry's opposition to early efforts to impose restrictions on mining. Complaints that mining debris was filling the Yuba River were already coming from communities like Marysville, prompting calls for curtailment of industry freedoms.

Up here in the mountains where we are all directly or indirectly connected with the business of gold mining..., we need no better laws and ask no better laws than those which our own experience and wisdom have enacted and sanctioned.... Our California miners wish to be let alone—by our legislators and by the federal government—and be permitted to manage their own affairs in their own way. A "Masterly inactivity" in all that regards mining and mining interests is what miners ask of legislators, and it is to be hoped that what is so modestly asked may not be churlishly denied.

Source: Mining and Scientific Press, December 21, 1860, p. 4.

Document 5.3   The California State Agricultural Society Echoes the Progress and Power of Gold Mining, 1865

Although farmers' fields had been feeling the destructive power of hydraulic mining for the previous decade, agriculture in California was not yet the economic generator it would one day be, nor, consequently, had farmers gained enough political power effectively to challenge the dominance of mining and water companies. Moreover, farmers understood well that much of their livelihood, indeed the prosperity of the entire state, as John Todd made clear, owed to the mining industry. Although individual farmers were making their objections to the industry clear in many quarters by 1865, the degree to which agriculture generally saw its fortunes tied to those of mining is reflected here in the 1865 "Mining Review" of the California State Agricultural Society. Beyond a customary reference to the "exhaustless" resource and the economic advantages of mining, however, there is an implication here of the industry's deleterious impacts. Still, the editors rebuked the growing calls for regulation of the industry.

Just eighteen years have now elapsed since the grand discovery of gold in California, this event having occurred on the fourth day of January, eighteen hundred and forty-eight.... This event, like many other important discoveries, was the result of accident; and though it failed, as often happens in cases of this kind, to enrich the party making it, produced at once a marked effect upon the trade, industry, and financial aspect of the whole civilized world. The energies of the nations were aroused, emigration was excited, new channels of transportation and travel were opened, and new enterprises were set on foot—every interest and department of labor being made to feel its quickening and invigorating influences....

The plan of working mines with a view to enhance or depress the prices of stocks as might best serve the interests of those having control of them, is not likely to be practiced to the same extent as formerly, it threatening to prove nearly as dangerous to those engaged in carrying it on as to the intended victims. That this business may speedily be purged of this and all other abuses is greatly to be hoped, since to it we must continue to look for those large and certain revenues which have thus far never failed us, as they are not likely to do, our mines being vast in extent and literally exhaustless, while the value and amount of their productions are less dependent on the seasons, the demands of a foreign market, and other incidental circumstances, than are our cereal crops, wines, wool, and other staple productions.

Neither rain nor drought, seasons of plenty or dearth, of financial ease or stringency, can ever wholly cut off or seriously diminish the yield of our mines or lessen the value of their products. In this feature of stability, apart from the extent and prolific character of our mines, we have a fund of wealth upon which we can always rely, even should our grain crop prove short, our herds perish with famine, and all our other resources fail. But that this element may be made to yield its full measure of advantage, it must obviously be prosecuted with a more careful economy and less with a view to large and immediate than to certain and permanent results. Wherever it has been carried on in a legitimate manner, being conducted with the same discretion and care evinced in most other callings, it has generally been proved a success; the failures mostly being attributable to lack of skill, extravagant expenditures, or some other sort of mismanagement. . . .

When you touch the mines with the hand of oppression [government regulation], you oppress every other interest, and when you encourage and stimulate the development of the mines, you encourage and stimulate every other pursuit. In this respect, if not in actual investment of money, we are all miners and cultivators of the soil. . . .

Source: Transactions of the California State Agricultural Society for the Year 1864 and 1865 (Sacramento: O. M. Clayes, 1866), p. 33.

Documents 5.4 and 5.5   **Two California Newspapers React to the Catastrophic Flooding of 1875 Caused by Hydraulic Mining**

Throughout the 1860s, periodic flooding caused by denuded hillsides (in part a result of two decades of logging to support the mining industry) and the collapse of company dams prompted valley communities to build protective levees. As flooding continued to fill the riverbeds ever higher with silt, the height of the levees rose, as did calls from farmers for legislative and court relief from the industry. A catalyzing event toward reform came on the morning of January 20, 1875, when a flood devastated the towns of Yuba City and Marysville. The first account from the generally pro-mining Nevada City Daily Transcript *acknowledged the tragedy, as well as the daunting challenge of finding a solution that would not impinge on the all-important mining industry that, presumably, was not going anywhere. By the end of the year, after a series of additional floods that fall, the* Sacramento Daily Union *spoke more determinedly for farmers' interest in calling for relief.*

Document 5.4

There is no doubt but a large share of the lands adjoining the rivers which carry the water from the mountains to the ocean have been flooded and irreparable damage has been the result. It is evident that no system of damming can prevent an overflow when such a freshet as the last occurs. What are the owners of the farms to do? It is evident mining can never be stopped. It is an industry the whole world desires to foster. The government will encourage it, notwithstanding agriculture may suffer.... Each year adds to the amount of sediment deposited in the valleys. Fifty years hence the whole surface of the country will be raised much above its present level by the accumulation of dirt washed down from above.... So, the question becomes one of serious import.... What relief can be afforded we can not apprehend.

Source: Nevada Daily Transcript, January 22, 1875.

Document 5.5

We published yesterday the report of a meeting held at Yuba City, to prepare a petition to the Legislature concerning the injury inflicted upon the valley lands at Yuba and Sutter counties by the debris washed down from the mining regions of the Sierra. The allegations of the petition which was adopted at this meeting are unquestionably true, and the subject is one of the greatest importance, and should obtain the most earnest attention from the Legislature. The effect of hydraulic mining upon the agricultural interest in the valleys has long been most prejudicial, and as science develops each year improved processes for washing away the bluffs of mountain claims, the amount of debris sent down the rivers is steadily increasing. It was long since pointed out by this journal that if no remedial measures were taken a time must arrive when the Sacramento river would cease to be navigable, and when the mass of detritus washed down would so fill its bed that it would spread over the adjoining country, resolve itself into a number of significant streams, and convert a vast fertile area into quagmire and morass.... For many years past the residents of the valleys have been compelled to extend their levees higher and higher up the stream, but since the flow of the mining detritus continues and becomes constantly greater, the effect upon the river beds far more than offsets the effect of the levees, and a period is already in view when these precautions will cease to be effective, and the evils which have been combated so long and so patiently will obtain the ascendancy. The matter is of such vital importance to the whole community that action upon it cannot be evaded save in deliberately neglecting a plain and pressing duty. Whether the proper resort is not to Congress, may perhaps be questioned, but even if the State Legislature cannot deal directly with the matter, it can impress upon our Senators and Representatives the urgent necessity of relief. In considering the best means of abating the nuisance caused by hydraulic mining it will naturally be suggested that the main desideratum is to prevent the mining debris from being washed down into the valleys, and that to accomplish this end a scheme is required by which the flumes and ditches of the mines shall be made to deposit the matter borne in solutions by their waters, before these waters are returned to the streams from which they are derived. In devising such a scheme we believe that no serious engineering difficulties will have to be surmounted, and indeed a practical method has already been suggested by a mining engineer.... He proposes that the desired end shall be obtained by constructing reservoirs in some of the innumerable small canyons and hollows among the mountains—places which are wholly useless for any purpose whatever, at present, and which would actually be utilized by the process suggested. Into these natural tanks or reservoirs the flumes or ditches should be emptied. There the waters would rapidly deposit their heavy detritus, and thence they could be reconducted to the rivers by convenient waste-weirs and sluices. In a few months the first series of reservoirs would be filled up, and the ditches could be conducted to fresh localities; but in drawing off the waters some acres of soil would be found deposited, and would afford the basis for cultivation. In this way the proceeds of hydraulic mining, instead of inflicting damage and destruction upon the valley lands, would gradually enlarge the cultivable area in the mountains, and by repairing the effects of systematic denudation ... might even tend to restore the climatic equilibrium at present so seriously threatened by the processes being carried out throughout the mining regions. Of course there can be no question of stopping the development of the mines, but there is a strong question of the rights of miners to destroy the valley lands in the way now proceeding....

Source: Sacramento Record-Union, December 24, 1875.

Document 5.6   *Nevada City Daily Transcript* Defends Hydraulic Interests

---

> *With continued resistance from the miner to such expensive engineering solutions, the conflict continued to simmer. By 1879, it had worked its way into the courts. In March that year, James H. Keyes won a judgment against the Little York Gold Washing and Water Company, declaring hydraulic mining to be a "public nuisance" that damaged the plaintiff's land, and hence his property rights. Emboldened by the decision, long-suffering Marysville filed suit against the North Bloomfield Gravel Mining Company, the most powerful of the mining companies. In response, the* Nevada City Daily Transcript, *the leading organ of the miners' interests, inveighed against the town and its threat to capital.*

It is an open question whether the existence of a half dozen villages like the city of Marysville is of as much importance to the state of California and the country at large as the existence of hydraulic mining.... The idea of Marysville bringing suits to abate the hydraulic mining companies on the Yuba [River] and its branches as a nuisance is preposterous; to do so would simply be the confiscation of millions of dollars of property.

Source: Nevada City Daily Transcript, November 8, 1879.

Document 5.7   **California Supreme Court, *James H. Keyes v. Little York Gold Washing and Water Company*, November 17, 1879**

A week later, the California Supreme Court reversed the earlier judgment in favor of James Keyes. The court ruled that there was no way to determine which of the mining companies had sent the debris down the mountain that caused harm to Keyes's land; without such certainty it was not possible to hold any single company liable for damages.

The complaint sets forth that the plaintiff is the owner of certain described premises known as bottom land, situate[d] in the valley, upon the banks of the Bear River, about ten miles from where that stream debouches into the Sacramento Valley, and midway between that point and the mouth of the river; that the defendants are miners severally engaged in hydraulic mining at points high up on Bear River and its tributaries—the several mining properties of the defendants lying within a radius of seven miles upon the hill-tops adjacent to the river, and being severally wrought and carried on by the respective defendants, and that the several dumps used by the defendants respectively in their mining pursuits are some of them in the bed of the river, others in the beds of steep ravines and gulches immediately contiguous to and leading into the bed of the river and its tributaries; that the tailings of the several mining claims deposited on these dumps are swept down by the force of the current until they reach the lands of the plaintiff below, upon which they are deposited, and which they cover so as to destroy the value of said lands. The prayer is that an injunction issue enjoining the defendants from depositing the tailings and debris of their several mining claims so that they reach the channels of the river, etc.

The defendants appeared to the action, and filed a demurrer to the complaint upon several grounds—and, among others, upon the ground that there is a misjoinder of parties defendant, in that it did not appear by the complaint that the defendants jointly committed any of the acts complained of, or are acting therein in concert or by collusion with each other, but that, on the contrary, it did appear by the complaint that the defendants had no interest in common in the subject-matter of the suit, but were acting severally and without any joinder or co-operation on the part of the defendants, or any of them. . . .

. . . The wrong complained of is that each of the defendants, acting for himself, and not in collusion or combination with any other, threatens to continue to deposit the tailings from the working of the mine in such position, on or adjacent to his own premises, as that, from natural causes, they will flow down or be forced down upon plaintiff's farm.

If a nuisance was created by the exposure of the dumps to the action of the waters of Bear River and its tributaries, a nuisance was committed by each of the defendants, when he—disconnected from the others—made or threatened such deposit; or, if it be said that the matter of the *reasonable use* of the stream can enter into the inquiry, there could be no nuisance by any of the defendants who had made only a reasonable use.

In either view of the case, there is a misjoinder of parties defendant. The bare statement would seem to prove the proposition, since the very essence of the objection of misjoinder of a defendant with others is that he is not connected with or affected by the single cause of action, if there is but one, or that he is not connected with or affected by one or more of several separate and distinct causes of action, if several are alleged. If any one of these defendants was liable to be enjoined, he could have been enjoined in a separate suit, the subject-matter of such suit being the alleged threatened wrong. If any one of the defendants is not liable to be enjoined in a separate suit, he cannot be made liable in an action like the present; for there is no principle of equity which would make a man responsible for a wrong which he has neither done nor threatened, merely by joining him with other defendants who may independently have threatened a similar wrong. . . .

Source: James H. Keyes v. Little York Gold Washing and Water Company, No. 6659 Supreme Court of California, 53 Cal. 724 (November 1879).

Document 5.8   Judge Lorenzo Sawyer, *Woodruff v. North Bloomfield Gravel Mining Company and Others*, 1884

On Friday, January 7, 1884, Judge Lorenzo Sawyer handed farmers and townspeople the decision for which they had been waiting. For three and one-half hours, Judge Sawyer read aloud his landmark 225-page decision that put an end to all hydraulic mining operations on the Yuba River. Although Judge Sawyer's decision was grounded in the legal principles of American property rights, both land and people were the beneficiaries. It is regarded as the first significant court decision in American history favoring environmental protection.

This is a bill in equity to restrain the defendants, being several mining companies, engaged in hydraulic mining on the western slope of the Sierra Nevada Mountains, from discharging their mining debris into the . . . Yuba River . . . whence it is carried down by the current into Feather and Sacramento rivers, filling up their channels and injuring their navigation; and sometimes by overflowing and covering the neighboring lands with debris, injuring, and threatening to injure and destroy, the lands and property of the complainant, and of other property owners, situate [*sic*] on and adjacent to the banks of these water-courses. . . .

Approximately . . . over 100,000,000 of cubic yards [of mining waste] in these mines have been washed out by the hydraulic process, and the debris deposited in the Yuba and its affluents; . . . This irruption from the mountains has *destroyed thousands of acres of alluvial land. . . .*

...before hydraulic mining operations commenced, the Yuba river ran through this part of its course in a deep channel, with gravelly bottom from 300 to 400 feet wide, on an average, with steep banks from 15 to 20 feet high.... From the top of the banks, on each side, extended a strip of bottom lands of rich, black alluvial soil, on an average a mile and a half wide, upon which were situated some of the finest farms, orchards, and vineyards in the state.... but this entire strip of bottom land has been buried with sand and debris many feet deep, from ridge to ridge of high land, and utterly ruined for farming and other purposes to which it was before devoted, and it has con-sequently been abandoned for such uses.

... The lands thus already buried and destroyed are over 15,000 acres, or 25 square miles.... The filling in the river bed is generally 25 feet or more ... [the] depth ... increasing year by year, and raising the bed of the river within the levees higher and higher above the surrounding country outside the levees....

The North Bloomfield Mining Company, defendant, has constructed a dam to impound its debris, 50 feet high, near the junction of Humbug canyon with south Yuba. The dam, not having been carried higher as it filled up, is now full, and the debris that has passed over the dam has filled the canyon and the south Yuba below the dam to a level with the debris above, so that now the debris passes along down the canyon over the dam without obstruction, as though no dam at all existed at that point....

The complainant has owned in fee for more than 20 years ... an undivided half of three parcels of land ... [much of which was] buried by debris in 1862 and subsequent years ... and are now useless for agricultural purposes....

About 1868 the people of Marysville found it necessary to build levees around the city and along the north bank of Yuba river to protect it from the rapid encroachment of the debris coming down the Yuba; ... It has been found necessary to increase these levees in height and thickness from year to year ever since. In 1875 the levee on the north side of the Yuba broke, some three or four miles above the city, and the city and other lands were not only flooded, but a large amount of debris was deposited. This was the first time Marysville was ever flooded, although the amount of water that fell ... was much less than in the great flood of 1862. So, in 1881, with much less water than at the great flood, it rose to a higher point at Marysville than ever before. This was doubtless owing in great part to the filling up of the channels and elevation of the beds and rivers.... At the break of the levee and flooding of Marysville, in 1875, complainant's Empire block, in Marysville, was materially injured....

The defendants have attempted to show that much of the danger from overflows results from the acts of the people themselves, in consequence of the improper system of leveeing adopted.... These works are always erected on the judgment of engineers, or other men presumed to be competent, and rarely without some difference of opinion, and it is scarcely possible that any plan wholly unobjectionable to all could be adopted. However this may be, there can be no possible doubt, not only that the deposit of the mining debris has greatly augmented the injuries heretofore received, but that ... it is the great source and cause of all or most of the evils which are suffered or threatened....

... The nuisance [of mining waste] is both public and private. If the unlawful filling up of a channel of a river, ... and burying with sand and gravel and utterly destroying all the farms of the riparian owners on either side...; if the sand and gravel so sent is... only restrained from working similar destruction to a large extent of farming country other than that already buried and destroyed... by means of levees erected at great expense by the land and other property owners of the county, and the inhabitants of the city, such levees continually... requiring to be enlarged and strengthened to keep pace with the augmentation of the mass of debris sent down...; and if the filling and narrowing... of the channels of the largest and principal waters of the state... to the injury of their navigation and danger of the riparian owners of the property—do not constitute a public nuisance of an aggravated character, then we confess that we do not know what a public nuisance is....

Defendants allege that both congress and the legislature of California have authorized the use of the navigable waters of the Sacramento and Feather rivers for the flow and deposit of mining debris; and having so authorized their use, all the acts of defendants complained of are lawful, and the results of those acts, therefore, cannot be a nuisance, public or otherwise.... It is one of the conditions always implied by the law, that one's rights, whether granted or regulated by the legislature, shall be exercised with due regard for the rights of others—so exercised as not to injure another; and certainly no authority to encroach upon the vested rights of others can be inferred without being in express terms clearly authorized;... But no intention can be properly inferred, from any act of congress brought to our notice, to permit the destruction or injury of the navigable waters of the state, or the destruction or injury of the towns and cities, or property of the riparian and adjacent owners along the water-courses of the state....

The state supreme court... [has] held that mining is not a public use, in favor of which this right of eminent domain [which defendants claimed] can be constitutionally exercised in the case of a private party. An elaborate argument has been made in favor of the constitutionality of the act, but... the statute... does not authorize the use of navigable waters of the state to the injury of navigation, or the discharge by miners of their debris upon the lands of riparian proprietors, without condemnation and payment.... Instead of inferentially authorizing the injuries complained of, the inference is directly the other way— that there is no authority to do an act which would work an injury to a public or private right, or, in other words, constitute a public or private nuisance, without first acquiring the right to use the property to be appropriated or injured, by purchase or condemnation of and payment for the property or right appropriated. It recognizes the constitutional right of every man to the undisturbed enjoyment of his property and all his legal rights....

Such use... of complainant's land, is a taking, *a fortiori*, a *damaging* of the property of complainant.... Conceding, then, that such use of the lands for deposit of mining debris is a public use [as defendants claimed in trying to assert rights of eminent domain to dump] still the legislature... could not make it lawful without taking them upon due process of law, and upon full compensation first paid. If the use is private... then they could not be taken at all without the consent of the owner; for there is no authority in the constitution or laws of the country to compel one man, unwillingly, to surrender his property for the use of another, either with or without compensation....

[With regard to *Keyes v. Little York*, above]: Is every property holder . . . bound to ascertain, or can he be presumed to know, every miner in the mountains who is contributing to the nuisance by which he is injured or threatened . . . ? and if he fails to ascertain the trespassers, and commence a suit against them all, separately, within the period prescribed by the statute of limitations, is an acquiescence in the nuisance to be inferred as to every one not sued in such sense as to give effect to a prescriptive right? It would obviously be impossible to maintain one's rights under such a rule; and it would be preposterous to hold that such a rule exists. . . .

. . . so long as hydraulic mining is carried on as now pursued it will continue to be, an alarming and ever-growing menace . . . threatening further injuries to the property of the complainant, as well as the lives and property of numerous other citizens similarly situated. Against the continuous and further augmentation of this nuisance the complainant must certainly be entitled to legal protection.

We are fully satisfied that acts of the defendants complained of are not authorized by any valid custom or usage, or by any valid law, statute or otherwise . . . ; and that complainant is entitled to such relief as shall fully and amply protect him from any other injuries to his property and any further encroachments upon his rights. What shall the remedy be? It would be difficult to appreciate too highly the importance of the mining interests. . . . The boldness with which capital interests . . . have invested large amounts of capital; . . . the vast enterprises they have undertaken and successfully carried out; the energy, perseverance, great engineering and mining skill displayed in pursuing these enterprises—excite wonder and unbounded admiration. . . . no one could possibly be more averse than we are to applying any remedy to the grievances complained of that must put an end to hydraulic mining. . . . We have therefore sought with painful anxiety some other remedy; . . . [on the suggested remedy to build larger impoundment dams]: . . . all the practical experiments heretofore made, at great expense, under the supervision of the state and of competent engineers, have been lamentable failures. . . . what guaranty have the court, and those whose lives and property are at stake, that any future works of the kind will not also be defective? . . . In view of past experience here and elsewhere . . . it is clear that we should not be justified in an attempt to prescribe in advance any kind of dam under which a large community should be compelled to live in dread of a perpetual, seriously alarming, and ever-present menace . . . there are no dams now of any appreciable service in protecting the rights of complainant from further injury . . . as may arise from a continuance of hydraulic mining as now pursued. There is, therefore, no alternative to granting an injunction. . . .

Source: Woodruff v. North Bloomfield Gravel Mining Company and Others, Circuit Court, D. California, 18 F. 753, U.S. App. (January 7, 1884).

NOTES

1. The definitive treatment of this story remains Robert Kelley, *Gold vs. Grain: The Hydraulic Mining Controversy in California's Sacramento Valley* (Glendale, CA: Arthur H. Clark, 1959). For the early development of the industry, see pp. 20–85.

2. John Todd, *The Sunset Land; or the Great Pacific Slope* (Boston: Lee and Shepard, 1870), pp. 54–55.

3. First quote from Kelley, *Gold vs. Grain*, p. 74; *Nevada City Daily Transcript*, December 28, 1875; both cited in J. S. Holliday, *Rush for Riches: Gold Fever and the Making of California* (Berkeley: University of California Press, 1999), pp. 255–56.

4. Hydraulic Miners Association Articles of Agreement and *San Francisco Daily Bulletin*, March 9, 1878; both quoted in Holliday, *Rush for Riches*, p. 258.

5. Judge Keyser's decision recounted in *Pacific Rural Press*, March 22, 1879.

ANNOTATED BIBLIOGRAPHY

Heizer, Robert Fleming. *The Destruction of California Indians: A Collection of Documents from the Period 1847 to 1865 in which Are Described Some of the Things that Happened.* Lincoln: University of Nebraska Press, 1993. Primary source collection documenting painfully the destruction of California's native population during the gold rush era, superseded somewhat by Trafzer and Hyer's collection (below).

Holliday, J. S. *Rush for Riches: Gold Fever and the Making of California.* Berkeley: University of California Press, 1999. Scholarly and richly illustrated narrative of the gold rush story, Holliday's interpretation takes the reader from the innocent heady days of pick-and-shovel through the era when capital interests invested heavily and profited handsomely. He traces well the challenge from the state's agricultural sector that was growing in importance and finally achieved its historic legal victory in 1884.

Isenberg, Andrew C. *Mining California: An Ecological History.* New York: Hill and Wang, 2005. Isenberg plunges brilliantly into the environmental history of the gold industry, tracking the relatively innocuous effects of the early years to the cascading impacts wrought by quartz and hydraulic mining.

Kelley, Robert. *Gold vs. Grain: The Hydraulic Mining Controversy in California's Sacramento Valley.* Glendale, CA: Arthur H. Clark, 1959. The early classic on this story now eclipsed by Holliday and Isenberg.

Orsi, Richard J., ed. *Contested Eden: California before the Gold Rush* (1998) by Ramon A. Gutierrez; *Rooted in Barbarous Soil: People, Culture, and Community in Gold Rush California* (2000) by Kevin Starr; *A Golden State: Mining and Economic Development in Gold Rush California* (1999) by James J. Rawls; and *Taming the Elephant: Politics, Government, and Law in Pioneer California* (2003) by John F. Burns. 4 vols. California History Sesquicentennial Series. San Francisco: California Historical Society. Each of these four books contributes something to our understanding of California's gold mining story, as scholars representing a range of disciplinary perspectives shed light on the racial, social, legal, political, and environmental dimensions of California's gold mining era.

Smith, Duane A. *Mining America: The Industry and the Environment, 1800–1980.* 1987. Reprint, Boulder: University Press of Colorado, 1993. A survey of the wider environmental impacts of the mining industry beyond California.

Trafzer, Clifford E., and Joel R. Hyer, eds. *"Exterminate Them": Written Accounts of the Murder, Rape, and Slavery of Native Americans during the California Gold Rush, 1848–1868.* East Lansing: Michigan State University Press, 1999. This collection of documents provides a necessary view of the grim experience of California natives during the gold rush era.

6

Wildlife Conservation: Slaughter and Salvation of the Bison

> No amount of scalping of the hunters would save the bison from extinction. He must follow the mammoth and the mastodon, and it does not matter much whether his inevitable fate is hastened or retarded.... When the clumsy, tough-fleshed creatures are all killed off, their room will be filled by good beef cattle.
>
> —E.V. Smalley, *The Northwest*, 1883[1]

> The destruction of the buffalo was a loss of wealth perhaps twenty times greater than the sum it would have cost to conserve it, and this stupendous waste of valuable food and other products was committed by one class of the American people and permitted by another with a prodigality and wastefulness which even in the lowest savages would be inexcusable.
>
> —William T. Hornaday, 1887[2]

Few episodes of American environmental history are more familiar than the story of the North American bison, commonly known as the buffalo. Most Americans appreciate this animal as an iconic symbol of both the "Old West" and the nation's provident policy of wildlife preservation and management. With the possible exception of the bald eagle, no species of American fauna has been more studied by historians and ecologists, or more burdened with cultural significance than the bison. Indeed, the history of its slaughter, near-extinction, and ultimate protection offers a revealing window on a complex set of issues critical to U.S. environmental history: nineteenth-century attitudes about the assumed supremacy of white American civilization, the evolving beliefs and values of that culture toward the natural world and animals in particular, and the limits of wildlife preservation on islands of wildness surrounded by an urban industrialized society.

It is impossible to determine with certainty the precise number of bison that once roamed the North American continent. However, based on recent studies of the likely carrying capacity of the grasslands of the mid-continent where populations were highest, ecologists and environmental historians have reduced prior estimates of as many as 75 million to somewhere between 25 and 30 million animals. One thousand years ago their range extended from Canada to present day northern Mexico. Though population pressures and hunting had taken their toll, as late as 1810 herds of bison roamed the valleys and hills of western Pennsylvania and southern Ohio.

The greatest concentration of bison wandered the short-grass prairies and plains between the Mississippi River valley and the Rocky Mountains. Like the passenger pigeons that filled the skies, bison herds, as George Catlin reported in 1832, "[blackened] the prairies for miles together." The Great Plains, as many Indians recalled, were "one big black robe." Since the early nineteenth century when the adoption of the horse allowed them to hunt bison more tenaciously and effectively, Plains Indians, whose existence had once been fortified by a greater admixture of agriculture, gathering, and hunting, had placed the bison at the center of their world.[3] Early explorers reported with astonishment that it took days for one herd to pass through an area. Spiritually revered as well, the bison—every ounce of it, from tongue and testicles to hooves and hide—provided material sustenance for a bewildering assortment of Indian needs. Their reliance on the fate of a single animal would prove fatal. By September 1883, this once "numberless" species had been reduced to three herds of fewer than 500 animals on the northern plains, and not coincidentally, the human populations that had grown so bison-dependent were now clinging to survival.

Although the period of accelerated bison slaughter happened overnight in historical terms, from roughly 1870 to 1883, the roots of the animal's demise extend much deeper. Further, while that final infamous episode of merciless killing was driven primarily by the profit motive, the causes of the bison's near-extinction go beyond the caricature of money-grubbing white men's avarice to a complex of historical and environmental factors. The truism that Indians were incapable of hunting beyond need is complicated first by the fact that although belief systems and ritualistic taboos admonished rapacious or recklessly wasteful hunting, other tribal myths held that if buffalo failed to appear one spring as they always had, it was because they had gone to wander in underground prairies; thus the hunting could (and did) continue unabated, at least for some tribes in certain areas. Still, even with some profligate hunting, estimates are that all Indian tribes on the Great Plains killed no more than half a million bison annually.

Other factors contributed to an increase in bison hunting by Indians. By 1840, Indian tribes who had been at war with one another and consequently had left bison herds in disputed areas relatively unmolested in fear of being attacked, reached peace agreements and accelerated their hunting. More importantly, as was the case with beaver in New England during the 1600s, Indians were drawn, willingly, into the Euro-American market that put a price on the animal's shaggy hide, and ultimately ensured its destruction in the wild. Paralleling in some ways the story of beaver hats, the buffalo robe became the fashion rage in eastern cities and in Europe. Because of the trade value of a bison hide, some, though certainly not all, Indians were lured to hunting for market value of the skin alone. This signaled an ominous departure from the Indian tradition of extracting use-value from the entire animal; like white hide hunters, Indians had come to sever from the animal its marketable portion, leaving the carcass for the wolves. Compounding this inauspicious trend by the 1850s was a period of drought, which caused the short "buffalo grass" of the prairies to wither, and along with it, the slowly diminishing numbers of bison. Drought, however, was cyclic on the plains and bison had withstood such periods for centuries. Even the buffalo-robe trade, as with beaver hats, might have been expected to fade as fashion changed.

By 1870 a more sinister and far more threatening force loomed on the bison's horizon: America's second Industrial Revolution. In a number of ways, the nation's surging industrial development that exploded following the Civil War brought the final denouement of this epic drama. There was first, on the demand side, an increased need for industrial leather belts for turning spindles in textile mills and other factory machinery. In the 1860s tanners imported them at great cost from as far away as Latin America. Millions of bison seemed to offer an American solution. For bison hides to solve the growing desire for industrial leather, however, a transformation in the processing of bison hides was required. Until this point, Indian women skinned the hides of bison flesh, curing them for shipment to long-distance markets. The time-consuming nature of this process often caused bottlenecks, holding up production. In a flash of innovative American genius, in 1870 a Philadelphia tannery discovered a method for turning bison skins into leather belts. Still, in order to be processed, hides had to be green, which meant heavy (as much as fifty pounds each)—far too heavy for a horse to carry efficiently to market. Enter the iron horse—the symbol and engine of American industrialization.

The railroad's arrival in the West in the 1860s and 1870s, besides triggering the climactic major episode of America's Indian Wars, also sealed the bison's fate. From the Union Pacific to the Santa Fe and Kansas Pacific, armies of railroad builders numbering in the thousands shot and gorged on bison. William F. "Buffalo Bill" Cody earned his moniker in this period, shooting in one twelve-month period 4,280 bison. Travelers on the newly built lines were then invited to stand atop railroad observation cars and take aim at the bison, leaving their bodies to rot in the summer sun.

The greatest impact the railroads had upon bison was of course their capacity to ship the staggering volumes of green hides that came off the plain and flooded railway terminals by the early 1870s. Professional market hunters took aim at an animal that was not biologically accustomed to predation; to the hunters' utter amazement, whole bison herds stood pat as their companions fell around them. The killing was stunning and merciless. Good marksmen could kill hundreds in a single day, thousands in a season. One man went deaf from the repetitious firing of his .50 caliber rifle on his way to a count of 6,000 in the summer of 1876. The southern herd, split by the Union Pacific Railroad in 1869 and estimated at between 12 and 15 million animals, was destroyed by 1878.

Hide hunters received encouragement from the U.S. Cavalry, whose campaign to subjugate the Plains Indians seemed to stall in the late 1860s after a series of both horrifying debacles and glorious victories raised moral and practical questions about Indian policy back east. In that context came both subtle and explicit support to the bison hunters from U.S. Army officers, who knew well that the demise of the Indians' main food supply would hasten the destruction of the tribes. If not through outright starvation, the loss of the bison would compel Indians who were still resisting reservation life to accept containment and the accompanying government handouts. By 1876 General Phil Sheridan declared to the Texas state legislature that market hunters had done more in the previous few years "to settle the vexed Indian question than the entire regular army has done in the last thirty years. They are destroying the Indians' commissary." He urged them to "send . . . powder and lead, if you will; but for the sake of lasting peace, let them kill, skin and sell until the buffaloes are exterminated."[4] The army indeed occasionally distributed free ammunition to the hunters.

Congressional efforts from 1872 to 1876 to stop the slaughter failed, the debate (Document 6.2) often turning on the polarizing issue of whether or not Indians should be exempt from the proposed prohibition. Further, opponents of the measure often claimed that Indians were just as guilty as were white hunters, and in any case exempting them from the prohibition would inhibit the army's effort to achieve a final military victory. The best evidence of that was the sounding of the absolute death knell of the bill following Custer's disastrous defeat at the Little Big Horn in June 1876. Until the early 1890s the larger societal debate over the fate of the bison, to the extent there was such a thing, swirled around the Indian's fate. To save the buffalo was to prolong the "savagery" in the Indian; and with a Darwinian twist, to save the buffalo was to fight the "inevitable fate" that doomed "an inferior race." So went the arguments as bison fell.

Only the smaller northern herd remained by 1879. Its destruction by 1883 resulted from a combination of hide-market (and "sport") hunting, drought, and the arrival of nearly a half million head of cattle in Wyoming alone, whose appetite for grass and water competed with that of the diminishing bison. By September 1883, when young Theodore Roosevelt arrived in Dakota Territory hoping for a bison hunt, millions of bones lay scattered across the plains, the only reminders of the once-mighty herds. These, too, would be gathered, shipped east, and pulverized into phosphate-rich fertilizer to be spread on southern cotton fields.

The largest remaining bison herd, numbering around four or five hundred, roamed the area of Yellowstone National Park and over the next twenty years became the focus of conservationists' attempts to rescue the animal from absolute extinction. Leading that effort was the Boone and Crockett Club, an organization of conservation-minded genteel sportsmen founded in 1887 by Theodore Roosevelt and *Forest and Stream* editor George Bird Grinnell for the purpose of encouraging "manly sport with the rifle" and the "preservation of the large game of this country." In that spirit, the organization led protectionist forces on behalf of Yellowstone, established as the nation's (and world's) first national park in 1872. Throughout the late 1880s and 1890s, the preserve was threatened continually by a number of forces, including the possible incursion of a railroad to serve a northern Montana gold mining operation. Through

Grinnell's influential magazine and as individuals (some of whom served the federal government in influential positions), Boone and Crockett Club members argued effectively for the park's preservation. Scientist and club member Arnold Hague, for example, successfully advocated the establishment of the nation's first forest preserve on Yellowstone's border as a way of protecting regional watershed and providing additional wildlife habitat.

To be sure, however, Boone and Crockett members, like most sportsmen generally, did not as a rule argue for preservation of "nature" in any modern ecological sense. The common denominator was big game protection. As Roosevelt remembered later: "We wanted the game preserved, but chiefly with the idea that it should be protected in order that there might be good hunting which should last for generations."[5] They saw themselves as self-appointed guardians of the manly virtues of America's frontier that, like the buffalo, was rapidly disappearing. As such, they exhorted the growing class of middle-class sportsmen across the country to adhere strictly to the "sportsmen's code" of hunting only in season, taking only the allowable limit of fish and game, and never killing for profit, nor for "the pot." Naturally, then, just as they went after hide hunters (albeit too late), they railed against alleged Indian hunting of elk and bison in and around Yellowstone Park and applauded the avalanche of state and local ordinances that prohibited lower-class immigrants from hunting game.

Thus could sportsmen conservationists seize upon the capture of poacher Edgar Howell in Yellowstone's Pelican Valley in March 1894. Howell was the classic villain, and this the perfect moment to galvanize popular opinion in favor of stronger measures to protect the remaining bison in Yellowstone. With Grinnell's leadership, the dramatic story of Howell's capture led to the quick passage of a bill that prohibited the killing of all animals in the park except those that posed a threat to humans (this loophole allowed for the massive killing of wolves and other predators, which was carried out by park rangers well into the twentieth century), stiffened penalties considerably, and authorized the appointment of a federal park commissioner to adjudicate cases of alleged violators.

Named for its author, Congressman John F. Lacey of Iowa, the Lacey Act established the legal precedent for wildlife protection in the United States, paving the way for the second Lacey Act, passed in 1900. That landmark law prohibited the interstate shipment of wildlife in violation of state game laws and also designated the first national wildlife refuges. The measure came in response to pressures erupting far from the bounds of Yellowstone Park. In the 1880s and 1890s women leaders of the Humane Society, the Audubon Society, and women's clubs had been working for an end to the market hunting of exotic birds. Add to their tenacious and effective organizational work the sudden, inexplicable disappearance of the passenger pigeon and the demise of the bison—symbol of a vanishing, increasingly romantic frontier—and the result was the Lacey Act.

Finally, it is worth noting that both the Lacey laws banned the trafficking of illegally killed animals. That suggests the important fact that neither Edgar Howell nor the hide hunters were the only, or even the most culpable, villains in the demise of the bison. They stood at one end of a chain of poachers, entrepreneurs, and consumers that even after Howell's capture continued to reduce the number of bison in Yellowstone to somewhere around 200 animals by 1900. Emblems of a western wilderness rapidly receding, bison heads—all the more prized as their numbers diminished—ornamented the late Victorian parlors of the genteel. By the beginning of the twentieth century, the juggernaut of urban industrial civilization could find a home for bison only within the bounds of Yellowstone National Park and, thanks to the efforts of William T. Hornaday's American Bison Society and other preservationists, similar public and private reserves. Americans in the modern age, increasingly separated from their frontier past and from nature, would look increasingly to zoos and museums (Document 6.8) to find artifacts of both.

DOCUMENTS

Document 6.1   U.S. Army Officers Recall the Bison Slaughter

Although debate among scholars continues over whether or not and to what extent the extermination of the North American bison was officially encouraged as part of the strategy of the U.S. Cavalry's war against Great Plains tribes, clearly soldiers witnessed and many participated in the slaughter of the 1870s and 1880s. The three excerpts from soldiers' accounts, published below, suggest the range of officers' opinions on the bison's nature and use. Colonel Homer W. Wheeler, an officer in the U.S. Fifth and Eleventh Cavalry for thirty-five years, recalled the once-great numbers of the bison and how the animal's habits seemed to ensure their wholesale slaughter. General George A. Custer remembered how bison hunting relieved the boredom of both officers and soldiers under their command. And Surgeon O. C. McNary offered a poignant recollection of the Cheyenne chiefs who awaited the animal's return.

Millions of Buffalo were slaughtered for the hides and meat, principally for the hide. Some of the expert hunters made considerable money at the occupation. . . .

Some of the habits of the Buffalo herds are clearly fixed in my memory. The bulls were always found on the outer edge, supposedly acting as protectors to the cows and calves. For ten to twenty miles one would often see solid herds of the animals. Until the hunters commenced to kill them off, their only enemies were the wolves and coyotes. A medium-sized herd, at that time, dotted the prairie for hundreds of miles, and to guess at the number in a herd was like trying to compute the grains of wheat in a granary. . . .

Buffalo hunting was dangerous sport. Although at times it looked like murder, if you took a buffalo in his native element he had plenty of courage and would fight tenaciously for his life if given an opportunity. Like all other animals, the buffalo scented danger at a distance and tried to escape by running away, but if he did not escape he would make a stand and fight to the last, for which every one must respect him. . . .

The stupidity of the buffalo was remarkable. When one of their number was killed the rest of the herd, smelling the blood, would become excited, but instead of stampeding would gather around the dead buffalo, pawing, bellowing and hooking it viciously. Taking advantage of this well-known habit of the creature, the hunter would kill one animal and then wipe out almost the entire herd. . . .

Source: Colonel Homer W. Wheeler, *Buffalo Days: Forty Years in the Old West: The Personal Narrative of a Cattleman, Indian Fighter, and Army Officer* (New York: Bobbs-Merrill, 1925), pp. 80–82.

GENERAL CUSTER

To find employment for the few weeks which must ensue before breaking up camp was sometimes a difficult task. To break the monotony and give horses and men exercise, buffalo hunts were organized, in which officers and men joined heartily. I know of no better drill for perfecting men in the use of fire-arms on horseback, and thoroughly accustoming them to the saddle, than buffalo-hunting over a moderately rough country. No amount of riding under the best of drill-masters will give that confidence and security in the saddle which will result from a few spirited charges into a buffalo herd.

Source: George A. Custer, *My Life on the Plains, Or Personal Experiences with Indians* (New York: Sheldon, 1874), p. 111.

ARMY SURGEON O. C. MCNARY

In the fall of 1885, when I, as a young acting assistant surgeon, United States Army, was stationed with A Troop, Fifth Cavalry for a short time at Cantonment, Indian Territory, we had several bands of Cheyennes under our care. Among the chiefs we had Stone Calf, Little Robe, Spotted Horse and White Horse. Having learned the sign language, I had many talks with these Indians. . . . Stone Calf and Little Robe were greatly troubled over the disappearance of the buffalo. They told me that the great spirit created the buffalo in a large cave in the Panhandle of Texas; that the evil spirits had closed up the mouth of the cave and the buffalo could not get out. They begged me to get permission from the great father at Washington for them to go and open the cave, and let the buffalo out. They claimed to know the exact location of the cave. They even wanted me to ac-company them.

Source: O. C. McNary account in Wheeler, *Buffalo Days*, p. 349.

Document 6.2   **Congress Debates Legislation to Protect the Bison, 1874–1876**

In his 1887 book, The Extermination of the American Bison, *William T. Hornaday, director of the New York City Zoological Park and later president of the American Bison Society, reproduced portions of the congressional debate from 1874–1876 centered on efforts to stop the slaughter of the bison. Despite the efforts of Illinois U.S. representa-tive Greenburg Lafayette Fort, the bison's most ardent champion, legislative efforts ended in failure when President Ulysses S. Grant killed the 1874 bill with a pocket veto. Because of the bison's strong association with the Plains Indians, a second legislative attempt in 1876 was doomed by the disastrous defeat of Custer's forces at the Battle of the Little Big Horn.*

On January 5, 1874, Mr. Fort, of Illinois, introduced a bill (H. R. 921) to prevent the useless slaughter of buffalo within the Territories of the United States; which was read and referred to the Committee on the Territories. . . .

The first section of the bill provided that it shall be unlawful for any person, who is not an Indian, to kill, wound, or in any way destroy any female buffalo of any age, found at large within the boundaries of any of the Territories of the United States.

The second section provided that it shall be, in like manner, unlawful for any such person to kill, wound, or destroy in said Territories any greater number of male buffaloes than are needed for food by such person, or than be used, cured, or preserved for the food of other persons, or for the market. It shall in like manner be unlawful for any such person, or persons, to assist, or be in any manner engaged or concerned in or about such unlawful killing, wounding, or destroying of any such buffaloes; that any person who shall violate the provisions of the act shall, on conviction, forfeit and pay to the United States the sum of $100 for such offense (and each buffalo so unlawfully killed, wounded, or destroyed shall be and constitute a separate offense), and on a conviction of a second offense may be committed to prison for a period not exceeding thirty days; and that all United States judges, justices, courts, and legal tribunals in said Territories shall have jurisdiction in cases of the violation of the law.

Mr. Cox said he had been told by old hunters that it was impossible to tell the sex of a running buffalo; and he also stated that the bill gave preference to the Indians.

Mr. Fort said the object was to prevent early extermination; that thousands were annually slaughtered for skins alone, and thousands for their tongues alone; that perhaps hundreds of thousands are killed every year in utter wantonness, with no object for such destruction. He had been told that the sexes could be distinguished while they were running. . . .

Mr. Cox wanted the clause excepting the Indians from the operations of the bill stricken out, and stated that the Secretary of the Interior had already said to the House that the civilization of the Indian was impossible while the buffalo remained on the plains.

The Clerk read for Mr. McCormick the following extract from the *New Mexican*, a paper published in Santa Fé:

> The buffalo slaughter, which has been going on the past few years on the plains, and which increases every year, is wantonly wicked, and should be stopped by the most stringent enactments and most vigilant enforcements of the law. Killing these noble animals for their hides simply, or to gratify the pleasure of some Russian duke or English lord, is a species of vandalism which can not too quickly be checked. United States surveying parties report that there are two thousand hunters on the plains killing these animals for their hides. One party of sixteen hunters report having killed twenty-eight thousand buffaloes during the past summer. It seems to us there is quite as much reason why the Government should protect the buffaloes as the Indians.

Mr. McCormick considered the subject important, and had not a doubt of the fearful slaughter. He read the following extract from a letter that he had received from General Hazen:

I know a man who killed with his own hand ninety-nine buffaloes in one day, without taking a pound of the meat. The buffalo for food has an intrinsic value about equal to a[n] average Texas beef, or say $20. There are probably not less than a million of those animals on the western plains. If the Government owned a herd of a million oxen they would at least take steps to prevent this wanton slaughter. The railroads have made the buffalo as accessible as to present a case not dissimilar.

... [Mr. McCormick] did not believe any bill would entirely accomplish the purpose, but he desired that such wanton slaughter should be stopped.

Mr. Cox said he would not have objected to the bill but from the fact that it was partial in its provisions. He wanted a bill that would impose a penalty on every man, red, white, or black, who may wantonly kill these buffaloes.

Mr. Potter desired to know whether more buffaloes were slaughtered by the Indians than by white men.

Mr. Fort thought the white men were doing the greatest amount of killing.

Mr. Eldridge thought there would be just as much propriety in killing the fish in our rivers as in destroying the buffalo in order to compel the Indians to become civilized....

Mr. Parker, of Missouri, intimated that the policy of the Secretary of the Interior was a sound one, and that the buffaloes ought to be exterminated, to prevent difficulties in civilizing the Indians....

The question being taken on the passage of the bill, there were—ayes 132, noes not counted. So the bill was passed.

On June 23, 1874, this bill (H. R. 921) came up in the Senate.

Mr. Harvey moved as an amendment, to strike out the words "who is not an Indian."

Said Mr. Hitchcock, "That will defeat the bill."

Mr. Frelinghuysen said: "That would prevent the Indians from killing the buffalo on their own ground. I object to the bill."

Mr. Sargent said: "I think we can pass the bill in the right shape without objection. Let us take it up. It is very important one" ...

The bill was reported to the Senate, ordered to a third reading, read the third line, and passed. It went to President Grant for signature, and expired in his hands at the adjournment of that session of Congress....

On January 31, 1876, Mr. Fort introduced a bill (H. R. 1719) to prevent the useless slaughter of buffaloes within the Territories of the United States, which was referred to the Committee on the Territories.

In support of it Mr. Fort said: "The intention and object of this bill is to preserve them [the buffaloes] for the use of the Indians, whose homes are upon the public domain, and to the frontiersmen, who may properly use them for food.... They have been and are now being slaughtered in large numbers.... Thousands of these noble brutes are annually slaughtered out of mere wantonness.... This bill, just as it is now presented, passed the last Congress. It was not vetoed, but fell, as I understand, merely for want of time to consider if after having passed both houses." He also intimated that the Government was using a great deal of money for cattle to furnish the Indians, while the buffalo was being wantonly destroyed, whereas they might be turned to their good.

Mr. Crounse wanted the words "who is not an Indian" struck out, so as to make the bill general. He thought Indians were to blame for the wanton destruction.

Mr. Fort thought the amendment unnecessary, and stated that he was informed that the Indians did not destroy the buffaloes wantonly.

The Clerk read for him a letter from A. G. Brackett, lieutenant-colonel, Second United States Cavalry, stationed at Omaha Barracks, in which was a very urgent request to have Congress interfere to prevent the wholesale slaughter then going on.

Mr. Beagan thought the bill proper and right. He knew from personal experience how the wanton slaughtering was going on, and also that the Indians were *not* the ones who did it.

Mr. Townsend, of New York, saw no reason why a white man should not be allowed to kill a female buffalo as well as an Indian. He said it would be impracticable to have a separate law for each. . . .

Mr. Hancock, of Texas, thought the bill an impolicy, and that the sooner the buffalo was exterminated the better.

Mr. Fort replied by asking him why all the game—deer, antelope, etc.—was not slaughtered also. Then he went on to state that to exterminate the buffalo would be to starve innocent children of the red man, and to make the latter more wild and savage than he was already. . . .

On February 25, 1876, the bill was reported to the Senate, and referred to the Committee on Territories, from whence it never returned.

Source: William Temple Hornaday, *The Extermination of the American Bison, with a Sketch of Its Discovery and Life History* (Washington, DC: Government Printing Office, 1887), pp. 515–19; citing the *Congressional Record*, 43rd Cong., 2, pt. 1:371; 43rd Cong, 1st sess., 2, pt. 3:2105, 2199; *Congressional Globe*, 43rd Cong., 1st sess., 2, pt. 6; 44th Cong., 1st sess., 4, pt. 2:1237–41; 44th Cong. 1st sess., 4, pt. 1:773.

Document 6.3   **George Bird Grinnell Mourns the Loss of "a Departed Race," 1884**

Along with Theodore Roosevelt and other genteel conservation-minded sportsmen, naturalist George Bird Grinnell cofounded the Boone and Crockett Club, which became a leading advocate for the preservation of bison and other big game. Grinnell also served as editor of Forest and Stream, *one of the prominent sportsmen's magazines of the era. Grinnell's pages continually took aim at crude, profit-driven traders and market hunters who, in the eyes of men like Grinnell, were responsible for the demise of the bison. In this particular diatribe, Grinnell included among the villains the bone hunters whose work completed the commodified slaughter of the bison.*

. . . The Indian, as a rule, is not wasteful nor improvident in the destruction of game. He realizes that it is the mainstay of his life, and if he waste this year it may cause him to suffer from hunger next year; hence he kills to provide meat for the present; and preserves for the future. The skins from animals so slain, after sufficing for his own wants, find their way to the trader, and thence into the channels of commerce. Thus began the trade in buffalo skins. As the white man became acquainted with the country he saw profit in it, and about 1830 traders began to reach out into the buffalo country, accompanied by professional white hunters, who made a life business of slaughter....

For two or three years after the opening of the [Union Pacific and Kansas Pacific] railways, a train seldom crossed the plains without passing in sight of buffalo, and it was not an uncommon thing for a train to have to wait for a moving herd to cross the track. Now buffalo are never seen from the trains,...But there remained one more harvest to be gathered from the departed native life and grandeur of the great plains; a poor, pitiful post-mortem harvest of stinking bones. After they had surfeited the East with odorous hams and glutted the markets of the world with "robes" killed in season and out of season, these gallant hunters turned scavengers and gathered the rotting bones and blistering horns of the countless dead. Railway trains that had in former years groaned under loads of meat and bales of hides were now loaded down with bones destined for Eastern manufactories of various kinds....

At length the work was done. Destruction was complete. No sign was left to show that a buffalo had ever existed in the country, and the vandals who had hounded them to their death and their bones to the sugar refinery, drifted off northward...to follow up the remnants of herds, to gather the bones along other railways, or to repeat the slaughter upon the noble elk that so recently peopled all the valleys and parks of the mountains.... [quoting another unnamed newspaper account]: 'It is said in St. Paul that hundreds of teams are now engaged near Bismarck in gathering buffalo bones, for which the sum of $6 a ton is paid by persons who send them to Philadelphia for grinding into fertilizing powders.'...

And yet the country is full of sportsmen who clamor for more deadly repeating rifles.

Source: George Bird Grinnell, "A Departed Race," *Forest and Stream* (July 10, 1884), p. 462.

Document 6.4   *Harper's Weekly* **Decries the "War of Extermination,"**
                      1884

As Custer's defeat receded in memory and the conquest of Indians became more complete, American opinion drifted back toward sympathy for the remaining bison. Thus by 1884, it was not just voices like Forest and Stream *that leveled damning indictments at those responsible for the bison's near-extermination. With just a few hundred animals still roaming the plains,* Harper's Weekly, *a popular middle-class publication, castigated market hunters, foreign parties of sportsmen, the U.S. Cavalry, and pleasure-seeking rail travelers—all of whom had a hand in the bison's destruction.*

. . . During these years [of slaughter] every man's hand has been raised against [the buffalo], and none has been lifted in their defense. The United States Government has even encouraged their extermination, by furnishing cavalry escorts to parties of titled foreigners who have visited the plains with the avowed and sole purpose of becoming buffalo butchers. . . . In two or three weeks [such parties] would return after having killed as many buffalo as would have supplied all the Indians on the plains with meat, and leaving the carcasses to feed the wolves or to rot where they fell. . . . Merely for the sake of afterward being able to boast that they had wantonly destroyed so many dozens, scores, or hundreds of inoffensive animals, these so-called sportsmen threw aside their manliness and descended to the level of pot-hunters and butchers. With no pretext save the satisfying of their lust for slaughter, they were more contemptible than the members of the army of white men who at this time infested the plains and made a living by killing the buffalo for their meats or hides. . . . What [the market hunters] carried away was not a hundredth part of what had been killed, for only the choicest portions of the best carcasses were deemed of sufficient value to transport even as far as the railway stations, and here hundreds of tons rotted before means for their further transportation could be obtained. . . . A hunter, armed with a magazine rifle and a brace of big revolvers, could and did destroy an average of from seventy-five to a hundred buffalo per day, . . . For a few years thousands of men were thus employed, and the doomed buffalo disappeared like dew before the summer sun. From time to time feeble protests have been made by the Indians, who have gazed aghast upon this wholesale destruction of their staple food supply; but the protests have been ignored, the protesters killed, and all has gone on as before. . . .

Still more contemptible than any of the buffalo butchers already mentioned are those who, from pure wantonness, have blazed away at him from the wagons of emigrant trains, from stagecoaches, and from railway cars, whenever he has come within range of his murderous weapons. . . . in No. 8 [of the illustrations accompanying the story] a group of dejected buffalo occupy the only asylum in which they can hope for life—behind the prison bars of a zoological museum.

Source: Kirk Munroe, "A War of Extermination," *Harper's Weekly* 27 (August 2, 1884): 499–500.

Document 6.5   A Western Champion of Progress Hails the "Far Superior" Farmer's Cow and Approves the Demise of the Bison, 1884

Unanimity of opinion with respect to the bison's pathetic fate there was not. Westerners, in particular, demonstrate the mixed sense of resignation and approbation that many expressed at the bison slaughter. Indeed, E. V. Smalley's The Northwest *saw the extermination of the bison as another propitious sign of the march of progressive civilization, like the coming of the biologically superior cattle and white men. Smalley was far from alone in linking the fall of the bison to that of the Plains Indian.*

Several attempts have been made within the past few years to perpetuate the blood of the American buffalo by crossing it with bovine blood. Careful and studied experiments have been made by fancy breeders in this line, but all efforts to improve the stock either on the one side or the other have proved futile.... Although the bison belongs zoologically to the herbivorous genus of the ox and its kindred, it is so far removed ... from the common bovine tribe as to make the successful amalgamation of the bloods highly improbable. Then again, from an economic and commercial standpoint, such a mixture is not desirable. The meat of the ox is far more desirable for all purposes than the meat of the buffalo. The former has become an important item of commercial traffic, and the latter can never rise above a limited sentimental demand for it as game. The incidental products of the beef (including hides, tallow, horns, bones and hoofs) are all worked up into useful articles of domestic use, far superior to the similar products from the buffalo. Then again, the most important difference manifests itself in the articles of milk, butter and cheese. Here the buffalo is completely outdone. His family could never be trained or improved to take the place of the farmer's cow.

Viewed, therefore, from the standpoint of the rationalist and optimist, the buffalo must rapidly disappear before the march of the ox and cow, just as the Indian disappears before the march of his superior, the Caucasian. His bleached bones and moldering horns which now dot the prairies will go to fertilize the soil over which he was wont to roam in times of old, and he will go to dwell forever with the mastodon as one of the extinct species of an ancient and honorable race.

Source: E. V. Smalley, *The Northwest* (September 1884), p. 6.

Document 6.6   George Bird Grinnell Editorializes on the Capture of Poacher Edgar Howell in Yellowstone National Park, 1894

By the mid-1880s, the effort to save the last remnants of the North American bison centered on the small herd of fewer than 500 that roamed Yellowstone National Park. Despite the presence of U.S. Cavalry troops who patrolled the park after 1886, illegal poaching persisted, feeding a lucrative market for heads, robes, and other bison parts. The illegal bison trade was hindered (though not ended) by the capture of poacher Edgar Howell in March 1894 in Yellowstone. George Grinnell had sent correspondent Emerson Hough and noted

Yellowstone photographer F. Jay Haynes to the park to investigate reports of poaching. Hough's story, along with photographs of "the butcher's work," soon appeared in publications across the country and transformed the capture into a cause celebre for bison protection. Grinnell and a cadre of influential conservationists pressed Congress for action, resulting in the first Lacey Act (Document 6.7), designed to protect all wildlife (save predators) in Yellowstone National Park. The definition of "our bison" as "government property," and Grinnell's appeal to democratic duty and the obligations of republican govern- ment with respect to the protection of animal life are noteworthy.

It is but a short time since we announced the capture of the poacher in the National park, and the fact that he killed eleven buffalo, . . .

There seems to be little doubt that within the last year or two a wholesale slaughter has been taking place among our buffalo preserved in the Yellow- stone park . . . we can well imagine that two hundred or two hundred and fifty is the outside limit for the [living] buffalo in the Park.

As we stated a few days ago, Congress has put a premium on the head of every one of these great beasts. Any man is free to enter the National Park and kill them, and knows that—even if taken in the act—no punishment can be inflicted on him. The chances against his capture are considerable, a[n]d even if taken, the only inconvenience [*sic*] that he suffers is a confiscation of his outfit, amounting to but a few dollars in value, and a few weeks discomfort in the guard house. Against this there is the prospect of selling for $200 or $300 the head of every buffalo he has killed, . . .

It is not surprising that sportsmen and many of the newspapers of the country are stirred up about this matter, nor that the number of police bills have been introduced in Congress to remedy the existing state of things. Most of the bills introduced thus far are entirely inadequate, . . . We have already said that these animals are Government property, and that injury to them should be punished in the same way as injury to any other Government property. The Yellowstone Park has by law been distinctly set aside as a public Park or pleasuring ground for the people, and the natural objects in it, whether animate or inanimate, belong to the public. It is the business of the Government, which acts for the people, to protect this property which belongs to those whom it represents. The executive branch of the Government has done and is doing all in its power to furnish this protection, but the legislative branch has failed and continues to fail to do its duty, for it refuses to provide methods and means for enforcing the protection which it has authorized in the organic [original] act establishing the Park.

We suggest that every reader of *Forest and Stream* who is interested in the Park or in natural history, or in things pertaining to America, should write to his Senator and Representative in Congress, asking them to take an active interest in the protection of the Park. In no other way can Congress be made to feel the force of public opinion, and be induced to enact the necessary laws for the protection of the National Park.

Source: "Save the Park Buffalo," *Forest and Stream* 42 (April 14, 1894): 1.

Document 6.7   The Lacey (National Park Protection) Act, 1894

The Lacey Act of 1894 provided the legislative mechanism to protect wildlife in Yellowstone. A full-time federal commissioner, along with the presence of the U. S. Cavalry, enforced the law (until 1916 when the newly established National Park Service assumed these duties). Its provision for fines and jail time for poaching wildlife in the park served to reduce significantly the number of offenses. More importantly, it established the precedent for protecting wildlife in all national parks, and later, on other federal lands such as wildlife refuges.

CHAP. 72.—An Act To protect the birds and animals in Yellowstone National Park, and to punish crimes in said park, and for other purposes. . . .

SEC. 4. That all hunting, or the killing or wounding, or capturing at any time of any bird or wild animal, except dangerous animals, when it is necessary to prevent them from destroying human life or inflicting an injury, is prohibited within the limits of said park; nor shall any fish be taken out of the waters of the park by means of seines, nets, traps, or by the use of drugs or any explosive substances or compounds, or in any other way than by hook and line, . . . That the Secretary of the Interior shall make and publish such rules and regulations as he may deem necessary and proper for the management and care of the park and for the protection of the property therein, . . . ; and for the protection of the animals and birds in the park, from capture or destruction, or to prevent their being frightened or driven from the park; . . . Possession within said park of the dead bodies, or any part thereof, of any wild bird or animal shall be prima facie evidence that the person or persons having the same are guilty of violating this Act. . . . Any person found guilty of violating any of the provisions of this Act or any rule or regulation that may be promulgated by the Secretary of the Interior with reference to the care and management of the park, . . . shall be deemed guilty of a misdemeanor, and shall be subjected to a fine of not more than one thousand dollars or imprisonment not exceeding two years, or both, and be adjudged to pay all costs of the proceedings.

Source: U.S. Statutes at Large, vol. 28, p. 73, approved May 7, 1894.

Document 6.8   William T. Hornaday Hails the Bison's Arrival
at the National Museum, 1887

The near-extermination of the bison is a landmark event for a number of reasons, not the least of which is William T. Hornaday's 1887 The Extermination of the American Bison. *Written by a former big-game hunter who became a leading and influential advocate for wildlife preservation, it was the first such book in America to denounce so forcefully and completely the assumed position of superiority and dominance of man over the animal world that was manifested most dramatically in the slaughter of the bison. Although his book called on the U.S. government to take steps to preserve the last remnants of the species, like many preservation advocates, by 1887 Hornaday was resigned to the loss of the bison. He did hope that the book, as he put it in the preface, could "point a moral that shall benefit the surviving species of mammals which are now being slaughtered in like manner." As the excerpt below suggests, he hoped the newly mounted bison exhibit at the Smithsonian Museum would aid the same purpose: to warn against the destruction of other species. The encasement behind glass (and inside the boundaries of Yellowstone Park) of the last vestiges of this central symbol of a vanishing "wild West" demonstrated poignantly and profoundly how tame the American wilderness had become over the course of three centuries.*

A little bit of Montana—a small square patch from the wildest part of the wild West—has been transferred to the National Museum. It is so little that Montana will never miss it, but enough to enable one who has the faintest glimmer of imagination to see it all for himself—the hummocky prairie, the buffalo-grass, the sagebrush, and the buffalo. It is as though a little group of buffalo that have come to drink at a pool had been suddenly struck motionless by some magic spell, each in a natural attitude, and then the section of prairie, pool, buffalo, and all had been carefully cut out and brought to the national Museum. All this is in a huge glass case, the largest ever made for the Museum. This case and the space about it, at the south end of the south hall, has been inclosed by high screens for many days while the taxidermist a[n]d his assistants have been at work. The finishing touches were put on to-day, and the screens will be removed Monday, exposing to view what is regarded as a triumph of the taxidermist's art. The group, with it accessories, has been prepared so as to tell in as attractive way to the general visitor to the Museum the story of the buffalo, but care has been taken at the same time to secure an accuracy of detail that will satisfy the critical scrutiny of the most technical naturalist.

Source: William Temple Hornaday, *The Extermination of the American Bison, with a Sketch of Its Discovery and Life History* (Washington, DC: Government Printing Office, 1889; first published as Smithsonian's Annual Report in 1887), p. 535.

NOTES

1. E. V. Smalley, "The Slaughter of the Buffalo," *The Northwest* (January 15, 1883): 1.

2. William Temple Hornaday, *The Extermination of the American Bison, with a Sketch of Its Discovery and Life History, Smithsonian Annual Report, 1887* (Washington, DC: Government Printing Office, 1887), p. 521.

3. George Catlin, *North American Indians: Being Letters and Notes on Their Manners, Customs, and Conditions, Written During Eight Years' Travel Amongst the Wildest Tribes in North America, 1832–1839* (Minneapolis: Ross and Haines, 1965; first printed in London, 1841), pp. 292–95.

4. Philip Sheridan, quoted in John R. Cook, *The Border and the Buffalo* (Topeka, KS: Crane, 1907), p. 113.

5. Theodore Roosevelt, *Works, Memorial Edition*, ed. Hermann Hagedorn (New York: Charles Scribner's Sons, 1923), p. xviii.

ANNOTATED BIBLIOGRAPHY

Barsness, Larry. *Heads, Hides & Horns: The Compleat Buffalo Book*. Fort Worth: Texas Christian University Press, 1985. Detailed and well-illustrated examination of the buffalo, including hunting methods, uses of the animal by both Indians and whites, the centrality of the buffalo in Plains Indian culture, and preservation efforts.

Belue, Ted Franklin. *The Long Hunt: Death of the Buffalo East of the Mississippi*. Mechanicsburg, PA: Stackpole Books, 1996. Interdisciplinary synthesis, fine scholarship, and a riveting narrative of this obscured part of the buffalo's story that takes place in America's "first far West," with George Washington, John Filson, and Daniel Boone among the characters who convey the slaughter that ended in the 1820s.

Callenbach, Ernest. *Bring Back the Buffalo! A Sustainable Future for America's Great Plains*. Washington, DC: Island Press, 1996. Makes a moving and convincing case that the quarter of a million buffalo who once again roam the Great Plains represent great potential for restoring ecological health and a sustainable agricultural economy to the region.

Dary, David. *The Buffalo Book: The Full Saga of the American Animal*. Athens, OH: Swallow Press, 1990. The cultural adaptation and significance of the buffalo is featured here, along with the history and a survey of contemporary ranching.

Geist, Valerius. *Buffalo Nation: History and Legend of the North American Bison*. Stillwater, MN: Voyageur Press, 1998. Thin survey of the natural and cultural history of the buffalo and the nineteenth-century slaughter waged against it.

Haines, Frances. *The Buffalo*. Norman: University of Oklahoma Press, 1995. Although eclipsed somewhat by Isenberg, this remains a valuable study, in part for its sweeping historical scope—from prehistoric times to the railroad-era slaughter to the preservation efforts of the late nineteenth century to contemporary efforts to return the animal to parts of its historic range.

Isenberg, Andrew C. *The Destruction of the Bison: An Environmental History, 1750–1920*. New York: Cambridge University Press, 2000. With interdisciplinary methodology and sophisticated analysis, this is the definitive scholarly treatment. Argues that the central cause of the bison's near-demise was fundamentally the cultural encounter between Native American tribes and European Americans. Isenberg maps the forces of drought, disease, and livestock introduction that compounded the intensified hunting of the buffalo by both Plains Indians and whites that led to its near-demise.

Matthews, Anne. *Where the Buffalo Roam: Restoring America's Great Plains*. 2nd ed. Chicago: University of Chicago Press, 2002. A fascinating and moving account of an effort beginning in the 1980s to create a vast "Buffalo Commons" on the Great Plains that would also restore ecological health and balance to the overgrazed West.

McHugh, Tom. *The Time of the Buffalo*. 1972. Reprint, Victoria, BC: Castle Books, 2004. Award-winning, though a bit dated, look at the natural and human history.

Robinson, Michael. *The Buffalo Hunters*. Abilene, TX: State House Press, 1995. A modestly successful exploration of the buffalo-hunting era.

Sample, Michael. *Bison: Symbol of the American West*. Billings, MT: Falcon Press, 1987. Easily digestible, concise look at the historic and contemporary buffalo.

7

"Reclaiming" the Arid West

There is a great space on the earth's surface nearly waste and barren now, which by reasonable and moderate expenditure can be converted into a fertile and blooming garden and can blossom as the rose. I have no doubt there are on this continent lands largely useless now, on which under proper development . . . ten and perhaps scores and perhaps hundreds of millions of human beings are within a century or less to be located in happy American homes . . .
—U.S. Senator George F. Hoar of Massachusetts, during the 1902 debate on the Reclamation Act.[1]

Of all pivotal moments in the nation's environmental history, few compare for lasting significance to the late nineteenth-century debate over how the arid and semiarid regions of the western United States were to be irrigated and developed—"reclaimed" in the language of the era. The question of *whether* they would be developed was rarely heard at the dawn of the new century, by which time an alliance of western politicians and government scientists had inspired a national consensus urging that the driest lands of the continent be cultivated and "civilized." For most politicians and interested observers, the only question was how these western lands were to be permanently settled. Although a few critics remained bitterly opposed to federal reclamation all the way to the impoundment of the first river, they were on the wrong side of history. America's industrial economy had become a juggernaut, and many of its leading architects had set their sights on the irrigation and incorporation of the dry American West—what one leading proponent termed "a vast store of wealth [that was] almost incomprehensible."[2] As Senator Hoar and others predicted, federally sponsored irrigation of western rivers positioned the region in the center of the national and global agricultural economy. However, the course of "proper development" by which western reclamation was ultimately pursued would dramatically impact not only the long-term economic development, but also the ecological health of the region. And despite the much-heralded promise that irrigation would democratize farm ownership, it instead strengthened preexisting patterns of concentrated landownership and wealth in the West. Critics argued that the winning strategy for reclamation, designed by political and economic elites, ensured that outcome. Moreover, the engineering of western water through massive dams and irrigation projects changed the way modern Americans got much of their food, further distancing them geographically and psychically from the ramifications of the modern agricultural system. The nation has only recently begun to acknowledge the hidden social, ethical, and ecological costs of the technologically engineered landscape of the arid West that is the legacy of the reclamation debate.

The monumental, though in many ways tragic, figure in this story is Major John Wesley Powell, a Civil War veteran who had lost an arm at the Battle of Shiloh. A trained scientist and geologist, Powell triggered the discussion over western development following his celebrated scientific expedition down the Colorado River in 1869, performed under the auspices of the Smithsonian Institution. Beyond confirming his theories about the geological origins of the region's dramatic landscape of canyons and mesas, that journey and a second one in 1871 advanced Powell's thinking about how the development of the entire arid region of the country should proceed. Through the 1870s he lectured widely on the natural features and scientific wonders of the Colorado River. His call to consolidate and reorganize rival surveys of the West led to the establishment of the U.S. Geological Survey in 1879. It was in his position as director of the survey from 1881 until 1894 that Powell attempted, ultimately unsuccessfully, to chart the course for western reclamation.

What placed Major Powell at the center of the debate over western irrigation was his famous *Report on the Lands of the Arid Region of the United States*, issued to the U.S. Congress in 1878. Based on more than a decade of first-hand scientific observation, Powell's document offered an environmentally sensitive—and politically revolutionary—vision of how development should proceed in the most arid section of the country. He had become convinced that the land laws that had guided the nation's westward development would never do in the arid West. From the beginning, the very American idea behind the nation's land laws was to subdivide and sell off 160-acre squares of the public domain, ostensibly to aspiring independent farmers. It was the great Jeffersonian vision that such free yeomen would best safeguard the economic independence and institutions of the republic. As the nation became an urbanized industrialized power in the last third of the nineteenth century, the ideal of free land for the enterprising pioneering American took on even greater significance. Proponents of western migration held that the West could always absorb the discontented, marginalized, and potentially rebellious underclass of eastern cities. Yet, Powell's report was premised in part on the widely recognized fact—certainly among aspiring farmers themselves—that western reality contrasted sharply with the myth. Despite the noble intent of the Homestead Act, much of the best arable land in the Great Plains had fallen under the control of the railroads, cattle barons, and other large corporate interests.

It appeared that the pattern was repeating itself further west. One year prior to Powell's report, the Desert Lands Act was signed into law, offering 640 acres of land in the arid West for $1.25 an acre with only 25 cents an acre down, provided the buyer irrigate the land within three years. The law implicitly acknowledged that lands lying west of the 100th meridian, unlike the more temperate, humid regions to the east, could not be made agriculturally productive without irrigation. Its vaguely written terms, however, invited fraud; virtually all of the lands claimed under the Desert Lands Act came through cheating. Bullying cattlemen and speculators were the chief beneficiaries. In Powell's view, the bogus law threatened to exacerbate the concentration of ownership of the most desirable (i.e., irrigable) lands in the far West. At the time Powell issued his report, the combination of existing land laws and the prevailing doctrine of riparian water rights conspired to dictate the control of water. A relatively few men managed to gain control—often nefariously—of water-fronting parcels of land in the upper reaches of western rivers and streams. Those who came along later and bought lands downstream were at the mercy of the upstream owner. Many surrendered and ultimately sold their lands to the dominant owners.

In his 200-page report, Powell did not call for the arid region to remain unsettled. He firmly believed in the popularly held promise that irrigation could make the desert bloom. "All the waters of all the arid lands" must be tamed for the "greatest possible development," he wrote. But he was equally convinced that such development should occur on but a small fraction of the desert. His declaration early on that this arid region—nearly 40 percent of the nation—could only become productive through irrigation, was followed by the more distressing argument that perhaps only 1 to 3 percent of each of the arid states and territories could actually be watered, or "redeemed," as he put it. Beyond the problem of monopolized land and water rights, the other major flaw in the existing land laws for this region, Powell argued, was the legislated size of the land parcels. A 160-acre irrigated farm was too large, and unnecessarily so, for a family to manage; his close examination of successful reclamation elsewhere in the West—the communitarian Mormon enterprise in Utah, and the well-watered, well-organized community of Greeley, Colorado—told Powell that eighty acres or less was sufficient. Conversely, for ranching purposes, 160 acres was far too small—as cattle barons knew well.

Moreover, the rational division of land into linear squares made no sense in a place where it was far from certain that such parcels would include access to water. Similarly, state boundaries were arbitrary and irrational. Powell therefore proposed that water serve as the fundamental organizing principle of the entire arid region. Watersheds, also referred to as "catchment" or "hydrographic basins," were areas of drainage for each western river by which lands should be both distributed to prospective settlers and reclaimed through irrigation projects. Powell's proposal was to allow settlers to form irrigation districts, the boundary lines for which were to be configured in accord with the watershed topography. Following the Mormons' successful experiment in collective water sharing, each settler would be afforded equitable access to sufficient water through impoundments and irrigation districts which they devised and constructed themselves. Mandated and ultimately enforced by federal law, such local control would guard against monopoly of both land and, more importantly in this region, water.

As Powell's critics soon made quite clear, the plan's flaws were many, not the least of which was that even collectively homesteaders did not have sufficient capital to construct the kind of reservoirs and delivery channels that would be necessary. Still, what is most striking and prophetic today about Powell's vision is that it explicitly recognized that human settlement, in this place at least, would have to live within the limits of nature. And, in stark contradiction with the rugged individualism that characterized the myth (if not the reality) of American frontier settlement, men would have to work cooperatively. What we in a more environmentally conscious era might find wise and forward thinking, Powell's opponents could dismiss as downright un-American.

It did not appear that way initially. Powell's call for the federal government to undertake a survey of the arid region to determine with scientific certainty the location of irrigable lands was enthusiastically supported by westerners of every stripe, including those who held a very different vision of the direction re-clamation should take following the survey. Most prominently, Nevada senator William Stewart provided critical support for Powell's idea to survey the entire region for its irrigation potential. But Stewart, allied personally and politically with powerful western forces including railroads and cattle, timber, and banking interests, believed the principal purpose of the survey was merely to locate the superior irrigation sites. The government should then get out of the way. Men of capital (like himself) would unleash the power of corporate capitalism and bring about the end vision they seemed to share, that of a fully developed West. As Donald Worster has summarized, Stewart and his western allies "wanted a West that would be wide open to men of large ideas and heavy pockets, a West that would be developed fast, where fortunes could be made tomorrow."[3] When a subsequent proviso from the General Land Office ordered that no sale or set-tlement of lands in the region take place while the survey proceeded, Stewart grew increasingly critical with the slow pace of the survey. He took particular aim at Powell's assertion that detailed topographic maps were necessary in order to plot the course of irrigation, arguing that the previously imposed linear di-vision of the General Land Office was sufficient for the engineering of re-clamation projects. Though it may appear as trivial political wrangling, the contentious issue of grid-line maps versus those that would reveal a truer por-trait of the region's natural contours and features illustrated two very different views of the same landscape. If one were interested in rapid, rapacious ex-ploitation, squared sections and quarter sections were all one needed.

His patience worn thin, Stewart launched an attack on Powell's survey and on Powell himself, pointing to the director's "scandalous habits with women" as one reason why he should be removed from his position. As chair of a special Senate Committee on Irrigation, in 1889 Stewart organized what was billed as a fact-finding tour of the arid states, but in truth served as a platform from which to criticize Powell and call for an expeditious conclusion to the survey. Fol-lowing the journey, Stewart sponsored legislation to turn control of the survey over to a new office that would be located in the Department of Agriculture. He charged that Powell's wrongful diversion of irrigation funds to mapmaking was nothing more than a self-indulgent, bureaucratic waste of the public treasury.

The debate continued throughout the 1890s, as irrigation proponents established a journal and met in a series of annual "congresses" to debate and promulgate their views. A beleaguered John Wesley Powell retired from the Geological Survey in 1894, the same year the U.S. Congress passed the Carey Act, an experimental effort to return to the states federal land with the promise of reclamation and the proceeds of lands sold going to the federal treasury. This attempt to improve on the dismal record of the Desert Lands Act failed miserably, mostly for lack of interest; the cost of the dam-building enterprise was simply prohibitive for states. Calls for the complete and total reclamation of the West were increasingly accompanied by a clear recognition that only the federal government could carry out this project on the scale imagined. Enthusiasts such as William Smythe trumpeted western irrigation with a mixture of bombastic nationalism and promises of endless industrial progress and American empire. The 1890 U.S. Census Bureau announcement that the progress of western settlement had effectively dissolved the frontier line separating wilderness from civilization hastened calls to irrigate the more remote arid and semiarid regions that once had been dismissed as uninhabitable.

Decades of deliberation culminated in the passage of the Newlands Reclamation Act of 1902. Named for its chief legislative sponsor, Francis Newlands (like Stewart, also of Nevada), the Reclamation Act established a Reclamation Service (later the Bureau of Reclamation) to direct the irrigation of the American West. The project was to be self-sustaining: proceeds from the sale of western public lands would establish a reclamation fund to construct irrigation projects. Lands within those projects were to be sold in allotments no larger than 160 acres, at prices determined by the cost of the irrigation projects. Land payments were to be made in full within ten years and would go into a revolving fund to be used to sustain continual reclamation projects elsewhere, in perpetuity.

More than a century later, the reclamation of the West stands as a stunning, spectacular success in modern engineering. The agency constructed more than 600 major dams and several thousand miles of irrigation canals. Those projects have delivered water to millions of acres of American farms and millions of urban residents from Phoenix to Los Angeles to Spokane. Hydroelectric power from many of the dams helped to power the factories that defeated the Axis Powers in World War II, and then fueled the region's explosive economic development after the war. Boulder (Hoover) and Grand Coulee dams were breathtaking monuments to American confidence and optimism in the depths of the Great Depression, as well as to its enduring engineering prowess. In the context of the cold war, influential Americans spoke triumphantly of a West fully watered and developed as the center of a benign American empire. To stand before the magnificence of one of these mammoth structures generations later is to behold the remarkable achievement of progressive government and to the reclamation enterprise in particular.

Yet, as critics in 1902 had predicted, the enterprise not only could not sustain itself; it in fact grew heavily dependent on federal largesse. Federal outlays to subsidize irrigation of the West exploded during the World War II– and cold war–driven development of the Southwest. The annual budget for western water development soared from $33 million in 1939 to nearly $250 million throughout the 1950s. But for most it was worth it, for the engineering genius of Grand Coulee and dozens more dams across sublime, vast western landscapes epitomized the larger American success in mastering the forces of nature—particularly when juxtaposed, as they often were during the early years of the cold war—with the presumed inferiority of Soviet society. "Total use for greater wealth," the Army Corps of Engineers confidently proclaimed.[4] From Los Angeles to Denver, champions of development had long decried the "waste" of any western river that still flowed unimpeded to the sea. They continued their work until there was only one that did so (the Yellowstone).

This suggests that at least that portion of John Wesley Powell's vision that called for not "wasting" one drop of western water was manifested in the Reclamation Act. Powell would surely be impressed with the century of American engineering achieved by the Bureau of Reclamation. He would not, however, applaud the degree of control over both land and water rights that now obtains throughout reclamation districts in the West. Studies as early as 1930 painted an early unflattering portrait of the agency's legislated restriction on the size of land parcels; they were routinely ignored. As had been the case since the beginning of America's westward movement, water rights and land development continued to be plagued by fraud and chicanery. Many of the fears raised by opponents in the 1902 debate proved all too accurate. The promise that reclamation would pay for itself proved illusory; by the end of the century, American taxpayers were paying nearly $1 billion annually to help the agency meet its budget. Despite its promise to help create a region filled with family farmers, the bureau's work only exacerbated the concentration of land ownership in the hands of fewer men—the majority of them, corporations growing alfalfa to feed cows, the most inefficient use of water on the planet. Not to be outdone (or outspent), the U.S. Army Corps of Engineers joined the western dam-building frenzy; unlike the Bureau, it was bound by not even the pretense that small landowners should be the primary beneficiaries of its projects. It built dams to control flooding. Incidental beneficiaries of the Corps' dams, however, turned out to be mainly corporate agribusiness. The interests of family farmers in other regions of the country were damaged with the spread of large corporate operations which, with the aid of enormous federal subsidies, could get potatoes to eastern markets far more cheaply than could a farmer in Pennsylvania. The agrarian democracy promised was not delivered.

Moreover, Powell could never have envisioned the environmental damage that has accrued to western lands as reclamation proceeded. Though his vision was riddled with self-contradiction, his instinct was toward what we today would term "sustainable development." Implicitly, his message cautioned against the kind of ecologically insensitive engineering that has unfolded across entire watersheds and produced a host of environmental ills. For example, the same dams on Idaho's Snake River that produced the phenomenal growth of the potato industry also led to the severe decline of the greatest salmon runs on the face of the earth. The story is the same elsewhere throughout the West. Irrigation canals dug from small streams in Montana's Bitterroot Valley have depleted the young population of westslope cutthroat trout that are critical to the survival of the species. Powell's beloved Colorado River has been so thoroughly dammed from end to end, its waters so drained by irrigation (primarily to grow hay and pasture forage for cattle), that it fails to reach the sea. A number of heavily irrigated river valleys face insidious exposure to pesticides used to keep irrigation channels open. Irrigation has also produced widespread salinization of soil, as well as river and ground waters. Leaching and "salt-loading" of the natural salinity of western waters in intensified concentrations into the soil and water sources has left a trail of habitat degradation, and in the worst areas, desertification and abandonment of lands. Finally, millions of head of cattle that feed on the irrigated range produce their own deleterious consequences, from destruction of riparian habitats where they congregate, to the generation of the greenhouse gas methane, to the continued pulverizing of the public grasslands. Like the glistening lights over Phoenix, these things also are part of the legacy of reclamation.

DOCUMENTS

Document 7.1   **John Wesley Powell's** *Report on the Lands of the Arid Region of the United States,* **1879**

Based on more than a decade of firsthand exploration and scientific study, Powell's landmark Report on the Lands of the Arid Region of the United States *called for a different system of land distribution and settlement in the American West than what had prevailed under all previous land laws. In these excerpts, he argues that the surveying and disposition of public lands in the arid West should carefully conform to the dictates of rainfall and topography. More radically, he calls for a system that would above all serve the needs of the aspiring "poor man." He would have limited the kind of coldly speculative, profit-driven impulses that had theretofore determined much of America's westward movement and left many of the most prized lands in the hands of corporations and other absentee ownership. His report ignited a national debate that would last a quarter century and ultimately result in the Newlands Reclamation Act—federal legislation that irrigated the arid lands while ignoring Powell's chief recommendations.*

. . . There are two considerations that make irrigation attractive to the agriculturist. Crops thus cultivated are not subject to the vicissitudes of rainfall; the farmer fears no droughts; his labors are seldom interrupted and his crops rarely injured by storms. This immunity from drought and storm renders agricultural operations much more certain than in regions of greater humidity. . . . It may be anticipated that all the lands redeemed by irrigation in the Arid Region will be highly cultivated and abundantly productive, and agriculture will be but slightly subject to the vicissitudes of scant and excessive rainfall. . . .

Small streams can be taken out and distributed by individual enterprise, but coöperative labor or aggregated capital must be employed in taking out the larger streams. The diversion of a large stream from its channel into a stream of canals demands a large outlay of labor and material. To repay this all the waters so taken out must be used, and large tracts of land thus become dependent upon a single canal. It is manifest that a farmer depending upon his own labor cannot undertake this task. To a great extent the . . . chief future development of irrigation must come from the use of the larger streams. . . . The volume of water carried by the small streams that reach the lowlands before uniting with the great rivers, or before they are lost in the sands, is very small when compared with the volume of the streams which emerge from the mountains as rivers. This fact is important. If the streams could be used along their upper ramifications while the several branches are yet small, poor men could occupy the lands, and by their individual enterprise the agriculture of the country would be gradually extended to the limit of the capacity of the region; *but when farming is dependent upon larger streams such men are barred* from these enterprises until coöperative labor can be organized or capital induced to assist.

These [arid] lands will maintain but a scanty population. The homes must necessarily be widely scattered from the fact that the farm unit must be large. That the inhabitants of these districts may have the benefits of the local social organizations of civilization—as schools, churches, etc., and the benefits of cooperation in the construction of roads, bridges, and other local improvements, it is essential that the residences should be grouped to the greatest possible extent. This may be practically accomplished by making the pasturage farms conform to topographic features in such manner as to give the greatest possible number of water fronts.... for poor men coöperative pasturage is necessary, or communal regulations for the occupancy of the ground and for the division of the increase of the herds. Such communal regulations have already been devised in many parts of the country....

If the irrigable lands are to be sold, it should be in quantities to suit purchasers, and but one condition should be imposed, namely, that the lands should be actually irrigated before the title is transferred to the purchaser.... If these lands are to be reserved for actual settlers, in small quantities, to provide homes for poor men, on the principle involved in the homestead laws, a general law should be enacted under which a number of persons would be able to organize and settle on irrigable districts, and establish their own rules and regulations for the use of the water and subdivision of the lands, but in obedience to the general provisions of the law....

The general subject of water rights is one of great importance. In many places in the Arid Region irrigation companies are organized who obtain vested rights in the waters they control, and consequently the rights to such waters do not inhere in any particular tracts of land.... [If] the land titles and water rights are severed, the owner of any tract of land is at the mercy of the owner of the water right.... If the water rights fall into the hands of irrigating companies... the farmers then will be dependent upon the stock companies, and eventually the monopoly of water rights will be an intolerable burden to the people.

The magnitude of the interests involved must not be overlooked.... practically all values for agricultural industries inhere, not in the lands but in the water. Monopoly of land need not be feared. The question for legislators to solve is to devise some practical means by which water rights may be distributed among individual farmers and water monopolies prevented....

Every man who turns his attention to this department of industry is considered a public benefactor. But if in the eagerness for present development a land and water system shall grow up in which the practical control of agriculture shall fall into the hands of water companies, evils will result therefrom that generations may not be able to correct, and the very men who are now lauded as benefactors to the country will, in the ungovernable reaction which is sure to come, be denounced as oppressors of the people.

Source: John Wesley Powell, *Report on the Lands of the Arid Region of the United States, with a More Detailed Account of the Lands of Utah,* 2nd ed. (Washington, DC: Government Printing Office, 1879), pp. 10, 11, 22–23, 27–28, 40–42.

**Document 7.2   Congress Authorizes Irrigation Survey
of Arid Lands, 1888**

*John Wesley Powell's buoyant, optimistic vision of an irrigated West
was advanced in 1888 with a joint congressional resolution "directing
the Secretary of the Interior by means of the Director of the Geological
Survey to investigate the practicability of constructing reservoirs for the
storage of water in the arid region of the United States." The General
Land Office subsequently ordered that all public lands in the region
would be off limits to settlement and irrigation until the completion of
the survey—a directive that became a central issue in the political
conflict between Survey Director Powell and his opponents in and out
of Congress.*

Whereas a large portion of the unoccupied public lands of the United States
is located within what is known as the arid region and now utilized only for
grazing purposes, but much of which, by means of irrigation, may be rendered
as fertile and productive as any land in the world, capable of supporting a large
population thereby adding to the national wealth and prosperity;

Whereas all the water flowing during the summer months in many of the
streams of the Rocky Mountains, upon which chiefly the husbandmen of the
plains and mountain valleys chiefly depend for moisture for his crops, has been
appropriated and is used for the irrigation of lands contiguous thereto,
whereby a comparatively small area has been reclaimed;

Whereas there are many natural depressions near the sources and along the
courses of these streams which may be converted into reservoirs for the storage
of the surplus water which during the winter and spring seasons flows through
the streams; from which reservoirs the water stored there can be drawn and
conducted through properly constructed canals, at the proper season, thus
bringing large areas of land into cultivation, and making desirable much of the
public land for which there is now no demand; therefore be it

*Resolved by the Senate and House of Representatives of the United States of
America in Congress assembled,* That the Secretary of the Interior by means of the
Director of the Geological Survey be, and he is hereby, directed to make an
examination of that portion of the arid regions of the United States where
agriculture is carried on by means of irrigation, as to the natural advantages for
the storage of water for irrigating purposes with the practicability of constructing reservoirs, together with the capacity of the streams and the cost of
construction and capacity of reservoirs, and such other facts as bear on the
question of storage of water for irrigating purposes; and that he be further
directed to report to Congress as soon as practicable the result of such investigation.

Approved, March 20, 1888.

Source: Congressional Record, 50th Cong., 1st sess., Resolutions 5–7 (Washington, DC:
Government Printing Office, 1888), p. 618.

Document 7.3   Report of the Special Congressional Committee on the Irrigation and Reclamation of Arid Lands, 1890

U.S. senator William Stewart of Nevada, chairman of a special Senate Committee on Irrigation and initially a supporter of the irrigation survey, soon turned against Powell. Stewart grew frustrated by the stay on settlement while the survey proceeded, by the length of time it was taking Powell to complete the work, and by Powell's focus on the time-intensive making of topographic maps. Less than two years into Powell's survey, Stewart introduced legislation to reassign the work to the Department of Agriculture. His bill would have expedited the survey of arid lands and accelerated their private development. Excerpts from the report of Stewart's committee appear here in two parts—the first from the majority represented by Stewart, and the second representing the views of the minority who continued to support Powell.

Mr. Stewart, from the Select Committee on Irrigation and Reclamation of Arid Lands, submitted the following REPORT: [To accompany S. 2104.]

The Director [Powell] contends that the segregation of the irrigable lands can be effected much more cheaply by a topographic survey than in any other manner. This is a statement upon which any member of Congress can form an opinion without any advice from either topographers or engineers. The law vests the administration of the public lands of the United States in the General Land Office. It has for nearly a century provided a system, and grown up under it, by which the public lands are parceled into townships, sections, and quarter sections. The people are thoroughly educated to it and understand it. Surveys have been provided which make the subdivision and mark the corners on the ground, and the law recognizes such marks as the true and only lawful metes and bounds. The Land Office has a record system of all surveyed parcels, and it is the only record which the law recognizes....

Now it is plain enough that in order to specify irrigable lands the irrigation engineers must first go over the country to find out what lands are irrigable. He must then identify what townships and sections include these irrigable lands and must identify the corners on the ground. He can then represent them on a transcript of the Land Office map, and report them, section by section, to the Land Office.

The engineers say that they find some convenience in topographic maps in the way of general information of a geographical character. But they can dispense with them without any serious inconvenience....

The maps already in existence... are all that is required for the engineering work for irrigation.

If it be admitted, however, that the views of the Director of the Geological Survey are correct as to the necessity for topographic surveys in advance of irrigation surveys, such views are no justification for the diversion of the money appropriated for irrigation....

A provision was inserted in the act of October 2, 1888, which is working great hardship to the people of all the arid States and Territories. It was necessary to reserve "all the lands which may hereafter be designated or selected by such United States surveys for sites for reservoirs, ditches, or canals for irrigation purposes." This reservation ... was inserted to prevent the occupation of reservoir sites and other places necessary for public use in connection with irrigation. But the following clause was unnecessary and the construction given to it has been disastrous. It did not come from the original friends of irrigation development. It adds to the provision above, quoting the following:

> And all the lands made susceptible or irrigation by such reservoirs, ditches, or canals are from this time henceforth hereby reserved from sale, as the property of the United States, and shall not be subject ... to entry, settlement, or occupation until further provided by law....

VIEWS OF THE MINORITY

It is a matter of prime importance that the irrigable lands shall be selected and defined and water rights established to such lands in advance of settlement, so far as that is yet possible, in order that the agricultural industries growing up in the arid lands may be permanent. It has already been shown that the amount of land which can be irrigated depends upon wise selection; if the selection is made at random, or improperly, the area which it may be possible to irrigate may be reduced....

The principle ... is exceedingly simple. It is that the arid lands depending for irrigation upon perennial streams shall be divided into irrigation districts so that each shall have a defined body of irrigable lands and a defined catchment area, and that the lands and waters shall thus be related, the lands being just sufficient, and no more, to use all the water which the catchment area will provide.... Nature has divided the arid lands into districts which are usually well defined. The entire region is composed of drainage basins, and through the midst of each one flows a stream, and it is bounded above and on either side by the crest where the waters divide. Such a district, therefore, is natural, and in such a district all of the conditions for prosperous agriculture exist and are unified....

The plan of the Director ... appears to be wise, and in all its parts to be necessary to carry out the provisions of the statute.

The survey also seems to be conducted in the interests of the farmers themselves rather than in the interests of the water companies. This fact has led to some criticism of the methods and results. In general, the water companies are disappointed because the statute provides for the reservation of the sites for works, including headwork sites, canal sites, and reservoir sites, and prevents their falling into the possession of monopolistic corporations. The statute also provides that the lands which can be irrigated by said works shall be withdrawn from the operation of the desert-land laws, the timber-culture laws, and the preemption laws, so that they cannot be acquired thereunder; ... This provision also seems to be obnoxious to companies and individuals desiring to acquire large tracts of land.... Believing that the statute of 1888 is wise and for the interests of the people settling in the arid lands, and generally for the good of the country, we earnestly recommend the continuation of the survey on the plans already adopted. . . .

The objections to this [S. 2104] bill are as follows:

(1) It seems to us to be in the interest of the great cattle companies that pasture their animals on the public domain, and opposed to the interests of the farmers who are making homesteads on the lands.

(2) It also appears to be in the interest of the great irrigation companies rapidly developing in the West, who seek to gain control of the land and the waters alike, and it practically excludes from ownership the poor man who settles upon the land . . .

Source: Report of the Special Committee of the United States Senate on the Irrigation and Reclamation of Arid Lands. Report of Committee and Views of the Minority. 51st Cong., 1st sess., Report 928, and Views of the Minority (Washington, DC: Government Printing Office, 1890), pp. 10–12, 108–109, 117–20, 134–38, 143–44.

Document 7.4   Excerpt from William E. Smythe's *The Conquest of Arid America*, 1900

Few boosters of western reclamation matched the zeal of William E. Smythe, founder of the journal The Irrigation Age. *In his book,* The Conquest of Arid America, *published in 1900, Smythe affixed to irrigation the kind of bombastic, religiously and racially charged rhetoric in the tradition of America's Manifest Destiny. Like many of his readers—and, on one level, like Powell himself—he saw the engineering of western waters leading to a more democratic, prosperous America. A classic work of the era of Progressive conservation, Smythe's book reveals the contradictory claims of that movement: to apply the genius of American science and technology to an ostensibly more prudent exploitation of finite resources.*

Imagine the Republic of the twentieth century, all its magnificent resources under process of development on lines of enlightened co-operation, approved alike by the sane business sense and the humanitarian instincts of the people!

Behold the out-swinging gates of the West, opening at last the wealth of surplus resources to the throngs of surplus people—the gates unlocked by the magic of surplus capital!

See how the "uneasy" have "planted new colonies," as Edward Eggleston said they did in all past stages of the American emigration; how, under the impulse of this new forward march, the Republic has again surpassed the monarchies of the Old World "with giant strides," as Andrew Carnegie has shown that it did in a past era; how "the desert has blossomed with the homes of men," as Thomas B. Reed predicted; . . .

Here are millions of free men who live upon their own soil, under their own roofs, and work for themselves. Here is a society which has mastered the machine and made it work for man rather than against him. Here is a people who have organized capital so that it works for the many rather than the few.

Here is the finest flower of Anglo-Saxon civilization, with personal independence and ambition still preserved as the robust inspiration of all progress, but with everything beyond the sphere of the individual firmly held by associated man....

Instead of crowded cities festering with vice and poverty, throughout Arid America are farms that blend into beautiful towns, and towns that shade almost imperceptibly into peaceful farms. Here are country people who enjoy all the advantages of town life, and townspeople who know the independence of the country. Here are social conditions where the entire population enjoys the privileges of the club and the blessings of the public library....

In a word, here is America, under the powerful dominance of the ancient Saxon spirit, engaged in the conquest of its waste-places and the making of new forms of civilization worthy of the race, the place, and the age....

The field, the opportunity, and the people are ready. The hour is ripe for the advance. The silent command that speaks to men's minds through resistless economic forces has gone forth.

The American people will press on...to illustrate the highest possibilities of democratic institutions.

Source: William E. Smythe, *The Conquest of Arid America* (New York: Harper and Brothers, 1900), pp. 308–309.

Document 7.5   **Excerpt from the Congressional Opposition to the Newlands Reclamation Act, 1902**

Congressmen debated the merits of the landmark Newlands Reclamation Act fiercely. Echoing Smythe, westerners' claims that unmatched prosperity would flow to the whole country from federally sponsored irrigation were met with, among other things, the allegation that it was an unmerited subsidy for large landowning railroads and cattle corporations who stood to profit from federal reclamation. An "insolent and impudent attempt at larceny," Representative Hepburn of Iowa thundered. This excerpt from the 1902 debate summarizes the main themes of opposition to the bill: the cost of reclamation, its perceived unconstitutionality, fears that irrigation would undermine farmers' interests elsewhere, and the charge that public money was solely or largely going to benefit private interests.

The cost of constructing, maintaining, and operating one of these reservoirs may be estimated, but any estimate will be far from the actual expense. If the Government commences the construction of such reservoirs at different points and the proceeds of sales of public lands are exhausted before they are completed and put in operation, a demand will immediately be made for an appropriation out of the public treasury on the plea that the Government having gone into the business of irrigation and having expended millions for incompleted work, such works must be preserved and completed in order to be of any value whatever. Such please [sic] are usually successful, but the result would be either that the Government must abandon its incomplete work or tax all the people for the benefit of a locality.

If we add millions of acres of productive land to our national possessions we shall surely diminish the value of the present farming lands throughout the Union, and we shall open new areas in the far West to compete in production with the farmers in the South, East, and middle West. The people in these sections will not consent, and ought to consent, to pay from the public treasury for the construction of such public works which, even if successful, will work injury to their interests.

Our present agricultural lands are not so overcrowded or so unproductive that we need to enter on this scheme in order to feed or accommodate the people of this nation even should the population double in the next fifty years.... Nor should we open up these lands for the purpose of encouraging immigration. The time is at hand when immigration should be limited and discouraged rather than encouraged.

It is conceded that if this bill is enacted into law the Secretary of the Interior will have the absolute disposal of at least $6,000,000 now on hand, with about $3,000,000 added each year thereafter until the sale of irrigated lands commences, when the sum will be much larger.

No sane man desirous of promoting the growth and prosperity of our whole country and of making permanent our institutions of free government will consent to the placing of this immense sum of money and the power of appropriation or expenditure thereof at the disposal of any one man in times of peace. In the mad scramble for this money corruption would run riot....

The land-grant railroads are behind this scheme and the real beneficiaries. These roads run through these arid lands and semiarid regions, and they own vast tracts of these lands. The construction of these irrigation works and reservoirs at the public expense will inure to their benefit, for it will bring their lands into the market at twenty times their present value. In our judgment the Congress of the United States will be false to its trust if it sanctions a scheme the benefits of which are largely, at least, to be reaped by these railroad corporations....

That Congress may pass laws authorizing the acquiring of lands by condemnation proceedings for a public use is not denied.

Here the use contemplated is the acquiring of lands and water rights which are to be improved and then sold again to private individuals and used for private purposes, or used for storage purposes, the property (water) collected from such water rights and stored to be sold to private individuals and corporations and all for purposes of speculation or supposed gain, not to the public treasury but to the State, by increasing its population, productive power, and taxable property.

There is no gain to the public treasury, for the proceeds of sales are to go into the construction and maintenance of the irrigation works; no benefit to the United States unless it be in the promotion of the interests and growth of a State or of a few States to the possible detriment of the many.... The United States is not a dealer in real estate and has not the constitutional power to become such. The objects and purposes mentioned [in the bill] are not governmental objects or purposes....

[The majority responds:]

To say that the National Government can not, within the Constitution, do its part in the development of the latent wealth that exists in a region that is nearly one-third the total area of the United States is to discredit the genius of the American people. To say that we may not utilize the waste waters that pour down from the mountain heights, and by applying these waters to public lands that would otherwise be worthless make two blades of grass grow where none grew before, is to admit that national progress has reached the end and we are henceforth doomed to decay.

Sources: Irrigation and Reclamation of Arid Lands. House Report No. 794. Part II. From Reports of Committees of the House of Representatives for the first session of the Fifty-seventh Congress, 1901–1902 (Washington, DC: Government Printing Office, 1902), pp. 4–6, 10, 13; and Congressional Record, 57th Cong., 1st sess. (Washington, DC: Government Printing Office, 1902), p. 1383.

Document 7.6   Excerpt from the Newlands Reclamation Act, 1902

Named for its chief legislative sponsor, Nevada representative Francis G. Newlands, the Newlands Reclamation Act is arguably the single most important piece of legislation in the modern development of the American West. Politically inspired by two decades of support from major western business and political interests, the law committed the federal government to construct and control massive irrigation projects that shaped much of the subsequent environmental, political, economic, and social history of the arid West. Though sometimes misinterpreted as the realization of J. W. Powell's call for an irrigated West, the actual terms of the law could not have been more different from Powell's vision of a more environmentally sensitive and democratically and locally controlled system of irrigation. The law created the Reclamation Service, initially within the Department of the Interior under the leadership of Frederick Newell; it later became an independent agency, and in 1923 was renamed the Bureau of Reclamation.

FIFTY-SEVENTH CONGRESS. Sess. I. CH. 1093—June 17, 1902 [Public, No. 161]

CHAP. 1093.—An Act Appropriating the receipts from the sale and disposal of public lands in certain States and Territories to the construction of irrigation works for the reclamation of arid lands.

Be it enacted by the Senate and House of Representatives of the United States of America in Congress assembled, That all moneys received from the sale and disposal of public lands in Arizona, California, Colorado, Idaho, Kansas, Montana, Nebraska, Nevada, New Mexico, North Dakota, Oklahoma, Oregon, South Dakota, Utah, Washington, and Wyoming, beginning with the fiscal year ending June thirtieth, nineteen hundred and one, ... shall be, ... reserved, set aside, and appropriated as a special fund in the Treasury to be known as the "reclamation fund," to be used in the examination and survey for and the construction and maintenance of irrigation works for the storage, diversion, and development of waters for the reclamation of arid and semiarid lands in the said States and Territories, and for the payment of all other expenditures provided for in this Act. ...

SEC. 2. That the Secretary of the Interior is hereby authorized and directed to make examinations and surveys for, and to locate and construct, ... irrigation works for the storage, diversion, and development of waters, including artesian wells, ...

SEC. 3. That the Secretary of the Interior shall ... withdraw from public entry the lands required for any irrigation works contemplated under the provisions of this Act, ... ; and the Secretary of the Interior is hereby authorized, at or immediately prior to the time of beginning the surveys for any contemplated irrigation works, to withdraw from entry, except under the homestead laws, any public lands believed to be susceptible of irrigation from said works. ...

SEC 5. That the entryman upon lands to be irrigated by such works shall, in addition to compliance with the homestead laws, reclaim at least one-half of the total irrigable area of his entry for agricultural purposes, and before receiving patent for the lands covered by his entry shall pay to the Government the charges apportioned against such tract, ... No right to the use of water for land in private ownership shall be sold for a tract exceeding one hundred and sixty acres to any one landowner, and no such sale shall be made to any landowner unless he be an actual bona fide resident on such land. ...

SEC. 6. That the Secretary of the Interior is hereby authorized and directed to use the reclamation fund for the operation and maintenance of all reservoirs and irrigation works. ...

SEC 7. That where in carrying out the provisions of this Act it becomes necessary to acquire any rights or property, the Secretary of the Interior is hereby authorized to acquire the same for the United States by purchase or by condemnation under judicial process, and to pay from the reclamation fund the sums which may be needed for that purpose, ...

SEC 8. That nothing in this Act shall be construed as affecting or intended to affect or to in any way interfere with the laws of any State or Territory relating to the control, appropriation, use, or distribution of water used in irrigation, ...

Approved, June 17, 1902.

Source: U.S. Statutes at Large, Vol. 32, Part 1, Chap. 1093, pp. 388–90. "An Act Appropriating the receipts from the sale and disposal of public lands in certain States and Territories to the construction of irrigation works for the reclamation of arid lands." [S. 3057]; Public Act No. 161.

Document 7.7   Excerpt from the Report of President Theodore Roosevelt's Conservation Commission, 1908

Chaired by Gifford Pinchot, President Roosevelt's National Commission on Conservation delivered an unequivocal message that the nation's resources—lands, minerals, forests, and waters—had to be properly managed, developed, and above all, harnessed for the continued industrial development of the nation. It was the quintessential message of the Progressive conservationists, led by Pinchot: that is, nature should be developed to serve the greatest good for the greatest number of Americans as far into the future as possible.

Of the total area of our lands, but little more than two-fifths is in farms, and less than one-half of the farm area is improved and made a source of crop production. The area of cultivated land may possibly be doubled. In addition to the land awaiting the plow 75,000,000 acres of swamp land can be reclaimed, 40,000,000 acres of desert land irrigated and millions of acres of brush and wooded land cleared. We must greatly increase our yield per acre. The average yield of wheat in the United States is less than fourteen bushels per acre; in England it is thirty-two bushels and in Germany twenty-eight.... Proper management will double the yield and produce more than three times our present population can consume.

Source: Report of the National Conservation Commission. February 1909. Special message from the President of the United States transmitting a report of the National Conservation Commission, with Accompanying Papers.... Edited under the direction of the Executive Committee by Henry Gannett, vol. 1 (Washington, DC: Government Printing Office, 1909), pp. 17–18.

Document 7.8   Dorothy Lampen Critiques Federal Reclamation Policy, 1930

Political economist Dorothy Lampen was among those who, in subsequent years, studied the progress of the Reclamation Service (Bureau of Reclamation from 1923), evaluating the extent to which the bureau had fulfilled the promise of its founders. In this excerpt from a 1930 study, Lampen remarks on two of the great points of contention in the years of debate—that is, the ability of irrigation projects to pay for themselves, and the susceptibility of the whole enterprise to fraud.

The repayment of the construction cost by the project settlers has always been a subject of controversy. Originally, the reclamation act provided for a revolving fund plan covering ten years, whereby the money as it was returned to the Federal treasury would be available for other irrigation projects.

Very soon after the first construction repayments were due from the project settlers, demands were made for lightened conditions of repayment in which the ten equal payments should be extended over a twenty-year period, or a system of graduated construction payments authorized. Despite the fact that the 1910 survey made by the army engineers had resulted in the conclusion that the general adoption of a relief measure was not believed to be either necessary or advisable, in 1914 the situation had so developed that relief was essential. . . .

As a further result of the demands for relief . . . means for more extended investigation were afforded. At this time, opposition to payments by water users and objections to the construction costs on projects became so serious that [Interior] Secretary Lane created the Central Board of Review, with authorization to conduct hearings and make recommendations as to what payments ought to be made by settlers.

Although the feeling had been that the charges were too high and that a large part of the cost ought to be written off, . . . this body found that high charges for water were not responsible for the evils of the projects, but "inflated land prices, high freight charges, high interest rates, alien landlordism, and normal and not actual compliance with the regulations fixing the size of farm units that closely verges on fraud," were the true causes of the difficulties. In the light of this, they advised that the Government should fix the project cost, rigidly enforce this payment on those able to pay, adopt measures to enforce cultivation of farm units, and put an end to the evasion of regulation fixing the size of farm units. . . .

"This remedial legislation [passed 1921–1923]," it was stated in 1924 [in the Bureau's annual report], "has not removed the troubles it was intended to cure. The deferment of charges does not touch the heart of the matter. The distressing symptoms of 1911 still obtain."

Source: Dorothy Lampen, "Economic and Social Aspects of Federal Reclamation," in *Johns Hopkins University Studies in Historical and Political Science* (Baltimore: The Johns Hopkins University Press, 1930), pp. 59–61; citing Twenty-third Annual Report of the Bureau of Reclamation for the fiscal year ended June 30, 1924, p. 3.

NOTES

1. Newlands Reclamation Act: Debates and Proceedings. Excerpted from the 57th Cong., 1st sess., *Congressional Record* 35 (March 1, 1902): 2282.

2. Senator William Stewart, Newlands Reclamation Act Debate, *Congressional Record*, 1 March 1902, 2278.

3. Donald Worster, *Rivers of Empire: Water, Aridity, and the Growth of the American West* (New York: Pantheon Books, 1985), p. 136.

4. Ibid., pp. 265–75.

ANNOTATED BIBLIOGRAPHY

DeBuys, William. *Seeing Things Whole: The Essential John Wesley Powell*. Washington, DC: Shearwater Books/Island Press, 2001. A skillfully edited collection of Powell's writings that delivers penetrating insight into a man who was (at least) a century ahead of his countrymen in his intellectual approach to sustainable regional development.

Martin, Russell. *A Story that Stands Like a Dam: Glen Canyon and the Struggle for the Soul of the West*. 1989. Reprint, Salt Lake City: University of Utah Press, 1999. Classic narrative of the epic battle waged by the Sierra Club's David Brower in the 1950s to stop Glen Canyon Dam. More resonant than ever as the dam has become a symbolic focal point of criticism of Western water policy.

Pisani, Donald J. *From the Family Farm to Agribusiness: The Irrigation Crusade in California, 1850–1931*. Berkeley: University of California Press, 1984. A survey of the transmogrification of California agriculture undergirded by subsidized water projects, somewhat superseded by several chapters in Reisner's *Cadillac Desert*.

———. *To Reclaim a Divided West: Water, Law, and Public Policy, 1848–1902*. Albuquerque: University of New Mexico Press, 1992. A fine study of the early development of western water law and public policy and its links to regional economic interests.

———. *Water and American Government: The Reclamation Bureau, National Water Policy, and the West, 1902–1935*. Berkeley: University of California Press, 2002. Centered on the critical early period when western dams first became the "mother's milk" of American politics. Readers understand how western politicians first succeeded in getting the nation to accept the enormous financial and social cost of heavily subsidized water projects.

Reisner, Marc. *Cadillac Desert: The American West and Its Disappearing Water*. 1986. Rev. ed. New York: Penguin Books, 1993. This popular history is recognized by many as the definitive work on the politics of western water development. Though not discounting the undeniably magnificent achievements of early engineering of western rivers, Reisner chronicles with meticulous detail (though without footnotes) the social, economic, political, and environmental costs subsequently paid by taxpayers, small farmers, and the environment for the thousands more projects that followed.

Stegner, Wallace. *Beyond the Hundredth Meridian: John Wesley Powell and the Second Opening of the West*. 1954. Reprint, New York: Penguin Books, 1992. A classic work offering insight into John Wesley Powell's career, from the legendary journey down the Colorado River, to the political conflict that led to his ultimate dismissal from the Geological Survey.

Worster, Donald. *A River Running West: The Life of John Wesley Powell*. New York: Oxford University Press, 2002. Scholarly treatment of Powell's philosophy and work as one of the most remarkable public servants in American history. His Colorado River runs and their impact on Powell's vision of the arid West are the centerpiece.

———. *Rivers of Empire: Water, Aridity, and the Growth of the American West*. 1985. Reprint, New York: Oxford University Press, 1992. Worster's sweeping history and probing analysis of western river engineering raises profound questions about the role of the West in our history and national mythology.

8

Preservation vs. Conservation: The Epic Fight over Yosemite's Hetch-Hetchy Valley

> Everybody needs beauty as well as bread, places to play in and pray in where Nature may heal and cheer and give strength to body and soul alike.
> —John Muir, 1907[1]

> I fully sympathize with the desire of ... Mr. Muir to protect the Yosemite National Park, but I believe that the highest possible use which could be made of it would be to supply pure water to a great center of population.
> —Gifford Pinchot to Theodore Roosevelt, 1907[2]

In the last quarter of the nineteenth century middle- and upper-class Americans demonstrated a growing fascination with the natural world that took many forms. Calendars, chinaware, and wallpapers featured nature scenery. Well-heeled Americans in increasing numbers traveled to picturesque locales and relocated to the first bucolic suburbs where many absorbed burgeoning volumes of travel books and wilderness literature. Sportsmen organized groups like the Boone and Crockett Club to preserve the virtues of a waning frontier era. Others would soon organize the Boy Scouts and similar children's outfits to pass on the skills and "character" associated with outdoor experience. These and other expressions mark the extent to which nature became suffused with aesthetic, moral, and spiritual values, and one's interest in fine scenery and wildlife came to signify good taste. Americans had become lovers and avid consumers of nature.

At the same time, increasing numbers of influential Americans began arguing for governmental policy to protect and conserve a natural world that seemed increasingly besieged. Two strains of thought emerged during the period.

Though bound together by an aesthetic sensibility that broadly celebrated the moral virtues of nature and its material importance in the nation's development, they were indeed two distinct philosophies. The first idea, to carefully manage the use of natural resources so as not to impair the capacity of future generations of Americans to similarly prosper, stemmed primarily from the destruction of much of the nation's forest cover (Chapter 6). Conservationists were called to action by George Perkins Marsh and led at the turn of the century by Gifford Pinchot, who became the nation's chief forester under President Theodore Roosevelt. Roosevelt and Pinchot oversaw the establishment of government agencies that employed scientists and other professionals to manage millions of acres of public grazing lands, national forests, and lands "reclaimed" through massive irrigation projects. They believed that only the combination of scientific managers working closely with large private corporate entities could extend the limits of nature, thereby sustaining the nation's economic growth indefinitely.

The designation of Yellowstone National Park, the world's first such preserve, epitomizes the second impulse of elite Americans regarding nature—that of setting certain lands aside entirely from extractive development. Though its origins derive ultimately from European romanticism of the eighteenth century, preservation assumed uniquely American forms. Key early prophets of the preservation idea include literary figures William Cullen Bryant and Henry David Thoreau and artists Thomas Cole and George Catlin. In letters and on canvas, depictions of landscapes from Concord to the Catskills figured prominently in the cultivation of America's cultural identity in the first half of the century. Americans with the means found picturesque and sublime landscapes a source of both national pride and a refuge from the harrying business of mastering the continent. Thus, the establishment of the 3,472-square-mile reserve of Yellowstone National Park in 1872 seems a logical culmination of decades of growing interest in and fascination with nature. However, Yellowstone National Park is less a sharp departure from previous exploitative attitudes regarding nature than this familiar story line of its creation suggests. Behind the scenes lay the Northern Pacific Railroad, one of the most dominant corporations in post–Civil War America. Envisioning increased traffic on its line and a possible spur to development of lands and resources it controlled through its vast federal land grant, the railroad promoted and helped fund and organize the 1870 and 1871 expeditions that led directly to the introduction of legislation establishing the park (indeed the first formal suggestion for the park was penned on railroad stationery).

More revealing of American attitudes regarding nature and the ensuing split between preservationists and conservationists that is the subject of this chapter was the conclusion of the 1871 expedition that Yellowstone's chief value lay in its exotic geothermal landscape of natural wonders and "curiosities." Ferdinand V. Hayden, head of the U.S. Geological Survey and expedition leader, assured congressmen voting on the bill that Yellowstone's volcanic origins and harsh climate rendered it without value for either agricultural settlement or mineral extraction. "Worthless" in utilitarian terms, Yellowstone would serve as a haven for those seeking moral uplift amid one of God's sublime creations, as well as an emblem of American nationalism. In subsequent years, however, park defenders would be hampered by the inherent limits of that economic justification for the park. Faced with repeated attempts by mining and railroad interests to penetrate or slice off a portion of the reserve to advance extractive development in the area northeast of Yellowstone, those defending the inviolability of the reserve championed the economic, utilitarian value of maintaining forest cover to farmers (hence the first forest "preserves" in the nation were established on the borders of the park). Politically influential sportsmen argued for the park's importance in maintaining valuable game populations. Most critically, preservationists appealed to national interest over western territorial provincialism, to the public good versus the assumed rapacious motives of shadowy corporate forces. And after 1890 they warned about the dangerous precedent that would be set in modifying park borders, for there were now additional parks—California's majestic Yosemite, King's Canyon, and Sequoia—with more to follow. Were the boundaries of national parks sacred or not?

By the turn of the new century, the question was resolved in Yellowstone in the preservationists' favor, but loomed larger than ever in Yosemite. Unlike the struggle in Yellowstone where proponents of reconfiguring park boundaries could be branded as invaders intent on the pillaging of a sublime landscape for shortsighted corporate greed, here the far more democratic issue was the water supply for the city of San Francisco. City engineers in the early 1880s had envisioned the possibility of damming the high-walled Hetch-Hetchy Valley, situated 150 miles to the east, as the best way to solve San Francisco's perpetual water supply problem. Damming the Tuolumne River at the lower end of the valley would create a reservoir that would serve the needs of a growing population. The problem was that Hetch-Hetchy was situated inside the boundaries of the new Yosemite National Park—established in 1890 by Congress after a long campaign led by naturalist and Sierra Club founder John Muir, *Century* magazine editor Robert Underwood Johnson, and other outdoor enthusiasts. For city fathers and most San Franciscans, the basic needs of a human population quite obviously were to take precedence over the preservation of wilderness. No matter how spectacular, Hetch-Hetchy was visited by relatively few people. The public good to be gained by damming the valley—for the benefit of the many—far outweighed the good of preserving it for the pleasure of a few.

That John Muir did not see it that way came as no surprise. He had first come to the attention of American nature lovers in the 1870s with his writings on the natural glories of Yosemite, which proved instrumental in the designation of the region as America's second national park. More surprising was Secretary of the Interior Ethan Allen Hitchcock's refusal in 1903 to grant the right of way for the dam and reservoir to the city. Hitchcock asserted that no argument the city had made compelled him to violate the intent of Congress in reserving the area.

However, the devastating 1906 earthquake that struck the city and the ensuing public health crisis gave the issue a new sense of urgency. With typhoid outbreaks related to unsafe supplies of drinking water common to many American cities, the argument made by city officials for a reliable source of clean, fresh water from the Sierra Nevada grew more compelling. Add to this the prevailing consensus of most Americans who thought about such things—including especially, leading conservationists such as John Wesley Powell and Gifford Pinchot—that western water that simply flowed into the sea was "wasted," and the damming of Hetch-Hetchy begins, at least in hindsight, to seem inevitable.

When the city's plea for the right of way to build the reservoir was made again in 1908, a new Secretary of the Interior, James R. Garfield, received it favorably. Garfield had been appointed Hitchcock's successor by President Theodore Roosevelt. In many ways, Roosevelt is the central figure in the two-headed movement to both preserve American landscapes *and* conserve natural resources in order to fully harness them for national development. Roosevelt embodied the contentious struggle between preservation and conservation shared by many men of his class and generation. Roosevelt cultivated a deep, lifelong affection for wild country from his time as a rancher and sportsman in Dakota Territory through more contemplative camping and hiking experiences with men such as John Burroughs and John Muir. The preservation impulse led him to set aside five new national parks, and to establish the nation's first wildlife refuges (fifty-one during his tenure) and the first eighteen national monuments. Yet no sentimentalist was Roosevelt. His pronouncements of the inherent value of wild forest, wild bird, or wild game protection were often accompanied by declarations of the more practical, material benefits of government management of the nation's natural bounty. Forested watersheds, for example, were to be protected for the benefits that would accrue to farmers, commercial navigation, and homebuilding. One hundred fifty new national forests and twenty-four reclamation projects testify to that more utilitarian conservationist legacy.

Theodore Roosevelt's vision was too expansive to be bothered by any contradiction between preservation and conservation. For ordinary men, however, the Hetch-Hetchy controversy rendered the divide between the two ideals an impassable chasm. In the fight over one valley's fate, the fundamental philosophical differences between preservation and conservation, and the nation's commitment to both policy goals, became seemingly irreconcilable. Garfield's approval of the city's request prompted Muir and Johnson to launch what became a five-year-long, national campaign to defend the valley, and as they saw it, the very integrity of the national park idea.

Led by Muir, Yosemite defenders appealed to the growing revulsion toward what many critics had long ago declared to be an excessively materialistic society. For preservationists, the proposal to flood Hetch-Hetchy Valley represented the most egregious sign of an overly commercialized, overly urbanized civilization slouching toward decadence. The outcry prompted congressional hearings over the Garfield decision, a forum in which defenders firmly embedded Hetch-Hetchy as a symbol of all things sacred, a bulwark against the overwhelming force of modernism. One Hetch-Hetchy camper posed these incisive questions: "is it never ceasing; is there nothing to be held sacred by this nation; is it to be dollars only; are we to be cramped in soil and mind by the lust after filthy lucre only; shall we be left some of the more glorious places?"[3] Invoking the divine association that such majestic places of grandeur had assumed in American culture, Muir and others condemned the proposal as an ungodly, satanic act that would destroy one of God's own "temples." Others clamored against the private interests that allegedly stood to profit from the control and sale of the water supply and the associated hydroelectric power that would be generated by the dam. Defenders of the valley also engaged the services of independent engineers who testified that other alternative sources, outside the bounds of Yosemite, could be tapped to solve the city's water problem. Opposition came from across the country in the form of letters and telegrams from civic groups, scientists and travelers, and editorials from leading newspapers and magazines. Although the proposal—essentially certifying Garfield's decision—passed the committee on a narrow vote, the popular groundswell of opposition prompted the House of Representatives in 1909 to allow the legislation to die.

Dam proponents would not surrender. Two sessions of Congress later, San Francisco's congressman John E. Raker introduced the bill that would ultimately be approved and grant the city the right of way it had long requested. Though some congressmen took the hearing as an opportunity to criticize all national forests and parks, they were in the minority. Raker himself grounded his argument on the market value of Yosemite that he believed would be *enhanced* by the dam. He trumpeted the enormous monetary value (in the millions, he estimated) that an impounded reservoir would have, versus the paltry $300,000 he affixed to the valley in its present "swampy" state." Indeed, most advocates of the city's proposal acknowledged their support for parks and the broader intrinsic value of wilderness—when not in conflict with other, more pressing human needs, as was the case here. Even Gifford Pinchot, while echoing the familiar premise that the highest purpose of natural resource conservation was to serve the greatest good for the greatest number, admitted that wilderness preservation should prevail when "nothing else [was] at stake." Such arguments always pointed out that the reservoir would hold recreational value, effectively replacing whatever natural qualities would be lost by impounding the river; indeed, most advocates argued that the reservoir would be *more* lovely than the "old barren rocks" and "swampy floor" of the valley.

One last hope for Muir and his allies was Congressman William Kent, who had been made an honorary member of the Sierra Club for his championing of the preservationist cause elsewhere in California. Yet, Kent had also proved himself a champion of public ownership of utilities. He feared that if the city's proposal did not succeed, the Pacific Gas and Electric Company, already a monopolistic force in control of the state's hydroelectric power, would gain control of Hetch-Hetchy. If the deed must be done, Kent reasoned, far better for the public to own the resource than a rapacious profiteering corporation.

After the measure passed the House of Representatives, opposition forces reprised their nationwide campaign of protest. Senators received thousands of letters each from constituents; newspapers and magazines railed against the proposal and the "sordid commercialism" the dam had long come to symbolize. Impressive though it was, the effort ultimately failed. On December 6, 1913, the Senate voted forty-three to twenty-five in favor of the proposal. Despite a personal plea from Robert Underwood Johnson for a presidential veto,

Woodrow Wilson signed the Raker Act that would flood Hetch-Hetchy, signaling a major defeat for the preservation movement.

Despite the final outcome, the campaign to save Hetch-Hetchy did more than drive old friends Gifford Pinchot and John Muir and their respective philosophies their separate ways. The controversy revealed the limits of the "worthless lands" rationale for establishing parks and wilderness areas—an issue with which today's preservationists must continually contend. Hetch-Hetchy forced the nation's elected officials to consider as they heretofore had not the higher value of untouched wilderness and demonstrated the overwhelming public support that ideal had acquired in American culture. And forty years later, when another proposed dam threatened to invade the sanctuary of a national preserve (this time Dinosaur National Monument in Colorado), preservationists would prevail. In Alamo-like fashion, the Sierra Club and other preservationists recalled the damage done to Yosemite through the damming of Hetch-Hetchy, once again rallying the support of the nation for preserving wilderness, and in that instance, they would succeed.

DOCUMENTS

**Document 8.1   John Muir Describes the Hetch-Hetchy Valley in
                      Yosemite National Park**

---

*In November 1909, the Sierra Club published a twenty-two-page
pamphlet urging continued citizen action against the proposed
damming of the Hetch-Hetchy Valley of Yosemite National Park. By
then the debate between a coalition of preservation forces led by
Sierra Club founder Muir and those arguing for the highest possible
human use of the valley and its water was approaching its final stages.
In this excerpt from the pamphlet (other versions of which appeared
earlier in* Century *magazine and in the* Sierra Club Bulletin*), Muir
describes in the romantic language typical of nature writers of the age
the natural features of the valley, compares the area favorably to the
better-known Yosemite Valley, and urges its protection.*

The fame of the Merced Yosemite has spread far and wide, while Hetch-
Hetchy, the Tuolumne Yosemite, has until recently remained relatively unknown, notwithstanding it is a wonderfully exact counterpart of the valley. As
the Merced flows in tranquil beauty through Yosemite, so does the Tuolumne
through Hetch-Hetchy. The floor of Yosemite is about 4,000 above the sea,
and that of Hetch-Hetchy about 3,700, while in both the walls are of gray
granite, very high, and rise precipitously out of flowery gardens and groves.
Furthermore, the two wonderful valleys occupy the same relative positions on
the flank of the Sierra, were formed by the same forces in the same kind of
granite, and have similar waterfalls, sculpture, and vegetation. Hetch-Hetchy
lies in a northwesterly direction from Yosemite at a distance of about eighteen
miles, and is now easily accessible by a trail and wagon-road....

The most strikingly picturesque rock in the valley is a majestic pyramid over
2,000 feet in height which is called by the Indians "Kolana." It is the outermost
of a group like the Cathedral Rocks of Yosemite and occupies the same relative
position on the south wall. Facing Kolana on the north side of the valley there
is a massive sheer rock like the Yosemite El Capitan about 1,900 feet high, and
over its brow flows a stream that makes the most beautiful fall I have ever
seen. The Indian name for it is "Tueeulala." From the edge of the cliff it is
perfectly free in the air for a thousand feet, then breaks up into a ragged sheet
of cascades among the shoulders of an earthquake talus....The only fall I
know with which it may fairly be compared is the Yosemite Bridal Veil; but it
excels even that favorite fall both in height and fineness of fairy airy beauty
and behavior....Imagine yourself in Hetch-Hetchy on a sunny day in June,
standing waist-deep in grass and flowers (as I have oftentimes stood), while
the great pines sway dreamily with scarce perceptible motion. Looking

northward across the valley you see a plain gray granite cliff rising abruptly out of the gardens and groves to a height of 1,800 feet, and in front of it Tueeulala's silvery scarf burning with irised sun-fire in every fiber. Approaching the brink of the rock, her waters flow swiftly, and in the first white outburst of the stream at the head of the fall there is abundance of visible energy, but it is speedily hushed and concealed in divine repose; and its tranquil progress to the base of the cliff is like that of downy feathers in a still room. . . .

So fine a fall might well seem sufficient to glorify any valley; but here as in Yosemite Nature seems in no wise moderate, for a short distance to the eastward of Tueeulala booms and thunders the great Hetch-Hetchy fall, Wapama, so near that you have both of them in full view from the same standpoint. It is the counterpart of the Yosemite Fall, but has a much greater volume of water, . . .

Hetch-Hetchy Valley is a grand landscape garden, one of Nature's rarest and most precious mountain mansions. As in Yosemite, the sublime rocks of its walls seem to the nature lover to glow with life, whether leaning back in repose or standing erect in thoughtful attitudes giving welcome to storms and calms alike. And how softly these mountain rocks are adorned, and how fine and reassuring the company they keep—their brows in the sky, their feet set in groves and gay emerald meadows, a thousand flowers leaning confidently against their adamantine bosses, while birds, bees, and butterflies help the river and waterfalls to stir all the air into music—things frail and fleeting and types of permanence meeting here and blending, as if into this glorious mountain temple Nature had gathered her choicest treasures, whether great or small, to draw her lovers into close confiding communion with her. . . .

Garden- and park-making goes on everywhere with civilization, for everybody needs beauty as well as bread, places to play in and pray in, where Nature may heal and cheer and give strength to body and soul.

It is impossible to overestimate the value of wild mountains and mountain temples. They are the greatest of our natural resources. God's best gifts, but none, however high and holy, is beyond the reach of the spoilers.

These temple destroyers, devotees of ravaging commercialism, seem to have a perfect contempt for Nature, and instead of lifting their eyes to the mountains, lift them to dams and town skyscrapers.

Dam Hetch-Hetchy! As well dam for water-tanks the people's cathedrals and churches, for no holier temple has ever been consecrated by the heart of man. . . .

Source: John Muir, "The Endangered Valley: The Hetch-Hetchy Valley in Yosemite National Park," in *Let Everyone Help to Save the Famous Hetch-Hetchy Valley and Stop the Commercial Destruction Which Threatens Our National Parks* (pamphlet) (San Francisco: Society for the Preservation of National Parks, 1909), pp. 14–17. Retrieved from the San Francisco Museum Web site, http://www.sfmuseum.org/john/muir10.html (accessed June 25, 2004).

Document 8.2   Secretary of the Interior Hitchcock Opposes Proposed Hetch-Hetchy Dam, 1903

Both proponents and those who resisted the dam employed the voices of engineering and hydrological experts and other authorities to support their case. In their 1909 pamphlet, opposition forces quoted the original 1903 denial of the permit application submitted by San Francisco city officials issued by former secretary of interior E. A. Hitchcock.

Hon. E. A. Hitchcock, December 22, 1903:

It is proposed to convert Lake Eleanor and Hetch-Hetchy Valley, respectively, into reservoirs for the storage of a water supply for the city. Both are admittedly scenic features of the Yosemite National park. . . .

If natural scenic attractions of the grade and character of Lake Eleanor and Hetch-Hetchy Valley are not of the class which the law commands the Secretary to preserve and retain in the natural condition, it would seem difficult to find any in the park that are, unless it be the Yosemite Valley itself. . . .

Presumably the Yosemite National Park was created such by law because of the natural objects, of varying degrees of scenic importance, located within its boundaries, inclusive alike of its beautiful small lakes, like Eleanor, and its majestic wonders, like Hetch-Hetchy and Yosemite Valley. It is the aggregation of such natural scenic features that makes the Yosemite Park a wonderland which the Congress of the United States sought by law to preserve for all coming time as nearly as practicable in the condition fashioned by the hand of the Creator—a worthy object of national pride and a source of healthful pleasure and rest for the thousands of people who may annually sojourn there during the heated months.

Having in view the ends for which the Park was established and the law which clearly defines my duty in the premises, I am constrained to deny the application.

Source: Let Everyone Help to Save the Famous Hetch-Hetchy Valley, and Stop the Commercial Destruction Which Threatens Our National Parks (pamphlet) (San Francisco: Society for the Preservation of National Parks, 1909), p. 10.

Document 8.3   Decision of Secretary of Interior James R. Garfield to Grant San Francisco Permit to Create Reservoir Sites and Rights of Way in Hetch-Hetchy Valley, 1908

The Interior Department position on Hetch-Hetchy had changed abruptly in 1907 when President Theodore Roosevelt appointed James R. Garfield to succeed Secretary Hitchcock. While acknowledging the merits of the preservationist argument, Garfield justifies his authority to grant the right of way for the reservoir. He grounds his reasoning on the central theme of the conservation movement: that natural resources should serve the greatest good for the greatest number of people. In this case, he determined that the domestic water supply of San Francisco outweighed the national interest of preserving the valley as it was and that even the goal of exposing scenic beauty to greater numbers of Americans would be served by building the dam.

Decision of the Secretary of the Interior Department, Washington, DC, granting the city and county of San Francisco, subject to certain conditions, reservoir sites and rights of way at the Lake Eleanor and Hetch-Hetchy Valley in the Yosemite National Park.

Washington, May 11, 1908.

...This application [for reservoir rights, by the city of San Francisco] was considered by the Secretary of the Interior and, on December 22, 1903, rejected on the ground that he did not have the legal power to allow such a right of way within the Yosemite National Park. From that time to this the city has, with practical continuity, pressed its request for a permit to use these reservoir sites....I have given the most careful consideration to this petition, and have decided...[to] reinstate the application of [Mayor] James D. Phelan....

Congress, on February 15, 1901, provided specifically:

"The Secretary of the Interior...is authorized...to permit the use of rights of way through...the Yosemite, Sequoia, and General Grant national parks, California, for...water conduits and for water plants, dams, and reservoirs used to promote...the supply of water for domestic, public, or other beneficial uses...provided that such permits shall be allowed within or through any of said parks...only upon the approval of the chief officer of the department, under whose supervision such park or reservation falls, and upon a finding by him that the same is not incompatible with the public interest."

By these words Congress has given power to the Secretary of the Interior to grant the rights applied for by the city of San Francisco, if he finds that the permit is "not incompatible with the public interest." Therefore I need only consider the effect of granting the application upon "the public interest."...

[The] words "the public interest" should not be confined merely to the public interest in the Yosemite National Park for use as a park only, but rather the broader public interest which requires these reservoir sites to be utilized for the highest good to the greatest number of people. If Congress had intended to restrict the meaning to the mere interest on the public in the park as such, it surely would have used specific words to show that intent. At the time the act was passed there was no authority of law for the granting of privileges of this character in the Yosemite National Park. Congress recognized the interest of the public in the utilization of the great water resources of the park and specifically gave power to the Secretary of the Interior to permit such use. The proviso was evidently added merely as a reminder that he should weigh well the public interest both in and out of the park before making his decision.

The present water supply of the city of San Francisco is both inadequate and unsatisfactory. This fact has been known for a number of years and has led to a very extensive consideration of the various possible sources of supply. The search for water for the city has been prosecuted from two diametrically opposite points of view. On the one side, the water companies, interested in supplying the city with water for their own profit, have taken advantage of the long delay since it was first proposed to bring water from the Yosemite to San Francisco to look up and get control, so far as they could, of the available sources in order to sell them to the city. On the other hand, both the National Government and the city of San Francisco have made careful study of the possible sources of supply for the city. Four or five years ago the hydrographic branch of the Geological Survey, after a careful examination by engineers of character and ability, reached the conclusion that the Tuolumne River offered a desirable and available supply for the city. The same conclusion was reached by the engineers of the city of San Francisco after years of exhaustive investigation.

I appreciate keenly the interest of the public in preserving the natural wonders of the park and am unwilling that the Hetch-Hetchy Valley site should be developed until the needs of the city are greater than can be supplied from the Lake Eleanor site when developed to its full capacity. Domestic use, however, especially for a municipal supply, is the highest use to which water and available storage basins therefore can be put. . . .

The only other source of objection, except that from persons and corporations who have no rights to protect but merely the hope of financial gain if the application of the city is denied, comes from those who have a special interest in our national parks from the standpoint of scenic effects, natural wonders, and health and pleasure resorts. I appreciate fully the feeling of these protestants and have considered their protests and arguments with great interest and sympathy. The use of these sites for reservoir purposes would interfere with the present condition of the park, and that consideration should be weighed carefully against the great use which the city can make of the permit. I am convinced, however, that "the public interest" will be much better conserved by granting the permit. Hetch-Hetchy Valley is great and beautiful in its natural and scenic effects. If it were also unique, sentiment for its preservation in an absolutely natural state would be far greater. In the mere vicinity, however, much more accessible to the public and more wonderful and beautiful, is the Yosemite Valley itself. Furthermore, the reservoir will not destroy Hetch-Hetchy. It will scarcely affect the canyon walls. It will not reach the foot of the various falls which descend from the sides of the canyon. The prime change will be that, instead of a beautiful but somewhat unusable "meadow" floor, the valley will be a lake of rare beauty.

As against this partial loss to the scenic effect of the park, the advantages to the public from the change are many and great. The city of San Francisco and probably the other cities on San Francisco Bay would have one of the finest and purest water supplies in the world. The irrigable land in the Tuolumne and San Joaquin valleys would be helped out by the use of the excess stored water, and by using the electrical power not needed by the city for municipal purposes to pump subterranean water for the irrigation of additional areas the city would have a cheap and bountiful supply of electric energy for pumping its water supply and lighting the city and its municipal buildings. The public would have a highway at its disposal to reach this beautiful region of the park heretofore practically inaccessible. This road would be built and maintained by the city without expense to the Government or the general public. The city has options on land held in private ownership within the Yosemite National Park, and would purchase this land and make it available to the public for camping purposes. The settlers and entrymen who acquired this land naturally chose the finest localities and at present have power to exclude the public from the best camping places, and, further, the city in protecting its water supply would furnish to the public a patrol to save this part of the park from destructive and disfiguring forest fires.

The floor of the Hetch-Hetchy Valley, part of which is owned privately and used as a cattle ranch, would become a lake bordered by vertical granite walls . . . practically full during the greater part of the tourist season in each year, and there would be practically no difficulty in making trails and roads for the use of the tourists around the edges of the valley above high-water mark. . . .

In considering the reinstated application of the city of San Francisco, I do not need to pass upon the claim that this is the only practicable and reasonable source of water supply for the city. It is sufficient that after careful and competent study the officials of the city insist that such is the case. . . .

Very respectfully,

James R. Garfield,

Secretary

Source: George J. Hesselman, ed., *Decisions of the Department of the Interior . . . June 1, 1907–June 30, 1908* (Washington, DC: Government Printing Office, 1908), pp. 410–13.

Document 8.4   The *New York Times* Opposes the Proposal to Dam the Hetch-Hetchy Valley, 1913

Garfield's 1908 decision vaulted preservationist forces into action. John Muir and Century *magazine editor Robert Underwood Johnson launched a national campaign to defend both Hetch-Hetchy and the very idea that national parks were inviolable. Though the effort failed, they succeeded in generating national opposition to the dam proposal. Here, in two excerpts from a series of editorials it published, the* New York Times *weighs in on the debate over the Raker Bill, which ultimately passed the U.S. Congress and authorized the flooding of Hetch-Hetchy Valley. Beyond the aesthetic value of the valley, the paper suggested that duplicitous tactics and ulterior motives were at work.*

A NATIONAL PARK THREATENED

Why the City of San Francisco, with plenty of collateral sources of water supply, should present an emergency measure to the special session of

Congress whereby it may invade the Yosemite National Park is one of those Dundrearian things that no fellow can find out. The Hetch-Hetchy Valley is described by John Muir as a "wonderfully exact counterpart of the great Yosemite." Why should its inspiring cliffs and waterfalls, its groves and flowery, park-like floor, be spoiled by the grabbers of water and power? The public officials of San Francisco are not even the best sort of politicians; as appraisers and appreciators of natural beauties their taste may be called in question.

It is the aggregation of its natural scenic features, the Secretary of the Interior declared to the would-be invaders of the park when a decade ago they presented their first petition, that "makes the Yosemite Park a wonderland, which the Congress of the United States sought by law to preserve for all coming time." Their application was rejected. Now they have obtained from the Board of Army Engineers a report approving their project as an emergency measure which is based on incomplete, erroneous, and false evidence. The engineers say in their report that they have merely passed on such data as were presented by the officials of San Francisco, since they had neither time nor money to investigate independently the various projects presented. But San Francisco's officials have withheld from these data the report upon the Mokelumne River and watershed submitted April 24, 1912, in which Engineers Bartel and Manson declare that this system is capable of supplying to the City of San Francisco between 280,000,000 and 430,000,000 gallons daily, the larger amount if certain extinguishable rights are disposed of. Even on their insufficient data, the army engineers report that San Francisco's present water supply can be more than doubled by adding to present nearby sources, and more economically than by going to the Sierras....

THE HETCH-HETCHY STEAM ROLLER

... The local strength behind the city's rushline is not difficult to understand when one realizes that the [Raker] bill involves contracts amounting to $120,000,000, with opportunities of "honest graft." For months, the project has been presented to Congress with persistence and serious misrepresentation. Urged first as a measure of humanity, it has been shown to be a sordid scheme to obtain electric power. Urged as providing the only available source, it is confronted by the conclusive statement of the Board of Army Engineers that "there are several sources of water supply" and that "the determining factor is one of cost." Urged on the ground that it cannot injure Hetch-Hetchy because that valley is inaccessible and altogether negligible, it is shown by Mr. Long, the city's attorney and advocate, that nine miles of roadway would make it accessible, and by Mr. Pinchot's confession that it is "one of the great wonders of the world." Its altogether reputable official sponsors are Secretary Lane, who ten years ago as attorney of San Francisco became an advocate of the project, and Secretaries Houston and Garrison, who half-heartedly join in approval, besides three bureau heads who have the temerity to agree with their chiefs. In Congress the bill finds strong support in the two Public Lands Committees, composed as they are preponderatingly [sic] of trans-Mississippians, who have a natural and proper bias in favor of the local use of the forest reserves, and who apply this theory illogically to the national parks.

The act creating Yosemite National Park sets forth the importance and duty of reserving these wonders "in their original state," and the world has a moral right to demand that this purpose shall be adhered to. The "beautiful lake" theory deceives nobody. An artificial lake and dam are not a substitute for the unique beauty of the valley. Senators cannot transfer to a committee the grave responsibility that rests upon them.

Source: New York Times, July 12, 1913; October 2, 1913.

Document 8.5   Debate on the Raker Bill, 1913

The era's most controversial environmental issue culminated in 1913 with the passage of the Raker Act, which granted federal approval for the flooding of a remote corner of federally owned land in California's Yosemite National Park to build the Hetch-Hetchy dam. Debate on the bill in the House of Representatives began in the Committee on Public Lands. Proponents, led by former San Francisco mayor James Phelan and Gifford Pinchot, the chief architect of America's conservation policy, argued that the material needs of San Francisco's citizens should take precedence over the aesthetic value of Yosemite as a pristine wilderness. In the end, Congress chose the utilitarian demands of San Francisco over the preservation of scenic beauty, voting 43–25 (with twenty-nine abstentions) to allow the Hetch-Hetchy dam to go forward.

Mr. PINCHOT: . . . So we come now face to face with the perfectly clean question of what is the best use to which this water that flows out of the Sierras can be put. As we all know, there is no use of water that is higher than the domestic use. Then, if there is, as the engineers tell us, no other source of supply that is anything like so reasonably available as this one; if this is the best, and, within reasonable limits of cost, the only means of supplying San Francisco with water, we come straight to the question of whether the advantage of leaving this valley in a state of nature is greater than the advantage of using it for the benefit of the city of San Francisco.

Now, the fundamental principle of the whole conservation policy is that of use, to take every part of the land and its resources and put it to that use in which it will best serve the most people, and I think there can be no question at all but that in this case we have an instance in which all weighty considerations demand the passage of the bill. There are, of course, a very large number of incidental changes that will arise after the passage of the bill. The construction of roads, trails, and telephone systems which will follow the passage of this bill will be a very important help in the park and forest reserves. The national forest telephone system and the roads and trails to which this bill will lead will form an important additional help in fighting fire in the forest reserves. As has already been set forth by the two Secretaries, the presence of these additional means of communication will mean that the national forest and the national park will be visited by very large numbers of people who cannot visit them now. I think that the men who assert that it is better to leave a piece of natural scenery in its natural condition have rather the better of the argument, and I believe if we had nothing else to consider than the delight of the few men and women who would yearly go into the Hetch-Hetchy Valley, then it should be left in its natural condition. But the considerations on the other side of the question to my mind are simply overwhelming, and so much so that I have never been able to see that there was any reasonable argument against the use of this water supply by the city of San Francisco. . . .

Mr. RAKER: [California Congressman] Taking the scenic beauty of the park as it now stands, and the fact that the valley is sometimes swamped along in June and July, is it not a fact that if a beautiful dam is put there, as is con-templated, and as the picture is given by the engineers, with the roads con-templated around the reservoir and with other trails, it will be more beautiful than it is now, and give more opportunity for the use of the park? . . .

Mr. PINCHOT: You might say from the standpoint of enjoyment of beauty and the greatest good to the greatest number, they will be conserved by the passage of this bill, and there will be a great deal more use of the beauty of the park than there is now.

Mr. RAKER: Have you seen Mr. John Muir's criticism of the bill? You know him?

Mr. PINCHOT: Yes, sir; I know him very well. He is an old and a very good friend of mine. I have never been able to agree with him in his attitude toward the Sierras for the reason that my point of view has never appealed to him at all. When I became Forester and denied the right to exclude sheep and cows from the Sierras, Mr. Muir thought I had made a great mistake, because I allowed the use by an acquired right of a large number of people to interfere with what would have been the utmost beauty of the forest. In this case I think he has unduly given away to beauty as against use. . . .

Mr. PHELAN: . . . I do not wish to delay the committee a moment longer than is necessary, so I will only emphasize the fact that the needs of San Francisco are pressing and urgent. . . .

A large number of our population has been lost to Oakland, Alameda, and Berkeley, by reason of the fact that we have never had adequate facilities either of transportation or of water supply. . . .

As Californians, we rather resent gentlemen from different parts of the country outside of California telling us that we are invading the beautiful natural resources of the State or in any way marring or detracting from them. We have a greater pride than they in the beauties of California, in the valleys, in the big trees, in the rivers, and in the high mountains. . . .

All of this is of tremendous pride, and even for a water supply we would not injure the great resources which have made our State the playground of the world. By constructing a dam at this very narrow gorge in the Hetch-Hetchy Valley, about 700 feet across, we create, not a reservoir, but a lake . . . so, coming upon it, it will look like an emerald gem in the mountains; and one of the few things in which California is deficient, especially in the Sierras, is lakes, and in this way we will contribute, in a large measure, to the scenic grandeur and beauty of California. I suppose nature lovers, suspecting a dam there not made by the Creator, will think it of no value, in their estimation, but I submit, man can imitate the Creator—a worthy exemplar. . . .

Mr. LA FOLLETTE: . . . I am looking at the matter from the broad viewpoint of the people. Not one hundredth of 1 per cent of the people of the United States will ever go in there. On the other hand, if one-fiftieth or a hundredth part of the people of the United States, or even of California, were to go in there, it would be a vast camp ground instead of a thing of beauty. That change would take place within a year. For that reason, looking at it from a practical viewpoint, I do not believe the people of the United States care very much whether it is kept for a playground or not, when in all probability only one hundredth of 1 percent of the people of the country would ever go in there.

If I had my way about it, they would build the dam immediately as high as they could, to store every gallon of water flowing there. . . . I can not believe that the flooding of 1,500 acres will destroy all that vast area of scenery. I think if they go in there to see it and if anything is said derogatory to the dam, their attention should be called to the fact that the water is required for the irrigation of thousands of acres of land, and is also required to meet the domestic and economic needs of a great city, and when they come to realize that I should think their aesthetic taste could stand a little shock. . . .

Mr. WHITMAN: You are asked to consider this park as it is at present, with almost nobody using it. Very little attention has been given to what may happen to this park by the year 2000. On the other hand, the city desires to focus your attention to the year 2000 for its water supply. They are getting along and can get along perfectly comfortably for a good many years for their local supply, but it is the year 2000 they want you to look to. If you look to the year 2000 in one way, I pray you to look to it in the other. What will that park be and what will the use of it be to the American public, winter and summer, in the year 2000? . . .

I have tried to put this thing on a practical ground, which will appeal to the American citizen, and I do not want to add anything as to nature. But I have a letter here addressed to the chairman of this committee from Robert Underwood Johnson, who was, with Mr. John Muir, the original cause of the establishment of this park. . . . He says:

. . . There never was a time when there was a more urgent necessity for our country to uphold its best ideals and its truest welfare against shortsighted opportunism and purely commercial and local interests. The history of the country presents a thousand examples of the sacrifice of the good of all to the advantage of a part, and the waste of national resources at the dictation of selfish parties under specious pretexts. . . .

What is at stake is not merely the destruction of a single valley, one of the most wonderful works of the Creator, but the fundamental principle of conservation. Let it be established that these great parks and forests are to be held at the whim or advantage of local interests and sooner or later they must all be given up. One has only to look about to see the rampant materialism of the day. It can only be overcome by a constant regard for ideas and for the good of the whole country now and hereafter. The very sneers with which this type of argument is received are a proof of the need of altruism and imagination in dealing with the subject....

The opponents . . . say if there were no other source of good and abundant water for the city they would willingly sacrifice the valley to the lives and the health of its citizens. . . . It has not been demonstrated that Hetch-Hetchy is the only available source, but only that it might be the cheapest. . . . [While] we are willing to die for the lives or the health of the citizens of San Francisco, we are not willing to die for their pockets. . . .

I am aware that in certain quarters one who contends for the practical value of natural beauty is considered a "crank," and yet the love of beauty is the most dominant trait in mankind. The moment anyone of intelligence gets enough to satisfy the primal needs of the physical man, he begins to plan for something beautiful—house, grounds, or a view of nature. Could this be capitalized in dollars, could some alchemy reveal its value, we should not hear materialists deriding lovers of nature, with any effect upon legislators. Without this touch of idealism, this sense of beauty, life could only be a race for the trough. . . .

I have the honor to remain, respectfully yours,
Robert Underwood Johnson

Source: House Committee on the Public Lands, *Hetch-Hetchy Dam Site*, 63rd Cong., 1st sess., 25–28 June 1913; 7 July 1913 (Washington, DC: Government Printing Office, 1913), pp. 25–29, 165–66, 213–14, 235–38.

NOTES

1. John Muir, "The Tuolumne Yosemite in Danger," *Outlook* 87 (1907): 488.

2. Gifford Pinchot to President Theodore Roosevelt, October 11, 1907, in "Water Supply for San Francisco," Record Group 95 (United States Forest Service), National Archives, Washington, DC; quoted in Roderick Nash, *Wilderness and the American Mind*, 3rd ed. (New Haven: Yale University Press, 1982), p. 164.

3. U.S. Congress, House of Representatives, Committee on the Public Lands, *Hearings on San Francisco and the Hetchy-Hetchy Reservoir*, 60th Cong., 2nd sess., January 9, 12, 20, 21, 1909, p. 179; quoted in Nash, *Wilderness and the American Mind*, p. 167.

ANNOTATED BIBLIOGRAPHY

Brechin, Gary A. *Imperial San Francisco: Urban Power, Earthly Ruin*. Berkeley: University of California Press, 2001. The taking of Hetch-Hetchy Valley by the city is presented convincingly as part of the long-standing pattern of rampant, egregious, often ruinous exploitation of northern California resources driven by San Francisco–based capitalists.

Cohen, Michael P. *The Pathless Way: John Muir and the American Wilderness*. Madison: University of Wisconsin Press, 1984. Biography that establishes Muir's vision, writings, and battle to save the Hetch-Hetchy Valley within the larger context of the emerging wilderness and conservation movements.

Fox, Stephen. *The American Conservation Movement: John Muir and His Legacy*. Madison: University of Wisconsin Press, 1986. Highlights the integral role of Muir as the first true environmentalist of the modern era.

Hundley, Norris, Jr. *The Great Thirst: Californians and Water—A History*. Rev. ed. Berkeley: University of California Press, 2001. The history of California's voracious, seemingly insatiable quest for water and the fight for the Hetch-Hetchy Valley is offered as an important, telling episode of that larger story.

Jones, Holway. *John Muir and the Sierra Club: The Battle for Yosemite*. San Francisco: Sierra Club Books, 1965. Though eclipsed by Righter's study, this remains valuable for its insights into the formation of Sierra Club founder John Muir's early leadership.

Nash, Roderick. *Wilderness and the American Mind*. 4th ed. New Haven: Yale University Press, 2001. Nash's acclaimed study of the transformation of wilderness in American culture from a feared place to one of virtue treats Hetch-Hetchy as a critical turning point in that history.

Righter, Robert W. *The Battle over Hetch-Hetchy: America's Most Controversial Dam and the Birth of Modern Environmentalism*. New York: Oxford University Press, 2005. With meticulous research and fresh analysis, Righter argues that the presentation of Hetch-Hetchy as simply a battle between preservationists who would keep the valley sacrosanct and business interests who would exploit it is overly simplistic.

Runte, Alfred. *Yosemite: The Embattled Wilderness*. 3rd ed. Lincoln, NE: Bison Books, 1997. Explores the larger questions that emerged from America's first wilderness debate, including the central issue of whether places like Hetch-Hetchy would be safe from development if they were found to have utilitarian value, and asks were places like Hetch-Hetchy Valley of any public good if relatively few people went there.

Wolfe, Linnie Marsh. *Son of the Wilderness: The Life of John Muir*. 1945. Reprint, Madison: University of Wisconsin Press, 1978. This Pulitzer Prize–winning volume remains a superior biographical portrait of John Muir.

9

Progressive Women and "Municipal Housekeeping": Caroline Bartlett Crane's Fight for Improved Meat Inspection

> There is an ancient idea ... That woman's sphere lies strictly within the precincts of the home; that the whole duty of woman is comprised in the operations of housekeeping. . . . The germ-laden dust from dirty streets invades our homes; impure water, infected milk, diseased beef, bring poison to the best appointed family board; . . . and to all suggestion, polite or otherwise, that [women] should mind their own business and keep in their own sphere, they are gaining courage to answer after the manner of one woman who, when reproached in this fashion for pernicious activity in the interests of pure milk, replied: "Sir, I would have you understand that woman's sphere extends not only outside of the home but inside of the baby."
>
> —Caroline Bartlett Crane, 1908[1]

The intellectual and legislative legacy of Theodore Roosevelt and Gifford Pinchot dominate most histories of the conservation movement's ascendancy during the Progressive Era. These towering figures led a generation of (mostly) men who delivered policies designed to bring more prudent management and preservation of the nation's public lands and resources, a story geographically centered in the rural and remote West. Only recently emerging is the history of Progressive Era middle-class women who directed their energies closer to home—toward reform of America's urban industrial environment. From small and midsized towns to large cities, on issues ranging from refuse management to the need for more playgrounds to the occupational health of industrial workers, women led the way in educating citizens and agitating public officials toward improving the public health and community welfare of Americans. Characterized then as "municipal housekeeping," the urban environmental stewardship cultivated by women of this era extended and redefined their traditional duties and responsibilities as keepers of home and family. Pushing the boundaries of late-Victorian propriety, they recast their role as guardians of domesticity and societal virtues. With deep conviction they assumed the charge to restore and protect a degraded urban-industrial environment, viewing it as central to the moral responsibilities of women in the modern age. Streets, neighborhoods, and factories far beyond their doors became realms of activity for women who organized to improve the well-being of their own children and of society at large.

Born into a rural-agricultural world, this generation of women came of age during the period of America's rapid urban-industrialization, and bravely proceeded to confront some of its worst abuses. Their practical idealism had roots in an earlier period; in 1851 Frederick Law Olmsted envisioned New York City's Central Park in part as a place of beauty that would cultivate moral and civic virtues among the city's increasingly lower-class workforce and ameliorate the worst effects of an already deteriorating urban environment for its middle- and upper-class denizens. Led by (male) landscape architects and the first generation of professional urban planners, women in the City Beautiful movement of the 1890s extended Olmsted's vision. Urban reformers, male and female, believed that parks, landscaped boulevards, Beaux-Arts architectural grandeur, and open green space could serve to beautify and redeem the urban environment, as well as foster social control and order. Beauty was an intrinsic good and a means to more practical goals that seemed urgent amid the class warfare of that decade and the political convulsions it generated.

Although women came to accept the challenge of reforming the urban environment with some of those same goals in mind, important differences distinguished their work. Fear of social disorder and political chaos motivated much of the City Beautiful movement, whose advocates lived well beyond such places as the "typhoid ward" of New York City's Lower East Side and Chicago's Packingtown. By contrast, women reformers, many of whom lived among the populations they cared for, were generally motivated by a sense of moral outrage, an incredulous disbelief that in a society of such wealth, profit, and prosperity, humans could be forced to live in their own filth. Leaders of the movement generally disavowed the Social Darwinism of the elite who believed that immigrant populations were fated by their racial-ethnic makeup to live in squalor, holding instead that remedying poor living conditions provided an essential step to a decent life. The Ladies Health Protective Association in New York City believed that reforming the city's abysmal system of refuse management and street sweeping was one means to improving the lives of the city's teeming immigrant population.

Central to the women's urban reform movement was the opening of Hull House in Chicago in 1889. Founded by Jane Addams, Hull House established the moral tone and practical agenda of the settlement house movement, served as an incubator for social reform and activism, and characterized the spirit of this generation of women. Although mostly associated with the charitable work of assisting immigrants with daily material needs and assimilating them into American life with English language classes, Hull House and subsequent settlement houses in Chicago became laboratories and clearing houses for surveying and studying the severe environmental problems that permeated the industrial communities of the city, particularly the persistent and occasionally fatal issue of water pollution. Settlement house leaders including Addams, Mary McDowell, and Alice Hamilton challenged local and state politicians to confront such issues that produced staggering rates of typhoid and other diseases.

Also of great importance nationally was the work of the General Federation of Women's Clubs. Established in 1890, the federation organized on an array of environmental issues from the killing of birds that adorned women's hats to urban parks and playgrounds. Their committees on waterways, rivers, and harbors lobbied for action both locally and on the national level to clean the nation's drinking water supply. Women saw, perhaps more clearly and earlier than any other urban constituency, the basic connection between clean water and human health; their efforts to educate the public and challenge often corrupt local power structures on the issue helped promote the emergence of a professional class of technical experts and engineers who began designing modern sewage treatment and water delivery systems for the nation's cities.

Caroline Bartlett Crane exemplifies this generation of Progressive women. "Carrie" Bartlett was born in Hudson, Wisconsin, in 1858. This, as one of her biographers has noted, was fortuitous for her public life ahead. In the Midwest, societal conventions for women were less rigid and possibilities more expansive.[2] In addition, her parents encouraged her independent spirit, though they hoped she would outgrow a teenage desire to become a Unitarian minister. She did not. Her liberal arts program at Carthage College (1876–1879) cultivated her interest in combining a spiritual life with the pragmatic work of making the world a better, more humane place.

Not surprisingly, there were few such openings in 1879. Crane thus served a brief stint in the traditional female occupation of teaching. Its strictures could not contain her passion to make a difference in the world. She then ventured into journalism, a profession that stood at the center of the broad movement for societal reform that came to be called Progressivism. As an assistant city editor of a newspaper in Oshkosh, Wisconsin, she interviewed some of the most prominent figures of the period, including the physician, minister, and suffrage leader Dr. Anna Howard Shaw. Shaw helped to convert the journalist to the suffrage cause, alerted her to links between private health and public welfare, and reawakened her call to the ministry.

Bartlett commenced theological training at the progressive Iowa Unitarian Conference and became an ordained minister in 1889. Assigned to the First Unitarian Church of Kalamazoo, Michigan, Reverend Bartlett over the next decade transformed what had been a moribund congregation into a vibrant churchly agent of social change. She was strongly influenced by the Social Gospel movement of the time that envisioned the church as a vehicle for improving the lives of the poor and the discontented who filled American cities. To deepen her understanding, she traveled to Europe where such intellectual and social change movements were more advanced and returned to school for sociology course work. She launched her renamed "People's Church" into the work of social improvement, initiating classes for girls and boys in a variety of subjects not covered in the public schools (some of which were so successful they were added to the local school curriculum).

Her marriage to Dr. Warren Augustus Crane in 1896 did not slow her down. Indeed, her new life motivated her to enroll in the class in household sciences offered at her church, an experience that only deepened her interest in social issues. From that point forward, the production, processing, and preparation of food became a central passion in her life and a subject of intense study. It led her to related matters of water purity, waste disposal, and the broader subject of public health. She plunged herself into a series of Unity Club research projects entitled "The Sociology of Kalamazoo." Reverend Crane led her congregants to investigate the whole of Kalamazoo's social environment: food supply, waste and sewage disposal, school sanitation, water supply, police and fire protection, recreation, charities, and sanitation in the public schools. With support from other prominent women of the city, Crane exposed the city's most blighted areas through illustrated lectures, sparking enough indignation and embarrassment that the mayor called for a citywide cleanup (which became an annual event). In 1904 she founded the Women's Civic Improvement League of Kalamazoo, whose first task was to lead a campaign to reform the city's street-cleaning methods. The league successfully convinced officials to adopt the methods of New York City, devised by the well-known sanitary engineer Colonel George Waring—and supported by the very active Ladies Health Protective Association.

Through these experiences, Crane acquired the skills and knowledge to launch a career as a municipal sanitarian. She articulated her clear vision of women's rightful role and responsibility for "public housekeeping" early on, which epitomized the larger vision of many women reformers of the period:

> We certainly should keep our city—that is to say, our common house—clean. The floor should be clean. The air should be clean. The individual houses and premises, the schools, the places of public assembly, the places of trade, the factories, the places where foods are prepared, sold, or served, should be clean. There should be sanitary collection and disposal of all the wastes that inevitably accumulate wherever human beings have a home. . . .[3]

In an attempt to translate this vision into public policy, Crane resigned her ministry in 1898 and began charting a career for herself as a pioneering expert in municipal sanitation. For much of the next decade and a half, she traveled to more than fifty cities from New York to Kentucky, conducting municipal surveys on a wide range of issues. Upon the invitation of community organizations and public officials (she would not visit a city without assurances that a broad segment of leadership wanted her there), Crane would send a questionnaire ahead of her visit pertaining to the wide range of issues she was to survey, including waste and refuse disposal methods, water supply, street construction, form of government, smoke-abatement programs, parks and playgrounds, and the nature of the public-school system. On the final day of her visit she delivered a public address on her findings and subsequently issued a detailed final report full of both praise for positive aspects of broadly defined public health policies, as well as her recommendations for change. Though success was far from universal, Crane's consultative visits did result in an impressive number of civic improvements: the dingy mining camp of Calumet,

Illinois, according to a public official there, had been transformed into a beautifully clean city within one year after Crane's visit; her survey of Uniontown, Pennsylvania, resulted in an investigation by the state board of health and subsequent improvements of a dangerously contaminated water supply; in the months following Crane's investigation of the state of Kentucky, the legislature there passed statute after statute aimed at remedying the environmental degradation of many towns and cities.

One issue that drew Crane's attention from the beginning of her career in public health was the condition of the local food and meat supply. She investigated where the meat came from, how butchers handled it, how and whether any animals suspected of being diseased might be disposed of, and the condition of the local slaughterhouses. This interest was derived from her experience in Kalamazoo. In 1902 Crane organized a series of meetings on public health topics for the Michigan State Federation of Women's Clubs. When the state board of health official scheduled to speak on the condition of the milk and meat supply canceled out, Crane resolved to probe the issue herself. She gathered a group of prominent women and men and led an unannounced tour of local slaughterhouses. What they found shocked the conscience and turned stomachs. Every surface was caked with "blood, grime, grease, hair, mold, and other quite unmentionable filth," she wrote. "In one pen we saw trampled into the mud the decomposing body of a very small calf, quite too young, I think, to have been born, and inevitably suggesting the previous slaughter of a pregnant animal." Most horrifying was that diseased carcasses were shipped along with healthy animals to city butchers.[4]

Foreshadowing the equally gruesome accounts soon to be offered by Upton Sinclair's *The Jungle*, Crane's report stunned Kalamazoo. Alarmed city officials were nonetheless powerless to do anything about such conditions since the slaughterhouses lay outside city limits, nor could they even regulate the quality of meat sold in the city. Undaunted, Crane appealed to the state, where the board of health encouraged her to recommend a statewide legislative solution. After studying every local, state, national, and international statute and regulation she could find pertaining to the meat industry, Crane drafted a bill empowering local municipalities to establish meat inspection laws. She testified on behalf of the bill and lobbied fiercely for its passage. Although Crane regretted its voluntary provisions, it was, she said, better than nothing.

The next few years saw the reformer focused on her municipal survey work. Meanwhile, President Theodore Roosevelt and a reform-minded Congress responded to public outcry over revelations in the meat-packing industry contained in *The Jungle* and passed the Meat Inspection Act of 1906. As with even the best laws, the federal statute's effectiveness depended upon the rigor of enforcement. In 1906 Florence Kelley of the National Consumers' League appointed Crane to a committee to monitor the enforcement of the new pure food and meat inspection laws. Crane's oversight found the administration of meat regulation by the U.S. Department of Agriculture (USDA) lacking. Employing journalistic skills acquired earlier in her career, she interviewed countless officials and employees of the packinghouses and obtained from inside the industry copies of USDA regulations issued surreptitiously to the packers that seemed to defy the law's intent to protect American consumers from unsafe meat products. Although USDA officials vigorously disputed Crane's charges, many of the "secret" regulations stipulated that carcasses "diseased and unfit for human food" that had been rightly rejected by foreign inspectors were to be instead "passed" and sent to American markets. Crane believed that discrepancies between the secret and published rules governing the act's enforcement were solely at the behest of the meat packers who had fought regulation of their industry from the start.

Despite support from other noted public health experts, Crane's efforts to launch an investigation of the department's actions stalled in 1909. A critically important attempt to have the American Public Health Association endorse her call for an investigation failed when a few high-ranking officials of that body (who Crane believed were beholden to interests in the packing industry) orchestrated a suspicious rejection of her argument by the organization. Repeated efforts to publish her findings in popular magazines failed—Crane believed, out of publishers' fears of the industry. A final effort to hold the department accountable came in 1912 when U.S. Representative John Nelson of Wisconsin agreed to hold a hearing on the issue. In a harbinger of the attack on Rachel Carson decades later, the USDA waged a preemptive frontal assault on congressmen and, in the media, on Crane's credibility and integrity. Attacking her motives and credentials, the department—through its pugnacious solicitor, George McCabe—suggested that she was warring against the department to advance her own interests and that USDA inspectors were honest public servants whose credibility was beyond reproach. Although other noted experts in the field supported Crane's contention of lax enforcement by the department, the hearing led to no meaningful reform.

Crane despaired at what could only be perceived as a failure to achieve tougher enforcement of meat inspection. It is worth noting that Upton Sinclair's book also failed at its author's intended central purpose, which was not to galvanize the public behind a meat inspection law, but rather to reform the working conditions of slaughterhouse employees.

Moreover, this episode does not diminish the legacy of a woman who devoted the better part of her life to seeking improvements in public health. Far beyond the specific changes her sanitary surveys produced in dozens of American cities were the more fundamental contributions she and thousands of other middle-class women of her generation made toward both revitalizing democracy and embracing a more comprehensive view of what came to be called in another generation *environmental protection*. Progressive-Era women reformers recognized the need for persistent citizen engagement and responsible government acting in the public interest to protect and restore the urban, industrial environment where modern Americans worked, lived, played, and consumed. It is significant that in 1909 Ellen Swallow Richards (the first female graduate of the Massachusetts Institute of Technology) became the first American scientist formally to apply the word *ecology* to an understanding of the human relationship with nature, doing so in her study of the "unsanitary" conditions of the industrial urban environment.

This underscores the point that women urban reformers were in some ways very much *of* their time even as they were far in front of it. Their work came at a time of restricted suffrage and a culture of assumed male supremacy, moving women's voices to the center of discussions on a wide range of policy matters and audaciously advancing the cause of women's political liberty. Through their own activism in civic affairs, they promoted a more activist—and invariably, larger—government that would be more honest and responsive to the needs of the majority of its citizens. Moreover, they presaged by more than half a century the age of ecology that urgently called for renewed attention to menacing, all-surrounding threats to public health and a more holistic understanding of our commonly shared urban environment.

One might argue, finally, that in the early twenty-first century the legacy of Caroline Bartlett Crane is carried forward in the work of scientists and environmentalists who rail against the dangers to human health and the environment posed by the modern beef industry. They warn of the unknown effects of eating cattle shot full of hormones and antibiotics and the environmental costs of draining precious western water, punishing degraded grassland to feed those animals, and raising cattle in industrial feedlots, effluent from which has on occasion spilled over and poisoned rivers and watersheds. And on the other side of this divide: a beef packing industry highly concentrated in the hands of a few corporations (and once again the most dangerous occupation in America) determined as they were a century ago to maintain the status quo.

DOCUMENTS

Document 9.1   **Caroline Bartlett Crane Calls for Stronger Meat
                      Inspection in Michigan, 1904**

*After six years of study and personal surveys of slaughterhouses,
Caroline Bartlett Crane had become a national expert on the safety
of the nation's food supply. Her local involvement in Kalamazoo,
Michigan, had led in 1903 to draft local and state laws that allowed
local municipalities to inspect and regulate slaughterhouses and meat
markets. In January 1904, she organized a program of expert speakers
for the Michigan State Board of Health on the issue of meat inspection.
The following excerpts from her address that evening make the case
for still stronger measures mandating inspection and regulation at the
local level. Her citing of experts—in this case, local (and male) health
authorities from around the country—would set an example for future
generations of community and environmental activists seeking to
make their case more credible to the public.*

... What protection have we, as residents of the State of Michigan, from the
dangers tonight described and illustrated? Do the dairy and pure food laws of
our State give us any protection? No....

Does the new law, passed by the State Legislature last winter, give us
any protection? It is a local option law. It gives to all cities and villages in
Michigan enlarged liberties and specified powers ... of protecting themselves, by
means of local meat inspection ordinances, such as I am here tonight to urge the
adoption of in your several communities. But unless cities and villages do avail
themselves of this enlarged liberty and these specific powers, their case is in no
wise different from what it was before the new law was passed....

This fact is clear: That the only means at hand for the protection of the great
mass of the people of Michigan from the dangers of diseased meat is by in-
stituting thorough inspection in our several local communities. This is the way
it has been done in other States.... In ... Massachusetts, the example set by
Boston thirty-three years ago, and gradually spreading to other cities, has so
educated the people that in 1901 a compulsory state law was passed requiring
the rigid ante-mortem and post-mortem examination of all animals slaughtered
for food anywhere in the [state]. The interstate commerce laws guarantee a
similar inspection of any meat coming from any other State; and thus the
citizens of Massachusetts are now fully protected....

This is no theory of mine.... It is a fact, demonstrated over and over
again ... in the words of Doctor D. E. Salmon, Chief of the Bureau of Animal
Husbandry on the United States.... "Since the federal inspection has been established for meat shipment in the interstate trade, the tendency is to send
known diseased animals to the slaughterhouses which kill for the local trade,

and have little, if any, inspection." "And," he adds, "unquestionably, many badly diseased animals get upon the market and are eaten."...

And not only do diseased and dead and new-born animals come to the local slaughterhouses in abnormal numbers. There are other abominations.... Dr. Guy L. Kiefer, the [Detroit] Health Officer, states...: "We catch butchers every now and then, selling 'slunts' or unborn calves."...

All slaughtering should be done in sanitary slaughterhouses, under the eye of a competent inspector. Every animal and carcass, or part thereof, found diseased in a manner to render it unfit for human food, should be condemned and destroyed; and all wholesome meats should be officially stamped or branded as such, and only those stamped or branded should be allowed to be sold. **This is meat inspection. Nothing short of this is meat inspection; because nothing short of this gives the consumer the protection he has a right to suppose he enjoys** [emphasis Crane's]... This is the standard of the United States government for all its export and interstate trade. It is the standard established by the more progressive cities of America, large and small. It is the standard in all the leading countries of Europe. Is disease and filth-contaminated meat less harmful to us than to other people? Are we less concerned than others with questions of wholesomeness and decency as affecting our food supply?...

Source: Rev. Caroline Bartlett Crane, "The Argument for Local Meat Inspection." Address at the Seventh General Conference of Health Officials in Michigan, Ann Arbor, January 7, 1904, pp. 1–3, 7. From the Papers of Caroline Bartlett Crane, courtesy Western Michigan University Library.

| Document 9.2 | **Department of Agriculture Solicitor Defends Regulation of Meatpacking Industry and Attacks Caroline Bartlett Crane, 1912** |

The Meat Inspection Act of 1906 had promised to fully ensure the safety of American consumers by establishing a system of inspection of slaughterhouses and meat packers and federal regulation of meat products shipped through interstate commerce. Caroline Bartlett Crane subsequently became one of a number of experts on the issue who monitored and increasingly criticized the Department of Agriculture's enforcement of the law. In 1912 that critique (illustrated in Document 9.3) led to the introduction in the U.S. House of Representatives of the Nelson Resolution that called for a full investigation of the department and its alleged complicity with the meat-packing industry. Before the Nelson investigation could begin, Solicitor George McCabe of the Department of Agriculture launched a preemptive attack on the premises of the resolution and upon Crane personally, impugning her professional integrity and questioning her credibility. McCabe employs the same tactic against Dr. Albert Leffingwell, whose 1910 book confirmed and extended much of what

Crane and other public health officials around the country had been saying about the enforcement of the law.

... The resolution contains 15 preliminary statements or "whereas" clauses, which are alleged statements of fact adduced to show the necessity for an investigation. The statements ... are, for the most part, either absolutely false or are mixtures of half truths with falsehood skillfully blended, producing a semblance of truth and creating erroneous impressions.... The charges are drawn in the main from two sources.

(1) Mrs. Caroline Bartlett Crane, who is now under contract to work for the National Cash Register Co., of Dayton, Ohio, at a compensation of $100 per day. Mrs. Crane *has been "investigating"* the meat-inspection service for some years and it would be interesting to learn *who is paying her for the work.* She has traveled extensively and well and the expense connected therewith has been large. *Who has stood the expense?*

Mrs. Crane presented similar charges to the American Public Health Association at [their] Richmond meeting ... in October, 1909. She appeared before the executive committee of that association and submitted documents, etc., but the ... committee found that "neither these documents nor her statements ... substantiate these charges," and recommended that the motion for an investigation be laid upon the table....

(2) Dr. Albert Leffingwell, of ... New York, in 1910 published a book on American meat. The book was published in England and is an appeal to the English workingman not to eat American meat. It would be interesting to know under what financial arrangement Dr. Leffingwell's book was published.... The book abounds in misstatements of fact....

THE "WHEREAS" CLAUSES IN THE RESOLUTION

... (2) Clause 4 reads:

> Whereas the Secretary of Agriculture ... by published regulations and other means, have specifically authorized nullifications of both the letter and intent of the meat-inspection act, contrary to the public health and in the interests of the meat packers.

This is absolutely false.... The regulations have the approval of not only the animal pathologist of the Department of Agriculture, but are in accord with the published opinions of the leading meat-inspection authorities of the world. The interest of the meat packers has never been considered where a question of public health or of the enforcement of the provisions of the law was involved....

(3) Clause 5 reads:

> Whereas the authorized nullifications are such that, even under faithful performance by inspectors of their prescribed duties, the Federal stamp, "U.S. Inspected and Passed," cannot safely be taken as a guarantee that the meats ... are in accord with the requirements of the meat-inspection act.

This is false. If the inspectors follow the regulations and their instructions, they pass only meat which is sound, healthful, wholesome, and fit for human food...This does not mean that if a sheep has the snuffles, or if a steer has the warbles, the meat of the animal is condemned. It means that...if the disease be slight and of such a character that the fitness of the meat for food is not affected, then, of course, the sound meat is passed. If the theory advanced by certain agitators...who have little or no scientific knowledge of the subject, had prevailed,... *there would have been taken from the food supply of the country more than 6,000,000 carcasses the meat of which was perfectly safe, wholesome food.* [emphasis original].... Would not this have had a tremendous effect upon the price of meat, which is already too high for the pocketbook of the average man, and would not the farmer who produced these food animals have been robbed,...?

(8) Clause 11 reads:

> Whereas a lowering of standards and practices of inspection has been brought about by the direct and demonstrable influence of packers....

There has been no lowering of standards and practices of inspection due to the influence of the American Meat Packers Association. This is an utterly unwarranted and outrageous libel upon the officials of the Department of Agriculture....

The Department of Agriculture in its administration of the meat-inspection law has committed no offenses endangering the health of consumers of packing-house products. On the contrary, all of the meat which the inspectors of the [department's] Bureau of Animal Husbandry have marked "Inspected and passed" has been sound, healthful, wholesome, and fit for human food. The injury to the faith and confidence of foreign nations in American meat is not wrought by the Department of Agriculture, but, on the contrary, is brought about by attacks made, not only by mercenary interests, but in some cases by well-meaning but uninformed people who have not taken the trouble to investigate the plausible but false statements of professional agitators....

Source: U.S. Department of Agriculture, Office of the Secretary, "House Resolution 512. A Discussion of the [Nelson] Resolution from the Standpoint of the United States Department of Agriculture" (Washington, DC: U.S. Department of Agriculture, 1912), pp. 1–10.

Document 9.3   **U.S. House Rules Committee Hearing on the "McCabe Circular" and Crane's Charges Against the Department of Agriculture**

George McCabe's circular proved to be the opening salvo of a broad assault waged in the press by the Department of Agriculture against Crane, Representative Nelson, and others who supported the need for

*an investigation of the department's meat-inspection practices. In a
hearing before the U.S. House Rules Committee, Nelson explains the
rationale for his resolution and charges the department with abusing
its charge to protect the public interest by launching its tirade.
Caroline Bartlett Crane also appeared before the committee to defend
her motives and respond to McCabe's charges.*

... Some months ago my attention was directed to the lax enforcement, putting it
mildly, of the meat-inspection law, by a lady of the highest standing in this country.
She is considered by those who know of her work, and I merely quote from
authority, one of "the great women of the world." She came to me recommended
by the wife of a United States Senator.... From facts furnished to me, at first by her
and since by others, I am convinced that the $3,000,000 that is appropriated an-
nually ... [to meat inspection] is largely going to waste, because it is paying salaries
to inspectors whose hands are tied, whose efforts to protect public health are
overruled.... Government officials ... are, to say the least, vastly more zealous in
promoting the profits of the packers than in protecting public health....

The day before the time set for the hearings [on the resolution] there appeared Solicitor McCabe's circular. I have it here. It is anonymous. There is no
name signed to it. It is published as "in the office of the Secretary," but not by
the Secretary. It first purports to give the sources of my information. The second
paragraph charges mercenary motives to this distinguished woman who
furnished me with information. It abounds with misstatements, insinuations,
and appeals to prejudice. It says I was imposed upon. This document ... printed
evidently by the Public Printer, was sent to Members of Congress, and to the
newspapers of the country, and otherwise franked [postmarked by the government at public expense]. The frank bears the penalty clause....

Now, I desire to call your attention to Mr. McCabe's tactics at the hearings.
He ... insisted upon the right to cross-examine witnesses. This was extraordinary.... Not content with this privilege, he would continually "butt in," ...
although he was warned by the chairman to desist, and when I announced a
witness, he would arise and make some remark reflecting upon the character
and integrity of that witness....

I have previously referred to the printed circular, but day by day ... garbled
reports ... inclosed in envelopes bearing the government frank, were sent out
by this press bureau to ... newspapers throughout the country. These depart-
mental messengers and this press service are made use of for private purposes
at public expense....

STATEMENT OF MRS. CAROLINE BARTLETT CRANE

... I appreciate the privilege of stating the facts, because ... it is a matter of
considerable importance to me to be cleared from the imputation in this
[McCabe] announcement. In February of this year, I was giving lectures in
New York under the auspices of the League for Political Education.... At
the close of [my last] lecture a gentleman whom I had never seen before ... approached and was introduced as Mr. Patterson, president of the
National Cash Register Co. He said to me, "I want you to come and make a
critical sanitary survey of my plant." I replied that from what I had heard I

did not suppose there was anything wrong about his plant. He said he had heard me give two or three lectures, and began to think perhaps something could be improved for the welfare of his employees. He engaged me then and there at $100 a day.... These are my usual terms for such work and have been my terms for more than a year.... Now that is the sole extent of my connection with the National Cash Register Co.... [May] I say a word about the statement that "Mrs. Crane failed to make good at the American Public Health Association in Richmond"?... the facts are these: On October 20, 1909, I gave an address before the American Public Health Association upon "What is happening to American meat inspection?" I had made known to the president the whole purpose of it in advance, and he had welcomed the disclosures, saying they would help the association to get a national bureau of public health. But during the progress of that address I was interrupted by Dr. Dorset, Chief of the Biochemic Division of the Bureau of Animal Husbandry, with the positive statement that what I said was not true. I had made the statement that the Department of Agriculture issued "service announcements" which materially lowered the published standards of meat inspection and that these documents were meant to be, and were in effect, secret documents, not available to the public. When... other statements of mine were challenged, I challenged these persons to come forward and see my proofs. I had with me a great many documents in proof of all the assertions I had made. It was moved that a committee should be appointed to investigate my charges....

Notwithstanding this... the committee was never appointed.... Instead of doing that, the leaders—and I would dislike very much to use names—but men profoundly and personally interested in suppressing this news—some of them connected with the Department of Agriculture, and others whom I believe to be beholden, for position, to the packing interests in Chicago—used most unfair and dishonorable methods to discredit me before the association and the country....

[The] next afternoon, after the convention had been brought to an abrupt and premature close which cut me off from all opportunity of appeal, I learned that... [the] executive committee—or a part of it, rather—had held a hurried meeting just before the evening public session of the association and had passed... [a resolution declaring that no investigative committee be formed].

So an investigating committee was never appointed; my charges were never investigated; my documents—except one of their own choosing—were never examined; I was lured into a meeting under false pretenses for the purpose of enabling them to pass a false resolution, and the methods employed to make it appear that the association had endorsed that resolution were so extraordinary that I have never held the real association morally responsible for the actions of the few who planned and engineered this most unworthy performance.

And now, after two years and a half, the Department of Agriculture lays hands upon this false resolution passed by the connivance of its own members and friends, to discredit me and my testimony in behalf of the Nelson resolution and the fight for honest and efficient meat inspection in the interests of the consumer....

I do not assume the department is honest, or the intentions are honest. I do assume these experts are honest and intentions are honest; but I say when two of the leading experts are selected after having just given public statements in regard to their opinions on meat inspection standards, and when three others at the time, or had been, in employ of the Department of Agriculture and whose opinions therefore must have been known, and still another is an official in another department . . . that is not the way to get a just and broadly representative opinion of the standards.

Now, this is important, gentlemen, because continually the department entrenches itself behind this "indorsement of the experts"; but the thing which I have proved is that by these secret documents they have continually lowered the standards of the experts, and that the standards of meat inspection to-day are not at all what the experts indorsed; yet they go on representing that they are following the opinion of the experts. . . .

THE CHAIRMAN. Are you in any way representing any interests that conflict with the packing interests of the country?

MRS. CRANE. I am so glad you asked me that question. . . . I will regard myself as under oath in making this statement: That never at any time in my life, in the past or present, have I had the slightest connection or interest, financial or otherwise, such as your question suggests, with any organization or individual in any way, shape, or manner which was or is antagonistic to the packers or the Department of Agriculture. I began to study local meat inspection more than 10 years ago and to try to clean up the dirty little slaughtering houses in the vicinity of my own town first, and then in my own state. I drafted a law, which was put in legal shape in the office of the Attorney General; a general enabling act for any city to control these places even if outside city limits. For years I believed implicitly in the Federal meat inspection, and said to every person, "Eat only inspected meat," and the butchers who did not have Federal inspected meat suspected I was working in the interests of the packers. I do not think they really suspected it, but they suggested it.

Not until the winter of 1905 and 1906 did I have any suspicion that standards of Federal meat inspection were not right. I first gained this suspicion reading the European criticism of our meat inspection and prior to the exposures of "the Jungle," etc., I had begun a study of these Federal meat standards. Then, upon invitation of Mr. [James Bronson] Reynolds [a member of the commission established by President Theodore Roosevelt to investigate the meat packing industry], . . . I continued this study, and this suspicion was enlarged and deepened into a certainty that our Federal meat inspection is vastly more in the interest of the producer—not the farmer, but the middleman, the packer—than of the consumer, and that it is demonstrable that this lowering of standards on the part of the Department of Agriculture had occurred, in many, many instances as the direct result of solicitation of the American Meat packers' Association. I can produce one document after another, in "Service Announcements" and in the packers' official organ, the National Provisioner, to show how the association asked that this and that and the other thing in the meat-inspection regulations should be changed, and then comes as announcement of a modification of the regulation, and then comes a statement in the National Provisioner that "now the thing is satisfactory." . . .

Published regulations say that any organ or part of a carcass which is the seat of a tumor, malignant or benign, shall be condemned, and that the head and tongue of all lumpy-jawed cattle shall be condemned. But secret instructions authorize inspectors to cut out mild ulcers from lumpy-jawed tongues, and pass the tongues.... secret instructions authorize the cutting out of "benign" tumors and passing the affected organs! The same of livers and other organs infested with flukes... though the "Regulations" condemn such affected organs; but they are passed for food by the secret instructions to inspectors.

...My whole contention is that the department is not justly administering this law; that it is being administered largely in the interests of the packers; and that the secret lowering of the standards occurred largely as a result of direct solicitation and pressure by the packers.

The CHAIRMAN. You have stated these things as you were under oath, and you have come here out of a patriotic sense of duty and as a public-spirited citizen?

Mrs. CRANE. I have come here for nothing else—for no other reason in the world. I was most reluctant to come. I have been undertaking to give these facts to the world through magazine publication. I did not want to bring them personally in this way to Congress.

The CHAIRMAN. The reason I asked the question is, I have seen some suggestion, in the press and otherwise, that probably some interest that you might be connected with clashed with the packers' interest, and that that was the origin of this investigation.

Mrs. CRANE. I assure you, Mr. Chairman, upon my word of honor, that I have absolutely no motive in any way except that which I have told you—to try to right a wrong.

Source: "Department Press Agents," *Hearing Before the Committee on Rules.* House of Representatives under H. Res. 545. May 21, 1912 (Washington, DC: Government Printing Office, 1912), pp. 4–5, 7, 18–27.

Document 9.4   Dr. H. W. Wiley Defends Caroline Bartlett Crane, 1912

Crane was not alone in her allegations of malfeasance on the part of the Agriculture Department. Among her defenders was Dr. H. W. Wiley, another expert in the field who had been studying the enforcement of the Meat Packing Act. This is an excerpt from his defense of Caroline Bartlett Crane, which appeared in Good Housekeeping, *a leading women's magazine.*

One of the foremost workers in sanitary science in the United States is Mrs. Caroline Bartlett Crane. She is the author of a number of sanitary inspection reports of various cities, giving her time almost entirely to such work.

Mrs. Crane made an investigation of the meat inspection service of the federal government, and when Representative Nelson of Wisconsin recently introduced in Congress a resolution calling for a thorough investigation of this service, Mrs. Crane made a dignified and extended statement before the committee.... She brought forward documentary evidence in support of her accusation that grave faults were permitted in the inspection service, and all of them in the interest of the packer. She showed, especially, that the provision of the act which requires that all pieces of flesh be stamped was persistently violated, and even that the seals which were placed on cans of meat had been broken....

In addition to Mrs. Crane's testimony, former employees of the inspection service gave evidence confirming, in every particular, the charges which Mrs. Crane presented....

The official attack upon Mrs. Crane sets a record in official documents which has never before been attempted by any department of the government. The Statements made in regard to Mrs. Crane are clearly libelous, and had they been made by a private individual, would be actionable in a court of justice.

Sitting at the table to look after the interests of the Department at the investigation was Solicitor McCabe, puissant genius of endless trouble and investigation, solicitor without Act of Congress, and contrary to the provisions of the [laws]; dominant in the secretary's office and defender of the besmirched faith of the Department on all occasions. In commenting on McCabe's appearance at this preliminary hearing, the editor of one of the Washington dailies made the following remark:

> If the Department has nothing to conceal and nothing to fear from an investigation, it ought not to be protesting against the passage of the resolution. Rather, it should welcome the chance to silence any charges. The activity and zeal of Mr. McCabe are calculated to give a bad impression to the public. Speaking broadly, Mr. McCabe does not enjoy such a fund of public confidence as to prejudice in favor of the side he so enthusiastically espouses in this sort of an affair....

It was shown by Mrs. Crane, from official documents, that the meat inspection was not nearly so rigid as the annual reports of the Bureau of Animal Industry [Husbandry] indicated. Within a very short time after an annual report had stated that the conditions were wholly satisfactory, a secret circular was issued asking inspectors to take a little more care in regard to permitting improper meats to be shipped to the South.

Another secret circular called attention to discrepancies between the number of animals condemned and those sent to the tanks to be worked into fertilizing materials. This circular did not make a plea to have more animals sent to the tanks, but suggested that steps be taken to make the reports more nearly agree. It was shown by documentary evidence that inspection of meats for foreign report was far more rigid than for domestic consumption. A secret circular called attention to the fact that tongues and other parts of animals from which diseased portions of the meat had been cut, should not be passed for shipment to foreign countries, although no objection was made to their use for home consumption. It was shown that tongues and other parts of the bodies from which ulcers and diseased tissues had been cut, went freely into domestic consumption.

It was shown that while the law requires each part of an animal to be separately stamped, the secret regulations permitted whole carloads of unstamped pieces of animals to be transported, the car alone being sealed and marked. It was further shown that these seals were often broken, and no attempts were made to punish those who violated the law by breaking the seals.

Mrs. Crane characterized the annual report of the Bureau of Animal Industry as a brief for the packers, and showed in a convincing manner how the actual conditions which obtain differ from the rosy conditions which are set forth.

Mrs. Crane also brought out the difficulty which she experienced in securing copies of the secret circulars. In these circulars, those receiving them are often cautioned against showing them to the public....

If the flesh of all these [diseased] animals were destroyed or used for fertilizing and technical purposes, the loss would not be of a character to increase the price of meat above one or two per cent, variations which are exceeded almost every week by manipulations of the packers.

Also, if the viscera [discarded parts] are the only parts by which disease can be ascertained, it is not fair to the consumer to pass the flesh of animals whose viscera disclose the presence of tuberculosis. The consumer should demand either that the flesh of all tuberculous animals be destroyed, or else that those portions of it which are supposed by the inspector to be fit for consumption be marked so that the consumer may know that they came from animals afflicted with tuberculosis. *This is not done*, and by reason of this failure, consumers are exposed to physical dangers.

Source: H. W. Wiley, "The Attack on Caroline Bartlett Crane," *Good Housekeeping* 55 (July 1912): 107–109.

NOTES

1. Caroline Bartlett Crane, "The Importance of Club-Women in Society," *Journal of the Michigan State Medical Society* v. 7 (1908): 199–200.

2. Lynda J. Rynbrandt, *Caroline Bartlett Crane and Progressive Reform: Social Housekeeping as Sociology* (New York: Garland Publishing, 1999), pp. 20–21.

3. Caroline Bartlett Crane, "The Making of an Ideal City," Crane Papers, Western Michigan University Library Special Collections. No publication date or place; quoted by Suellen Hoy, "'Municipal Housekeeping: The Role of Women in Improving Urban Sanitation Practices, 1880–1917," in *Pollution and Reform in American Cities*, ed. Martin Melosi (Austin: University of Texas Press, 1980), p. 183.

4. "The Local Slaughter-House Meat Inspection," Michigan State Board of Health, *Teachers Sanitary Bulletin* 6 (February 1903): 9–11; and Caroline Bartlett Crane, "Interest in Meat Inspection," Typescript, 1909, pp. 1–13; Crane Papers.

ANNOTATED BIBLIOGRAPHY

Brown, Alan S. "Caroline Bartlett Crane and Urban Reform." In *Michigan Perspectives: People, Events, and Issues*, edited by Alan S. Brown, John T. Houdek, and John H. Yzenbaard. Dubuque, IA: Kendall/Hunt, 1974, pp. 167–78. A concise history of Crane's sanitary surveys and urban-reform efforts.

Clarke, Robert. *Ellen Swallow: The Woman Who Founded Ecology*. Chicago: Follett, 1973. Among the first, and still one of the best, full biographies of any of the women progressive reformers.

Crane, Caroline Bartlett. *Everyman's House*. Garden City, NY: Doubleday, Page, 1925. Crane's insightful autobiography chronicling her role in and vision of progressive urban reform.

Frankel, Noralee, and Nancy S. Dye, eds. *Gender, Class, Race, and Reform in the Progressive Era*. Lexington: University Press of Kentucky, 1995. Fine collection of essays surveying the role of women in Progressive reform; includes a chapter on Alice Hamilton.

Hamilton, Alice. *Exploring the Dangerous Trades: The Autobiography of Alice Hamilton*. Boston: Little, Brown and Company, 1943. Reprinted with an introduction by Jean Spencer Felton. Boston: Northeastern University Press, 1985. Self-portrait documents Hamilton's overlooked central role in the early occupational health movement.

Hoy, Suellen. *Chasing Dirt: The American Pursuit of Cleanliness*. New York: Oxford University Press, 1996. Excellent chronicle of America's war on dirt, with women in the center of the story, particularly since the era of Caroline Bartlett Crane.

———. "'Municipal Housekeeping': The Role of Women in Improving Urban Sanitation Practices, 1880–1917." In *Pollution and Reform in American Cities, 1870–1930*, edited by Martin V. Melosi, Austin: University of Texas Press, 1980. Hoy's brief but important survey of key women like Caroline Bartlett Crane, Mary McDowell, and Jane Addams.

Leavitt, Judith Walzer, ed. *Women and Health in America: Historical Readings*. Madison: University of Wisconsin Press, 1999. A terrific collection of historical essays chronicling an array of issues, including a section on public health reformers of the late nineteenth and early twentieth centuries.

Muncy, Robyn. *Creating a Female Dominion in American Reform, 1890–1935*. New York: Oxford University Press, 1994. Sheds light on the role of women in defining Progressive reform, and the professional standardization of the welfare state.

Rickard, O'Ryan. *A Just Verdict: The Life of Caroline Bartlett Crane*. Kalamazoo: Western Michigan University Press, 1994. A solid biography, with extended treatment of Crane's efforts to ensure rigorous enforcement of meat inspection.

Rynbrandt, Linda J. *Caroline Bartlett Crane and Progressive Reform: Social Housekeeping as Sociology*. New York: Garland, 1998. A sociologist analyzes Crane's important contributions to the birth of American sociology.

Sicherman, Barbara, ed. *Alice Hamilton: A Life in Letters*. Cambridge, MA: Harvard University Press, 1984. Invaluable for the insight it provides into Hamilton's pioneering work on issues of lead exposure and occupational health.

10

Getting the Lead Out: Public Health and the Debate over Tetraethyl Leaded Gasoline

> You will see by it, that the Opinion of the mischievous Effect from Lead is at least above Sixty Years old; and you will observe with Concern how long a useful Truth may be known and exist, before it is generally receiv'd and practic'd on.
>
> —Benjamin Franklin, 1786[1]

Few environmental stories raise as many troubling and enduring questions as the chronicle of how and why the federal government allowed lead, one of the most useful but toxic metals on earth, to get into the nation's gasoline supply and stay there for some sixty years. Although ethanol had emerged early as the preferred antidote to the jarring "knock" or "pinging" in the automobile's internal combustion engine, it was tetraethyl lead, a neurologically toxic compound, that came to rule the market of gasoline antiknock additives. This story brings to the surface key themes of modern U.S. environmental history, not the least of which is the sheer dominance of both the automobile and petrochemicals in the twentieth century. Americans have ostensibly come to accept certain costs and possible risks in exchange for the convenience and pleasures afforded by auto travel. Yet the history of leaded gasoline brings disquieting questions: How does a society balance consumer desire with product safety? What is an acceptable level of risk to public health, and who decides? In particular, to what extent should corporations be permitted to influence the government's determination of exposure to a potentially harmful substance—particularly when the pressures of the market do not encourage the study of its chronic, long-term toxicity?

Central to this story is the role of corporations—specifically, the petrochemical and auto industries that in the 1920s moved to the center of the American economy—in deciding these questions and ultimately in formulating public health policy. How is it possible that the Ethyl Corporation came to control a federal agency's inquiry into the endangerment of occupational and public health and safety due to exposure to tetraethyl-leaded gasoline? How can it be that a government increasingly charged in the modern era with safeguarding public health leaned solely on corporate-funded research in continuing to sanction leaded gas, and consequently, lead in the air Americans breathed? Why did it choose essentially to give industry the benefit of the doubt, rather than compel corporate leaders to prove that leaded gasoline exposure was not harmful? Readers will find in this chapter neither simple nor reassuring answers to these matters.

At the time Dr. Benjamin Franklin made the above observation to Sir George Baker, the "mischievious" effects of working with lead had actually been known for several thousand years. In the second century B.C., Greek poet and physician Nikander described in detail the symptoms of lead poisoning. Pliny, the Roman naturalist and author, warned of the toxic effects of lead smelting, as had architect and engineer Vitruvius. Centuries later, Baker determined that a malady known as "Devonshire colic" had been caused by local cider having been produced in leaden presses and stored in lead-lined cisterns. Franklin's personal knowledge had been derived sixty years earlier from his time as a printer's apprentice in England, where he had noticed that the process of cleaning the lead type by heating it produced symptoms he described as the "dangles."

Though crude by modern standards, most of this early scientific and medical theorizing correctly ascertained that heating and processing of lead and exposure to lead particles produced ferocious attacks of colic and a range of brain and neurological diseases—all of which in their most acute form could be fatal. Also determined, albeit imprecisely, was lead's tenacious presence; once extracted, processed, and deposited into natural and human environments (including the body itself), lead is extremely resistant to conversion or dissolution into more benign forms. In short, lead lasts.

Despite the known hazards, by the early twentieth century, industrialists had discovered a plethora of new uses for the malleable metal, as well as for a number of lead compounds containing carbon and hydrogen. Munitions for World War I, storage batteries, cigar wrappers, food-can seals, and enamel paints were among the dozens of products containing some form of lead. New manufacturing processes and tens of thousands of workers employed in lead-related industries made possible a proliferation of commercial and industrial applications for lead. Predictably, such labor-intensive mass processing of a known toxic metal produced widespread ill effects among the workforce.

No one had any idea how serious the health impacts and how pervasive the ill effects were among the workers until 1911, when industrial hygiene pioneer Alice Hamilton produced her report on the Illinois lead industry as part of the survey conducted by that state's Commission on Occupational Diseases. Regarded as the first large-scale study of occupational disease in the nation, the Illinois survey was historic. Hamilton's lead investigation in particular broke new ground in directly linking medical records with specific occupations. The detective work of determining the health effects of dozens of new industrial lead processes took Hamilton to more than 300 business establishments. In her search for information, she frequently encountered resistance from plant managers and company doctors. Undeterred, she turned to hospitals, other physicians, apothecaries, labor halls, and to workers' homes.

Her painstakingly thorough documentation of nearly 600 cases of lead poisoning in Illinois led to an invitation from the U.S. Department of Labor to conduct a broader investigation of lead industries elsewhere. She began by investigating the horrifying conditions in the "white lead" industry, where men were exposed to extraordinarily large volumes of lead dust continuously in a process that transformed metallic lead into basic (white lead) carbonate. Here, men breathed lead dust all day, every day. Men drank water and ate sandwiches sprinkled with lead dust, and men went home sick. Hamilton's study documented 358 cases of severe (less perceptible, not including chronic) lead poisoning, including the deaths of sixteen workers. Subsequent investigations led her to the pottery, tile, porcelain, and battery industries, as well as to lead smelters and refineries, where she scrupulously documented more of the same.

Although many company managers complied with her recommendations to improve plant conditions, other owners and the physicians employed by the companies bitterly denounced her reports. Dr. H. T. Sutton, for example, a member of the Ohio State Board of Health and also the physician for the American Encaustic Tile Works of Zanesville, Ohio, publicly decried her 1912 report, which had cited the company (among dozens) for needlessly exposing men to injurious conditions. "This woman," he railed, had produced "a striking example of exaggeration, either a false and apparently a malicious and slanderous report, or an erroneous one."[2] Taken aback by this public attack, Hamilton responded to her superior at the U.S. Department of Labor:

> ...I hardly know what to say as to Dr. Sutton's accusations. He is the physician employed by the American Encaustic Tile Works of Zanesville...and this fact may color his opinions. I have been going over the notes I made in Zanesville and I find the following jotted down during my talk with Dr. Sutton. "Member of the State Board of Health. He has seen a good deal of lead colic and is often called to the American Encaustic to treat cases of hysterical convulsions in girls,... Dr. Sutton sees about a dozens cases a year and he thinks that a good deal of lead poisoning is not recognized as such...." You will see that he made no denial of the existence of lead poisoning in Zanesville.[3]

Hamilton's cautious intimation that Dr. Sutton's position may have been compromised by his association with the company anticipated a central theme that lay at the center of the controversy over leaded gasoline that began to unfold the following decade.

Although the lead compound tetraethyl had first been discovered in 1854, the distressing fact that prolonged casual exposure to it produced respiratory distress, hallucinations, convulsions, spasms, asphyxiation, and even death steered chemists away from any possible industrial applications. It was rediscovered as a result of the decade-long search for a gasoline additive to cure the "knock" in the internal combustion engine of the automobile. Solving this jarring annoyance would not only allow cars to run more smoothly, but also deliver higher compression in the engine's cylinders and consequently, more power to the vehicle and possibly even greater fuel economy. Until 1921, ethanol—high-octane alcohol produced from farm crop surplus—seemed to be the answer, either as a gasoline additive or as straight fuel. Henry Ford was so convinced of ethanol's future that early Model A cars could run on either gasoline or alcohol.

General Motors engineer Thomas Midgley Jr. sang ethanol's praises as well— until 1922, shortly after the discovery of the antiknock properties of tetraethyl lead, and more importantly, following big internal changes at GM. The DuPont corporation, flush with munitions' profits from World War I and looking to branch out into petrochemicals, purchased a controlling financial interest in GM by 1920. From the standpoint of GM's new DuPont leadership, ethanol had two fatal flaws: it could not be patented, nor would it ever be profitable. Tetraethyl lead, with no such deficiencies, suddenly leaped over ethanol as the antiknock solution. By October 1922, DuPont had signed an agreement with GM to supply it with tetraethyl from plants in Dayton, Ohio, and Deepwater, New Jersey. Production commenced despite immediate reports of lead poisoning at the latter facility, prompting a warning of this "serious menace to public health" from an official at the U.S. Public Health Service.[4] Rather than conduct its own investigation into the safety of tetraethyl, the agency made the precedent-setting decision to rely on the company for all data regarding both workers' health and exposure to the public of a known poison. Meanwhile, Thomas Midgely became a tetraethyl convert, writing a letter to the U.S. Surgeon General personally assuring him that the public would suffer no harm. This confidence came not only after Midgley began receiving letters from public health and medical experts around the country warning of tetraethyl's dangers; incredibly, it came immediately following Midgley's acknowledgment that he himself had been poisoned after several months of tetraethyl exposure in the laboratory.

In August 1923, several workers died of lead poisoning at DuPont's Deepwater plant. Though the deaths went largely unreported, there was enough unease in the public mind with any product containing lead to compel DuPont and GM to agree to a study to prove the safety of tetraethyl lead. The inquiry, however, was to be paid for by the General Motors Research Corporation and conducted by the U.S. Bureau of Mines, giving the study the authoritative stamp of approval sought by corporate leaders. With a previous track record of subservience to the mining industry, the bureau proved more than compliant with the extraordinary demands imposed on it by the new GM-DuPont–created Ethyl Gasoline Corporation (an entity that also included Standard Oil, which had developed and patented a better tetraethyl production method). Ethyl demanded absolutely no press coverage from bureau officials about the investigation while it was underway, and no use whatsoever of the word "lead" in reference to the product being investigated (hence the brand sobriquet Ethyl). Most astonishingly, Ethyl requested "that before publication of any papers or articles by your Bureau, they should be submitted to them [Ethyl] for comment, criticism, and approval." Ethyl was to control both content and the timing of the report's release. All requests were granted, giving the new corporation, as David Rosner and Gerald Markowitz have summarized, "veto power over the research of the United States government."[5] Ethyl would get what it was paying for. Strenuous protests from public health experts that the bureau's cozy relationship with GM fatally compromised its integrity proved futile.

While the study was still underway, on October 26, 1924, the first of five deaths of tetraethyl workers took place at Standard Oil's Bayway plant in Elizabeth, New Jersey. Unlike the previous casualties at the Deepwater plant (and others at DuPont's Dayton plant), the Bayway disaster, which ultimately affected forty-nine employees or 80 percent of the workforce, received major coverage. Grim reports of horrific deaths and injuries tumbled out of the plant day after day. Standard Oil initially attempted to blame the workers, and then days later, following a ban on the sale of leaded gas in New York City, Philadelphia, and other municipalities and states around the nation, a company spokesman admitted tetraethyl's inherent toxicity and that there had been previous injuries and death at other plants. In the midst of this public relations crisis, the Bureau of Mines released a summary of its findings, which, not surprisingly, exonerated tetraethyl. Local health officials were skeptical, particularly following severe criticism of the report from renowned public health authorities at major universities, and publications like *Scientific American* and the *Journal of Industrial Hygiene*. The Workers Health Bureau, a consortium of union officials and other labor activists focused on occupational safety and health issues, damned the report as a corporate-funded whitewash. Dr. Yandell Henderson, a well-known physiologist and public health expert from Yale University, denounced the scientific methodology of short-term animal testing in the study, arguing it had no bearing on real-life conditions of human exposure. Keeping Ethyl on the defensive, Henderson assisted the Workers Health Bureau in investigating and revealing the deaths and injuries of the other workers at the Deepwater and Dayton plants. Alice Hamilton joined the anti-ethyl chorus in a coauthored article for the *Journal of the American Medical Association*.

Fallout from Bayway and the reaction to the Bureau of Mines report led the U.S. surgeon general to stage a conference in May 1925 on the safety of tetraethyl-leaded gasoline. As one might imagine in this polarized atmosphere, conference participants were bitterly divided. Alice Hamilton declared that no lead-related industry or product could ever be made completely safe. Yandell Henderson delivered the most pointed, prescient criticism of the continued manufacture and sale of leaded gasoline. Henderson worried less about the continued deaths of more workers in the plants, than of the insidiously intensifying effects of chronic lead exposure to millions of Americans as automobile use increased. The latter, virtually impossible to clinically study and quantify with absolute certainty, was, nonetheless, potentially far more threatening to human health in the long run. Further, he and other opponents argued, just because there was no quantifiable proof of negative health effects derived from street exposure to tetraethyl was not an argument that there was none. The burden of proof, they claimed, was on the companies to prove tetraethyl's safety, not on the public to demonstrate the long-term threat of exposure, something that was impossible. Other public health professionals at the conference disagreed sharply with Hamilton and Henderson, claiming that after two years of ethyl's use, injury to the public would have manifested itself in reported lead poisoning. Ethyl officials, naturally, opposed any suggestion of prohibiting the sale of tetraethyl-leaded gasoline.

The major result of the conference was the recommendation to the surgeon general that he appoint a committee of esteemed public health experts from the nation's leading universities to conduct a more thorough independent examination of the effects of tetraethyl exposure. This inquiry was to be funded by the federal government, presumably resulting in more credible conclusions than the GM-funded Bureau of Mines report. To the amazement of opponents, Ethyl announced at the end of the conference that it was suspending production and distribution of its product pending the resolution of all questions surrounding the use of leaded gasoline.

What appeared to be a win for opponents became instead the climactic victory for tetraethyl's advocates. Instead of an extended, thorough examination, the committee, given only a few months to complete its work, conducted what opponents claimed was a limited study short-circuited by quiet pressure from Ethyl. Its recommendation to allow the continued production and use of tetraethyl-leaded gasoline did come with this important, though ultimately ignored caveat: continued use of leaded gas by more and more automobiles, said the committee, called for further studies by the U.S. Public Health Service as lead exposure levels increased.

That never happened. The agency never strongly advocated for such studies, and the Congress failed to seek appropriations for them. For the next forty years, all Ethyl research was conducted by the corporation's lead consultant, Dr. Robert Kehoe of the University of Cincinnati (the same Kehoe who helped to exonerate flouride following the 1948 Donora air pollution disaster—Chapter 12). In 1928 Kehoe dismissed the conference's recommendation for further investigation by magnanimously suggesting that the industry most affected financially should bear the expense of further studies, not the public. He said nothing about the possible cost to public health, except to note that his own study "[failed] to show any evidence for the existence of such hazards."[6]

For the next forty years, Robert Kehoe's theory held that any abnormally high lead levels in his test subjects were within the "normal" range of what occurs "naturally" in humans. This was the cornerstone of Ethyl's defense against all further attempts to curtail production and distribution. It began to lose credibility in the 1960s with additional studies by other researchers, most notably the geochemist Clair Patterson, who shattered Kehoe's theory of "normal" lead levels. With the added political force of the environmental movement, and still more studies of what Patterson called "chronic lead insult" resulting from emissions and other sources including lead-based paint, leaded gasoline was phased out beginning in 1976 and was effectively banned by 1986. To the surprise of few researchers, data from the Center for Disease Control showed that blood-lead levels in Americans aged 1–74 declined 78 percent between 1978 and 1991. A 1992 article in the *New England Journal of Medicine*, however, cautioned against over-elation: researchers investigating the bones of pre-Columbian inhabitants of North America revealed that our ancestors enjoyed average blood-lead levels 625 times lower than the current "safe" level designated by the Environmental Protection Agency (EPA).[7] A further sobering fact is that the last remaining producer of tetraethyl continues to market and distribute this toxin to Third World nations.

Indeed, the sixty-year life of Ethyl left plenty of residue: not only lead in the bodies of three generations of Americans but also serious policy questions which, as promised, are not answered satisfactorily here. More than anything perhaps, the lead controversy reminds us again that environmental history matters, for ultimately entangled here are issues still very much with us: the potential perfidy of men whose overriding interest is profit, the role of government in regulating the private sector in an industrial age, and the fundamental issue of how public trust and confidence in a healthy environment can best be ensured.

DOCUMENTS

Document 10.1   **Excerpts From the *New York Times* Reporting on Fatalities at Standard Oil's Tetraethyl Plant in New Jersey, October 1924**

Public alarm about the possible dangers of using leaded gasoline was first sounded in late October 1924 following the disaster at Standard Oil's Bayway tetraethyl plant in Elizabeth, New Jersey. "Odd Gas Kills One, Makes Four Insane" understandably shook American confidence in the wondrous new product that had eliminated engine "knock." In the face of daily grim reports of dead and injured workers, company officials steadfastly denied any wrongdoing on the part of management, instead shifting blame for the accident to the workers themselves for failing to employ safety practices such as gas masks to avoid inhalation. In one excerpt, Standard Oil vehemently protests the call of Yale professor Yandell Henderson to cease the sale of tetraethyl-leaded gasoline. Henderson and other critics argued that tetraethyl posed a threat to human health not only in the workplace but also the atmosphere beyond. New York City, along with other cities and states, responded to the warning by forbidding the sale and distribution of leaded gas. Such prohibitions proved temporary, however, as public anxiety began to wane, evidenced by the New York Times *editorial that came just one month later.*

OCTOBER 17, 1924—"ODD GAS KILLS ONE, MAKES FOUR INSANE"

Four men were under treatment for delirium in Reconstruction Hospital here yesterday and another was dead from the effects of breathing a gas used to increase the efficiency of gasoline in experiments at the research laboratory of the Bayway plant of the Standard Oil Company at Elizabeth, N. J. . . .

Ernest Oelgert . . . suddenly became delirious while at work at the plant. Convulsions set in. Milder symptoms appeared in seven other patients. Some seemed slightly deranged and others delirious. One had to be put in a strait-jacket before he could be brought to the hospital here. . . .

Dr. [Joseph] Funk, who treated Oelgert at the Alexian Brothers Hospital, said:

"We treated the patient in the hope of eliminating the poison and administering sedatives to check the convulsions, but the action of the poison increased and his life could not be saved.

"From my observation of the case and from what I have learned, I believe that the breathing of the gas had gone on for a period of days and weeks, during which the poison had been gradually accumulated in the system. There apparently were no early symptoms, but as soon as the man's blood became saturated with the poison the violent attack took place. Apparently as soon as the poison was present in the body in sufficient strength it attacked the brain and nerves."

...Employes [sic] at the plant revealed that the experiment building was known as the "loony gas building." Men who took up work in this building came in for "undertaker jokes" and serio-comic handshakings and farewell greetings when their comrades learned of their action. So far as could be learned, no special warnings were given employes working with the "loony gas," nor apparently did they sign documents relieving the company of responsibility....

No investigation of Oelgert's death or of the causes of the illness of the other men is intended by the Union County authorities. Walter C. Tensey, assistant prosecutor, said there appeared to be no cause for criminal action....

Dr. C. O. Johns, who has been in charge of the research work at the Bayway laboratory, said he had been away ... and knew nothing about the gas accident. "I have been trying my best to discover what happened, but I can't find anybody who seems to know anything about it," he said. "You might obtain information from our physician, Dr. W. Gillman Thompson, in New York."

Dr. Thompson was asked about the matter and replied:

"Nothing ought to be said about this matter in the public interest."

D. Mann, who has had charge of some of the research at the plant ... prepared this:

"These men probably went insane because they worked too hard."

Source: New York Times, October 27, 1924, pp. 1, 11.

OCTOBER 29, 1924—"THIRD VICTIM DIES FROM POISON GAS"

... Inspectors from the Trenton staff of Charles H. Weeks, Deputy Commissioner of Labor, began an investigation of the Bayway Laboratory to ascertain whether State laws governing ventilation had been violated and if workmen had been subjected to conditions endangering their health.

"We shall have a report later as to the conditions," [Weeks] said, "and if it is found that laws regulating the ventilation of buildings have been violated we shall make charges immediately, either against the company or those officials responsible for the unlawful conditions...."

William L. Dill, New Jersey State Motor Vehicle Commissioner, said that he had no evidence that [tetraethyl] gasoline ... was being sold in New Jersey. Officials in this city were positive that it was not being sold or used here.

Commenting on the statement of Dr. Yandell Henderson, Professor of Applied Physiology at Yale, who evolved the tetra-ethyl theory, charging that use of the modified gasoline might under certain conditions menace the health of persons in the street, Dr. Frank Monaghan, Health Commissioner, said that he had been investigating gasoline and its relation to health for some time.

"...I read Dr. Henderson's conclusion about the danger of releasing the fumes in the open street. I agree that if a person were immediately near the released fumes at the moment of their discharge he might inhale sufficient of the gas to become ill."

"We are not taking Dr. Henderson's statement seriously," said a representative of the Standard Oil Company, yesterday at 26 Broadway....

Jacob Freeman of the Workers' Health Bureau, 799 Broadway, last night made public the following telegram from Professor Henderson:

"Sale to the public of gasoline containing lead is now reported in New Jersey, Maryland, the Middle West and elsewhere. It should be stopped immediately and prohibited until the subject is fully investigated by scientific experts. Otherwise there is a great danger of widespread poisoning among men at gasoline filling stations, garages, repair shops, and even among the general public. Public health authorities everywhere should take immediate action."

Source: New York Times, October 29, 1924, p. 23.

OCTOBER 31, 1924—"BAR ETHYL GASOLINE AS 5TH VICTIM DIES"

Herbert Fuson of 516 Grier Avenue, Elizabeth, N.J., died in a straitjacket violently insane at Reconstruction Hospital yesterday morning, the fifth victim of the deadly tetraethyl lead fumes generated in the Standard Oil plant at Elizabeth, N.J....

Thirty-six persons were under treatment or under observation in hospitals and eight in their homes yesterday because of exposure to the gas. With the five dead, this made a total of forty-nine persons who had been placed in the peril of this insanity-producing substance.

In an official statement yesterday the Standard Oil Company of New Jersey denied that the poison which had wrought this havoc was a "mystery gas" and said that its qualities were well known. It was admitted that it was known that this gas had collected a previous toll of death and insanity before the forty-nine employees were exposed to it at the Elizabeth plant....

Although the perils involved in making the lead-gasoline were admitted by the Standard Oil Company yesterday, it denied that such perils existed in the use of this gas in automobiles. Such gasoline, greatly diluted, is in use in more than 10,000 filling stations and garages and no ill effects have thus far been reported, according to the Standard Oil Company. Acting on information that this product was dangerous, however, the health authorities of this city barred it yesterday. Dr. Yandell Henderson of Yale, whose opinion on the action of the gas on human breathers was sought by the manufacturers and then rejected, asserted that the absence of reports of injury due to breathing this gas in automobile exhaust fumes was no indication that those fumes were not dangerous. He said that this poison was so insidious that the breakdown in health might occur long after the breathing of the poison, so that insanity or milder symptoms might not be connected with the true cause....

These deaths, together with the warnings of Yandell Henderson and other investigators of the alleged dangers lurking in the use of tetraethyl lead gas, caused the calling of a special meeting of the Board of Health of New York, at which this resolution [banning the sale and use of tetraethyl-leaded gasoline] was adopted:...

Thomas Midgley Jr., discoverer of the use of tetraethyl lead for increasing power in gasoline, defended his compound at an interview yesterday.... To prove that the substance was not dangerous in small quantities he rubbed some of the tetraethyl on his hands....Mr. Midgley said the Bureau of Mines had been asked to make a most thorough investigation of the effects of tetraethyl lead gas poisoning, and that the bureau had been conducting tests in this connection for about ten months. According to an official of the Standard Oil Company, the bureau will make a statement on the results of these tests in two or three days....

Dr. J. Gilman Thompson, consulting physician for the Standard Oil Company...gave out the following typewritten statement on the subject:

"...It should be emphasized that the product as destined for final use in gasoline engines has to be greatly diluted, usually with 1,000 parts of gasoline. This extremely diluted product has been for more than a year in public use in over 10,000 filling stations and garages, and no ill effects have thus far been reported."

...Asked what would be the reaction of the Standard Oil Company to possible claims of families of men who died from the poison that the stricken men were never aware of danger involved in their work, officials of the company replied that the rejection of many men as physically unfit to engage in the work at the Bayway plant, daily physical examinations, constant admonitions as to wearing rubber gloves and using gas masks and not wearing away from the plant clothing worn during work hours should have been sufficient indication to every man in the plant that he was engaged "in a man's undertaking."

Source: New York Times, October 31, 1924, pp. 1, 13.

NOVEMBER 28, 1924—EDITORIAL: "NO REASON FOR ABANDONMENT"

Both the report of Dr. McBride, the New Jersey Commissioner of Labor, and that of the American Chemical Society on the manufacture of tetra-ethyl lead as an additive to gasoline are of great as well as varied interest. Both take with proper seriousness the dangers incidental to the manufacture of this peculiar substance, and Dr. McBride, while he admits that the company fully met all the requirements of the law as to the protection of the workmen, calls attention to the fact that it is one thing to provide the facilities for such protection, but the enforcement of their constant use is quite another, as is shown by the deaths that occurred among the men employed at the Bayway factory. Human nature is such that familiarity with such perils almost always results, after a while, in disdain of them and a carelessness which easily can have fatal results. The men found themselves inconvenienced in their work by the gas masks which at least would have decreased the perils of their occupation, and therefore did not wear them as persistently as they should. Herein, in Dr. McBride's opinion, evidently lies such responsibility as rests on the company; it did not see to it that the needful precautions it had prepared always were taken, though it knew and should have remembered, that its employes were skilled workmen, not trained scientists who thoroughly understood the situation. This responsibility was moral rather than legal, but it was no lighter on that account. The Chemical Society's report was along another line. It saw in the deaths at the Bayway factory not a sufficient reason for abandoning the use of a substance by means of which a large economic gain could be effected—that is, a considerable increase in the value of gasoline as a source of power. The report recalls that in many other instances just such a price has been paid in learning how to achieve like results, and it holds that with the knowledge now available there is little or no fear of further fatalities in making tetra-ethyl lead; and as there is no measurable risk to the public in its proper use as a fuel, the chemists see no reason why its manufacture and sale should be abandoned. That is the scientific view of the matter, as opposed to the sentimental, and it seems rather cold-blooded, but it is entirely reasonable....

Source: New York Times, November 28, 1924, p. 14.

**Document 10.2   Alice Hamilton Summarizes the Case against
                       the Use of Leaded Gasoline, 1925**

The debate over the use of tetraethyl gasoline continued long after the furor over the Bayway tragedy had waned. With extensive experience acquired from years of studying the health impacts of men and women working in lead-related industries, renowned occupational disease expert Alice Hamilton weighed in on the debate. She is joined here by colleagues Paul Reznikoff and Grace Burnham of the Workers Health Bureau in an article for the Journal of the American Medical Association (*the AMA defended the use of lead for decades*). *Appearing on the eve of the pivotal conference to decide the fate of tetraethyl gasoline, the article criticized the 1924 Bureau of Mines report that exonerated tetraethyl gasoline. Not included in the excerpt are the authors' scientifically detailed criticisms of the report. In sum, they deconstruct the methodology of the bureau, arguing that the conditions under which animals were exposed did not approximate those endured by humans exposed to tetraethyl-leaded gasoline, and further, that the analytical technique used by the bureau to interpret symptoms exhibited by the animals was faulty. Although the authors acknowledged that the science was still ambiguous as to the precise extent of the danger to public health posed by leaded gas, they argued that there was enough evidence to err on the side of caution by prohibiting its manufacture and use until further, more thorough studies were conducted.*

THE PRESENT-DAY PROBLEM

There are four questions that must be answered before we know whether the manufacture and distribution of tetra-ethyl lead and its use in gasoline carry with them a danger serious enough to warrant prohibition by public health authorities....

1. *The Danger to Men Manufacturing Tetra-Ethyl Lead.*—Within the last seventeen months, eleven men have died and one man has become insane through tetra-ethyl lead poisoning. All were engaged in the manufacture of this compound. . . .

Eldridge's paper [W. A. Eldridge, a scientist with the Chemical Warfare Service] contains a summary of the symptoms in the Standard Oil cases. . . . The first symptom noticed is a marked fall in blood pressure . . . an accompanying fall in body temperature . . . and a low pulse rate. . . . Then symptoms of profound cerebral involvement appear, persistent insomnia, extraordinary restlessness and talkativeness, and delusions. The gait is like that of a drunken man, but there are no paralyses or convulsions. Finally, after a period of exaggerated movements of all the muscles of the body, with sweating, the patient becomes violently maniacal, shouting, leaping from the bed, smashing the furniture, and acting as if in delirium tremens; morphine only accentuates the symptoms. The patient may finally die in exhaustion. In fatal cases, the body temperature rose to 110 F. just before death occurred. One of these was a young man of fine physique who had been at work only five weeks. He is said to have suffered terrible agony. "He died yelling." . . .

2. *The Danger to Men Handling Ethyl Fluid.*—Ethyl fluid is sold in one quart steel receptacles with pointed necks, sealed with soft tin caps. The service station operator who is to add ethyl fluid to the gasoline in automobile tanks breaks the seal over an upright spike as he places the receptacle over the cup of the delivery tube of the gasoline tank. When the receptacle is empty, he takes it off and substitutes another. There is a recognized danger involved in this process, for the liquid may be splashed over the face and hands of the worker. . . .

3. *The Danger to Filling and Distributing Station Employees and to the Public from Handling Ethyl Gasoline.*—A study covering this problem is being conducted at present by the Laboratory of Industrial Hygiene of the Columbia University College of Physicians and Surgeons . . . and as yet the data collected are insufficient for the formation of a definite statement.

4. *The Danger to Garage Employees and to the General Public from Exhaust Gases from Engines Using Ethyl Gasoline.*—The exhaust gases generated by the combustion of ethyl gasoline contain lead compounds in the form of more or less fine dust. The danger here would be from repeated small doses resulting in chronic lead poisoning. The importance of this problem was realized by the General Motors Research Corporation . . . and the corporation requested the United States Bureau of Mines to investigate the question. . . . The fact that the report was issued by a government agency gave it an authority and an air of finality, as shown by the fact that immediately after its publication the ban on the manufacture, distribution and sale of ethyl gasoline was lifted by the states of New York and New Jersey, and also by recent articles from the pens of two public officials. . . .

CONCLUSIONS

We believe that these conclusions are not warranted and that the evidence so far available seems to show a real danger of chronic lead poisoning connected with garage work when ethyl gasoline is used and a possible danger to the public from lead dust in the streets of large cities. The compounds of lead formed by the combustion of ethyl gasoline are the chloride or bromide, . . . and the sulphate. . . . Now, the chloride and bromide of lead are among the most soluble of the lead salts, far more soluble in water than are those usually encountered in industry. . . .

The statement, therefore, that only 15 per cent of the inhaled lead is retained is not entirely reassuring, even if one accepts it as proved. A finely divided soluble lead compound can be readily absorbed from the respiratory tract, beginning with the nasal mucosa, and may constitute a serious danger if administered in repeated doses, even if these are small.

It seems to us that the investigators have devoted their attention to the fine particles of lead suspended in the air and have not attributed enough importance to the discharge of "large particles of scale which fall to the ground," and which, in garages, in taxi stands under cover in the large railway stations, and even on the crowded streets of cities, might constitute a far from negligible danger. These particles will be ground fine by passing feet and swept up by currents of air, and when dissolved by rain and washed away, it is certainly possible that they may contaminate surface waters. . . .

SUMMARY

. . . Experiments carried on by Eldridge . . . show that tetra-ethyl lead passes readily through the skin and that rapid acute poisoning may follow skin application or the inhalation of fumes. In animals so poisoned, the lead is found chiefly deposited in the skeleton. A cumulative effect also was noted, when animals were given repeated small doses by these two routes, death occurring in more than half. . . .

The mixing of ethyl fluid with gasoline constitutes a danger, the extent of which is as yet undetermined, to employees of refineries and service station employees.

The use of gasoline to which ethyl fluid has been added constitutes a probable risk to garage workers and a possible risk to the public, of chronic lead poisoning, because the combustion of tetra-ethyl gasoline results in the formation of soluble compounds of lead, the chloride and bromide (as well as the less soluble sulphate), which compounds pass out with the exhaust gases in the form of light and heavy particles.

The states of New York and New Jersey prohibited for a time the use of ethyl gasoline, but rescinded this order when a report was issued by the United States Bureau of Mines declaring that tests made on animals with exhaust gases from engines using ethyl gasoline had shown no evidence of plumbism in any of these animals.

This report of the Bureau of Mines has been critically examined and found to be inadequate in scope, in technique, and in conclusiveness. It cannot be accepted as the final word on the question as to the toxicity of exhaust gases from cars using ethyl gasoline. The further question, of the risk to garage workers, is only lightly touched on in this report, and it also must await a more thorough handling.

Because of the enormous and increasing use of automobiles, the question of the danger to industrial workers and to the public which is involved in the production and handling of tetra-ethyl lead and the use of ethyl gasoline is of the highest importance and calls for a study which will be beyond criticism. Such an investigation must include an intensive survey of a selected group of individuals who have already been exposed to the gas, under known and varying calcium diet and varying exposure to sunlight. Their excreta should be analyzed for lead. Only in this way can absorption of lead and possible lead poisoning be ruled out. Perhaps of even greater significance is the possibility that the gonads may be injured and posterity be affected.... This would necessitate studying the progeny of pedigreed animals. Until investigations of this character have been made, it would seem to be in the interest of public health to suspend the use of tetra-ethyl lead in gasoline.

Source: Alice Hamilton, Paul Reznikoff, and Grace Burnham, "Tetra Ethyl Lead," *Journal of the American Medical Association* 84 (May 16, 1925): 1481–86. Reprinted with permission of the American Medical Association.

Document 10.3   **Frank A. Howard Defends Tetraethyl Gasoline as a "Gift of God"**

Lingering questions led the U.S. Surgeon General to call for a conference in May 1925 to decide whether to continue to allow the manufacture and sale of tetraethyl gas. The list of conference speakers was long and inclusive, representing the views of chemists, engineers, workers, public health experts, and of course the Ethyl Gasoline Corporation. The most notable representative for the company was executive Frank A. Howard, who subtly dismisses the public health dangers of leaded gas as a "remote probability." More significantly, he pointedly lays out what was at stake in determining the fate of tetraethyl lead: Howard smartly subsumes the company's interest into a more profound and altruistic concern for the future of American industrial civilization. Included also in his comments is the more fallacious notion that lead was essential to the conservation of gasoline, which, Howard observes, was already coming from around the globe (fuel efficiency in fact declined with the use of leaded gasoline). Finally, this rather remarkable address rhetorically raises the risk-benefit question that would be at the center of debates over environmental health and scientific-technological progress for the rest of the century—from pesticide use to the threat of global warming.

... Relatively speaking, the responsibility of Doctor [Yandell] Henderson, and of you gentlemen of the Public Health Service, is rather simple; that is, you have but one problem, and that is, Is this a public-health hazard? Unfortunately, our problem is not that simple. We can not quite act on a remote probability. We are engaged in the General Motors Corporation in the manufacture of automobiles, and in the Standard Oil Co. in the manufacture and refining of oil. On these things our present civilization is supposed to depend. I might refer to the comment made at the end of [World War I]—that the Allies floated to victory on a sea of oil—which is probably true. Our continued development of motor fuels is essential in our civilization. And our dependence upon a continuing supply of petroleum has been a subject which interests everyone who has the interest of his country at heart. The President has gone so far in the past few months as to appoint a special committee . . . to see if they could not exhaust all the possibilities of conserving petroleum in every direction.

Now, as a result of some 10 years' research on the part of the General Motors Corporation and 5 years' research by the Standard Oil Co. . . . we have this apparent gift of God—of 3 cubic centimeters of tetraethyl lead—which can be produced at a low figure, an inconsequential figure ultimately, and which will permit that gallon of gasoline, which we have recovered from the earth all over the world, because we import much of our supply and hope that we will import more in the future so that we will use less of our own supply, to go perhaps 50 percent further, and, if our optimistic engineering friends are correct will make it go 100 per cent further in the long run.

Now, there is that situation. We are presented with that gift of God which enables us to do that. . . .

And we are presented with this question at the start concerning the use of tetraethyl lead, the question of the health hazard. What is our duty under the circumstances? Should we throw this thing aside? Should we say, "No; we will not use it," in spite of the efforts of the Government and the General Motors Corporation and the Standard Oil Co. toward developing this very thing, which is a certain means of saving petroleum? Because some animals die and some do not die in some experiments, shall we give this thing up entirely?

Frankly, it is a problem that we do not know how to meet. We can not justify ourselves in our consciences if we abandon the thing. I think it would an unheard-of blunder if we should abandon a thing of this kind merely because of our fears. We could not justify an attitude of that kind; I do not think anybody could. Possibilities can not be allowed to influence us to such an extent as that in this matter. It must be not fears but facts that we must be guided by. I do not think we are justified in trying to reach a final conclusion in this matter on fears at all; nor are we justified in saying that we will cease this development because of fears we entertain. This development must be stopped, if it is stopped at all, by proofs of the facts. . . .

Source: United States Public Health Service, "Proceedings of a Conference to Determine Whether or Not There Is a Public Health Question in the Manufacture, Distribution or Use of Tetraethyl Lead Gasoline," *Public Health Bulletin No. 158* (Washington, DC: Government Printing Office, 1925), pp. 105–106.

Document 10.4   U.S. Public Health Service Committee Sanctions Tetraethyl's Use, Calls for Continued Monitoring, 1926

The most significant result of the 1925 conference was the recommendation to appoint a special committee to conduct a fuller examination of the possible dangers to garage and industrial workers and the general public from tetraethyl-leaded gasoline. Ethyl's opponents were heartened by the formation of the committee and by the lead industry's willingness to suspend the manufacture and sale of the product pending the results of the study. They were sorely disappointed, however, with what they believed was an abbreviated and inconclusive study of a relatively limited number of subjects under conditions not approximating the levels of leaded gas fumes to which both employees and the general population would be subjected over time. The committee's conclusions, excerpted here, included the important, though ultimately ignored, recommendation to continue monitoring the health effects from tetraethyl-leaded gasoline as use of the product increased.

On the basis of this investigation, the committee feels that the following general conclusions are justified:

1. Drivers of cars using ethyl gasoline as a fuel and in which the concentration of tetraethyl lead was not greater than 1 part to 1,300 parts by volume of gasoline showed no definite signs of lead absorption after exposures approximating two years.
2. ... In garages and stations in which ethyl gasoline was used the amount of apparent absorption and storage [in workers] was somewhat increased, but the effect was slight in comparison with that shown by workers in other industries where there was a severe lead hazard ... and for the period of exposures studied was not sufficient to produce detectable symptoms of lead poisoning.
3. In the regions in which ethyl gasoline has been used to the greatest extent as a motor fuel for a period of between two and three years no definite cases have been discovered of recognizable lead poisoning or other disease resulting from the use of ethyl gasoline.

In view of these conclusions your committee begs to report that in their opinion there are at present no good grounds for prohibiting the use of ethyl gasoline of the composition specified as a motor fuel, provided that its distribution and use are controlled by proper regulations. The committee feels that the formulation of specific regulations in regard to the manufacture, distribution, and use of tetraethyl lead, ethyl fluid, and ethyl gasoline for adoption and enforcement by the several states belongs properly to the office of the Surgeon General and the Public Health Service. ...

In conclusion we beg to say that we are conscious of the fact that the conclusions to which we have come in this report, although based upon most careful and conscientious investigations, are subject to the criticism that they have been derived from the study of a relatively small number of individuals who were exposed to the effects of ethyl gasoline for a period of time comparatively brief when we consider the possibilities in connection with lead poisoning. A more extensive study was not possible on account of limited time. It remains possible that, if the use of leaded gasolines becomes widespread, conditions may arise very different from those studied by us which would render its use more of a hazard than would appear to be the case from this investigation. Longer experience may show that even such slight storage of lead as was observed in these studies may lead eventually in susceptible individuals to recognizable lead poisoning or to chronic degenerative diseases of a less obvious character. In view of such possibilities the committee feels that the investigation begun under their direction must not be allowed to lapse.... With the experience obtained and the exact methods now available, it should be possible to follow closely the outcome of a more extended use of this fuel and to determine whether or not it may constitute a menace to the health of the general public after prolonged use or under conditions not now foreseen.

Outside the question of ethyl gasoline it would seem from this investigation that wherever automobiles are housed together there is an accumulation of lead dust which may prove to be a source of danger to the workers involved, in addition to the hazards arising from the production of carbon monoxide gas. The vast increase in the number of automobiles throughout the country makes the study of all such questions a matter of real importance from the standpoint of public health, and the committee urges strongly that a suitable appropriation be requested from Congress for the continuance of these investigations under the supervision of the Surgeon General of the Public Health Service, and for a study of related problems connected with the use of motor fuels.

W. H. Howell, Chairman (et al.)

Source: United States Public Health Service, "The Use of Tetraethyl Lead Gasoline in Its Relation to Public Health," *Public Health Bulletin No. 163* (Washington, DC: Government Printing Office, 1926), pp. 109–11.

Document 10.5   **Lead Industries Association President Extols Use and Safety of Lead, 1948**

In the wake of public alarm over the use of leaded gasoline in the 1920s, the lead industry established the Lead Industries Association (LIA), the purpose of which was to launch a public relations counterattack to still American fears about lead poisoning. Like other private foundations and trade groups, the LIA buttressed its positions by deploying industry-friendly scientists and government agencies to debunk the work of scientists who had long published studies warning of the dangers of lead. In this 1948 opening address to the LIA's "Lead Hygiene Conference," Felix E. Wormser, the group's president (also an executive with the St. Joseph Lead Company) speaks of the growing importance of the metal in the modern economy. By invoking the work of such distinguished (and lead-friendly) institutions as the American Medical Association and the United States Public Health Service, Wormser attempts to discredit those "alarmists" who continued their criticism of lead's increasingly ubiquitous presence in American society. Even as he acknowledges lead's toxicity and calls for eliminating atmospheric exposure in the manufacture of lead products, Wormser indirectly criticizes those who called for ending public use of leaded gasoline which poisoned the air far more pervasively. Also striking is Wormer's admission that cleaning up industrial lead emissions can lead to greater efficiency and an improved financial condition for the company; this concept was embraced by an increasing number of major corporations by the end of the twentieth century.

...It would take 200 freight trains each 100 cars long to move the lead that is consumed in our country each year. A simple calculation will show that this amounts to about one million tons. In fact, consumption today...is about 1,200,000 tons a year. It may be that the thoughts of this volume of lead being consumed annually in the United States is petrifying to those alarmists about the toxicity of our metal, as a million tons of lead, or two billion pounds, is a consumption of around 13 lb. per capita. On the contrary, my own interpretation is that this record shows that, despite contact with lead in nearly all our daily activities, some of it remote to be sure, the absence of reported injury on any other but an extremely modest scale, is one of the best evidences we have of the comparative safety to health under which lead can be produced and used today.

...Some of you [lead industry executives] serve mining companies, others smelting and refining companies, and some of you attend factories where pig lead is converted into white lead, cable sheathing, storage batteries, ammunition, and dozens of other important lead articles. Today, lead assumes an even more important role in industry than ever before, because we are on the threshold of great developments in the field of atomic power where lead will be protecting the lives of human beings from the effects of dangerous secondary radiation. I like to stress this point, because lead is so often condemned by virtue of its admittedly toxic properties, that it is refreshing to discover that it also has great value in the medical field as a preventive material...to prevent damage to the body from dangerous penetration of X-rays and other harmful electrical manifestations. Also, [sic] that its toxic quality is used to protect our food supply as an ingredient of insecticides.

...When I first became seriously interested in the problem of lead hygiene quite a few years ago, I was inclined to accept without much questioning many of the pronouncements that were made about lead in hygienic and medical circles, but it soon became apparent to me that our knowledge was not as thorough as it should be. Thanks to the perfectly enormous amount of work that has been done in medical circles over the past 35 years in more places than I can conveniently give credit to here, I feel that like a good many fears that plague humanity, this one can be dissipated in the light of our growing knowledge. For example, during the war, in an effort to economize on scarce tin, all of which had to be imported into the United States, and to consume lead...I suggested to an officer of the Food and Drug Administration that shaving cream might well be packed in lead instead of tin or aluminum collapsible tubes. He disagreed because he said, "Suppose someone shaved and cut his face? He would be apt to contract lead poisoning." Comment is superfluous. Events subsequently made it necessary to use lead for the purpose and that it has been done with perfect safety I have no doubt. As a matter of fact, tooth paste was added to the list of products eligible for packaging in lead, and I am sure millions of people used it with complete safety.... Here then was a large public experiment in the use of lead, where a hazard had been thought to exist, without any ill effects.

Some years ago I had a visit from two eminent professors of agriculture from western colleges who had been delegated by the apple-growing industry in the northwest to investigate the [lead arsenate insecticide] spray residue problem. They told me that the apple industry was threatened with extinction unless something were done to establish a tolerance for lead which they could meet. I urged a complete and impartial investigation, and, because of the public interest involved, suggested the use of the U.S. Public Health Service. Most of you know that this was subsequently done and the Public Health Service issued an excellent report, the conclusion of which was that they did not find a single case of lead poisoning among the 1,231 persons examined in the field, some subjected to high exposure of the lead arsenate spray....

Although I realize that great progress has been made, I do not think industry will ever rest content until we reach perfection and that no one is hurt by the production or use of any lead product. In this battle the prevention of exposure is our principal weapon. That is also where great improvement has been registered. Be keeping lead out of the atmosphere and by personal cleanliness, the lead hazard in manufacturing operations has been largely overcome, as you well know. This progress, I am confident, will be continued as more people realize that, not only from a humanitarian standpoint, but from a practical dollars and cents standpoint, it pays to improve hygienic practices.

Source: Felix Edgar Wormser, "Opening Address," *Proceedings of Lead Hygiene Conference Held at Bismarck Hotel, Chicago, Ill., November 15–16, 1948* (New York: Lead Industries Association, 1948), pp. 6–9.

Document 10.6   Dr. Clair C. Patterson Denounces Decades of "Chronic Lead Insult," 1965

For four decades, the lead industry rested its case for continued manufacture and distribution of its products upon a theory (often referred to as the "threshold for damage" concept) put forward by Robert Kehoe of the corporate-funded Kettering Laboratory at the University of Cincinnati. Kehoe argued that lead appeared naturally in relatively high levels in the human body. From the time of the 1925 conference, his premise had been denounced by medical and toxicological experts from the nation's leading universities. Still, Kehoe continued to use it to explain high blood-lead levels in human subjects exposed to leaded gasoline. The theory began to collapse in part with the 1965 publication of Dr. Clair Patterson's article, "Contaminated and Natural Lead Environments of Man," published in the Archives of Environmental Health. *Patterson was a California Institute of Technology geochemist previously known for his work on the Manhattan Project and for providing the most accurate estimate of the age of planet earth. His work on the latter scientific problem led him to the discovery that humankind in the industrial age had raised by a factor of 100 the naturally occurring level of lead in the body (which turned out to be grossly underestimated), and by 1,000 times over lead levels in the atmosphere. Patterson led the shaping of further scientific investigation that ultimately resulted in the ban on leaded gasoline in the United States.*

CHRONIC LEAD INSULT

The latest view of existing lead states in this country officially sanctioned by the United States Department of Health, Education and Welfare, is that they "... are well within the presently accepted range of lead levels for humans and are not significant in terms of a threat of the occurrence of lead intoxication ...". This view has prevailed in the state and Federal Public Health Services for decades. It is based upon a threshold for damage concept which has been applied to industrial workers, and which involves the axiom that a worker must be either perfectly healthy or classically intoxicated with lead but cannot be neither. This is a seriously unfortunate situation for the following reasons.

An average level of 0.25 ppm [parts per million] of lead in the blood of our population fails by an order of magnitude to provide an adequate margin of safety even from classical lead poisoning when the crudely significant range of lead levels in our population lies between 0.05 and 0.4 ppm and the threshold for acute lead intoxication lies in the uncertain range of 0.5 to 0.8 ppm.

The above acceptance of typical lead levels in humans in the United States today as normal and therefore safe or natural is founded on nothing more than an assumption that these terms are equivalent. No acceptable evidence exists which justifies this assumption. On the contrary, ... such an assumption may be in gross error. The 0.25 ppm level of lead in the blood, which has been and is still regarded with ill-founded complacency, actually seems to lie between an average natural level of about 0.002 ppm and an acute toxic threshold of 0.5 to 0.8 ppm. This suggests clearly and strongly that the average resident of the United States is being subjected to severe chronic lead insult.

The threshold for damage concept, as it applies to lead, is an ill-defined opinion unsupported by any evidence. . . .

Economic pressures for expedient exposure to lead should be opposed and brought into suitable balance by pressures for healthy populations unafflicted by lead poisoning. These latter pressures will originate from a thorough understanding of mechanisms of lead metabolism, but this kind of knowledge does not exist today and will be acquired slowly. It would be tragic if, many decades from now, it were recognized from accumulated evidence that large segments of populations in ours and other nations had suffered needless disability and torment because early warning signs like those recognized in this report went unheeded.

This crucial problem has been a matter of concern to some toxicologists. Monier-Williams, for example, said "It cannot be emphasized too strongly that in discussing the amount of lead which may be considered as negligible in food, consideration of the toxic limits, so far as these are defined by the appearance of symptoms of poisoning, is beside the point, and tends to obscure the real question. What we want to know is not so much the toxic limit, as the safe limit, if indeed any limit, however small, for a cumulative poison can be regarded as safe. We cannot assume that there is a sharp dividing line between what is obviously toxic, giving rise to lead colic or other symptoms, and what is completely harmless. In all probability there is a range of lead intake between these two extremes in which some effects, however slight, are produced upon metabolism, effects which, clinically, may be difficult or impossible to detect or to ascribe to their real cause." . . .

SUMMARY

There are definite indications that residents of the United States today are undergoing severe chronic lead insult. The average American ingests some 400 pg of lead per day in food, air, and water, a process which has been viewed with complacency for decades. Geochemical relationships and material balance considerations show that this ingestion of about 20 tons of lead per year on a national basis is grossly excessive compared to natural conditions. . . .

Source: Clair C. Patterson, "Contaminated and Natural Lead Environments on Man," *Archives of Environmental Health* 11 (September 1965): 344, 356–58. Reprinted with permission of the Helen Dwight Reid Educational Foundation. Published by Heldref Publications, 1319 Eighteenth St., NW, Washington, DC 20036-1802. Copyright © 1965.

NOTES

1. Benjamin Franklin, letter to Sir George Baker, 1786; quoted in Marjorie Smith, "Lead in History," in Richard Lansdown and William Yule, eds., *Lead Toxicity: History and Environmental Impact* (Baltimore: Johns Hopkins University Press, 1986), p. 21.

2. Columbus, "Federal Report Is Held to be Wrong," *Ohio State Journal* (January 24, 1913): 10.

3. Alice Hamilton to Charles H. Verrill, February 12, 1913, in Barbara Sicherman, *Alice Hamilton: A Life in Letters* (Urbana: University of Illinois Press, 2003), pp. 170–71.

4. Quote from Jamie Lincoln Kitman, "The Secret History of Lead," *Nation*, March 20, 2000; quote from *The Nation* on-line edition, http://www.thenation.com/doc.mhtml? i=20000320&c=1&s=kitman (accessed July 31, 2005).

5. David Rosner and Gerald Markowitz, "'A Gift of God'?: The Public Health Controversy over Leaded Gasoline during the 1920s," in David Rosner and Gerald Markowitz, eds., *Dying for Work: Workers' Safety and Health in Twentieth-Century America* (Bloomington: Indiana University Press, 1987), p. 124; quote from C. A. Straw to R. R. Sayers, August 22, 1924, National Archives, Record Group 70, 101869, File 725, in Rosner and Markowitz, *Dying for Work*, p. 124.

6. Quoted in Rosner and Markowitz, *Dying for Work*, p. 137.

7. Kitman, "Secret History of Lead."

ANNOTATED BIBLIOGRAPHY

Kitman, Jamie Lincoln. "The Secret History of Lead." *Nation* (March 20, 2000): 21–29.
    Investigative journalist Kitman offers a sharp critique of Ethyl's history, along with a useful timeline of lead in human history.

Kovarik, William Joseph. "The Ethyl Controversy: The News Media and the Public Health Debate over Leaded Gasoline, 1924–1926." Ph.D. diss., University of Maryland, College Park, 1993. Kovarik offers a thorough examination of the public discourse surrounding tetraethyl lead. He makes clear that industry officials knew the stakes in this critical public health debate.

Lansdown, Richard, and William Yule, eds. *Lead Toxicity: History and Environmental Impact*. Baltimore: Johns Hopkins University Press, 1986. A fine survey of the uses of lead and its resultant environmental and public health impacts in history, from ancient times through the very recent past.

Loeb, Alan P. "Birth of the Kettering Doctrine: Fordism, Sloanism, and the Discovery of Tetraethyl Lead." *Business and Economic History* 24 (Fall 1995): 72–88.

———. "Paradigms Lost: A Case Study Analysis of Models of Corporate Responsibility for the Environment." *Business and Economic History* 28 (Winter 1999): 95–107. These two articles by an economic historian probe the rationale for and consequences of corporate decision making inside the auto and oil industries with respect to the decision to develop tetraethyl and not more environmentally benign gasoline additives.

Rosner, David, and Gerald Markowitz, eds. *Dying for Work: Workers' Safety and Health in Twentieth-Century America*. Bloomington: Indiana University Press, 1987. A superb collection of essays examining the history of occupational disease in the United States since the late nineteenth century, along with the efforts to study and ultimately limit workers' exposure to toxic substances including lead and asbestos.

Sicherman, Barbara, ed. *Alice Hamilton: A Life in Letters*. Chicago: University of Illinois Press, 2003. This smartly edited volume of the distinguished public health physician and occupational health pioneer provides a fascinating look inside Hamilton's professional relationships with colleagues in government agencies. Her pivotal early years studying and attempting to reform the lead industry are a highlight.

11

Causes and Consequences
of the Dust Bowl

God speed the plow.... By this wonderful provision, which is only man's mastery over nature, the clouds are dispensing copious rains... [the plow] is the instrument which separates civilization from savagery; and converts a desert into a farm or garden....To be more concise, Rain follows the plow.

—Land speculator Charles Dana Wilber, 1881[1]

July has gone, and still no rain. This is the worst summer yet. The fields are nothing but grasshoppers and dried-up Russian thistle. The hills are burned to nothing but rocks and dry ground. The meadows have no grass except in former slough holes, and that has to be raked and stacked as soon as cut, or it blows away in these hot winds. There is one dust storm after another. It is the most disheartening situation I have seen yet. Livestock and humans are really suffering. I don't know how we keep going.

—Anne Marie Low, August 1, 1936[2]

No event in modern American environmental history struck with such dramatic force as the massive dust storms of the mid-1930s that turned a vast section of the southern Great Plains into a "Dust Bowl" and blew Oklahoma soil into the streets of Chicago, the halls of the White House, and onto the decks of ships positioned off the East Coast. Nor has any single event raised more fundamental questions about Americans' relationship with the Earth. The debate over the causes of the Dust Bowl that emerged during and following the disaster revealed sharply different interpretations of the event, often dividing Americans living in the East from those in the affected region of the Great Plains. Questions raised then by farmers and ranchers, by government scientists, and by other observers have yet to be definitively answered: was this the fault of a sustained period of unprecedented drought and fierce winds, or had the region faced those natural forces before? Could the farmers themselves be blamed, as much of the eastern press suggested, and some in the federal government seemed to confirm? Did the severe erosion of 500,000 square miles of the Great Plains demand a stronger role of the federal government in managing the nation's public lands—most of them located in a West long resistant to such overbearing bureaucratic administration? And was it not true, as many westerners were quick to point out, that federal policies had invited the kind of excessive plowing and grazing that exposed millions of acres of former grassland to drought and wind?

For a number of policymakers in the New Deal administration of President Franklin D. Roosevelt, the catastrophic dust storms offered apocalyptic evidence that nothing less than a shift in values was in order: away from the acquisitive, endlessly expansionary impulse that they believed had, more than anything else, brought on the disaster, and toward an ecological sensibility that drew from nature's bounty more mindfully and respectfully. For New Dealers charged with studying the causes and remedies of the Dust Bowl, the disaster provoked unprecedented questioning of the nation's economic faith in endless progress through technology. Ideas from the maturing discipline of ecology were infused into natural resource policies. In the eyes of many critics, however, most of the solutions proposed and all that came to pass represented compromise politics and governmental bureaucracy that failed to seize the opportunity presented by the Dust Bowl crisis to resolve its root causes and prevent another such calamity from ever recurring.

Misunderstanding the Great Plains climate and geography did not begin with the Dust Bowl generation. Explorer Zebulon Pike had first categorized the region in 1806 as best suited for the array of Native American tribes who lived there. In 1820 explorer Stephen H. Long affirmed Pike's view, determining that it was "almost wholly unfit for cultivation, and of course uninhabitable by a people depending upon agriculture for their subsistence." Long's labeling of the region as "The Great American Desert—Unexplored," stuck, appearing on maps for decades afterward.

It was not until the middle of the century that another view of the region emerged. At the height of America's expansionist fever, when the religiously, racially charged ideology of Manifest Destiny was at its height, a number of influential Americans began to reconsider the prospects for the Great Plains. As historian Henry Nash Smith brilliantly revealed, enterprising "American frontiersmen went to work transforming the image of the desert," most notably by repeating in the popular literature of the West the folk wisdom that settlement was transforming the climate of the southern plains. Cultivation of farms and planting of trees, wrote Missourian and Santa Fe Trail trader Josiah Gregg, had produced a wetter climate, according to the locals in New Mexico. If it indeed was true that frontier Hispano settlers produced a climate more hospitable to farming, surely the Americans, with their ambition and advanced science and technology could make it a veritable garden. As land speculator Charles Dana Wilber put it, "Rain follows the plow," a maxim that became popular myth in the latter decades of the century. Other forces propelled Americans westward. Further emigration into this previous no-man's land also would provide a "safety valve" for the discontented laboring classes and im-migrants who longed for a fresh start. So went the mythology, seized upon by railroads, land speculators, the General Land Office, and eventually affirmed by government explorers and scientists such as Ferdinand V. Hayden. If Hayden harbored scientific doubt about the fantasy that "rain [followed] the plow," he laid them aside in order to advance the larger national interests.[3] The proof seemed to be in the skies, as the region enjoyed sustained periods of heavier-than-normal precipitation during parts of the 1870s and 1880s. Adding to the allure of the Great Plains was the Homestead Act of 1862, generously offering 160 acres of free land to any prospective farmer after five years' set-tlement. Though it drew thousands more to the region, the law's promise proved nearly as chimerical as the illusion that steady rainfall would follow cultivation; the railroads and other large corporations continued to dominate the sale of land throughout the West.

Who would have guessed that it would quit raining? Tragically, American settlers' knowledge of the natural history of the Great Plains extended as far back as the railroad or land agent's literature that brought them there. They had little understanding that the region had always been subject to cyclic periods of drought and heavy rainfall. In this case, rain *preceded* the plow.

The wet years had also produced a veritable beef bonanza, as the northern range of the Great Plains filled with cattle by the hundreds of thousands, driven north from Texas following the demise of the bison. The most powerful cattle barons owned or controlled land covering several thousand square miles, though not enough, for the massive herds soon ate the short grass prairie to stubble. By 1887 the same drought that afflicted farmers, combined with a brutal winter, decimated the herds and shattered the buoyant hopes of aspiring cattlemen, if only for a time. As with so many other ecological disasters, the lessons proved temporary; cattle returned to private and public rangelands by the turn of the century, albeit in somewhat lesser numbers.

Over the course of millennia, the grasslands west of the 100th meridian had survived periods of drought as well as the pounding of bison and antelope hoofs (in part because bison, the dominant animal in this environment, did not graze in one place for too long). What it could not endure, it turned out, was the punishment of an intensified largely single-crop agricultural system of plowing and planting. Like the cattle bonanza, mile after linear mile of wheat paid huge dividends when weather and market conditions were right (as they were for a while), but they reaped dust storms and debt when the rains went away, as they did in 1894–95—the first catastrophic drought to hit the region in the modern era. Farmers by the score abandoned their homesteads. Some starved to death.

But as historian James Malin later recounted (Document 11.8), the farmers of the Great Plains—those who remained anyhow—adapted with new crops and new species of the old. Mennonite settlers from Russia brought hard red winter wheat that thrived in the subhumid conditions of central Kansas; spring wheat and sorghum proved fine substitutes in other areas. Drought-resistant crops were only one element of what was dubbed "dryland farming" (the railroads preferred "scientific"). The dryland regime also included fallowing of fields to allow moisture to accumulate underneath the packed soil, and a technique called "listing," which was essentially "double-plowing" so as to protect with rough furrows and ridges both soil and fragile crop. It worked famously for a time. Add tractors, combines, and gas-powered machinery to the mix, along with nearly continuously high and stable prices (aided by World War I) and the result was the second Great Plains wheat boom. Easterners and foreign investors (some of whom were called "suitcase farmers" for their alien ownership and seasonal management) cashed in, making profit many times over their relatively small investment. By 1929 the Great Plains states harvested more than 100 million acres of mostly wheat and corn—a nearly ten-fold increase from fifty years before. The Great Plains Committee established by President Roosevelt to investigate the causes of the Dust Bowl indicted this "strong speculative urge" as the leading culprit in the disaster.

The "great plow-up" bore countless bushels of wheat and fat profits for nearly two decades. Gone, however, were the native grasses, which once held the region's soil in place. And when the wet years predictably disappeared in the early 1930s, catastrophe arrived. Several years of drought arrived nearly simultaneously with the Great Depression, exposing the southern Great Plains' once rich soil to extreme wind erosion. During the worst of it in the spring of 1934, wind blew soil miles into the sky, covering farms and barns with dust twelve feet high. Women and children perished from "dust pneumonia."

Like a biblical plague, mere men could not stop, or even explain, it. The overwhelming majority of the region's residents naturally blamed the drought. Dry farming, it turned out, "worked best in wet years." As another farmer put it plainly, "that drought put the fixins to us." Eastern observers, particularly influential media organs like the *Saturday Evening Post* and *New York Times*, cast blame on the plainsmen themselves. Chambers of Commerce throughout west Texas rallied to defend their region's reputation and business climate. Newspaper editor John L. McCarty of Delhart waged verbal war on the uppity eastern establishment that knew nothing, he declared, of the Great Plains, or of its people's courageous history in settling the region.

While the public debate raged on, the activist New Deal administration of Franklin D. Roosevelt based its study of the region's plight on the emerging theory of ecological succession first espoused by biologist Frederick Clements several decades before. Clements's theory essentially held that the grasslands habitat of the Great Plains region had evolved over the course of several millennia to reach a stable, "climax"—and implicitly optimum—state that humans had brutally disrupted at their own peril in a mere half-century of time. Over time, the plains had become the most biologically diverse region on the continent, home to more species of flora and fauna than anywhere else. Clements's suggestion that the climax state of ecological maturity was the *preferred* state— a theory to which many if not all members of Roosevelt's committee subscribed—raised all sorts of troubling questions about the proper human role in this, or any, environment. Here it was: the essential core of what Clements's disciple Paul Sears called the "subversive" science of ecology. As Donald Worster, the preeminent historian of the Dust Bowl has argued, many who sat on the Great Plains committees and on the various incarnations of FDR's Natural Resources Planning Board had reached the conclusion that the American economy had reached a "matured" state that demanded that some of its agricultural land be retired to other more ecologically sensible purposes. Some subscribed to the radical notion implicit in Clements's theory that humans just might not be biologically central to life on the planet, and that the human economy had to surrender to the limitations of the natural world. Furthermore, individuals such as Lewis Gray (author of the *Future of the Great Plains* report) had become convinced that the era of an endlessly expansionist America had ended; in such a world, private property rights (alien corporate ownership of millions of acres of grassland, for example) would have to give way to the collective social good of the nation that paralleled sound ecological thinking.[4]

The New Deal response to the Dust Bowl offered the clearest evidence of how different the conservation of the 1930s was from that of the Pinchot-Theodore Roosevelt era. Whereas the approach of that first generation of conservationists had centered on how to manage America's resources in order to extend them for production forever, FDR conservationists often maintained that there had been too much production. This un-American heresy could only have been found in a decade when not only was ecology as a science maturing and gaining credibility, but perhaps equally important, other pillars of America's economic system were under withering attack from all sides.

Ecological principles receded in importance (or were eliminated entirely) in the final version of *The Future of the Great Plains*. The committee's fundamental recommendations began with the premise that the disaster of the Dust Bowl resulted not from a culture where more was never enough, but from having carried an agricultural system from an eastern humid climate into a subhumid region where it simply did not work. The inappropriateness of particular farming methods served as the foundation of the committee's findings, not an ecologically grounded challenge to the fundamental American belief of more production. Still, some ecological language and idealism remained, particularly when it came to the rhetoric of the Roosevelt administration. Produced by the Farm Security Administration (FSA), the propaganda film *The Plow That Broke the Plains* still stands as the most famous example of Rooseveltian ecological idealism that seemed to call for greater American humility with regard to natural resources.

As for policy, the legacy was mixed from both the standpoint of ecology and the famous egalitarian economics upon which the New Deal was ostensibly based. The Department of Agriculture spent much of the decade hurriedly trying to arrest the fifty-year process that had resulted in the Dust Bowl. The Soil Conservation Service (SCS) established seventy-five Conservation Districts to better assist and oversee farmers as they carried out soil conservation measures like contour planting (farming with the natural terrain of the land, as opposed to straight rows to minimize wind erosion). The SCS returned to the public domain by purchasing more than 11 million acres of badly abused or unused private agricultural lands. The original target was 75 million, however, suggesting that programs such as this and more radical suggestions to remove farmers from existing and degraded lands simply faced too much opposition and were by the end of the decade either defunded or terminated entirely. The Civilian Conservation Corps planted hundreds of millions of trees in "shelter belts" to provide greater protection from wind. To confront the problem of deflated farm prices, the government paid farmers to stop producing and to retire lands from production. In a telling sign that the end of the frontier had truly come, the federal government, under the Taylor Grazing Act of 1934, withdrew the remaining public range lands from sale. A new Grazing Service (renamed the Bureau of Land Management in 1946) began regulating use of those lands for ranching and all other extractive purposes.[5]

Indeed, management of the public lands by the federal government increased significantly as a result of the Dust Bowl disaster. But whether these agencies and regulations served the interest of small farmers and ranchers or not remained in question decades later. Furthermore, the extent to which they have served the ecological health and integrity of those lands also has been seriously questioned by environmentalists, by environmental historians, and by, as Great Plains historian James Malin called them, "common men" throughout the region. Programs that ostensibly recognized the natural limits of the region in actuality did little to force the postwar farm economy to live within them. Federal agencies did not constrain the activities of corporate agribusiness, but rather served them. Even as Malin lambasted government management of his region, corporate agriculture was well on the way to becoming the dominant force of both the economics of American agriculture and environmental change in the Great Plains, and arguably the greater menace faced by independent farmers and ranchers. Once challenged by New Dealers, the economic logic of agricultural corporate capitalism rolled on in the postwar era, as greater and cheaper production continued to marginalize small operators. Its controlling management regime was dictated by science, technology, and decision making in the halls of government and corporate boardrooms that increasingly excluded the voices and interests of small farmers throughout the nation.

Perhaps most disturbingly, the natural limits of the Great Plains were solved less by planting crop species that demanded less water than by drawing greater volumes of water from the underground aquifer that lies under a vast expanse of the Great Plains. The Ogallala aquifer irrigated 3.5 million acres of farmland in 1950; by the end of the century it was irrigating more than 16 million acres. Beginning the 1970s, Great Plains farming operations had been consuming groundwater at a rate conservatively estimated as ten times that of natural recharge. Being sucked dry at an unsustainable rate, the Ogallala demonstrated for many critics of U.S. agricultural policy that the wrong lessons were learned from the Dirty Thirties, that the nation had merely postponed another day of environmental reckoning. By the late 1990s, parts of the region had been so intensively irrigated that once-productive soils had become salinized (permeated by residual salts) and were approaching Dust Bowl conditions. At bottom, the debate that followed the Dust Bowl failed to overturn a set of values deeply embedded in the culture. Not surprisingly, Americans refused to steer from a course of more production to satisfy the insatiable urges of the marketplace—no matter how environmentally or socially irresponsible they may be.

DOCUMENTS

Document 11.1   **Ferdinand V. Hayden Confirms "Rain Follows the Plow" Myth, 1867**

Missourian Josiah Gregg, who made a lucrative career as a trader on the Santa Fe Trail, in 1844 first popularized the idea that "extensive cultivation of the earth" by American settlers might transform the arid region west of the Missouri River—what had been known for decades as the "Great American Desert"—into a garden. The myth held that bravely planting farms and trees would increase the humidity and therefore the precipitation of the subhumid region and render it hospitable to farming and the extension of American civilization. Railroads, land speculators, and regional newspapers seized upon the idea, reiterating it endlessly in an effort to lure settlers to the region. In 1867 Ferdinand V. Hayden, recently named Director of the Geological and Geographical Survey of the Territories, affixed the imprimatur of scientific authority on the idea in his first official report to the Secretary of the Interior. It turned out to be a leap of scientific faith, for the wet period to which Hayden referred was tragically followed by a period of drought, as it always had been.

It is believed . . . that the planting of ten or fifteen acres of forest-trees on each quarter-section will have a most important effect on the climate, equalizing and increasing the moisture and adding greatly to the fertility of the soil. The settlement of the country and the increase of the timber has already changed for the better the climate of that portion of Nebraska lying along the Missouri, so that within the last twelve or fourteen years the rain has gradually increased in quantity and is more equally distributed through the year. I am confident that this change will continue to extend across the dry belt to the foot of the Rocky Mountains as the settlements extend and the forest-trees are planted in proper quantities.

Source: Report of the Commissioner of the General Land Office for the Year 1867 (Washington, DC: Government Printing Office, 1867), pp. 135–36.

Document 11.2   **Cattleman T. C. Henry Debunks "Rain Follows the Plow" Myth, 1882**

Several periods of drought had already disproved the notion that rain would follow pioneering agricultural settlement. Kansan T. C. Henry had profited by the earlier wheat boom on the Kansas frontier, but by 1882 he had concluded that the subhumid environment of his state did not lend itself well to farming but rather to grazing cattle. In this address to the Central Kansas Stock Breeders' Association in Manhattan, Kansas, he acknowledges the region's climatic limits and argues that the grasslands be used for grazing purposes.

I apprehend that some, possibly many, of the propositions I shall advance on this occasion will subject me to criticism.... But I believe we are just upon the threshold of an era of substantial growth and real prosperity. We are wiser: drouths, grasshoppers, chinch-bugs and winds have taught us,—how much, and what, let us see.

... The attempt to sustain a population, then, wholly or mainly by grain—growing alone, must be conceded, I am sure, after a ten years' effort, to be unsuccessful. Only so far as the system of farming adopted is auxiliary to the stock interests, can it be recommended. The news paper, the railway and free homesteads are powerful agencies in building up a State now; but even more mighty is the withering, scorching, south wind. The former have more or less wittingly decoyed thousands and tens of thousands of honest, earnest people into a determined effort to settle the plains of western Kansas; and the latter has steadily blasted their hopes and wrested their fortunes.

... No industry, no energy, no enterprise can ever make it possible for an average 160 acres in western Kansas to yield such a support as American civilization demands for a family. The soil is fertile, and the climate unobjectionable; but the rainfall is insufficient to sustain general farming. Nor has there been any material increase in the annual rainfall; ... but so long as the Rocky Mountains border us on the west, so long will the natural humidity of the atmosphere be lessened.

... If ever any general climatic changes occur in our State, it will be effected by some great organic law wholly outside of any merely human agency. I conclude, therefore, that the present physical phenomena of the plains and prairies of Kansas will continue practically unchanged, and every successfully organized industry must be conformed to them. Here and there among the eastern counties of western Kansas, where the chemical constituents of the soil are particularly favorable, wheat growing may be made profitable. Even in such counties it should be a subordinate crop, and in all others wholly abandoned. Dry winters, late spring frosts, hot winds, chinch-bugs, and occasionally, grasshoppers, involve risks which no prudent farmer will confront. Corn is a safer crop, and its culture may be pushed further west.... Rye is very valuable, particularly for winter grazing. Oats, barley, and millet do well in a "wet year." Confident, therefore, that stock growing must be the leading and almost sole industry of western Kansas, I purpose directing the balance of this essay to the consideration of such measures as will, in my opinion, most wisely protect and advance that interest.

First—Preserve our native grasses.... No artificial grass has yet been supplied which can be relied upon as a substitute for them. They appear late in the spring, and they frost early in the fall; but they are bulky, abundant and nutritious. At any rate, they are all we have, all we are likely to have, and if once destroyed our plains would be a desert indeed....

Source: The Industrialist, February 4, 1882, pp. 1–3.

Document 11.3   *Collier's* Magazine Indicts Great Plains Farmers
for Dust Bowl

*The ensuing decades saw countless farm families learn the painful
lesson that "rain follows the plow" was more myth than scientific fact.
Severe drought in 1894–95 drove tens of thousands of settlers to
abandon their homesteads and return east. In the early twentieth
century a wet cycle returned, and "the big plow-up" of the World
War I and postwar era prepared the way for a disaster of unprecedented proportions. In this 1937 article in* Collier's *magazine, writer
Walter Davenport rails at "heedless greed," an inept federal government, and the ignorance of the farmers themselves.*

As long as men and machines pulverize dry range land to plant wheat, the
Dust Bowl will grow deeper and wider. As long as heedless greed . . . is pitted
against the natural laws we shall have more and bigger dust storms with all
their miserable train—famine, violent death, private and public futility, insanity
and lost generations.

Fifty federal agencies and half that many state bureaus have puttered around
the Dust Bowl for nearly four years, spending nearly $300 million to encourage
hapless farmers to go on farming hardpan farms which wouldn't and don't
support lizards. All that talking, dreaming, exhorting and political hook-
worming has brought us just more and bigger dust storms, less and lower
morale and only one net gain. And that increase is in the number of acreage
owners whose only possible crops are federal bounties, state subsidies, emergency legislation and an abiding conviction that it is no longer their privilege
but their right to "farm the government." . . .

Farmers, too many of whom have no more talent for agriculture than we
have, told us old wives' tales of changes in the world's weather, in the earth's
interior, in the deterioration of grain seed—that all these fabulous factors
contributed to their woe. None admitted that he had plowed the land to death,
that he was in any way responsible. We heard the radio blamed. Airplanes too.
They told us that the mountains had moved. . . .

Source: Walter Davenport, "Land Where Our Children Die," *Collier's*, September 18,
1937, pp. 14, 73.

Document 11.4   Texan John L. McCarty Defends His Region
from "Vicious Libel"

*Many westerners were indignant at the charges leveled at them and
the region largely by the eastern press. Newspapers and Chambers of*

Commerce throughout Texas in particular challenged the image of a blighted, beleaguered Great Plains and struck back with defensive editorials such as this one, written by the editor of the Dalhart Texan *as "An Open Letter" to the Associated Press.*

This is a protest against the misshapen, lopsided, downright harmful publicity that the Associated Press is giving this area which some hare-brained individual, in an abortive fit a year or two ago, named the "dust-bowl." ...

Does the Associated Press know, or does it care, that the Dalhart area has a 75 per cent better vegetative cover than it had last year, according to high Soil Conservation Service officials? Does the Associated Press know or care that two Hartley County, Texas citizens said the other day that on the basis of present prospects the county wheat crop would be about 75 per cent normal? Does the AP know that everybody is talking about getting back to normalcy, that we're heading out of the woods, that payrolls are picking up, that farm equipment sales are going ahead steadily? Or would the Associated Press rather nurse a decrepit has-been news story?

Will the Associated Press publish a feature story on the WHOLE TRUTH about this country? ...

Does the Associated Press care to redeem itself or will it just let a courageous people and a great country that are now fighting back from a bad situation suffer on account of Associated Press bungling?

Source: A.H.L., "An Open Letter," *Dalhart Texan,* May 18, 1937.

Document 11.5   President Franklin D. Roosevelt on the Use of Natural Resources, 1935

Responding to the Dust Bowl crisis, President Roosevelt, harkening back to the work of his second cousin decades before, established a broad program to inventory and more wisely use the nation's natural resources. In this 1935 address to the Congress, he articulates both an ecological sensibility that Theodore Roosevelt's conservation administration never espoused and the classically optimistic American belief that perseverance and ingenuity can overcome the malevolent forces of nature. This effort had actually begun in 1931 with the National Conference on Land Utilization, which evolved ultimately into the Natural Resources Planning Board. Although FDR does not explicitly declare it, one of the chief findings of that body was that America's agricultural economy had become overgrown, and that millions of acres currently under cultivation could and should be retired. Implicit in the message of the board and the president was a radical questioning of the assumption that more production and parochial Western interests should continue to guide the nation's public land use policies.

January 24, 1935
To the Congress:

DURING the three or four centuries of white men on the American continent, we find a continuous striving of civilization against Nature. It is only in recent years that we have learned how greatly by these processes we have harmed Nature and Nature in turn has harmed us.

We should not too largely blame our ancestors, for they found such teeming riches in woods and soil and water, such abundance above the earth and beneath it, such freedom in the taking, that they gave small heed to the results that would follow the filling of their own immediate needs. Most of them, it is true, had come from many-peopled lands where necessity had invoked the preserving of the bounties of Nature. But they had come here for the obtaining of a greater freedom, and it was natural that freedom of conscience and freedom of government should extend itself in their minds to the unrestricted enjoyment of the free use of land and water.

Furthermore, it is only within our own generation that the development of science, leaping forward, has taught us where and how we have violated Nature's immutable laws, and where and how we can commence to repair such havoc as man has wrought.

In recent years little groups of earnest men and women have told us of this havoc: of the cutting of our last stands of virgin timber; of the increasing floods; of the washing away of millions of acres of our top soils; of the lowering of our water-tables; of the dangers of one-crop farming; of the depletion of our minerals—in short, of all the evils that we have brought upon ourselves today and the even greater evils that will attend our children unless we act.

Such is the condition that attends the exploitation of our natural resources if we continue our planless course.

But another element enters in. Men and Nature must work hand in hand. The throwing out of balance of the resources of Nature throws out of balance also the lives of men. We find millions of our citizens stranded in village and on farm—stranded there because Nature cannot support them in the livelihood they had sought to gain through her. We find other millions gravitated to centers of population so vast that the laws of natural economics have broken down.

If the misuse of natural resources alone were concerned, we should consider our problem only in terms of land and water. It is because misuse extends to what men and women are doing with their occupations and to their many mistakes in herding themselves together that I have chosen, in addressing the Congress, to use the broader term "National Resources."

For the first time in our national history we have made an inventory of our national assets and the problems relating to them. For the first time we have drawn together the foresight of the various planning agencies of the Federal Government and suggested a method and a policy for the future....

In this inventory of our national wealth we follow the custom of prudent people toward their own private property. We as a Nation take stock of what we as a Nation own. We consider the uses to which it can be put. We plan these uses in the light of what we want to be, of what we want to accomplish as a people. We think of our land and water and human resources not as static and sterile possessions but as life-giving assets to be administered by wise- provision for future days. We seek to use our natural resources not as a thing apart but as something that is interwoven with industry, labor, finance, taxation, agriculture, homes, recreation, good citizenship. The results of this interweaving will have a greater influence on the future American standard of living than all the rest of our economics put together....

A permanent National Resources Board, toward the establishment of which we should be looking forward, would recommend yearly to the President and the Congress priority of projects in the national plan....

Our goal must be a national one. Achievements in the arts of communication, of transportation, of mechanized production, of agriculture, of mining and of power, do not minimize the rights of State Governments but they go far beyond the economics of State boundaries.

Only through the growth of thought and action in terms of national economics, can we best serve individual lives in individual localities.

It is, as these Reports point out, an error to say that we have "conquered Nature." We must, rather, start to shape our lives in more harmonious relationship with Nature. This is a milestone in our progress toward that end. The future of every American family everywhere will be affected by the action we take.

Source: President Franklin D. Roosevelt, January 24, 1935, reprinted in *The Public Papers and Addresses of Franklin D. Roosevelt*, vol. 4, 1935 (New York City: Random House, 1938), p. 59.

**Document 11.6   The Great Plains Drought Area Committee and the
                      Future of the Great Plains Committee
                      Report to the President, 1936**

After personally surveying the region in 1935, President Roosevelt established a committee to investigate more fully the causes of the Dust Bowl, plan short-term relief measures for the people afflicted, and recommend long-term solutions that would prevent future disasters. The initial report included grim descriptions of the condition of the region as well as a history of the ill-considered human decisions that led to the Dust Bowl. It called for agricultural decision-makers, from farmers to state and local government officials, to reconcile agricultural development in the region to the defining limitations of rainfall. Although some members of this and the Future of the Great Plains Committee argued for it in their deliberations, the committee's final report failed to indict the fundamental assumptions of America's economic culture, instead laying blame at the imposition of an agricultural system not fitted to the subhumid climate of the plains.

REPORT OF THE GREAT PLAINS DROUGHT AREA
COMMITTEE, SEPTEMBER 1936

The Nature of the Problem

...A trip through the drought area, supplementing data already on record, makes it evident that we are not confronted merely with a short term problem of relief, already being dealt with by several agencies of the Federal Government, but with a long term problem of readjustment and reorganization.

The agricultural economy of the Great Plains will become increasingly unstable and unsafe, in view of the impossibility of permanent increase in the amount of rainfall, unless over cropping, over grazing and improper farm methods are prevented. There is no reason to believe that the primary factors of climate temperature, precipitation and winds in the Great Plains region have undergone any fundamental change. The future of the region must depend, therefore, on the degree to which farming practices conform to natural conditions. Because the situation has now passed out of the individual farmer's control, the reorganization of farming practices demands the cooperation of many agencies....

Mistaken public policies have been largely responsible for the situation now existing. That responsibility must be liquidated by new policies. The Federal Government must do its full share in remedying the damage caused by a mistaken homesteading policy, by the stimulation of war time demands which led to over cropping and over grazing, and by encouragement of a system of agriculture which could not be both permanent and prosperous....

CAUSES OF THE PRESENT SITUATION

...The basic cause of the present Great Plains situation is an attempt to impose upon the region a system of agriculture to which the Plains are not adapted to bring into a semi arid region methods which, on the whole, are suitable only for a humid region.

The Great Plains area has climatic attributes which cannot be altered by any act of man, although they may slowly become changed, for better or worse, by natural weather cycles which we cannot yet predict.

With respect to plant growth, however, the stripping off of the mellow top soil, by unrestrained erosion, down to less absorptive, less tractable sub soil, is the equivalent of an unfavorable soil climate change. Adoption of soil conserving farm practices based on increased use of the rainfall by increase of its absorption, results in conservation not only of the soil but also of the water without which the soil cannot be utilized with maximum efficiency....

These lands have been held in place chiefly by such natural growths as buffalo grass and grama grass. One primary source of disaster has been the destruction of millions of acres of this natural cover, an act which in such a series of dry years as that through which we are now passing left the loose soil exposed to the winds. This destruction has been caused partly by over grazing, partly by excessive plowing....

As the ranges were enclosed feed crops were raised to fatten stock, requiring intensive cultivation, and the ranges themselves were overstocked. Thus there was not only a progressive breaking up of the native sod but a thinning out of the grass cover on lands not yet plowed.

The settlers lacked both the knowledge and the incentive necessary to avoid these mistakes. They were misled by those who should have been their natural guides. The Federal homestead policy, which kept land allotments low and required that a portion of each should be plowed, is now seen to have caused immeasurable harm....

Water has not been adequately conserved. In many parts of the area there has been a decline in the ground water level, though how much of this effect is due to excessive use and how much to the decline in rainfall is not yet certain, ...

Source: Hugh H. Bennett, Frederick H. Fowler, et al., *Report of the Great Plains Drought Area Committee* (Washington, DC: Government Printing Office, September 1936), pp. 1–3, 5–7, 12.

FUTURE OF THE GREAT PLAINS COMMITTEE, DECEMBER 1936

Nature has established a balance in the Great Plains by what in human terms would be called the method of trial and error. The white man has disturbed this balance; he must restore it or devise a new one of his own.... It is an inherent characteristic of pioneering settlement to assume that Nature is something of which to take advantage and to exploit; that Nature can be shaped at will to man's convenience. In a superficial sense this is true; felling of trees will clear land for cultivation, planting of seed will yield crops, and applications of water where natural precipitation is low will increase yields. However, in a deeper sense modern science has disclosed that fundamentally Nature is inflexible and demands conformity.... We know now, for instance, that it is essential to adjust agricultural economy on the Plains to periods of deficient rather than of abundant rainfall, and to the destructive influence of wind blowing over dry loose soil rather than primarily to a temporary high price for wheat or beef; that it is our ways, not Nature's which can be changed....

Source: The Future of the Great Plains: Report of the Great Plains Committee (Washington, DC: Government Printing Office, December 1936).

Document 11.7   ***The Plow That Broke the Plains* Indicts the Farmer and His Tools**

Working under the auspices of the New Deal Farm Security Administration, in 1936 filmmaker Pare Lorentz produced a documentary film that still stands as one of the most brilliant pieces of propaganda in the nation's history. With an award-winning musical score and Whitmanesque imagery, Lorentz's film indicted the farmer's aggressive use of plow and tractor to the Great Plains as the chief villain of the Dust Bowl. The final minutes of the film, which was shown in movie theaters across the country, touted the virtues of the New Deal's agricultural programs that were already, Lorentz suggested, taming the excesses and mistakes of America's farmers.

I: PROLOGUE

This is a record of land ... of soil, rather than people—
a story of the Great Plains:
the 400,000 acres of wind-swept grass lands that spread up
from the Texas Panhandle to Canada ...
A high, treeless continent, without rivers, without streams ...
A country of high winds, and sun ... and of little rain ...

II: GRASS

The grass lands ... a treeless wind-swept continent of grass
stretching from the broad Texas Panhandle
up to the mountain reaches of Montana and to the Canadian border.
A country of high winds and sun ...

III: CATTLE

First came the cattle ...
an unfenced range a thousand miles long ...
an uncharted ocean of grass,
the southern range for winter grazing
and the mountain plateaus for summer.
It was a cattleman's Paradise.
Up from the Rio Grande ... in from the rolling prairies ...
down clear from the eastern highways
the cattle rolled into the old buffalo range.
For a decade the world discovered the grasslands
and poured cattle into the plains.
The railroads brought markets to the edge of the plains ...
land syndicates sprang up overnight and the cattle rolled into the West.

IV: HOMESTEADER

But the railroad brought the world into the plains ...
new populations, new needs crowded the last frontier.
Once again the plowman followed the herds
and the pioneer came to the plains.
Make way for the plowman!
High winds and sun ...
High winds and sun ...
a country without rivers and with little rain.
Settler, plow at your peril!

V: WARNING

Many were disappointed.
The rains failed...
and the sun baked the light soil.
Many left...they fought the loneliness
and the hard years....But the rains failed them.

VI: WAR

Many were disappointed, but the great day
was coming...the day of new causes—
new profits—new hopes.
"Wheat will win the war!"
"Plant wheat..."
"Plant the cattle ranges..."
"Plant your vacant lots...plant wheat!"
"Wheat for the boys over there!"
"Wheat for the Allies!"
"Wheat for the British!"
"Wheat for the Belgians!"
"Wheat for the French!"
"Wheat at any price"
"Wheat will win the war!"

VII: BLUES

Then we reaped the golden harvest...
then we really plowed the plains...
we turned under millions of new acres for war.
We had the man-power...we invented new machinery...
the world was our market.
By 1933 the old grass lands had become the new
wheat lands...a hundred million acres...
two hundred million acres...
More wheat!

VIII: DROUGHT

A country without rivers...without streams
with little rain...
Once again the rains held off and the
sun baked the earth.
This time no grass held moisture against the
winds and sun...this time millions of acres
of plowed land lay open to the sun.

IX: DEVASTATION

Baked out—blown out—and broke!
Year in, year out, uncomplaining they fought
the worst drought in history
their stock choked to death on the barren land...
their homes were nightmares of swirling dust

night and day.
Many were ahead of it—but many stayed
until stock, machinery, homes, credit, food,
and even hope were gone.
On to the West!
Once again they headed into the setting sun . . .
Once again they headed West out of
the Great Plains and hit the highways
for the Pacific Coast, the last border.
Blown out—baked out—and broke . . .
nothing to stay for . . . nothing to hope for . . .
homeless, penniless and bewildered they joined
the great army of the highways. . . .
The sun and winds wrote the most tragic chapter
in American agriculture.

Source: Pare Lorentz, Script for *The Plow That Broke the Plains* (Washington, DC: Farm Security Administration, 1936), available at the Web site of the New Deal Network: http://newdeal.feri.org/search_details.cfm?link=http://newdeal.feri.org/nchs/doc01.htm.

Document 11.8   James Malin Challenges New Deal Ecological Views and Policies, 1956

Native Kansan and distinguished professor of history James C. Malin represented the views of many natives of the Great Plains region who resented "outsiders," whether academics or government experts, telling them how—or, indeed, whether—to make a living from the land they had long inhabited. In the 1940s and 1950s Malin challenged the view of man as a destructive force in the Great Plains region, holding, elsewhere, for example, that Kansas farmers had ingeniously, instinctively adapted to the subhumid climate of their region by planting soft winter wheat. Individual initiative of the "common man," not interference from an overbearing federal government, held the key to the future of the Great Plains. Here he skewers New Deal propagandists and the ecological "climax" theorists who had faulted white men for the Dust Bowl disaster and had commended Native American tribes for their role in maintaining the ecological balance of the region. His defense of modern man includes an allusion to the recurrence of Dust Bowl conditions in much of the region in the 1950s. Dust storms, he maintains, had always happened in the region and always would—no matter the dominant culture or agricultural regime.

Whenever and wherever a discussion is proposed of man-earth relations, or of man-food relations, certain fundamental conceptual barriers usually tend to block a free and effectual meeting of minds about even the nature of the problem. One of these is the assumption . . . that, as differentiated from plants and other animals, man's relation with the earth and all its properties is always destructive. A second barrier . . . is that the imperative responsibility of any student of these matters is to provide the bases for restoring what man, especially "civilized" man, has supposedly destroyed. The overtones, if not the explicit assumption, are those of urgency of decision and action to forestall disaster. . . . The grassland of North America is conspicuously the product of destruction, and as applied to this problem, destruction and creation are merely different aspects of the same thing. All areas of the earth's surface present a similar process to challenge the curiosity and understanding of men, but possibly a grassland reveals to the observation of contemporary men a more direct opportunity to study certain of the forces actively at work than do some other areas.

As the first draft of this paper was being written, March 11, 1955, a thermonuclear bomb had just been exploded in the Nevada desert. Afterward, red dust, falling over Baltimore, Maryland, some 2,200 miles eastward, aroused fears of radioactive fall-out from the explosion. In undertaking to allay that alarm by assuring the public that the red particles were nothing more dangerous than red dust blown from the Texas range country, the Weather Bureau inadvertently created another alarm about the destruction of the Great Plains by dust storms, supposedly caused by overgrazing and by plowing up the grass for wheat, cotton, and sorghum. Man is not happy unless he is worrying about something.

The Great Plains dust storms are a case in point that illustrates the problem and its overtones—the immediate push-button reaction in terms of a supposed solution to dust storms—to restore the Great Plains to their "original" grassland equilibrium as supposedly enjoyed in the state of nature. According to this stereotype, aboriginal man was a superior being, endowed with the wisdom of nature and of nature's God of the so-called "Enlightenment" of the eighteenth century—only civilized man was evil. . . .

The question does not appear to occur to historians that the Indian culture might have been headed for a major crisis, possibly disaster, even if displacement by white culture had not intervened to give disaster a different form as well as to provide the Indian with a good alibi. In fact, there is reason to assert that these Indian cultures were already off-balance and were running into trouble prior to any definite "pressure" being placed upon them by the actual invasion . . . by white men. . . .

Proof is yet forthcoming that imitation of the Indian culture would have been a safe course. But under no circumstances could such a course have prevented dust storms in this grassland. No more vivid description of dust storm has been recorded than that of Isaac McCoy, written on the spot in what is now north-central Kansas during the fall of 1830 (not 1930), when the so-called "native Plains Indians" were still in full possession. And dust storms in Kansas (1850–1900) have been described from contemporary records by the present writer. No more brazen falsehood was ever perpetrated upon a gullible public than the allegation that the dust storms of the 1930s were *caused* by the "plow that broke the Plains."

Source: James C. Malin, "The Grassland of North America: Its Occupance and the Challenge of Continuous Reappraisals," in William L. Thomas, Jr., ed., *Man's Role in Changing the Face of the Earth* (Chicago: University of Chicago Press, 1956, for the Wenner-Gren Foundation for Anthropological Research and the National Science Foundation), pp. 353, 355–56. Reprinted with permission of The University of Chicago Press.

NOTES

1. Charles Dana Wilber, *The Great Valleys and Prairies of Nebraska and the Northwest* (Omaha, NE: Daily Republican Print, 1881), p. 69; cited in Henry Nash Smith, *Virgin Land: The American West as Symbol and Myth* (Cambridge, MA: Harvard University Press, 1950), p. 182.

2. Ann Marie Low, *Dust Bowl Diary* (Lincoln: University of Nebraska Press, 1984), p. 136.

3. Smith, *Virgin Land*, pp. 178–83.

4. Donald Worster, *Dust Bowl: The Southern Plains in the 1930s* (New York: Oxford University Press, 1979), chap. 12. See especially pp. 184–93.

5. Ibid., and Donald Worster, *Nature's Economy: A History of Ecological Ideas* (Cambridge: Cambridge University Press, 1977), pp. 221–53.

ANNOTATED BIBLIOGRAPHY

Brant, Irving. *Adventures in Conservation with Franklin D. Roosevelt*. Flagstaff, AZ: Northland, 1989. Makes a strong case that Franklin Roosevelt's conservation legacy rivals that of his second cousin.

Hurt, R. Douglas. *The Dust Bowl: An Agricultural and Social History*. Chicago: Nelson-Hall, 1981. Though largely superseded by Worster, this remains a good history of the mechanized agricultural transformation of the Great Plains and the traumatic impacts of the Dirty Thirties on the region's people.

Lookingbill, Brad D. *Dust Bowl, USA: Depression America and the Ecological Imagination, 1929–1941*. Athens: Ohio University Press, 2001. Richly interdisciplinary, explores the photographs, books, songs, journalism, and films through which Americans understood the event and analyzes how the Dust Bowl became thoroughly embedded in the American psyche as a dystopic man-made landscape of agony and suffering.

Low, Ann Marie. *Dust Bowl Diary*. Lincoln: University of Nebraska Press, 1984. A powerful, moving diary of a woman who lived on the plains of North Dakota in the 1930s.

Malin, James C. *History and Ecology: Studies of the Grassland*. Edited by Robert P. Swierenga. Lincoln: University of Nebraska Press, 1984. A history of the Great Plains from one of the great historians of the twentieth century and arguably the first environmental historian.

Sears, Paul B. *Deserts on the March*. 1935. Reprint, Washington, DC: Island Press, 1989. Written by a pioneering ecologist at the worst point of the crisis, the book indicts modern agriculture, the capitalist system, and human arrogance as the primary Dust Bowl culprits. Among the first books to call for a serious, ecologically centered reassessment of the human relationship with the environment.

Svobida, Lawrence. *Farming the Dust Bowl: A First-Hand Account from Kansas*. 1941. Reprint, Lawrence: University Press of Kansas, 1986. A vivid, moving account of the Dust Bowl from the rare perspective of a farmer who lived through it. Svobida recorded the anguish of the era and called for the application of sound and sustainable agricultural practices.

Worster, Donald. *Dust Bowl: The Southern Plains in the 1930s*. 1982. Reprint, New York: Oxford University Press, 1979. Classic work of social and environmental history, chronicling both the human and ecological suffering of the disaster. The book helped to define the emerging field of environmental history. He contends that capitalist values, particularly the logic of modern, corporate agriculture that emerged early in the twentieth century, led to the Dust Bowl.

———. *Nature's Economy: A History of Ecological Ideas*. 1977. Reprint, Cambridge: Cambridge University Press, 1990. This brilliant treatise includes a chapter probing the response of Franklin Roosevelt's New Deal administration to the Dust Bowl and the long-term impact of the disaster on the evolution of ecological thinking.

12

The Donora Disaster and the Problem of Air Pollution

> I have felt the fog in my throat—
> The misty hand of Death caress my face;
> I have wrestled with a frightful foe
> Who strangled me with wisps of gray fog-lace.
> Now in my eyes since I have died.
> The bleak, bare hills rise in stupid might
> With scars of its slavery imbedded deep;
> And the people still live—still live—in the poisonous night.
> —"Death in Donora," a ballad by John P. Clark,
> whose mother was killed by the 1948 killer
> smog in Donora, Pennsylvania[1]

Some events in U.S. environmental history are marked by ambiguity—significant for the changes they did *not* produce as for any legislative results or modest shifts in popular attitudes toward nature they might have yielded. Emblematic of these is the "killer smog" that fell upon the towns of Donora and Webster, Pennsylvania, during the last days of October 1948, when air polluting emissions, long an accepted fact of life in these western Pennsylvania industrial communities, became trapped by a temperature inversion at concentrated levels so high that they proved lethal. The smothering blanket of sulfur and carbon oxides and heavy particulate matter killed twenty persons (seventeen of them in Donora) and made more than 6,000 people ill—both conservative estimates, according to a number of scientists who have contested the official version of the event. The Donora tragedy prompted waves of shock and sympathy from around the nation and the world as well as calls for stronger air pollution laws. However, in the wake of the tragedy, local residents were reluctant to blame their illness and the deaths of loved ones on emissions coming from one of the town's main employers. Thus, the kind of pressure that might have yielded immediate stringent regulations imposed by either the state or the federal government did not come from the community. The official investigation of the tragedy conducted by the U.S. Public Health Service echoed that caution, scientifically confirming, by lack of any conclusive proof that would have definitively implicated the leading industrial polluter in Donora, the need to severely curtail emissions. Independent scientists have long argued that complicity on the part of government and industry officials suppressed scientific information that would have revealed that fluorine poisoning from the Zinc Works served as the catalyst in producing the deadly atmospheric witch's brew that sickened and killed residents. The U.S. Public Health Service carefully avoided such conclusions, laying greater blame on the capricious whims of weather and topography—marking it as an "acute" atmospheric anomaly that was unlikely to recur.

Further complicating the significance of the Donora disaster was that although the event was part of the continuing national debate over air pollution that ultimately did produce strong clean air legislation by the 1960s and 1970s, what purified the air of the Monongahela River Valley was the flight of industry from the region. The American Steel and Wire Company's Zinc Works—the plant long suspected as the major culprit of the lethal mix of noxious gases—closed within a decade of the disaster. And despite the lack of a cause-effect relationship, in the decades that followed, many local residents were inclined to join the national chorus of voices blaming increasing environmental regulation for the loss of industrial jobs.

Notwithstanding these complicating factors, what happened in Donora energized a postwar debate about environmental threats to public health and suspected links between industrial urban society and potentially preventable chronic disease. Advocates for stronger environmental legislation continually invoked the tragedy, and in this way Donora did become legendary in the annals of global environmental history. Although its actual legacies remained ambiguous, Donora unquestionably became a watershed event.

Nestled in a horseshoe bend of the Monongahela River, Donora sprang to life as an industrial community shortly after the turn of the twentieth century. Mountain ridges that reached 600 feet in places created a narrow river valley that left just enough room for the town's steel and wire-making mills, a narrow business district, and modest industrial housing that was reached by steep brick and cobblestone streets and community staircases typical of Pittsburgh-area industrial communities. In 1915 the industrial boom of World War I led the American Steel and Wire Company, a U.S. Steel subsidiary, to establish a zinc works in Donora for the smelting and production of zinc-iron alloys and other byproducts used by U.S. Steel facilities in the region. Sprawling some forty acres along the river, the plant was one of the largest such facilities in the world when built. Yet it was already antiquated, for zinc works elsewhere were already shifting to electricity to fire their furnaces, while the Donora plant relied (as did most industries in the region) on the region's famously abundant supply of coal—cheaper but far more polluting.

All industry inherently emits water and air pollution, but zinc production in this era generated a particularly noxious mix of contaminants. Relative to other industries, technological and industrial processes at the Zinc Works released substantial amounts of particulate heavy metal dusts, sulfurous fumes, and carbon monoxide into the air above Donora and the neighboring community of Webster. Picturesque though it may have been, the valley's topography had not proven conducive to dispersing industrial pollution. Beyond the fact that the zinc smelter's smoke stacks reached upward only 150 feet (less than half the height of the hills), the surrounding hills naturally acted as a barrier to the cleansing action of prevailing winds. Worse, meteorological conditions occasionally conspired with the land to create a temperature inversion, where the cooler air of the hills traps the warmer air near the surface—air that normally rises, carrying particulate matter and polluting gases into the atmosphere. In such circumstances, naturally occurring fog on the valley floor became permeated by smoke from nearby industrial facilities, resulting in the very unnatural condition of smog. Thomas Bell, a former employee of the Zinc Works, described the environmental conditions of the valley this way in his classic novel of immigrant labor, *Out of This Furnace*:

> Freshly charged, the zinc smelting furnaces, crawling with thousands of small flames, yellow, blue, green, filled the valley with smoke. Acrid and poisonous, worse than anything a steel mill belched forth, it penetrated everywhere, making automobile headlights necessary in Webster's streets, setting the river-boat pilots to cursing God, and destroying every living thing on the hills.[2]

Like the majority of western Pennsylvanians, Donora and Webster residents generally accepted these conditions as the price of progress. More than 1,500 men made a good living from the plant. Still, while belching fumes meant food on the table, they also meant a degraded environment and deteriorating human health. As early as 1918, the company settled a claim for damages from local residents who charged that certain respiratory diseases stemmed from production at the mill. After less than a decade of the Zinc Works' operation, residents of the adjacent, more agrarian community of Webster filed suit against American Steel and Wire, seeking damages from the smelter's toxic fumes, which, they argued, had killed crops, livestock, and fruit trees. Destruction of vegetation had brought erosion of topsoil. Denying any wrongdoing, the company fought back in court—even as it seemingly admitted culpability by providing limestone to farmers to neutralize the acidification of soil and taking nominal measures to reduce and monitor their effluent. Even at the height of the Great Depression, dozens of Webster families filed suit against the company claiming damage to their health. Thus did zinc production in Donora become a powerful, polarizing local symbol of all that was both good and grim about America's industrialization.

Fairly typical smoky haze greeted local residents on the morning of Tuesday, October 26, 1948. A large mass of cold, stable air had settled over the entire region, preventing the escape of Donora's smoke-filled warmer air. Well-known science writer Berton Roueche later described the air as having "stiffened adhesively into a motionless clot of smoke." The air, he wrote, "began to have a sickening smell, almost a taste."[3] By Friday, the superintendent of the Zinc Works was concerned enough to check the effluent from his plant but found nothing unusual. Even as the community Halloween parade took place that evening, hundreds of residents were filling the beds of local hospitals, complaining of shortness of breath and acute coughing. Doctors made dozens of house calls and advised those elderly residents with chronic heart and respiratory problems to leave town. By midday Sunday, as rain mercifully fell and cut through and dispersed the smog, twenty people had died of asphyxiation and hundreds had been made ill. Walter Winchell broadcast the dreadful news from Donora to his national radio audience. It was Winchell who first pronounced the causes of the event as primarily meteorological, an act of God. Nevertheless, that this was an industrial town was an inescapable fact. The community began to assume its place as an international symbol of pollution, alongside the Meuse River Valley of Belgium, where in 1930, a similar "killer smog" had killed dozens of people.

Some nearby residents immediately directed their ire toward the Zinc Works. Local Board of Health member Dr. William Rongaus called pollution from the zinc smelter "just plain murder." He and a number of farmers who had lost livestock called for the plant to close. In a series of public meetings, plant officials reminded city officials that this was the first such incident in more than three decades of operation, and that the incident could well have been caused by a variety of sources, including the freak-of-nature fog that descended like the plague upon the valley. Moreover, argued U.S. Steel officials, pollution in the valley emanated from many sources other than their mills, including coal burning by trains, steamboats, and thousands of domestic users. The lead chemist from Pittsburgh's smoke control bureau agreed, lending credence to both those whose primary interest was in defending the leading industrial employer in town and those who argued for a smoke control ordinance modeled after Pittsburgh's recently passed law that would apply to all businesses and residents.

Despite fears that an investigation could lead to regulation of the mill that might in turn lead to a loss of jobs, borough councilmen—six of seven of whom were also officials in the United Steelworkers of America (USW) local—voted to make an unprecedented request to the federal government for an official inquiry into the causes of the tragedy. Workers at the zinc plant knew well the hazards of the facility. For years many had voiced complaints about a variety of health problems they believed associated with the highly toxic fluoride gas that came from zinc smelting. The federal agency in question, the U.S. Public Health Service (USPHS), rejected the request, echoing the company's declaration that the disaster was a singular "atmospheric freak" unlikely to recur. Officials insisted that the announced state response to the event—monitoring air quality, and establishing air sampling stations and a warning system for local residents—was adequate. Undeterred, the USW offered $10,000 to the community for the purpose of conducting an "independent and unbiased" investigation into the causes of the tragedy. The borough council accepted the grant. Upon the advice of medical researcher and public health expert Clarence A. Mills, they used the funds to conduct a survey of the impact of the event upon residents' health.

In the meantime, executives of the Mellon Institute, whose industry-funded Industrial Hygiene Foundation had accepted successful smoke control efforts in Pittsburgh, persuaded American Steel and Wire to undertake its own investigation. The company, anxious for an opportunity to exonerate itself legally, also saw an inquiry as an opportunity to manage public perception of the event. Led by Dr. Robert Kehoe of the Cincinnati-based Kettering Laboratory of Applied Physiology (who had formerly done work for the Ethyl Corporation defending the use of lead additives in gasoline), the inquiry based its conclusions on Kehoe's theory that human physiology had adapted to relatively low levels of long-term exposure to ubiquitous contaminants in the modern industrial environment. "Only sustained, highly concentrated exposures could cause permanent damage" to the well-defended human system.[4] Unless there was clear and documented evidence of a sudden release of high levels of effluent, the theory made it virtually impossible to prove unequivocally that the Donora smog had been caused by the zinc plant, or any other causal agent.

Neither the announcement of a company inquiry nor the local survey could quiet continued calls for a more comprehensive and independent investigation of the episode by the USPHS. Nearly three weeks after the incident, the agency reversed its decision and announced that its Division of Industrial Hygiene would conduct an investigation. One month later, Dr. Mills completed his investigation, declaring that not hundreds, but nearly 6,000 persons—almost half the population—had been made ill by the smog. Further, the Mills study revealed that employees of the Zinc Works had long been underreporting various illnesses. Late that winter, Mills publicly named the Zinc Works as the villain in the disaster. Mills quickly became a pariah in Donora and a hero to residents of Webster who had organized the Webster Society for Better Living and leaned on the Mills study to call for local stringent smoke control measures. Webster residents bitterly criticized the approach being taken up that winter by USPHS researchers, whom they saw as conducting a whitewash for the company. Eschewing the linkage between health effects and the Zinc Works, the USPHS employed an array of scientific methods such as air sampling, weather modeling, and extensive epidemiological surveys. Webster residents won a small victory when American Steel and Wire agreed in the spring of 1949 to a two-week "test smog" period that would simulate conditions of the previous late October. Yet, lacking independent verification that effluent levels had been matched and without a repeat of the meteorological conditions, few in Webster were satisfied. They continued to argue for a local smoke control ordinance to be accompanied by research and funding and a larger strategy to control air pollution while minimizing economic losses—an approach that had been supported in Pittsburgh by industry leaders.

Webster residents were particularly incensed when the 172-page preliminary USPHS report (there never was a final report), released one year following the event, recommended not a smoke control ordinance but voluntary reductions by industrial facilities. In terms of causal agents, fingers pointed not at the Zinc Works but at the synergistic combination of multiple sources. The concluding upshot: if everyone was to blame, no one was to blame. As Devra Davis has summarized, "the absence of definitive evidence of air pollution's harm was taken as proof of its safety."[5] It was not the first, nor the last time that such blithe conclusions would be reached in the matter of an environmental threat. Laden with air sampling and meteorological data, the USPHS report made causes diffuse and remedies vaguely voluntary. In terms of the Zinc Works, it seemed to echo what the Kehoe-led company inquiry had urged: regulation of production at the plant according to the well-measured capacity of meteorological conditions on any given day to disperse effluent.

Lurking behind the Donora studies were large questions that would confront industry leaders, politicians, and community activists in the decades ahead: what level of sustained exposure to air polluting effluent was an acceptable risk? Who would make that determination and on the basis of what science? The questions suggest that the model of community environmental activism established by Webster residents served as a harbinger of things to come: by the 1960s and 1970s citizens in communities across the nation would engage their own scientific experts to challenge what they often believed was a government-sanctioned cover-up of industry misdeeds threatening their health.

In Donora, it did not aid the credibility of the USPHS report when researchers noticed that Oscar Ewing, administrator of the Federal Security Agency within which lay the USPHS, had been a lead attorney for Alcoa—a corporation that at the time was facing lawsuits involving their own fluorine emissions. Philip Sadtler, a leading national expert on fluorine poisoning, had conducted research in Donora and Webster immediately after the disaster and examined the Mills health effects study. Eyewitness reports of the dead and dying immediately convinced Sadtler that fluorine had been the killer, and he published his findings in the leading journal of professional chemists, the *Chemical and Engineering News*. For decades afterward Sadtler maintained that the USPHS had deliberately avoided the fluorine issue, not only to serve the interests of Alcoa, but also because the financial implications of indicting fluorine as a threat to public health were ominous indeed. That many vital USPHS records were "lost" only fueled the theory of sinister complicity between industry and government in undermining the public interest.

Donora was significant in other ways. Despite the failure of the USPHS definitively to determine the cause of the tragedy and recommend conclusions that would have satisfied the anxious residents of Webster, the event did usher in an unprecedented wave of research by the agency into the causes and health effects of air pollution. Donora became a rallying cry for advocates of stronger air pollution control measures nationwide (particularly after the far more lethal London smog of 1952), ultimately leading to the Air Pollution Control Act of 1955. Conservative legislation very much in keeping with the business-minded politics of the 1950s, the law did nothing to control pollution. Its chief significance lay in acknowledging air pollution as a national problem that crossed community and state lines (as the folks in Webster would have agreed). A $5 million authorization to the Public Health Service for additional research would confirm much of what independent scientists—not to mention community residents—had been saying for years. The ongoing air pollution inquiry at the federal level led to increasingly more stringent clean air legislation of the mid and late 1960s, and ultimately to the landmark Clean Air Act of 1970. Industry's concern with the unknown cost of air pollution controls—always just beneath the surface of the conflict—would be addressed in those laws.

Answers to a number of other questions emerging from Donora have been elusive. The issue of "acceptable risks" posed by a given air pollutant would continue to be a matter of contentious debate, as would the issue of jobs versus the environment. Unlike Pittsburgh and other smoke-afflicted communities who were seeking to diversify their economy and rehabilitate their smoky image, Donora was beholden to one major employer. Residents wanted desperately to believe in the company and its defense—upon which their livelihoods rested.

It became a popular slogan in the 1960s struggle for clean air laws to say that "We all live in Donora." That was true in more ways than one, for whether fluorine was the killer or not, all humans have accepted—willingly or not—a certain level of exposure to a staggering number of environmental contaminants—some of which we can see and avoid but many others we cannot. Whether invisible fluorine was the killer in Donora and Webster or not, we are left with two incontrovertible facts most distressing: the genius of urban industrial civilization had turned the weather itself into a weapon capable of killing us; and finally, there is far more that we do not understand about environmental threats than what we do know.

DOCUMENTS

**Document 12.1   Webster Resident Lois Bainbridge Appeals
                    to the Governor**

---

*Sensing that officials of Donora would be reluctant to impose tough new
pollution controls on an industrial facility that was the main employer in
town, Lois Bainbridge, a resident of the adjacent community of
Webster, appealed to Governor James H. Duff for state intervention.
Her plainspoken and occasionally sardonic petition lays bare the threat
to both the environment and to human health that many residents,
particularly in Webster, saw in the Zinc Works.*

Webster, Pa.
Oct. 31, 1948
Hon. James H. Duff
Harrisburg, Pa.
Dear Sir:

I am writing for "Smoke Control" in Washington County. Pittsburgh has it,
why can't Donora after the tragedy of Oct. 30 & 31st.

The Zinc Works has ruined Donora & Webster. The company has talked
about moving it for years but nothing has been done about it. Perhaps this will
awaken some of the high officials who have built beautiful homes outside of
Donora in the surrounding country where vegetation will grow.

The towns of Monessen, Charleroi and Monongahela, adjacent to Donora &
Webster had fog but there weren't 20 deaths as Donora & Webster had. There is
something in the Zinc Works causing these deaths.

The Zinc Works is very old fashioned. It could be moved & electric furnaces
installed. That would help consume the fumes & do away with that awful acid &
smoke. It eats the paint off your houses. Even fish cannot live in the Monongahela
River, the bank on which the mill is situated.

I would not want men to lose their jobs but your life is more precious than
your job.

They closed the smeltering plant today. We found that you could breathe
normally without having the air polluted with acid fumes.

Webster was here before the Donora Zinc Works was constructed, so why
should we suffer? A once beautiful town is now almost a "Ghost Town."

I know you are quite a busy person but will you please consider this letter a
little bit?

Thanking you, I remain,
Respectfully yours,
Mrs. Lois Bainbridge
Webster, Pa.

Source: Letter of Mrs. Lois Bainbridge of Webster, PA, to the Governor, October 31, 1948. Manuscript Group 190: James H. Duff Papers, Subject File (Harrisburg, PA: Pennsylvania State Archives, Pennsylvania Historical and Museum Commission). Available at: http://www.docheritage.state.pa.us/documents/donoratrans.asp (accessed July 26, 2004).

Document 12.2   **Donora's *Herald-American* Decries "Radical and Biased Opinions," Calls for Confidence in Expert Scientists, 1948**

The Donora Herald-American *adopted a more moderate posture than most newspapers in the region. Acutely sensitive—some argued too sensitive—to the economic health of the community, the editors called for calm and measured restraint in the community's response to the tragedy and confidence in the experts' ability to produce the necessary recommendations to avert a recurrence. Here they criticize the "radical and biased opinions" provoked by the outrage many directed at the Zinc Works, views that seemed to be leading to calls to shut down the plant or so radically alter its operation that the company might seek to move its facility. The jobs issue aside, such unequivocal confidence in scientific expertise and governmental authority very much reflected larger attitudes of Americans in the postwar era.*

TEN DAYS AGO

Ten days ago, Donora was just an average industrial town—producing steel and athletes. There was nothing spectacular about us—we went about our daily tasks in much the same manner as any other small community. Suddenly tragedy visited nineteen homes over night. Our plight became known from coast to coast, from border to border. Here was another Liege, Belgium disaster, many thought. Newsmen found the story of the year. Every industrial center sat up and took notice. It did happen here.

Almost at once theories were advanced and as many theories were exploded.

Today Donora is the laboratory of the world—the test tube which scientists will use to probe for the cure for air pollution. What these men will find remains to be seen. While fault may lie with our local industry, it must be remembered that there are other factors involved. Factors that the average person failed to stop and consider.

Our task as citizens at the moment is not to hamper science nor industry with radical and biased opinion, but to follow recommendations of men of science and to cooperate to the fullest with suggestions that they have to make. Difficult though it may be to restrain ourselves, it is important that we meet this problem with open minds and with fortitude.

True, nineteen persons died, but they did not die in vain for aside from the tragic aspects of this catastrophe, there is the problem of saving other lives, not only here but in every locality where heavy industry is centralized.

Scientific surveys cannot be completed in a day. . . . As it has been pointed out this problem is a complicated one—so complicated that it may take months of study, calculation and testing. The answer, however, will be found for State and federal investigators now on the job expect to be here for some time. They are and will continue to carry on tests with exactness for upon their findings rests the lives of thousands of others which may be endangered, not only in Donora but in every locality where industry is concentrated.

The study of smog control and air pollution is still in an evolutionary stage. It is a new problem that confronts, not only industry but science as well and efforts are being directed toward remedial measures . . .

In this emergency, it is only natural that every man in the street express his opinion, but when opinions become radical and biased, there is every possibility that our purpose will be defeated. This is no time for gross accusations and threats—but rather a time for open mindedness.

We have had air pollution for many years. Metropolitan districts all over the nation are becoming cognizant of the danger due to polluted air. Their problem, too, is a difficult one.

Given time, science will track down the unknown quantity or unknown quantities that have been termed as "silent killers" and until then, our duty as citizens, individually and collectively, is to cooperate to the fullest.

Source: "Ten Days Ago," *Donora Herald-American*, November 8, 1948, p. 4.

Document 12.3   Industrial Chemist Blames Donora Tragedy on Fluorine from Zinc Works, 1948

Philadelphia chemist Philip Sadtler was among the experts brought to Donora by local officials to study levels of toxicity in the bodies of the deceased. Sadtler was among the foremost experts in fluorine and fluoride pollution in the nation. [NOTE: Fluoride is a salt of hydrofluoric acid consisting of two elements, one of which is fluorine. In these documents, the terms seem to be used interchangeably, but appear as in the original documents.] Although industry officials disputed the charge, Sadtler was convinced that excessive amounts of fluorine in the effluent produced by the Zinc Works led to the Donora catastrophe. Sadtler's conclusions about the Donora tragedy are summarized here in an article for Chemical and Engineering News, *the publication of the American Chemical Society, the professional association of chemists.*

Circumstantial and actual proof has been found of acute fluorine poisoning by the smog in the Monongahela River Valley to persons who already had chronic fluorine intoxication, states the official report of investigations of the cause of the deaths of 17 people in Donora, Pa., and of 3 in Webster during the last weekend in October. Most of the well-known symptoms of acute fluorine poisoning were found by members of the medical professions who examined victims of the smog, Philip Sadtler, consultant, discovered.

The fog bank across the tops of the valley walls surrounding the towns for four days had permitted little movement of air and allowed the gaseous waste products of several plants and the railroads to accumulate. Besides being saturated with soot, the fog blanket also contained sulfur dioxide, carbon monoxide, and hydrofluoric acid. It has not yet been shown that the first three were present in quantities sufficient to kill. Numerous factors, however, indicated fluorine poisoning, Mr. Sadtler states. Fluorine-containing substances are used in several plants in the vicinity. Analysis of blood of deceased and hospitalized victims showed 12 to 25 times the normal quantity of fluorine. Corn crops, very sensitive to fluorine, were severely damaged and all of the vegetation north of the town was killed. One of the primary symptoms of acute fluorine poisoning in human beings, dyspnea (distressed breathing similar to attacks of asthma) has been found in hundreds of cases. Although those who were affected were of all ages, those who died had displayed symptoms similar to those of chronic fluorine poisoning much earlier. Conspicuous evidence of such chronic poisoning in young persons in the vicinity is the high incidence of mottled tooth enamel and dental caries. Moreover, many effects of secondary fluorine poisoning are to be seen in herbivorous animals in the region. Lastly, inanimate objects show evidence of attack by acid gases.

Recommendations for improvements call for completion of the study in order to single out the plants, materials, and processes causing the trouble. Changes should be made in suspect processes to prevent emission of fluorine-containing fumes, and improvements in combustion are needed. Cottrell precipitators to collect dust and scrubbers to absorb the acid gases are also essential, Mr. Sadtler concludes.

Source: Reprinted with permission from "Industrial News: Fluorine Gases in Atmosphere as Industrial Waste Blamed for Death and Chronic Poisoning of Donora and Webster, Pa., Inhabitants," no author (unidentified *Chemical and Engineering News* staff), *Chemical and Engineering News* 26 (1948): 3692. Copyright © 1948 American Chemical Society.

Document 12.4   **U.S. Public Health Service, Preliminary Report on the "Unusual Smog Episode" at Donora, 1949**

Although independent scientific inquiries into the cause of the Donora tragedy continued, it was the U.S. Public Health Service that conducted the official government investigation of what had happened. Published one year following the disaster, the agency's report featured excerpts from exhaustive door-to-door interviews conducted by nurses and health officials with afflicted residents, details of the extensive epidemiological blood sampling of the ill, x-ray images of the autopsied lungs of the deceased, and excruciatingly detailed information regarding the meteorological conditions that triggered the event. Impressive in scope and substance though it was, the report provoked questions among public health professionals that lingered for decades. Most notably, the mysterious disappearance of the detailed medical histories gathered by nurses in the investigation fueled suspicions of a whitewash report that they believed deliberately exonerated fluorine poisoning as a leading culprit. Its great significance, as the opening comments from the Federal Security Administrator suggest, lay in the precedent it established for conducting research into the scourge of air pollution and applying the full weight of the federal government toward solving what had become a national problem afflicting communities far beyond Donora.

The whole Nation was shocked when 20 persons died and several thousand more became ill during the smog that enveloped the town of Donora, Pa.... To most of us this was a new and heretofore unsuspected source of danger. Although we have been concerned for many years with the general problem of pollution of the air in connection with smoke, we have regarded that as a nuisance and annoyance rather than a serious hazard to health.

Our scientists tell us that the Donora episode was a rare phenomenon.... This study by the Public Health Service into the Donora episode, the most exhaustive ever made on a problem of air pollution, is a step toward positive assurance that such a thing will not happen again.

There is another way we may now use the knowledge we have gained at Donora. The episode has focussed [*sic*] our attention on the larger problem; that is, the almost completely unknown effects on health of many types of air pollution existing today. We must move to an attack on this new frontier of atmospheric pollution.

—Oscar R. Ewing, Administrator

BIOLOGICAL STUDIES—THE ACUTE EPISODE

Summary of Findings

1. A total of 5,910 persons or 42.7 percent of the total population of the Donora area reported some affection from the smog of October 1948.
2. Of these, 2,148 persons were mildly affected, 2,322 were moderately affected, and 1,440 were severely affected...
3. Incidence of smog affection was relatively little influenced by sex, race, or occupational status.
4. Incidence rates show marked variation with age. For all degrees of affection, the percent of persons affected increased from 16 percent of children under 6 years of age to 60 percent, or almost two-thirds, of all persons 65 years of age and over. Of all adults in the Donora area one-half experienced some affection from the smog....
10. The single symptom most frequently reported was cough,... Both sore throat and constriction of chest were reported by more than 20 percent of

exposed persons, and dyspnoea with or without orthopnoea was reported by over 20 percent. . . .

LONG-TERM EFFECTS—ORAL STRUCTURES

Conclusions

1. Fluoride intake during the period of tooth development of the 427 children was insufficient to cause mottled enamel. Fluoride exposure from sources other than water was insufficient to alter the normal inverse variation of caries attack rate and fluoride content of the communal water.
2. The fluoride content of the urine from persons examined from Donora was within normal limits, . . . which is evidence that a fluoride exposure from sources other than water was not sufficiently high to alter this direct variation.
3. Quantitative analyses of human and animal bones for fluoride showed that amounts stored in the skeletal structures were within normal limits which fails to demonstrate an abnormal exposure by inhalation or ingestion. . . .

MORBIDITY AND MORTALITY—SUMMARY AND CONCLUSIONS

Age-specific morbidity and mortality rates failed to show causes of illness and death which were significantly higher for Donora than other areas nearby. Sickness experience for a 3-year period revealed that the number of absences per one thousand males on account of different kinds of sickness was 65.0 for the Donora steel and zinc company compared with 66.5 and 79.4 for the other two western Pennsylvania steel companies used as controls. . . .

Seasonal mortality and morbidity rates in Donora follow the usual pattern with an increase during the winter. . . . Apparently only in periods of crisis was the Donora health different from other nearby towns. . . .

DISCUSSION OF CAUSE OF EPISODE

The data presented in the biological studies indicate that the clinical syndrome was characterized essentially by irritation of the respiratory tract which was especially severe in elderly persons and those with known chronic cardiorespiratory disease. The data indicate, furthermore, that the episode was not due to an accidental occurrence but rather resulted from the accumulation of atmospheric pollutants during an unusually intense and prolonged stable air condition. While the weather alone cannot be blamed for the episode, the fact that it played a significant role cannot be denied.

Following analysis and study of all available data, it is believed that unequivocal identification of the specific agent responsible for the illness is not justifiable. Nevertheless, with the assumption that the air contaminants during the smog period were no different from those of the period of the study [November 1948–March 1949], except in a quantitative sense, it is of moment to consider the various substances studied with reference to the syndrome. . . .

FLUORIDE

Fluoride, possibly as hydrogen fluoride and sodium fluoride, was found in the engineering study to be present in exceedingly small amounts in the atmosphere during the sampling periods. The best available information indicates that such low levels of fluoride...would not cause the respiratory irritation that was observed. Corroborative data were supplied by the biological studies since no evidence of chronic effects from fluoride was found. It seems reasonable, therefore, to say that since the concentration of fluoride found in the atmosphere was relatively low, and further since no evidence of chronic effects was found, the possibility is slight that toxic concentrations of fluoride accumulated during the October 1948 episode.

CHLORIDE

The concentrations of chloride, possibly as hydrogen chloride and zinc chloride, found in the atmosphere during the investigation were of such low order of magnitude that the possibility is remote that levels accumulated during the October 1948 episode were capable of producing the syndrome observed.

OXIDES OF NITROGEN

The concentrations of oxides of nitrogen found in the atmosphere during the investigation were of such low order of magnitude that the possibility is remote that levels accumulated during the October 1948 episode were capable of producing the syndrome observed....

SULFUR DIOXIDE AND ITS OXIDATION PRODUCTS

The amounts of sulfur dioxide and total sulfur discharged into the atmosphere from various sources in the community were significant constituents of the over-all atmospheric pollution load. However, the levels of sulfur dioxide found in the general atmosphere *during the investigation* (emphasis in original) are not considered capable of producing the syndrome observed. It is, of course, not known what levels were reached during the smog period, and hence, whether or not levels capable of producing the syndrome were reached at that time. Further, it is known that sulfur dioxide can be oxidized to sulfur trioxide in the atmosphere. It is not possible, however, to estimate the extent of oxidation and the role sulfur trioxide may have played. That it could have had a significant effect is a possibility. It appears doubtful, however, that either sulfur dioxide or sulfur trioxide, acting individually or together, reached levels that were capable of producing the syndrome.

SUMMARY

It does not appear probable from the evidence obtained in the investigation that any one of these substances (irritant or nonirritant) *by itself* (emphasis in original) was capable of producing the syndrome observed. However, a combination of two or more of these substances may have contributed to that syndrome....

It is important to emphasize that information available on the toxicological effects of mixed irritant gases is meager and that data on possible enhanced action due to absorption of gases on particulate matter is limited. Further, available toxicological information pertains mainly to adults in relatively good health. Hence, the lack of fundamental data on the physiologic effects of a mixture of gases and particulate matter over a period of time is a severe handicap in evaluating the effects of atmospheric pollutants on persons of all ages and in various stages of health.

RECOMMENDATIONS

1. Reduce the gaseous contaminants especially sulfur dioxide and particulate matter discharged from the sinter plant Cottrell stacks [a nearby metals processing facility].
2. Reduce the particulate matter and carbon dioxide from the zinc smelters.
3. Reduce the particulate matter and sulfur dioxide discharged from the waste heat boiler stacks.
4. Reduce the discharge of oxides of nitrogen and acid mists from Gay-Lussac stacks.
5. Reduce the amount of particulate matter and carbon monoxide from the waste blast furnace gas.
6. Reduce the amount of carbon monoxide discharged from the stove and sinter stacks.
7. Reduce the amount of particulate matter discharged from the sinter plant and open hearth stacks.
8. Reduce the amount of particulate matter discharged from the waste heat and blast furnace boilers and the sulfur dioxide from the waste heat, steel and wire plant boilers.
9. Reduce the amount of particulate matter discharged from domestic heating systems, steam locomotives and steamboats.
10. Establish a program of weather forecasts to alert the community of impending adverse weather conditions so that adequate measures can be taken to protect the populace.

Source: H. H. Schrenk et al., *Air Pollution in Donora, PA: Epidemiology of the Unusual Smog Episode of October 1948* (Washington, DC: Federal Security Agency, 1949), pp. 29–30, 65, 77, 161–62, 165.

Document 12.5   *Monessen Daily Independent* **Expresses Frustration over Lack of Action, 1949**

Despite the impressive report submitted by the U.S. Public Health Service, many citizens continued to express frustration that no concrete action had yet been taken to prevent or ameliorate the conditions that could lead to a recurrence of the Donora tragedy. Especially tough in its call for stringent measures was the Monessen

Daily Independent. *The questions raised here by newspaper editors in this nearby industrial community centered on which level of government could most effectively take action. That question continued to be asked in the years ahead by citizens nationwide, leading inexorably to federal legislation and regulation of industry.*

WHOSE MOVE IS IT?

It seems to us that the officials of the local governments in this immediate section of the Monongahela Valley are taking far too lightly their responsibilities to protect their citizens from a recurrence of the Donora smog of just a year ago.

The U.S. Public Health Service announced yesterday afternoon that weather conditions much like those it regarded as partly responsible for the 1948 disaster are building up again. But for the fact that the steel and coal strikes have virtually suspended manufacturing and transportation in the Valley, we could be in for another death smog.

Yet no machinery is in existence to protect the public and none of the duly constituted local authorities, including the Monessen City Council, seems in the least disposed to provide such machinery!

While its massive report on the smog disaster did not name any specific cause, the PHS has nevertheless identified several of the major sources of air pollution in Donora, and a number of these sources must likewise exist in Monessen. The PHS also made a number of specific recommendations which, it seems to us, ought to be put into effect at the earliest possible moment as a matter of public safety....

What we want to know is who is going to do these things and when? Or do we have to depend upon strikes?

Our suggestion . . . is that there should be immediate consultation among the city and borough officials of Charleroi, Donora, Monessen and Monongahela to see whether they cannot take some cooperative and uniform steps to protect their citizens. Obviously, it would not do much good for Monessen to act if Donora fails to act. Smoke and fumes pay no attention to city lines....

The PHS has no powers but to investigate and recommend. Neither is much good if those responsible refuse to act or keep waiting for someone else to act.

AFTER A YEAR

. . . [We] know enough now, it seems to us, to be moving intelligently and forthrightly towards some positive corrections. Certainly we know the danger exists. We know, at least in general outline, what the causes are. And we know there are remedies, scientific, legal and other.

When any community is confronted with a danger to the life and health of its people, and when the community knows the causes of the danger, is it not the essence of the spirit of community life that something shall be done about the danger? Is that not the whole purpose of governments and laws—to protect the people against common dangers, to assure that the few shall not jeopardize the lives and happiness of the many? . . .

It is unthinkable that we in this Valley shall not come to grips at the earliest possible moment with this menace. Communities all over the nation are pointing the way to clean air and still keeping their industries. It is not a dream; it is a practical possibility.

The Independent thinks there should be immediate consultation among the local governments of the municipalities of the Valley district. They may find that they already have sufficient powers to deal with the situation. If they haven't, they should begin now to demand state or perhaps Federal legislation. At the very least they can insist that something be done and soon. . . .

Sources: Monessen Daily Independent, October 21, p. 4; October 22, 1949, p. 4.

Document 12.6   Public Health Scientist Clarence Mills Criticizes Official Report on Donora, 1950

A physician from the University of Cincinnati, Clarence A. Mills had been studying the problem of air pollution in Donora years before the lethal 1948 incident. He had argued fruitlessly for an intensive study of the long-term effects of both visible and unseen toxic contaminants contained in the valley's air pollution. Now, following the year-long study of the U.S. Public Health Service, he takes aim at the agency's failure to pinpoint the cause of the deadly episode. The PHS report, he argues, was laden with scientific evidence that should have led investigators to more definitive conclusions and calls for stiffer legislative remedies. Perhaps most significant is his claim that the quiet, nondramatic, long-term exposure to air pollution represents the greatest threat posed by air pollution.

One year ago 20 persons lost their lives at Donora, Pennsylvania, in America's first mass killing from industrial air pollution. Now the U.S. Public Health Service has released a preliminary report on its year-long study of the Donora tragedy. This represents the Public Health Service's first foray into the field of community air pollution. Two years ago they were not even interested in making a small grant to help studies already well along in opening up this health field. Today they suddenly find the field so important they quickly request $750,000 from Congress to enlarge upon their studies! Just what did their year's work, with a staff of 25 investigators, show?

They found that 42.7% of the people living in the Donora-Webster area were affected in the poison smog of a year ago. The quick survey made by local Donora workers at our request soon after the tragedy showed 43.2%. They found—as did we—that the percentage affected rose rapidly with age, was greatest at higher levels than down along the river, and was highest across the river in Webster. They found in the valley air the same irritants to the respiratory tract that were pointed out in our December report, but they found no dangerous concentrations and hence were unable to identify the killing agent.

The most valuable part of their year's work—analysis of poison output from the steel and zinc plant stacks—remains unused and unevaluated in their written report. They spent months analyzing the valley air for poisons, but failed to calculate the concentrations probably present during the killing smog a year ago, when an inversion blanket clamped a lid down over the valley's unfortunate people. Had they made such calculation, they would have found that even one day's accumulation of the very irritating red oxides of nitrogen from the acid plant stacks would have caused concentrations almost as high as had long been set as the maximum allowable for safety of factory workers exposed only for an 8-hour work day. At the end of 4 days of last year's blanketing smog, concentrations reached were probably more than four times higher than the 10 milligrams per cubic meter of air listed as the upper limit of safety! And the Donora people breathed the poison air not for 8 hours a day but for 4 whole days. *More than 4 tons* of this poison gas were poured out into the valley air every day during the April test period, even though the brownish-red plumes from the acid plant stacks were then very much less dense than those commonly seen up to the time of the October tragedy.

Stack output of zinc and the sulfur oxides were also found much too high for safety under smog conditions, while the amounts of carbon monoxide emitted were enormous. Because accumulation in the valley air of all carbon monoxide emitted over a 4-day period would probably have been fatal to the whole population, and because no signs of carbon monoxide poisoning were evident in Donora at any time, the Public Health Service investigators concluded that it would be unjustifiable to clamp a hypothetical lid down over the valley. This was a serious error on their part, for their own report (meteorology section) showed a gentle southward drift of the valley air throughout the critical part of the October smog period. Ninety percent of the carbon monoxide arose from blast furnace stacks located at the extreme southern end of the town and was thus carried away from the Donora residents. This gentle southward air movement also accounted for the same high illness rate throughout all parts of Donora as prevailed in its northern edge alongside the zinc plant.

There are now available up-to-date methods of cleansing such stack gases of harmful materials and the burning of carbon monoxide should be considered as a fuel-saving measure in plant economy. The operators of the Donora zinc smelter and sulfuric acid plant should have taken warning at the time of the Belgian disaster of 1930, when 60 persons lost their lives and many thousands were made ill under conditions almost identical with those at Donora. Yet, almost two decades later, the outmoded smelter at Donora was still operating as it and its Belgian counterpart were doing in 1930. Let us hope that the Donora tragedy may prove such an object lesson in air pollution dangers that no industrial plant will feel safe in the future in pouring aloft dangerous amounts of poisonous materials. Furthermore, safety standards to be set up should be those that will give safety under the most adverse weather or smog conditions.

The U.S. Public Health Service investigation of animal deaths in the surrounding countryside was merely cursory, and the report fails to consider at all the terrible devastation and erosion that have resulted from the killing of nearly all plant life within more than a mile radius of the zinc smelter. Surely these were important features of the local air pollution problem. The Federal Security

Administrator and the Surgeon General (in their forewords to the report) claim that the Service has here opened up a *new* field in the nation's health, blandly ignoring the years of work others had put in.

Let us hope that the Donora disaster will awaken people everywhere to the dangers they face from pollution of the air they must breathe to live. These 20 suffered only briefly, but many of the 6,000 made ill that night will face continuing difficulties in breathing for the remainder of their lives. Herein lies the greatest health danger from polluted air—continuing damage to the respiratory system through years of nonkilling exposure.

Millions of Americans and most medical scientists had been aware of this important public health hazard for several years before the Donora episode spotlighted the community dangers of industrial air pollution. But the U.S. Public Health Service focused its interest on the health of workers *within* the plants. Only after the Donora disaster was it drawn into the much more important aspect of the problem—the relation of industrial air pollution to *community* health [all italics in original].

Source: Reprinted with permission from Clarence A. Mills, "The Donora Episode," *Science* 111 (January 20, 1950): 67–68. © 1950 AAAS.

NOTES

1. Donora area resident John P. Clark, "Death in Donora," collected by folklorist Dan G. Hoffman. Reprinted in Earth Island Institute, *Earth Island Journal* (Fall 1998): 37.

2. Thomas Bell, *Out of This Furnace* (Pittsburgh, PA: University of Pittsburgh Press, 1977, first edition 1941), pp. 356–57.

3. Berton Roueche, *Eleven Blue Men* (Boston: Little, Brown, 1953), p. 196; quoted by Devra Davis, *When Smoke Ran Like Water: Tales of Environmental Deception and the Battle against Pollution* (New York: Basic Books, 2002), p. 16.

4. Lynn Page Snyder, "Revisiting Donora, Pennsylvania's Air Pollution Disaster," in Joel A. Tarr, ed., *Devastation and Renewal: An Environmental History of Pittsburgh and Its Region* (Pittsburgh, PA: University of Pittsburgh Press, 2003), pp. 136–37.

5. Davis, *When Smoke Ran Like Water*, p. 24.

ANNOTATED BIBLIOGRAPHY

Boubel, Richard W., Donald L. Fox, D. Bruce Turner, and Arthur C. Stern. *Fundamentals of Air Pollution*. 3rd ed. London: Academic Press, 1994. An essential primer on the causes, science, and technological and engineering solutions for air pollution.

Brimblecombe, Peter. *The Big Smoke: A History of Air Pollution*. New York: Taylor and Francis Group, 1989. A less technical, more readable survey than Halliday's.

Davis, Devra. *When Smoke Ran Like Water: Tales of Environmental Deception and the Battle against Pollution*. New York: Basic Books, 2002. Highly acclaimed book by one of the world's leading epidemiologists and public health scientists. Places Donora in context of other incidents where industry and government somehow conspired to hide truth from the public and avoid costly measures that would have better protected public health.

Dewey, Scott H. *Don't Breathe the Air: Air Pollution and U.S. Environmental Politics, 1945–1970*. College Station: Texas A & M University Press, 2000. Provides the most comprehensive look at the impact of Donora and other air pollution incidents of the postwar era upon the policy-making process.

Halliday, E. C. *An Historical Review of Atmospheric Pollution*. New York: World Health Organization, 1961. Although dated, this broad survey of the history of air pollution remains valuable, in part because it came at a time when studies of the killing events in London and Donora were beginning to shape political action to confront the problem.

Markowitz, Gerald, and David Rosner. *Deceit and Denial: The Deadly Politics of Industrial Pollution*. Berkeley: University of California Press, 2002. Damning indictment of polluters (and governments in some cases), who, the authors argue, learn the wrong lessons from incidents such as Donora—not how to better protect the public from emissions but how to defend more assiduously their own interests and reputations.

Stradling, David. *Smokestacks and Progressives: Environmentalists, Engineers, and Air Quality in America, 1881–1951*. Baltimore: Johns Hopkins University Press, 2003. Tracks the movement of air pollution onto the public agenda of industrial cities, as well as the gendered shift from female social activism to the engineering expertise of men to deal with the issue.

Tarr, Joel, ed. *Devastation and Renewal: An Environmental History of Pittsburgh and Its Region*. Pittsburgh, PA: University of Pittsburgh Press, 2003. Lynn Page Snyder's chapter on the Donora episode is one of a number of chapters in this fine regional environmental history.

13

Rachel Carson, Cesar Chavez, and the Pesticide Debate

> The question is whether any civilization can wage relentless war
> on life without destroying itself, and without losing the right
> to be called civilized.
> —Rachel Carson, *Silent Spring*, 1962[1]

> [Rachel Carson is] a fanatic defender of the cult of the balance of nature.
> —"The Desolate Year," Monsanto Corporation, 1963[2]

Few books have had the power to change American history. Such works have done so by challenging a combination of powerful forces resistant to change, or by raising the awareness or pricking the conscience of Americans on a particular issue that lies just beneath the surface. One of them is Rachel Carson's *Silent Spring*, published in 1962. The author's most immediate purpose in writing this landmark book was to expose the dangers of reckless, indiscriminate use of pesticides and insecticides. She achieved that and far more, eloquently confronting one of the central but largely unchallenged themes of modern life: the ecological price of scientific and technological progress. For all the debate about the specific merits of pesticide regulation that Carson's work ultimately produced, at bottom her profoundly radical and most enduring argument was that corporate and governmental institutions of power—whether out of arrogance or ignorance, or for base profit motives—had disrupted the balance of the natural world and now threatened human health. In doing so, *Silent Spring* linked the fate of "nature" with the well-being of humanity. Despite the savage attack leveled against both the book's science and its author, *Silent Spring* ushered in a modern environmental movement that within a decade not only brought the passage of a wave of new laws. More importantly, the book pronounced that the search for a new relationship with the natural world, one characterized by greater knowledge, understanding, and ultimately humility, had indeed arrived.

This book exemplified—and helped to create—the early 1960s spirit of, as one political manifesto of the era put it, "participatory democracy." Breaking with the "trust the experts" mantra that defined much of postwar American society, *Silent Spring*, like others of the period, called for active civic engagement on urgent matters of public policy. By doing so herself, Rachel Carson implicitly urged citizens to scrutinize the facts and motives of authorities whose responsibility it was to safeguard public health and the environment. In the Carson tradition, citizens' organizations for decades to come would often battle corporate or government officials with facts gathered independently by their own scientific experts.

One early such struggle was the movement of Mexican American farm workers for social, economic, and environmental justice that transpired in the sprawling grape orchards of California. As pivotal as Carson's book was to cultivating a modern environmental sensibility, she said very little in *Silent Spring* about the dangers posed to migrant farm workers who came into contact on a daily basis with an array of dangerous pesticides. The farm workers' union organizing effort, which began coincidentally the same year of *Silent Spring*'s publication, by 1969 became centered on securing protection from many of the same pesticides about which Carson had written. Cesar Chavez, leader of the farm workers' crusade, faced tenacious resistance from major agricultural growers and business interests opposed to the very idea of admitting that chemicals posed a danger. His activities invited the enmity of the fervent anticommunist leader of the FBI, J. Edgar Hoover, whose agency compiled a 2,000-page file on the union organizer. Although the specific issues and figures involved in these contentious episodes obviously differed, they were linked by the concern that pesticides posed a danger to public health and by their respective challenges to institutions that in the 1950s had seemed beyond reproach: big business, government agencies, and science itself. The work of Carson and Chavez by the early 1970s helped to drive increasing numbers of Americans to see the goal of a safe and healthy workplace as inseparable from the national commitment to a cleaner environment, and far too important to be trusted to authorities, private or public. Ultimately, only citizens of a rejuvenated democracy could ensure the protection of their environment.

This story begins not with Carson or Chavez but with World War II, the watershed event of the twentieth century in many ways, not the least of which is its importance in propelling the growth of the petrochemical industry. Wartime shortages of critical materials prompted the federal government to subsidize the efforts of chemical companies such as Union Carbide and Monsanto to conduct research and develop alternative substitute materials. The result was an endless cascade of new products derived from synthetic organic chemical compounds, including Acrylic, synthetic rubber, an astonishing array of plastics, and an equally stunning variety of synthetic pesticides. Although dichloro-diphenyl-trichloroethane (DDT) was not among them (its origins dating to 1874), the insecticidal properties of the most famous of the chlorine-based pesticides were only discovered in 1939. Allied forces immediately deployed DDT effectively against mosquitoes in the South Pacific and in Europe to combat malaria and typhus.

Like so many other wartime innovations, DDT found a place in postwar America. The United States Department of Agriculture (USDA), the U.S. Forest Service, the U.S. Public Health Service (which for a time believed it effective against polio), state departments of agriculture, local authorities, and individual farmers deployed DDT and other newly developed pesticides and herbicides on crop lands, forest lands, roadways, and in neighborhoods nationwide. DDT became the pesticide of choice because of its price and effectiveness on a wide array of pests and diseases—the "atomic bomb of the insect world," according to one gardening magazine. In the three decades following World War II, Americans sprayed 1,350,000,000 pounds of DDT. Total use of all pesticides, insecticides, and herbicides increased tenfold in the 1950s.

Suburbanites applied chemical pesticides, insecticides, and herbicides to anything that might threaten the bug- and crabgrass-free model of lawns and shrubbery to which they aspired. They did so with little caution for little was required in those years. They paid less attention to the minimal warnings that appeared on the labels and far more to the bug-killing features of the product. An ad for chlordane, for example, promised to eliminate "not only crabgrass but also grubs, ants, moles, night crawlers." Weedanol cyanol was "deadlier than ever to weeds!"; apparently not deadly enough, however, for the product soon added the ingredient Sodar that "would knock out your lawn's worst enemy. Kill it so it stays killed," the ad urged. The militaristic metaphor of the war on bugs is telling: among the popular herbicides of the era was 2, 4-D, one-half the mix of the deadly Agent Orange that soon went to work on the forest canopy of Vietnam. As historian Virginia Jenkins has written, "the public's naiveté about the environment and the long-term effects of indiscriminate use of chemicals on lawns was phenomenal."[3] "Better Things for Better Living Through Chemistry"—the old DuPont slogan—captured well the spirit of an age when Americans were far more inclined to be trusting than skeptical. For many, that naiveté was shattered first by the appearance of dead robins on front lawns. It was just such an image that would ultimately spark the publication of *Silent Spring*.

By the end of the 1950s Rachel Louise Carson had already become an internationally renowned author of three highly acclaimed, best-selling books about the sea: *Under the Sea Wind*, *The Sea Around Us*, and *The Edge of the Sea*. She had long since left her position as an aquatic biologist with the U.S. Fish and Wildlife Service and assumed the life of a full-time writer at her cottage on the coast of Maine. In 1958, as she began work on a book on the subject of ecology, she learned that *Reader's Digest* planned to publish an article lauding the benefits of aerial spraying. Carson was among a number of scientists at the Fish and Wildlife Service who had since the 1940s been observing the deleterious effects of pesticide use upon wildlife populations. Thus, she appealed to the magazine's editor-in-chief, advising him of the dangers posed to wildlife and to public health from such insect control efforts. The magazine opted not to publish the article.

Soon thereafter she received a letter from Olga Owens Huckins, a good friend who lived near Duxbury, Massachusetts. Huckins reported to

Carson on a recent aerial spraying that had horrific effects on Huckins's bird sanctuary:

> The mosquito control plane flew over our small town last summer. Since we live close to the marshes we were treated to several lethal doses, as the pilot criss-crossed over our place.... The "harmless" shower bath killed seven of our lovely song-birds outright. We picked up the three dead bodies the next morning, right by the door.... The next day three were scattered around the bird bath.... On the following day one robin dropped suddenly from a branch in our woods.
>
> We were too heart-sick to hunt for other corpses. All of these birds died horribly, and in the same way. Their bills gaping open and their splayed claws were drawn up to their breasts in agony.
>
> Air spraying where it is not needed or wanted is inhuman, undemocratic, and probably unconstitutional. For those of us who stand helplessly on the tortured earth, it is intolerable.[4]

Simultaneously, citizens elsewhere were raising similar concerns regarding the safety of pesticides; most notably, Long Island residents had filed suit to stop a spraying program. Soon thereafter Carson transformed a book on the general subject of ecology into one that took dead aim at the issue of the dangerous effects of indiscriminate pesticide use.

The focus allowed Carson to express the essence of ecology tangibly and with immediacy. As a well-trained scientist, and as a citizen who anticipated well the furious assault with which her book would be met, Carson researched the book meticulously. Drawing on anecdotal but pervasive evidence from citizens and other unofficial reports, she made a damning case that reckless spraying of pesticides had inflicted egregious damage on wildlife and posed an unknown but potentially serious threat to human health as well. Contamination of the food chain, extinction of entire species, and the grim specter of genetic mutation and cancer—all would prove too frightening for readers to ignore. Carson filled the book's final fifty pages with source notes referencing the scientific reports and experts that seemed, to most readers at least (though certainly not the industry), to confirm her charges.

In hindsight, Carson's argument seems reasonable, even conservative from the point of view of many environmentalists. She did *not* argue that pesticides could or even *should* be banned, merely that they ought to be used far more judiciously and prudently and that their use ought to be more honestly and stringently regulated by the government agencies charged with that function. That those agencies *had not* done so and that industry executives had not been truthful with the public, often shielding the dangers of their products—those were the allegations that drew the fierce ire of both government and industry officials.

Their blistering assault on Rachel Carson aimed to destroy her credibility and raise the grim specter of a world overridden by insects. To surrender to the "cult of the balance of nature" represented by "Miss Carson," they suggested, would roll back human progress more than a century. Industry officials impugned her science by suggesting that she took great liberties with the pharmacological and other experts cited in the book, inappropriately taking scientific expertise out of context conveniently to support her arguments and not citing other experts with other views. Carson made no apologies for the fact that she had become a passionate advocate for this cause. But she insisted on the soundness of her facts, as did her defenders in the scientific community. Though well grounded in hard science, Carson's eloquent, poetic style made the book accessible for readers—but for her critics, more easily damnable as "popular science." The masses were not supposed to understand biology or allowable tolerance levels of complicated synthetic chemical formulations; *Silent Spring* invited ordinary citizens into the inner sanctum of the scientist and the government regulator, where, Carson suggested, they might not like what they saw.

Inviting more unsavory, base levels of criticism was the fact of Carson's gender. Although Carson was not the first woman to step into the dangerous intersection of science and public policy (see Chapters 9 and 10), she was the first to so compellingly, brazenly challenge both the powerful cultural myth of technology and science as sacred instruments of progress, and specific institutions of corporate and bureaucratic power determined to resist at all costs any incursion into their world. "Emotional" and "hysterical," her critics ranted. Why would a "spinster" worry about genetic mutations? Rumors of lesbianism spread; anything to discredit the book and its writer.

Despite (and in part *because* of) the campaign against the book, *Silent Spring* gained critical and popular acclaim, in the U.S. and abroad. President John F. Kennedy appointed a study to investigate the issue of pesticide use, which in 1963 confirmed that indeed more judicious use and better labeling were prudent first steps to take, and that further, more thorough investigation was merited. It came, as did more contentious debate over the specific possibility of increased regulation of pesticides that seemed more likely by the end of the decade.

Passage of the Pesticide Control Act in 1972 is often considered, along with the ban on DDT use the same year, the crowning achievement of *Silent Spring*. Some voices in the environmental movement, however, have argued that this law, dozens of other environmental laws, and the entire regulatory system that Carson's book helped to bring about, represent on another level a tragic failure to fully realize the heart of the message of *Silent Spring*. As many ecologists argue, Carson's real challenge to humankind was, as she put it, "to prove our maturity and our mastery, not of nature, but of ourselves." Although the industry, much to its consternation, is regulated, industrial production of chemicals roll on. Consider that 70,000 chemical products are produced annually, the average person comes into contact with more than 500 chemicals and toxic substances daily, and that traces of more than 200 of these are found in the average person's body fat. As they were in 1962, the ubiquity of pesticides and chemicals are measures of the most technologically advanced civilization in history. For the heirs to Carson's legacy, they remain symptomatic of the larger ecological crisis that concerned her and which faces us still. Despite its momentous and real historic legacy, the real lessons of *Silent Spring*, one might somberly conclude, have not been learned. Regulation, Carson would have argued, will never be enough without a fundamental change in human values with respect to the natural world.

Proponents of a laissez faire economy continued assiduously to hammer away at Carson and what they disparaged as her "alarmist" warnings. In the four decades that followed *Silent Spring*, defenders of unfettered technological and scientific progress and development have put forth their own scientific studies disputing Carson's arguments about the specific danger of DDT. They have argued that only wildlife, not humanity, was ever endangered by the pesticide, and that far more harm (in the form of lives lost to malaria and the substitution of DDT with more dangerous chemicals) than good resulted from the DDT ban. Despite the elevated place Carson attained in American life (or *because* of it), conservative proponents of unregulated corporate capitalism have singled her out for unnecessarily frightening the American public and damaging economic growth. Environmental organizations and a clear consensus of the scientific community have answered those criticisms with a clear and passionate defense of Carson's science. They acknowledge that the precise threat to human health from DDT remains unknown, but insist that more than enough is known to warrant caution and that malaria control in tropical areas of the Third World can be achieved by alternative means. Moreover, they say, worsening global environmental crises affirm the urgent necessity of continuing to advance Carson's fundamental message.[5]

That point is reinforced by a visit to the farm fields of California, where, in the late 1960s, Cesar Chavez made protection from pesticide exposure a top priority in organizing the United Farm Workers of America. Only a union contract, Chavez and others insisted, could guarantee protection for workers; that, more than state and federal regulations that he knew from experience would be weakly enforced, would leave the workers' fate in their own hands. In what millions of Chicanos today recall as a legendary, heroic effort, Chavez persevered and won partial recognition for thousands of farm workers and modest health and safety provisions. The farm workers' struggle also helped to place occupational health on the agenda of the environmental movement by the early 1970s. The danger of relying on government regulation that Chavez foresaw could be found decades later in the continued widespread problem of dangerous pesticide exposure for those workers not covered by union contracts. In 2000, farm workers' organizations and the AFL-CIO charged that 4,069 violations of Worker Protection Standards mandated by the Environmental Protection Agency (EPA) had resulted in just 520 fines, with most fines under $400. Worse still, they argued, was the EPA's decision in 2003 to reduce even that minimal level of enforcement.

Although it occurs out of sight and mind of most Americans, the pervasive dependency of American corporate agriculture on pesticides continues to threaten the health and safety of thousands of workers. Meanwhile, the rest of us who enjoy the benefits of the global agricultural system face what many experts say are more insidious dangers associated with cheap food grown on industrialized farms, including residual pesticides on produce and genetically engineered crops. Honoring the tradition of Carson and Chavez, critics of corporate agriculture advocate a more environmentally sustainable and socially just agricultural system. The persistence of these and other unresolved issues are reminders that perhaps the most important legacy of Rachel Carson—to *have* the debate at all—lives on.

DOCUMENTS

Document 13.1   **Rachel Carson Declares Pesticides "Elixirs of Death,"
1962**

---

*Rachel Carson knew well the power of words. Several award-winning
books on the world's oceans had by 1962 won her international
acclaim and stirred scientific discussion about the health of the seas.
Still, nothing could have prepared her for the firestorm of controversy
that greeted the publication of* Silent Spring. *In this excerpt from the
third chapter of the book, Carson lays bare what were in 1962 the
startling facts of a chemical-laden world. As a scientist, she carefully
built her case upon a foundation of evidence gathered from around
the country and verified by expertise in several fields, including
ecology, pharmacology, epidemiology, and toxicology. To read a
passage like this one, however, even decades later, is to recall why
Carson was so bitterly attacked by the complex of interests threatened
by her book. Especially effective is her description of the food chain
passage of chemicals. Most alarming to many readers was the
declaration that one could not trust at face value the confident
reassurances of chemical safety that came from government or
industry experts, and that there was still much that we did not know
about the capacity of the human body to safely absorb life-altering
chemicals. She was effectively issuing a call for citizens to become
their own experts.*

ELIXIRS OF DEATH

For the first time in the history of the world, every human being is now
subjected to contact with dangerous chemicals, from the moment of concep-
tion until death. In the less than two decades of their use, the synthetic pesticides have been so thoroughly distributed throughout the animate and
inanimate world that they occur virtually everywhere. They have been recovered from most of the major river systems and even from streams of
groundwater flowing unseen through the earth. Residues of these chemicals
linger in soil to which they have been applied a dozen years before. They have
entered and lodged in the bodies of fish, birds, reptiles, and domestic and wild
animals so universally that scientists carrying on animal experiments find it
almost impossible to locate subjects free from such contamination. They
have been found in fish in remote mountain lakes, in earthworms burrowing
in soil, in the eggs of birds—and in man himself. For these chemicals are now
stored in the bodies of the vast majority of human beings, regardless of age.
They occur in the mother's milk, and probably in the tissues of the unborn
child.

All this has come about because of the sudden rise and prodigious growth of an industry for the production of man-made or synthetic chemicals with insecticidal properties. This industry is a child of the Second World War. In the course of developing agents of chemical warfare, some of the chemicals created in the laboratory were found to be lethal to insects. The discovery did not come by chance: insects were widely used to test chemicals as agents of death for man.

The result has been a seemingly endless stream of synthetic insecticides. In being man-made—by ingenious laboratory manipulation of the molecules, substituting atoms, altering their arrangement—they differ sharply from the simpler insecticides of prewar days. . . .

What sets the new synthetic insecticides apart is their enormous biological potency. They have immense power not merely to poison but to enter into the most vital processes of the body and change them in sinister and often deadly ways. Thus, as we shall see, they destroy the very enzymes whose function is to protect the body from harm, they block the oxidation processes from which the body receives its energy, they prevent the normal functioning of various organs, and they initiate in certain cells the slow and irreversible change that leads to malignancy.

Yet new and more deadly chemicals are added to the list each year and new uses are devised so that contact with these materials has become practically worldwide. The production of synthetic pesticides in the United States soared from 124,259,000 pounds in 1947 to 637,666,000 pounds in 1960—more than a fivefold increase. . . .

A Who's Who of pesticides is therefore of concern to us all. If we are going to live so intimately with these chemicals—eating and drinking them, taking them into the very marrow of our bones—we had better know something about their nature and their power. . . .

Scientists do not agree upon how much DDT can be stored in the human body. Dr. Arnold Lehman, who is the chief pharmacologist of the Food and Drug Administration, says there is neither a floor below which DDT is not absorbed nor a ceiling beyond which absorption and storage ceases. On the other hand, Dr. Wayland Hayes of the United States Public Health Service contends that in every individual a point of equilibrium is reached, and that DDT in excess of this amount is excreted. For practical purposes it is not particularly important which of these men are right. Storage in human beings has been well investigated, and we know that the average person is storing potentially harmful amounts. . . .

One of the most sinister features of DDT and related chemicals is the way they are passed on from one organism to another through all the links of the food chains. For example, fields of alfalfa are dusted with DDT; meal is later prepared from the alfalfa and fed to hens; the hens lay eggs which contain DDT. Or the hay . . . may be fed to cows. The DDT will turn up in the milk in the amount of about 3 parts per million, but in butter made from this milk the concentration may run to 65 parts per million. Through such a process of transfer, what started out as a very small amount of DDT may end as a heavy concentration. . . .

The poison may also be passed on from mother to offspring. Insecticide residues have been recovered from human milk in samples tested by Food and Drug Administration scientists. This means that the breast-fed human infant is receiving small but regular additions to the load of toxic chemicals building up in his body. It is by no means his first exposure, however; there is good reason to believe this begins while he is still in the womb. In experimental animals the chlorinated hydrocarbon insecticides freely cross the barrier of the placenta, the traditional protective shield between the embryo and harmful substances in the mother's body. While the quantities so received by human infants would normally be small, they are not unimportant because children are more susceptible to poisoning than adults....

All these facts—storage at even low levels, subsequent accumulation, and occurrence of liver damage at levels that may easily occur in normal diets—caused Food and Drug Administration scientists to declare as early as 1950 that it is "extremely likely the potential hazard of DDT has been underestimated." There has been no such parallel in medical history. No one yet knows what the ultimate consequences may be....

So experienced a pharmacologist as Dr. Lehman has described chlordane in 1950 as "one of the most toxic of insecticides—anyone handling it could be poisoned." Judging by the carefree liberality with which dusts for lawn treatments by suburbanites are laced with chlordane, this warning has not been taken to heart. The fact that the suburbanite is not instantly stricken has little meaning, for the toxins may sleep long in his body, to become manifest months or years later in an obscure disorder almost impossible to trace in its origins. On the other hand, death may strike quickly. One victim who accidentally spilled a 25 per cent industrial solution on the skin developed symptoms of poisoning within 40 minutes and died before medical help could be obtained. No reliance can be placed on receiving advance warning which might allow treatment to be had in time.

Document 13.2   The Chemical Industry Goes on the Attack, 1962

Even before the publication of Silent Spring *in book form, the chemical industry, along with their allies in state and federal departments of agriculture, launched an aggressive defense of the use of insecticides and pesticides. In this scathing review of the book for* Chemical and Engineering News, *a distinguished biochemist and nutritionist deploys many of the main arguments used by others in the industry and in government to refute "Miss Carson's" charges.*

[The book] will appeal to those readers who are as uncritical as the author, or to those who find the flavor of her product to their taste. These consumers will include the organic gardeners, the antifluoride leaguers, the worshipers of "natural foods," those who cling to the philosophy of a vital principle, and pseudo-scientists and faddists....

The author ignores the sound appraisals of such responsible, broadly knowledgeable scientists as the President of the National Academy of Sciences, the members of the President's Scientific Advisory Committee, the Presidents of the Rockefeller Foundation and Nutrition Foundation, the several committees of the National Academy of Sciences . . . who have long given thoughtful study to these questions, and the special advisory committees appointed by the governors of California and Wisconsin. . . .

All of these groups of scientists have recognized the essentiality of use of agricultural chemicals to produce the food required by the expanding world population and to sustain an acceptable standard of living and health. They have recognized the safety of proper use of agricultural chemicals and, indeed, the benefits to the consumer which accrue from their proper use in food and agricultural production.

Miss Carson's book . . . does confuse the [already known] information and so mix it with her opinions that the uninitiated reader is unable to sort fact from fancy. In view of the mature, responsible attention which this whole subject receives from able, scientific groups . . . (whom Miss Carson chooses to ignore); in view of her scientific qualifications in contrast to those of our distinguished scientific leaders and statesmen, the book should be ignored. . . .

Her thesis is revealed by the dedicatory quotations: "Man has lost the capacity to foresee and to forestall. He will end by destroying the earth." (Albert Schweitzer) "Our approach to nature is to beat it into submission. We would stand a better chance of survival if we accommodated ourselves to this planet and viewed it appreciatively instead of skeptically and dictatorially." (E.B. White)

Such a passive attitude as the latter coupled with such pessimistic . . . philosophy as the former, means the end of all human progress, reversion to a passive social state devoid of technology, scientific medicine, agriculture, sanitation, or education. It means disease epidemics, starvation, misery, and suffering incomparable and intolerable to modern man. Indeed, social, educational, and scientific development prefaced on the conviction that man's lot will be and is being improved by greater understanding of and thereby increased ability to control or mold those forces responsible for man's suffering, misery, and deprivation. . . .

. . . Miss Carson has effectively used several literary devices to present her thesis and make it appear to be a widely held scientific one. She "name-drops" by quoting or referring to renowned scientists out of context. A statement divorced from its original meaning is then appropriated to an opinion of the author or else to a question posed by her with an implied answer. The reader is led to conclude thereby that the authority mentioned is in accord with the author's position. . . .

Another useful device is that of a confusion of the reader with (to him) unintelligible scientific jargon or irrelevant discussions of cellular processes.

Miss Carson's failure to distinguish between the occupational and residue hazards is common to almost all popular writers on this subject. The occupational hazard associated with the manufacture and application of agricultural chemicals is similar to that of other work and can, should be, and is being reduced. That accidents have occurred is well known, but this is no more reason to ban useful chemicals than is the lamentable occurrence of preventable automobile or airplane accidents reason to ban these modern modes of transportation. Despite all of the implications of harm from residues on foods, Miss Carson has not produced one single example of injury resulting to man from these residues.

Miss Carson is infatuated with biologic control and the balance of nature. Despite her statement that the really effective control of insects is applied by nature, one must observe that the very ineffectiveness of such control is the raison d'etre of chemical pesticides. . . .

The toxicologists in industry, in the Food and Drug Administration, in our universities and research institutes have, as consumers, equal stake in protecting the nation's health as does Miss Carson—and are, I believe, better qualified to make those judgments necessary to assure this protection.

Her ignorance or bias on some of the considerations throws doubt on her competence to judge policy. . . .

The public may be misled by this book. If it stimulates the public to press for unwise and ill-conceived restrictions on the production, use, or development of new chemicals, it will be the consumer who suffers. If, on the other hand, it inspires some users to read and heed labels more carefully, it may aid in the large educational effort in which industry, government, colleges, and many other groups are engaged (despite Miss Carson's implication that they are not).

The responsible scientist should read this book to understand the ignorance of those writing on the subject and the educational task which lies ahead.

Source: Reprinted with permission from Dr. William J. Darby, "Silence, Miss Carson," *Chemical and Engineering News* 40 (October 1, 1962): 60, 62–63. Copyright © 1962 American Chemical Society.

Document 13.3   Another Scientist on the Pesticide Danger

There was no unanimity in the scientific community on the veracity of Carson's arguments. Generally speaking, among independent scientists not employed by any of the companies or government agencies with a financial or bureaucratic stake in the regulation or banning of certain chemicals, professionals trained in biological and zoological fields generally viewed the book more favorably, while those with degrees in chemistry, toxicology, and physics tended to find greater fault with her arguments. Here, Dr. Robert L. Rudd, a leading zoologist and author of a work of distinction of his own on the subject, Pesticides and the Living Landscape, *surveys and responds to some of the arguments of Carson's critics. Especially notable is his commendation of Carson for having brought the debate over pesticides, and, more generally the technological control of nature, out of the narrow province of scientific disciplines and onto the public agenda.*

The technological society in which Americans live has provided a level of health, ease, and comfort unparalleled in history. We have set the pattern and the goals toward which the rest of the world strives. Loud voices proclaim the value of our achievements and promise an ever-changing, ever-better future. True, there have always been doubters and there have even been those who would reverse our social directions. Yet, on balance, we have come to accept technological innovation as an inherent feature of our culture and to dismiss—sometimes with contempt and ridicule—the arguments of the doubters.

But a second category of doubt has lately appeared; this doubt is neither imagined nor easily dismissed. We have cause to suspect that the products of our technology may be unwisely applied, and in the long run harm us more than help us. . . .

Pesticides—now largely synthetic chemicals—are designed to kill or inhibit the plants and animals that interfere with our health, comfort, or production of foods and fibers. Some 200 chemicals are commonly used in agriculture. . . . Most can be considered "biocides"—they kill living things. . . . The purposes of pesticidal use are clear and widely accepted. But, if these purposes are acceptable, then why should anyone argue against their use?

Here are a few reasons:

1. Most pesticides are non-selective; they kill forms of life other than their targets.
2. Their manner of use, though often increasing in selectivity, is in most cases not precise enough, being restricted neither as to pest species nor area applied.
3. Insufficient attention has been given to other means of crop protection. . . .
4. Many kinds of pesticides . . . are chemically incredibly stable; their survival in soil, water, and living tissue is assured.
5. Insidious pathways of biological transfer of toxic chemicals are now well known. These channels of potential harm include delayed toxicity, . . . and potentially at least, mutagenic and carcinogenic effects. Yet many chemically-oriented persons continue to deny the importance of these biological consequences of pesticide use.
6. Their use is entirely too single-minded in relation to the manifold effects they produce. . . .
7. The technically supported viewpoints of the conservationist, the resource analyst, the biologist, and the sociologist are too frequently overlooked in pest control recommendations and in governmental programming.
8. Equally lacking is overt concern for esthetic and moral values that inevitably figure in the applications of technology to the satisfaction of human needs and desires. . . .

No one denies the value of pesticides in safeguarding ourselves and our food supply. All the points listed above have been debated in the limited circles of technologists, regulatory officials, agriculturalists, industrial representatives, and governmental policymakers. However, the era of closed debate has ended. Miss Carson's book has made the debate public property. . . .

Silent Spring is a credit to its writer. But while conceding her literary abilities, her critics challenge her technical competence in the subjects she covers. Are they correct? I should say, "Yes, in part, if what is expected is an ultimate knowledge of every aspect of the problem." However, no reviewer, including her critics, has that knowledge today. Among specialists there is far too much equivalence given to all facts and far too little venture into matters of judgment and conceptual thought. Miss Carson is a trained biologist and has worked professionally for many years in the U.S. Fish and Wildlife Service. Her interest in pesticidal chemicals dates from World War II.... In my opinion, she is eminently qualified to present facts, synthesis, and argument she has in *Silent Spring*. I leave it to her critics to do as well....

Source: Robert L. Rudd, "The Chemical Countryside," *Pacific Discovery* (now *California Wild*), published by the California Academy of Sciences, vol. 15, n. 6 (November, December 1962): 10–11. Reprinted with permission.

**Document 13.4   Economic Entomologist Assails "Hysteria"
of Pesticide Critics**

Like the scientific expertise, the passion in this argument ran both ways. Here, George C. Decker, head of the Economic Entomology section of the Illinois Agricultural Experiment Station, denounces generally all critics of pesticide use, dismissing their arguments as the ravings of emotional, uninformed, or misinformed amateurs. As a professional scientist employed by a government agency whose bureaucratic fortunes were deeply tied to the rise of the chemical industry, Decker did not write without his own bias.

...Pesticide manufacturers and users frequently are accused of using the human race as guinea pigs, which is by no means true. They do, however, rightly contend that since tolerances are based on toxicity studies involving life-span or at least long-time feeding studies, the occasional ingestion of some one item in the diet bearing a residue slightly above or possibly well above the established tolerance will not endanger the life or health of the individual.... [One] wonders if present-day pesticide residues can possibly do as much damage to human health and well-being as does the state of hysteria that has been created through ill-advised publicity and sensational journalism....

Obviously, the information given on pesticide labels represents the end result of very extensive research carried on by the manufacturer and others. The recommendations have been carefully scrutinized for safety and effectiveness.... it is safe to say that, when properly used in full accord with label directions, pesticides not only present no threat to the safety of the consumer of treated crops and produce but they involve few if any hazards to the user. Therefore, in the field of operational hazards, as in the case of food contamination, there have been no cases of death and few if any cases of illness in either man or his domestic animals traceable to pesticides *used in accord with label instruction* (emphasis Decker's)....

The real hazards—irresponsibility, carelessness, ignorance, delusion, and skepticism—involve mental reactions and human judgments and are not toxicological in nature. Perhaps such problems can best be approached and resolved through education rather than through further legislation and regulation....

Source: George C. Decker, "Pros and Cons of Pests, Pest Control and Pesticides," *World Review of Pest Control* (Spring 1962): 1, Part 1, pp. 14–16.

Document 13.5   Cesar Chavez Testifies on the Health Effects of Pesticides Among Migrant Farm Workers, 1969

Silent Spring triggered a decade-long debate about the danger to human health and to the environment from chemical pesticides and insecticides. In 1968 pesticide exposure became a dominant issue in the campaign led by Cesar Chavez to organize the United Farm Workers of America. This excerpt from Chavez's 1969 testimony before the U.S. Senate Subcommittee on Migratory Labor includes evidence of the severe health effects that had been suffered for more than a decade by a minority population whose plight had long been easily ignored by most Americans. When it reached the national agenda, the farm workers' struggle helped to make more immediate for American consumers the connections between occupational and environmental health. Senator Walter Mondale's opening question goes to one of the issues that would unite environmentalists, community activists, and labor leaders in the 1970s—that is, the "Right to Know" what hazardous materials existed both in the workplace and in communities across the country. Much of the rest of the testimony seemed to confirm allegations made by Rachel Carson regarding the danger to human health from reckless misuse of pesticides.

Senator Mondale. As I gather from testimony from Mr. Cohen (the farm workers attorney), it is almost impossible to find out from official government records what kind of pesticides are being used by commercial applicators. And, the growers themselves refuse to respond where there is no [union] contract. Thus, your workers really don't know what is being used, what quantity, or what kind of risks they are taking when they work in these fields. Is that correct?

Mr. Chavez. That is correct. That is where the danger lies. We are convinced that it is as much to the benefit to the employers as it is to the benefit of the workers to put some kind of protection in there so that we can protect them. . . .

PREPARED STATEMENT OF CESAR CHAVEZ, UNITED FARM WORKERS ORGANIZING COMMITTEE

On August 1st, 1969

The real issue involved here is the issue of the health and safety not only of farm workers but of consumers and how the health and safety of consumers and farm workers are affected by the gross misuse of economic poisons.

The issue of the health and safety of farm workers in California and throughout the United States is the single most important issue facing the United Farm Workers Organizing Committee. In California the agricultural industry experiences the highest occupational disease rate. The rate is . . . three times as high as the average rate of all industry in California. Growers consistently use the wrong kinds of economic poisons in the wrong amounts in the wrong places in reckless disregard of the health of their workers in order to maximize profits. . . .

In California an estimated 3,000 children receive medical attention annually after having injested pesticides. There are over 300 cases of serious nonfatal poisonings annually, most of which occur in agriculture. . . . In addition to this, literally thousands of workers experience daily symptoms of chemical poisoning which include dermatitis, rashes, eye irritation, nausea, vomiting, fatigue, excess sweating, headaches, double vision, dizziness, skin irritations, difficulty in breathing, loss of fingernails, nervousness, insomnia, bleeding noses, and diarrhea. . . .

Dr. Lee Mizrahi . . . has recently conducted a study relating to nutrition, parasites and pesticide levels. [He] has reported that though the results of the test are not complete, based on the findings already received there are pesticide levels which can only be described as epidemic. Thus far . . . 32 of the 84 reported values have fallen outside normal limits. Dr. Mizrahi has informed me that as a practicing physician he would be greatly worried if he found 10% of reportedly normal children outside normal limits. In this case he is frightened. These farm worker children are suffering from high levels of DDT in their blood and from low cholinesterase in their blood plasma. . . .

During this past summer in the grapes alone and largely in the Delano area the following incidents have been brought to the attention of our legal department.

On May 16th, 1969, Mrs. Delores Lorta was working for labor contractor Manuel Armendariz in a table grape vineyard owned by Agri-Business Investment Company. Without warning, an Agri-Business spray rig sprayed the row she was working on, and Mrs. Lorta was sprayed all over her body with an unknown mixture of chemicals. Shortly thereafter, she experienced difficulty in breathing. She told her forelady, who responded that the spraying had nothing to do with that; that she must have had that difficulty before. . . . She has suffered from continuing sores and rashes all over her body, headaches, dizziness, loss of weight, and her condition still continues. She has received no compensation from her employer as yet, and she has had to pay for her medical care herself. . . .

While working the vineyards of George A. Lucas & Sons this summer, Mrs. Beatrice Roman developed trouble breathing, sore throat, difficulty in speaking, and stomach pain. Each day her condition would worsen as she began work the following morning. There was a heavy white powder on the vines [where] she was working. . . .

After working in the vineyards of D. M. Steele for several days, Mr. Juan Q. Lopez developed trouble breathing, rashes on his neck and face, numbness in his left arm and upper left chest, headache and irritated eyes. There was a white powder on the vines. Mr. Lopez's condition began to improve when he stopped working in these fields.

While working picking grapes in a Caric vineyard about 10 days ago, Mr. Abelardo Hernandez ate some grapes from the vine. Shortly thereafter, he began to vomit and bleed from the nose. His foreman refused to take him to a doctor until other workers finally convinced him to do so. The doctor who treated him said his illness was due to the grapes and the chemicals on them. . . .

The United Farm Workers Organizing Committee (UFWOC) is attempting to solve this pervasive problem by the collective bargaining process. We have recently attained what is for farm workers an historic breakthrough in our negotiations with the Parelli-Minetti Company. We have completed negotiating a comprehensive health and safety clause which covers the subject of economic poisons. . . .

Source: Hearing Before the Subcommittee on Migratory Labor of the Committee on Labor and Public Welfare. United States Senate. 91st Congress. 1st and 2nd sessions on Pesticides and Farm Workers, September 29, 1969 (Washington, DC: U.S. Government Printing Office, 1970), part 6-B, pp. 3396–3400.

Document 13.6   Grape Growers Refute Charges of Cesar Chavez on Pesticides

---

A war of words between the UFWOC and the grape growers' industry ensued throughout the subcommittee's hearings that summer. In particular, charges of duplicity and outright deceit flew back and forth regarding the allegation by the union that grapes found in a Washington supermarket had levels of the pesticide Aldrin far in excess of what was allowable. A laboratory confirmed the union's charges, findings that were confirmed by a second independent test ordered by the supermarket. The incident provoked the grape growers to issue a press release, which was subsequently entered into the record of the committee's proceedings.

Two major California table grape growers today charged Cesar Chavez and the United Farm Workers Organizing Committee with mounting a false pesticide scare to cover UFWOC's failure to organize the nation's farm workers and to sustain a sagging grape boycott effort. . . .

[John] Giumarra, general counsel for Giumarra Vineyards Corporation of Edison, and [Anthony] Bianco, president of Bianco Fruit Corporation of Fresno, issued this statement; . . .

". . . [We] of the table grape industry have had to listen too long while Cesar Chavez has misled the American people and the Congress.

Mr. Chavez has come to Washington to testify before the highest legislative body in the land in an effort to use this revered place as the staging ground for a traveling sideshow which he had hoped would whip the farmers and stores of the nation to their knees.

"Mr. Chavez and his representatives have appeared before Congress and in the marketplaces of the country to charge that California table grapes are contaminated by pesticides. The hearings . . . will prove that those charges are false, and that they have been deliberately raised as a tactical weapon in a losing battle.

"They will prove that Mr. Chavez is the greatest threat to the American consumer in the history of agriculture and his pious trumpeting of the pesticide charge will be shown for what it is—a bogeyman campaign to keep his failing 'La Causa' alive.

"On August 1, the Subcommittee . . . heard Jerome Cohen, UFWOC general counsel, charge that Mr. Bianco's grapes contained 18 parts per million of the pesticide aldrin, a level far in excess of permitted tolerances. . . . Then with a broad brush but no specifics, he painted a black picture of growers poisoning farm workers and the American consumer. . . .

"Evidence will show that Mr. Cohen's charge is false. . . . Mr. Chavez has failed in his last desperate attempt to grab control of the nation's food production. California table grapes are being harvested, shipped and marketed and the American public is buying them."

Source: Hearing Before the Subcommittee on Migratory Labor of the Committee on Labor and Public Welfare. United States Senate. 91st Congress. 1st and 2nd sessions on Pesticides and Farm Workers, September 29, 1969 (Washington, DC: U.S. Government Printing Office, 1970), part 6-C, pp. 3706–707.

Document 13.7   Federal Environmental Pesticide Control Act of 1972

The continuing debate over the health and safety of farm workers and the safety of produce reached a legislative plateau in 1972 with the passage of the Pesticide Control Act. Although agribusiness and the chemical industry objected to what seemed at the time to be onerous regulations, the law has fully satisfied neither worker advocates nor environmentalists, who say its broad provisions and enforcement have only minimally slowed the onslaught of chemicals into the environment.

Digest [synopsis] of Federal Environmental Pesticide Control Act of 1972 . . . as amended.

The Federal Environmental Pesticide Control Act of 1972, enacted as P.L. 92-516, amended the 1947 Federal Insecticide, Fungicide, and Rodenticide Act (P.L. 80-102, June 25, 1947, 61 Stat. 163).

The 1947 statute (FIFRA) prohibited the sale or distribution of "economic poisons," provided for the registration of such materials, and authorized penalties for violation of the Act.

The 1972 amendments established, under the Administrator of EPA, a program for controlling the sale, distribution, and application of pesticides through an administrative registration process. The amendments provided for classifying pesticides for "general" or "restricted" use. "Restricted" pesticides may only be applied by or under the direct supervision of a certified applicator.

The amendments also authorized experimental use permits and provided for administrative review of registered pesticides and for penalties for violations of the statute. States were authorized to regulate the sale or use of any pesticide within a state, provided that such regulation does not permit any sale or use prohibited by the Act. . . .

The 1975 amendments to FIFRA (P.L. 94-140, November 28, 1975, 89 Stat. 751) required that the EPA Administrator consider the impacts of regulatory actions on production and prices of agricultural commodities and to notify the Secretary of Agriculture in advance of related rulemaking. Experimental use permits were also authorized for agricultural research activities.

Source: U.S. Fish and Wildlife Service. Digest of Federal Resource Laws of Interest to the U.S. Fish and Wildlife Service. http://laws.fws.gov/lawsdigest/fedenvp.html (accessed July 29, 2004).

Document 13.8   Occupational Safety and Health Act, 1970

Along with the struggles of the Oil, Chemical and Atomic Workers Union, the United Mine Workers of America, and uranium and asbestos workers, the increased focus on pesticide exposure by the United Farm Workers of America helped to win passage of OSHA, the law regulating worker safety and health in the United States. Again, enforcement of the law has been erratic, particularly with respect to migrant farm workers.

AN ACT

To assure safe and healthful working conditions for working men and women; by authorizing enforcement of the standards developed under the Act; by assisting and encouraging the States in their efforts to assure safe and healthful working conditions; by providing for research, information, education, and training in the field of occupational safety and health; and for other purposes.

Be it enacted by the Senate and House of Representatives of the United States of America in Congress assembled, **That this Act may be cited as the "Occupational Safety and Health Act of 1970."**

Source: Public Law 91-596; 84 STAT. 1590; 91st Congress, S.2193. December 29, 1970, as amended through January 1, 2004. (1).

NOTES

1. Rachel Carson, *Silent Spring* (Boston: Houghton Mifflin, 1987), p. 99.

2. "The Desolate Year" (New York: Monsanto, 1963). Cover letter to distributors, cited in Linda Lear's Rachel Carson Web site, www.rachelcarson.org. Lear is the author of the definitive Carson biography, *Witness for Nature* (New York: Henry Holt, 1997).

3. Virginia Jenkins, *The Lawn: A History of an American Obsession* (Washington, DC: Smithsonian Institution Press, 2003), pp. 146–54.

4. Cited in Philip Sterling, *Sea and Earth: The Life of Rachel Carson* (New York: Thomas Y. Crowell, 1970), pp. 147–48.

5. Leonie Haimson et al., *A Moment of Truth: Correcting More Errors in Gregg Easterbrook's "A Moment on the Earth"* (Washington, DC: Environmental Defense Fund, 1996). See especially pp. 21–35.

ANNOTATED BIBLIOGRAPHY

Ashworth, William. *The Carson Factor*. New York: Hawthorn Books, 1979. Offers one telling case study of the effect the book had on local citizens' struggles to contest spraying programs.

Colburn, Theo, Dianne Dumanoski, and John P. Meyers. *Our Stolen Future: Are We Threatening Our Fertility, Intelligence and Survival—A Scientific Detective Story*. New York: Plume Books, 1997. Extending Carson's legacy, this is a meticulously researched, extraordinarily well-documented, and terrifying argument linking reproductive disorders, sexual abnormalities, and birth defects in wildlife to exposure to a wide range of synthetic chemicals permeating our environment.

Dunlap, Thomas. *DDT: Scientists, Citizens, and Public Policy*. Princeton: Princeton University Press, 1983. A well-regarded history of the public policy debate over the regulation of this pesticide.

Easterbrook, Gregg. *A Moment on the Earth: The Coming Age of Environmental Optimism*. New York: Viking Press, 1995. Challenges scientific consensus on the dangers of pesticides and a host of other environmental threats, subsequently deconstructed and denounced by numerous scientists.

Ferriss, Susan, and Ricardo Sandoval. *The Fight in the Fields: Cesar Chavez and the Farmworkers Movement*. San Diego, CA: Harvest/HBJ Books, 1998. Comprehensive and compelling history of the struggle to organize the migrant farm workers.

Lear, Linda. *Rachel Carson: Witness for Nature*. New York: Henry Holt, 1997. The definitive biography of the biologist's life, recounting Carson's childhood, education, and early career as a marine biologist, tracing the maturation of the scientific thinking and aesthetic sensibility that inform her early books about the oceans, and ultimately *Silent Spring*.

Levy, Jacques. *Cesar Chavez: Autobiography of La Causa*. 1969. Reprint, New York: W. W. Norton, 1975. The Chavez-farm workers story, with substantial treatment of the pesticide issue.

Lomborg, Bjorn. *The Skeptical Environmentalist: Measuring the Real State of the World*. Cambridge: Cambridge University Press, 2001. Embraced enthusiastically by conservatives and the mainstream press as proof that Carson and environmentalists generally have had it all wrong. Factual basis for his arguments has been roundly disputed by the international scientific community.

MacGillivray, Alex. *Rachel Carson's Silent Spring: Words that Changed the World*. Hauppauge, NY: Barron's Education Series, 2004. Succinct but useful commentary and analysis on the impact of *Silent Spring*.

Matthiessen, Peter. *Sal Si Puedes: Cesar Chavez and the New American Revolution*. 1969. Reprint, Berkeley: University of California Press, 2000. An account of three years spent by the author with Chavez, provides a compelling glimpse of the organizer's vision and commitment to social justice that remains vital as ever.

Moses, Marion. *Harvest of Sorrow: Farm Workers and Pesticides*. San Francisco: Pesticide Education Center, 1992. The best overview of links between pesticides and the health of farm workers, written by a physician and worker health advocate.

Murphy, Priscilla Coit. *What a Book Can Do: The Publication and Reception of Silent Spring*. Amherst: University of Massachusetts Press, 2005. Chronicles the history of the book's publication, its serialization by the *New Yorker*, and Carson's relationship with her editors. Also details the assault on Carson and the book from the chemical industry, the role of the media and the public in the contentious debate over the book.

Steingraber, Sandra. *Living Downstream: A Scientist's Personal Investigation of Cancer and the Environment.* 1997. Reprint, New York: Vintage Books, 1998. Written very much in Carson's style of poetic eloquence and scientific precision, Steingraber skillfully weaves a personal story of surviving cancer with thorough scientific investigation of the chemical contamination of the human environment.

14

Love Canal and the Grassroots Movement Against Toxic Waste

> If you think you're safe, think again.
> —Lois Marie Gibbs, 2004[1]

> With the press and the homeowners screaming, the federal government apparently felt compelled to "do something" about the matter, and Hooker turned out to be the most suitable punching bag under the circumstances.
> —Eric Zuesse, 1981[2]

As is clear by now, few episodes of American environmental history are as simple as they might appear. The meaning of the late 1970s toxic waste nightmare at Love Canal is complex and contested still—despite its heroic and seemingly straight-forward narrative. When residents of a quiet working-class neighborhood of Niagara Falls, New York, discovered that they were living on top of a former toxic waste dump, they launched a citizens' struggle for justice that ultimately took them to the White House. Their campaign led the nation to confront the pervasive problem of hazardous waste disposal. At its most basic level, Love Canal is the story of how one community organized against the menace of toxic waste that had permeated its neighborhood. Yet that hard-won victory resulted in more than justice, albeit delayed, for the community, even more than the Superfund law to clean up thousands more potential Love Canals throughout the nation. It pow-erfully demonstrated that the threat posed by hazardous waste to communities in the United States could and would be challenged by citizens who increasingly turned their fear and anger into determined, effective activism. Grassroots organizing on environmental issues was not new, but Love Canal suffused it with urgency by making clear the links between environmental and human health.

Beyond the quest for justice, however, was the more troubling and complex issue of who ought to bear legal liability and financial risk for the staggering volumes of hazardous waste generated by industries that generate consumer goods and economic benefits for society at large.

Though it ended in a nightmare, Love Canal began as a utopian dream. In 1892 industrial visionary William T. Love arrived in Niagara Falls with great hopes of establishing a progressive industrial complex fueled by water power. He planned to build a seven-mile-long navigable canal that would connect the lower and upper levels of the Niagara River and provide power. Love's vision of a model city of 600,000 attracted investors and a charter from the state granting him the power to condemn property and divert unlimited amounts of water from the Niagara River—even to the point of turning off Niagara Falls. Two events killed Love's dream: the economic depression of the 1890s and the discovery of alternating electrical current, which allowed industrial facilities to locate away from the river. Love had completed just 3,000 feet of the canal, which was soon abandoned. The partially completed channel subsequently became a popular swimming hole for local residents.

The story took an ominous turn in the 1920s when part of the canal became a repository for Niagara Falls municipal waste and for highly toxic industrial waste from chemical companies in the vicinity. By far the largest volume came from Hooker Chemical Corporation, which buried its waste in the canal until 1954. By then more than 200 different chemicals and a total of 22,000 tons of waste had been dumped into the canal, including some of the most toxic substances ever devised: dioxin, polychlorinated biphenyls (PCBs), lindane, and multiple solvents and pesticides.

Hooker Chemical buried the wastes mostly in metal drums, some of which were old and rusty. Some drums broke open as they were dumped. Smaller amounts of waste were dumped directly into the canal. When the drums and waste filled portions of the canal to within a few feet of the surface, they were covered over with layers of fly ash and dirt. The company dug ancillary pits adjacent to the canal to dispose of excess waste. Hooker employees visiting the site during the dumping era reported to management the deteriorating condition of the drums and the infiltration of some waste into the portion of the canal still used as a swimming hole by local children. Despite strong recommendations from its own general counsel, the company refused to erect a fence to keep children from the waste-filled areas. By the mid-1950s, Hooker became aware that the ground above the deteriorating drums was subsiding, exposing some of the waste. Local residents reported occasional fires spontaneously erupting from the canal.

In 1952 the local school board approached Hooker with a desire to purchase a portion of the property. Concerned about potential liability, the company at first refused, but soon agreed to donate the property for one dollar. The deed contained foreboding stipulations: the school board had to take the entire property and indemnify Hooker against all liability. Further, the company retained dumping rights until the school was built. Hooker warned the board that it had used the canal "for plant refuse containing some chemicals," although it did not acknowledge the dangers of possible surface subsidence or of waste infiltration through the subsurface. The company affirmed that sections of the property would be appropriate for a school and proposed playground. School board officials planned to develop the balance of the property as single-family homes, adding to the dozens of homes that already existed near the abandoned canal.

Problems emerged before construction of the 99th Street School was even completed. The school's location was shifted when contractors encountered two waste-filled pits. Periodic ground subsidence exposed some of the waste to children and residents. Still, construction of the school and the new housing went forward.

From the late 1950s through the early 1970s, residents issued regular complaints to city officials about noxious odors permeating the air and "substances" surfacing in backyards. Also surfacing were the first reports of health problems among children in the area, ranging from skin rashes to respiratory conditions. Niagara Falls officials responded by throwing additional layers of dirt or clay on top of the exposed substances. The complaints persisted, and the city hired an outside consultant to investigate. The consultant's 1976 report confirmed the presence of toxic residual odors and liquids in the sump pumps of some residents' basements at the southern end of the neighborhood, along with high levels of highly toxic PCBs in the storm sewers. Recommendations included imposing a clay cap over the entire canal site, sealing home sump pumps, and most importantly, installing a tile drainage system to control the migration of wastes from the canal proper. The advice was ignored.

Not surprisingly, the waste continued to migrate underground into the basements of many of the 800 single-family home dwellers in the area. By 1978 what had been an incessant but mysterious nuisance had become a fully disclosed public health crisis. Michael Brown, a reporter for the local *Niagara Gazette*, wrote a series of articles on the problem of hazardous waste disposal throughout the area, focusing on Love Canal. His series included disturbing accounts of the severe maladies linked to chemicals deposited in the canal.

That series moved Lois Gibbs to act. A young mother of two children, Gibbs had moved into the neighborhood in 1972. Soon afterward her son Michael developed violent seizures that turned out to be epilepsy, along with a falling white blood cell count. She learned in Brown's articles that the 99th Street School had been built on top of the canal. Knowing her family health history and her son's previous good health, she became convinced that the school was making him sick. Gibbs promptly asked the school board to transfer him to another school. They refused, fearing the precedent it would establish for other families who might make the same request. After being refused help by city and state representatives as well, Gibbs went door to door with a petition to shut down the school. Her canvas of the neighborhood revealed multiple illnesses that appeared obviously linked to the waste: disproportionate numbers of similar cancers, respiratory, skin and urinary tract diseases, and a high rate of recent miscarriages, still births, and birth defects.

The petition drive shattered the reserve of residents and brought greater attention to the problem. It also increased pressure on the New York State Department of Health (NYSDOH) to take further action. Simultaneous to Brown's series, NYSDOH had conducted air and soil samples and health studies of the neighborhood. In April 1978, the agency issued its initial determination of a problem, declaring the canal "an extremely serious threat to the health and welfare" of residents. State health commissioner Robert Whalen called upon local officials immediately to remove exposed chemicals, restrict access to the site, and with his office, conduct a further examination of the health problems and potential engineering solutions.

Further study did ensue, resulting in Commissioner Whalen's August 2 declaration of a state of emergency. The NYSDOH accompanied that determination with not only an order that the 99th Street School be closed—a victory for Gibbs and her terrified neighbors—but also a recommendation that pregnant women and children under the age of two be evacuated. For citizens of Love Canal, the two-year-old threshold seemed arbitrary. Upon persistent questioning of NYSDOH medical and scientific experts, it appeared scientifically indefensible. Their outcry over the decision forced the evacuation order to be extended to all 239 families living in closest proximity to the canal. President Jimmy Carter signed a federal disaster order allowing emergency funding for the families' relocation.

Whalen ordered initial remedial cleanup to begin that fall. In an urgent attempt to arrest the migration of waste into neighbors' yards and basements, workers installed a drainage trench around the perimeter of the canal. They imposed a clay cap over the canal to reduce water infiltration from rain and snow and removed waste from sewer lines and nearby Black Creek.

Meanwhile, more than 600 families remained behind living in terror. As with the two-year-old threshold, their homes remained outside the evacuation zone. A November 1978 report revealed more than 200 chemicals were buried in the canal—more than twice the number declared by the state just months before. This disclosure, coupled with repeated obfuscation and stonewalling on the part of NYSDOH and local officials on a number of health, engineering, and evacuation issues, prompted a series of forceful protests from residents and stormy confrontations with authorities.

Led by Gibbs, families sought and received help from cancer researcher Dr. Beverly Paigen, who led residents in conducting an additional survey of local health problems. The Paigen study confirmed statistically shocking high rates of illness, birth defects, and miscarriage that residents had long suspected, triggering a second evacuation order from NYSDOH in February 1979. Once again, the order was limited in scope: pregnant women and children under the age of two from the 600-plus families. Moreover, it had come only after the state had denied relocation for nineteen families with documented illnesses so severe they were living in motels—a relocation that had been promised publicly by the governor. For these residents, there seemed to be no end to the nightmare. Feeling betrayed and deceived by local and state officials (and by Occidental Petroleum, Hooker's parent company), the community pressed for federal action. Congressional hearings in the spring of 1979 produced powerful testimony from afflicted residents. And still for more than another year the pace of action proved torturously slow. By the fall of 1979 more than 800 lawsuits had been filed against Hooker, the city, the county, and the board of education. The state of New York and the U.S. government, having already spent millions in remedial work and relocation costs, filed suit against Hooker, which countersued. The pitched and highly complex legal battle continued for well over a decade.

Legal action, years of scientific study, public education, and agitation of public officials at all levels had yet to produce complete evacuation of the community. In the spring of 1980 residents' frustration boiled over. They detained two officials from the U.S. Environmental Protection Agency (EPA) for six hours at the offices of the Love Canal Homeowner's Association, demanding declaration of a national emergency and evacuation of the remaining families. Within days, the hostage situation moved President Carter to issue the order. That fall he signed the bill authorizing funds for permanent relocation for all families who wished to leave. All but sixty-seven did so.

Love Canal focused national attention on the issue of hazardous waste. The scope of the problem was immense. Investigative reporting revealed tens of thousands of hazardous waste sites scattered across the country; a significant percentage of them in close proximity to communities. All were ticking time bombs, potential Love Canals, activists warned. Congress responded by passing, in December 1980, the Comprehensive Emergency Response, Compensation, and Liability Act (CERCLA). Better known as Superfund, the law established a system for identifying, managing, and funding the cleanup of the nation's hazardous waste sites.

In practice and enforcement, the law did not end the problems posed by improper hazardous waste disposal. Superfund has been criticized by community and environmental activists for many of the same reasons Love Canal residents grew frustrated: the law is highly technical, governed by a bureaucracy that is slow to move, and subject to legal challenge and resistance by the polluting parties. The business sector attacked it as well, for many reasons, not the least of which were the high costs associated with cleanup and the science used to target a site for remediation. Funding proved the biggest point of contention. The largest percentage of cleanup funds came from polluting industries, with a lesser portion from taxpayers. In 2004 President George W. Bush supported a long-standing effort by industry to terminate industry's contribution to Superfund, a move that shifted the entire burden of cleaning up the remaining sites onto the public at large.

The degree of remediation each site had to undergo was also a matter of continued debate. How clean did a site have to become in order to be redeveloped? After nearly two decades of litigation, as well as successful cleanup of hundreds of Superfund sites across the country, that question would turn largely on the practical matter of what function (e.g., industrial, residential, a parking lot, etc.) the remediated site was to serve. The difficult process of reaching a pragmatic consensus on redeveloping industrial "brownfields" unfolded in communities, in courtrooms, and in the policy-making arena. That war of words also played out at Love Canal. After a decade of demolition and remediation, the state and federal governments in 1988 declared the area "habitable." Despite 20,000 tons of buried waste that were never removed, Love Canal by the 1990s was born anew as a residential community. Some asserted that the scope and degree of the threat had been overstated in 1980.

Nevertheless, by then Love Canal had altered the nation's environmental politics and environmentalism itself. The event made frighteningly real the consequences of an "out of sight, out of mind" attitude toward hazardous industrial waste. Love Canal became synonymous with the public fear of the ubiquity of toxics in the environment. The environmental movement, long criticized by working people and people of color for ignoring *their* environments, was forced to pay heed to the issue that seemed disproportionately to affect those communities. Many of the local groups emerging out of Love Canal in the anti-toxics movement were situated in poor and minority communities, giving credence to the claims of civil rights activists that people of color disproportionately suffered from the siting of polluting industries and toxic dumps. Indeed, simultaneous to the nightmare at Love Canal was the less infamous episode of PCB waste-dumping along the roads of Warren County, North Carolina. Activists there made a convincing case that the area had been deliberately targeted because it was overwhelmingly poor and minority. Though the episode received little national attention, along with Love Canal it helped spark the "environmental justice" movement that joined issues of race, class, and environmental health. Often disparaged as the Not In My Backyard (NIMBY) syndrome, the phenomenon of community resistance to polluting facilities or waste dumps seemed strongest in poor and minority communities because that was disproportionately the locus of such pollution.

Not counting on mainstream environmental organizations to take up the issue of hazardous waste (for they had theretofore shown little or no interest), Lois Gibbs devoted her life to the cause. She founded the Citizens Clearinghouse for Hazardous Waste (later the Center for Health, Environment and Justice) to assist tens of thousands of people in hundreds of communities across the nation in their struggles with similar public health threats. Organizations such as the Sierra Club were compelled to devote energy and resources to the issue, though their work was focused on the regulatory process, legal challenges, and on lobbying officials in Washington. By contrast, Gibbs's organization and community groups with whom she worked employed the same tactics and strategies of making themselves experts and confronting authorities when necessary.

By the turn of the twenty-first century, environmentalists and some corporate leaders began calling for more constructive, less contentious solutions to the problem of toxics. They argued that reducing toxic effluent would save industry money, produce less risk to public health, and generate fewer economic costs on the cleanup end. Twenty years after Love Canal, American industry still generated 700 billion pounds of hazardous waste in the production of chemicals. One hundred pounds of product produced 3,200 pounds of waste, translating to the least efficient manufacturing economy in the world. Until those numbers could be improved significantly, the problem first confronted at Love Canal was not likely to go away.

Finally, the horrifying image of mothers holding children made ill by environmental contamination raised questions about responsibility. Was Love Canal a simple moral tale of villainous corporate irresponsibility and unaccountable, incompetent government? Or does the event suggest something deeper and larger about the costs and risks incurred by a consumer culture? If industrial production is inherently wasteful, then ought not the society at large that benefits from economic growth and cheap consumer goods bear some burden for that afflu-ence? If so, what level of risk to human health is acceptable, and in what com-munities? Since Love Canal, Americans have labored to resolve these and other questions. They weigh as heavily now as then, and not only on business profit-ability and governmental responsibility, but as matters of life and death.

DOCUMENTS

**Document 14.1   Hooker Chemical Company Deeds Abandoned Canal
to Niagara Falls School Board**

---

*On April 28, 1953, the Niagara Falls School Board acquired title to the
Love Canal property from Hooker Chemical for the nominal fee of $1.
The candid admission of hazardous waste having been dumped into
the canal has led some to argue that the culprit in the Love Canal
nightmare was the school board, not the Hooker Chemical Company.*

... This Indenture [is] made the 28th day of April, Nineteen Hundred and
Fifty Three, between Hooker Electrochemical Company ... and the Board of
Education of the School District of the City of Niagara Falls, New York. ... Prior
to the delivery of this instrument of conveyance, the grantee herein has been
advised by the grantor that the premises above described have been filled, in
whole or in part, to the present grade level thereof with waste products resulting from the manufacturing of chemicals by the grantor at its plant in the
City of Niagara Falls, New York, and the grantee assumes all risk and liability
incident to the use thereof. It is therefore understood and agreed that, as a part
of the consideration for this conveyance and as a condition thereof, no claim,
suit, action or demand of any nature whatsoever shall ever be made by the
grantee, its successors or assigns, against the grantor, its successors or assigns,
for injury to a person or persons, including death resulting therefrom, or loss of
or damage to property caused by, in connection with or by reason of the
presence of said industrial wastes. It is further agreed as a condition hereof that
each subsequent conveyance of the aforesaid lands shall be made subject to the
foregoing provisions and conditions.

Source: Deed recorded July 6, 1953, City of Niagara Falls, Niagara County Clerk's Office,
Lockport, New York.

**Document 14.2   New York State Health Commission Report on Love
Canal, 1978**

---

*After several months of intensive study prompted by the investigative
journalism of Michael Brown and the activism of Love Canal residents,
the Commissioner of the New York State Department of Health reported
his agency's findings on the situation to the governor and the state
legislature. The report's grim acknowledgment of the crisis and the
specific scientific findings confirmed much of what residents had been*

saying. However, the recommended actions, particularly the provision that only pregnant women and children under the age of two be relocated, left residents furious. Moreover, they took great issue with the commissioner's assertion that the response of public officials had been "swift and compassionate." Although much was not known at the time of the report, residents contended that the severity of what was known made it imperative that a complete evacuation take place. Why risk people's lives, they argued, when everything that was being learned suggested the need for more aggressive action.

The profound and devastating effects of the Love Canal tragedy, in terms of human health and suffering and environmental damage, cannot and probably will never be fully measured.

The lessons we are learning from this modern-day disaster should serve as a warning for governments at all levels and for private industry to take steps to avoid a repetition of these tragic events. . . .

We must improve our technological capabilities, supplant ignorance with knowledge and be ever vigilant for those seemingly innocuous situations which may portend the beginning of an environmental nightmare.

The issues confronting our citizens and their elected and appointed leaders in the Love Canal situation are unprecedented in the State's health annals. We can be proud of the swift and compassionate response to the crisis by our leaders and the agencies they direct in easing the plight of those affected and removing the hazards to their health and safety.

Under Governor Carey's personal direction, State agencies moved with dispatch to deal with a variety of complex problems associated with the Love Canal. . . .

Described as an environmental time bomb gone off, Love Canal stands as testimony to the ignorance, lack of vision and proper laws of decades past which allowed the indiscriminate disposal of such toxic materials. . . .

For those responsible for containing the problem . . . Love Canal represents what may very well be the first of a new and sinister breed of environmental disasters. . . .

ENVIRONMENTAL SAMPLING

The State Departments of Health and Environmental Conservation in the early spring of 1978 launched an intensive air, soil and groundwater sampling and analysis program following qualitative identification of a number of organic compounds in the basements of 11 homes adjacent to the Love Canal.

The new data collected by the two agencies confirmed not only the presence of a variety of compounds but established precise levels for many of the chemical constituents. It became immediately apparent from the data that the problem was not limited to a few homes and that a potential health hazard existed from long term exposure to the chemicals.

Based on this latest information, the Commissioners of Health and Environmental Conservation instructed their respective staffs to explore every remedy available to the State to protect the public's health and safety.

Commissioner Whalen's order [of April 25, 1978] set into motion a coordinated plan of attack by local, State and Federal agencies to further delineate the nature and extent of environmental and public health hazards. . . .

As data flowed in, it became evident that unacceptable levels of toxic vapors associated with more than 80 compounds were emanating from the basements of many homes in the first ring directly adjacent to the Love Canal. Ten of the most prevalent and most toxic compounds—including benzene, a known human carcinogen—were selected for evaluation purposes and as indicators of the presence of other chemical constituents. . . .

Armed with additional information showing the extensive contamination of homes directly adjacent to the Canal, Commissioner Whalen ordered an extension of basement air sampling to include homes across the street from the Canal—approximately 138 residences. The preliminary basement air data indicate much lower levels of selected contaminants compared to the first ring. . . .

The full extent of migration of chemical leachate is being determined . . . by extensive analyses of soil samples, shallow wells and sump drains at intervals extending in all directions beyond the Canal. A review of results for a small number of soil samples . . . suggests migration of chemicals, including lindane and toluene, outside the immediate Canal area. . . . [The] U.S. Environmental Protection Agency on August 23, 1978, [reiterated] our recommendation that remedial action be undertaken immediately to prevent future contamination of private property and additional human exposure to unacceptable health risks.

It should be restated that basement air samples taken from homes in the outlying area have thus far shown significantly lower levels of contaminants as compared to the first ring of homes, both in numbers of compounds and concentrations present. . . .

As part of the . . . investigation, radiological health specialists conducted a scan of the Canal surface for radioactivity and found three spots . . . where radiation levels slightly exceeded normal background radiation activity. Additional samples were being taken at various depths to ascertain the source of the radioactivity. It should be emphasized that the radioactive readings found did not exceed safe levels and are not hazardous to health.

Hydrogeological analyses of deep groundwater aquifers are being conducted in the Canal area but sufficient information is not yet available to permit any definitive conclusions. . . .

EPIDEMOLOGIC INVESTIGATION

HUMAN TOXICITY OF CHEMICALS: . . . [Virtually] all of man's physiologic systems can be pathologically influenced by exposure to chemicals identified to date at the Love Canal site—a list which must be viewed as incomplete since the types of chemicals dumped into the landfill and the chemical reactions which may have occurred over time cannot be fully documented. . . .

No conclusions relative to residence on the Canal can be drawn at this time with regard to the significance of minor abnormalities detected. Efforts will be made to confirm and more fully investigate abnormal test results. . . .

FINDINGS OF FACT

1. Seven of the chemicals identified in the air samples taken by the Division of Laboratories and Research are carcinogenic in animals and one, benzene, is a known human carcinogen.

2. In one home, in particular, the concentration of organic chemicals in the living space was well beyond the concentrations measured in the basement of any other house.

3. An epidemiologic study to determine whether residents presently living adjacent to the Love Canal are at increased risk for certain disorders was conducted . . . utilizing spontaneous abortions and congenital defects as indicators of potential toxicity.

4. Based upon information obtained relating to maternal age, pregnancy order, and number of spontaneous abortions observed and expected . . . the following was determined:

   a. A slight increase in risk for spontaneous abortion was found among all residents of the Canal and for the northern and southern sections, with the overall estimated risk 1.5 times greater than that expected.

   b. A significant excess of spontaneous abortions was localized among residents of 99th Street South.

   c. The miscarriage experience in the 99th Street North and 97th Street North and South sections approximated that which could be expected. . . .

CONCLUSIONS

5. A review of all of the available evidence respecting the Love Canal Chemical Waste Landfill site has convinced me of the existence of a great and imminent peril to the health of the general public residing at or near the said site as a result of exposure to toxic substances . . . the existence of an emergency should be declared. . . .

8. That further studies should be made to:

   a. delineate chronic diseases afflicting all residents who lived adjacent to the Love Canal landfill site, with particular emphasis on the frequency of spontaneous abortions, congenital defects, and other pathologies, including cancer;

   b. delineate the full . . . boundaries of the Love Canal with respect to possible toxic effects;

   c. determine . . . the extent that leachate has moved . . . to the surrounding neighborhood;

   d. identify which groundwater aquifers, if any, have been contaminated by leachate;

   e. determine the possibility of minimizing the introduction of noxious odors and chemicals by way of drainage from outside the homes and to consider the utility or feasibility of installing customized fans or the special venting of sumps. . . .

RECOMMENDATIONS

6. That the families with pregnant women living at 97th and 99th Streets and Colvin Boulevard temporarily move from their homes as soon as possible.

7. That the approximately 20 families living on 97th and 99th Streets south of Read Avenue, with children under 2 years of age, temporarily move from the site as soon as possible. . . .

12. That residents living on 97th and 99th Streets avoid use of their basements as much as possible. . . .

13. That consumption of food products home-grown by residents of 97th and
    99th Streets and Colvin Boulevard be avoided. . . .
DATED: August 2, 1978

Robert P. Whalen, M.D.
Commissioner of Health

Source: University of Buffalo Library On Line Collection of Love Canal Documents,
http://ublib.buffalo.edu/libraries/projects/lovecanal/disaster_gif/records/feder1.html
(accessed July 23, 2004).

**Document 14.3   Lois Gibbs Recalls Residents' Response to Health
                   Department Report**

---

*Residents grew frustrated with the technical nature of the health and
engineering experts' findings that seemed to them designed deliberately to obfuscate the real issues of their health and safety. Critics then
and ever since have disparaged the "emotionalism" of Lois Gibbs and
the rest of the leadership of the Love Canal Homeowner's Association,
who were largely mothers, often subordinating and dismissing their
concerns in light of the "rational, objective" science of government
experts. This is an excerpt from the book she later wrote about the
episode.*

Commissioner Robert Whalen, Dr. Vianna, Dr. Axelrod . . . Dr. Kim, and a
few others were sitting on the stage. Commissioner Whalen stopped up and
began the meeting. He read an order stating that the residents of Love Canal
were not to eat food from their gardens and that the 99th Street School would
be closed during remedial construction. The bombshell came when he recommended the evacuation of pregnant women and children under two because, he said, the state was concerned about a danger to their health. Whalen
backed up this statement with data and statistics. He didn't say the state
would move all those people, just that they *should* move. The state order
stipulated only pregnant women and children under the age of two. What, I
wondered, were the rest of their families supposed to do—leave them
there? . . .

I was furious. I jumped up and said to Commissioner Whalen, "If the dump
will hurt pregnant women and children under two, what for God's sake, is it
going to do to the rest of us? What do you think you're doing?" . . .

Debbie [Cerillo] joined in, "Wait a minute, wait a minute. My kids are over
two. Are you trying to tell me my children are safe?" (Debbie's backyard was
right on the canal. . . .) Between the two of us, we kept the meeting in an uproar
for some fifteen minutes. "We can't eat out of our garden. We can't go in our
backyard. We can't have children under two. We can't be pregnant. You're
telling us it's safe for the rest of us!" . . .

I talked to Dr. Vianna. He walked up and down, up and down, insisting that he couldn't find any problem. There just wasn't that much abnormality. I told him I thought he was dead wrong. I had learned about five crib deaths myself, just by walking around, and I wasn't doing a health survey. Many women told me they had miscarried. I found sick people all around the canal....

When the meeting reconvened, Frank Rovers...was on the stage to explain the remedial construction plan. He was the engineer who had drawn it up. I was still boiling from my talk with Dr. Vianna, and now I attacked Rovers. "Wait a minute," I said, "What about the underground streams?" He said they would be taken care of and gave me a technical explanation I didn't understand. "Excuse me," I replied. "I'm just a dumb housewife. I'm not an expert. You're the expert. I'm just going to use a little common sense. You will have underground streams running through the canal beneath those pipelines. The chemicals will get out. There's no way they are going to go into your pipe. They will be under it. Now, how do you take care of that?" He answered with some incomprehensible engineering terms.

The meeting had been scheduled to last half an hour, but we made it last until well after the lunch hour.... Commissioner Whalen had walked out of the meeting, and these guys were giving us a bunch of baloney. I had a list of fifty questions, but all I got was engineering jargon and political answers that made no sense: "Well, we're going to check on that...." "We haven't got everything completed yet...." "You're going to have to be patient...." Yet the newspaper reports said they had been doing studies since 1976, or even before then, and here it was two years later, and they were telling us they needed to study the problem some more....

Dr. Axelrod told me he would hold a public meeting the following day in Niagara Falls to explain the situation to the residents. He asked me if I would have any people there. I told him I would pack the auditorium.... As it turned out, Commissioner Whalen's order guaranteed a full house. I don't know what else they thought would happen....

The meeting that night lasted until well after eleven. Commissioner Whalen said only about two words through the whole thing.... I just stared back at him and thought: *Where do you get off judging everybody's future, telling people what they can and cannot do. You're not God.* It was the way they sat up there, so arrogant and so righteous. *This is the way it's going to be. Too bad about your two-and-a-half-year-old. Too bad about your three-year-old.*

Source: Lois Marie Gibbs, *Love Canal: The Story Continues* (Stony Creek, CT: New Society Publishers, 1998), pp. 49–51, 57. Reprinted with permission.

**Document 14.4   Love Canal Homeowners Association Flyer
Demanding Complete Relocation**

Here is an even more vivid illustration of the anger and frustration that began to boil over in the community after nearly two years of what they increasingly perceived as governmental incompetence and outright duplicity.

LOVE CANAL
ASK THOSE WHO REALLY KNOW!
Ask the victims of Love Canal why they need immediate permanent relocation, and why some will refuse to leave their motel rooms once funds are cut off. Ask the innocent victims of corporate profits.

The reasons are simple. We cannot lead a normal life. We
Cannot go in our basements because of contamination from Love Canal.
Cannot eat anything from our gardens because of soil contamination.
Cannot allow our children to play in our yards because of contaminated soils.
Cannot have our children attend a school in the area—two have been closed due
  to Love Canal contamination.
Cannot breathe the outside air—because of contamination we are now in hotels.
Cannot become pregnant—miscarriage rate is state defined....
Cannot have normal children because of a 56% risk of birth defects.
Cannot sell our homes. Love Canal was not mentioned in our deeds....
Cannot get a VA or FHA loan in Love Canal, even the government is reluctant....
Cannot have our pregnant daughters or our grandchildren visit—it's unsafe for them.

We need your support and your help to end the suffering of men, women, and especially children of Love Canal. We have lost our constitutional rights of life, liberty, and the pursuit of happiness. Justice for all but not Love Canal Victims.
We Cannot Live at Love Canal—We Cannot Leave Love Canal.

Source: Gibbs, *Love Canal: The Story Continues*, p. 72.

**Document 14.5   Cancer Research Scientist Affirms Love Canal
                        Victims' Claims**

Offering a model for future grassroots activism, Love Canal residents engaged their own scientific experts to contest the evidence used by the state of New York to deny and delay evacuation of the community. They would use the study conducted by Dr. Beverly Paigen to continue to press for a complete evacuation.

Testimony Presented to the House Sub-Committee on Oversight and Investigation March 21, 1979 by Dr. Beverly Paigen, Roswell Park Memorial Institute

INTRODUCTION

...I have a Ph.D. in biology and my research interest is genetic susceptibility to environmental toxins. I served on the Environmental Protection Agency's Toxic Substances Advisory Committee from 1977–1979....

SUMMARY OF HEALTH EFFECTS

The studies that I will present concern the health hazards experienced by the people still living from one to five blocks from the Love Canal dump site. I will present information that leads me to conclude that toxic chemicals are presently migrating through the soil along the paths of old streambeds that once criss-crossed the neighborhood. Families whose homes border these old streambeds show an increase in several health problems including miscarriages, birth defects, nervous breakdowns, asthma and diseases of the urinary system. These studies have led me to conclude that a minimum of 140 additional families should be evacuated immediately and [that] evacuation may need to be extended to as many as 500 more families. In addition, the results raise questions about whether the presently planned remedial construction to prevent further outflow of toxic wastes is adequate.

METHODOLOGY

...Older residents suggested that the clusters [of disease] seemed to follow the path of old streambeds that had intersected the Love Canal many years ago and had been filled when houses were built. At this point the residents contacted me for help since I am known locally as an environmental scientist. I discussed with area residents how to collect health information in a scientifically acceptable way. They put aside all the information they had gathered and started making a systematic phone survey to each home, collecting information about the number of persons in each family, the length of time they had lived in the Love Canal area, and the health problems experienced by the family....

RECOMMENDATIONS

1. Serious thought should be given to the purchase of some or all of the homes affected,... resulting in the homes being torn down and the basements filled in. This would minimize complaints and prevent further exposure to people. This action would compliment partial or minimal cleanup....
3. *Maximum Cleanup Method—*
    A. Remove all *chemical* fill, contaminated earth and debris in the area....

IN CONCLUSION

There is no immediate relief for the people concerned, other than moving them out by buying their homes or placing them in other facilities until the problem is corrected. The problem will not be corrected unless the fill and the surrounding earth around the private property are totally removed and ground water flow is directed away from the homes....

Source: University of Buffalo Library On Line Collection of Love Canal Documents, http://ublib.buffalo.edu/libraries/projects/lovecanal/science_gif/records/paige1.html (accessed July 25, 2004).

Document 14.6   Testimony of Love Canal Victims, 1979–1980

More than scientific study, the impassioned heartbreaking public testimony of mothers whose children had suffered severe health problems or who had died as a result of exposure to the Love Canal waste site helped gain for residents the national attention that finally brought the resolution they were seeking. Here are two examples, one a statement delivered to stockholders of Occidental Petroleum (the holding company of Hooker Chemical), and the other testimony to a U.S. Senate committee hearing held near Love Canal, an event that brought residents one step closer to an emergency declaration and evacuation of their community.

STATEMENT TO THE ANNUAL MEETING
OF OCCIDENTAL PETROLEUM SHARE HOLDERS
CORPORATE RESPONSIBILITY RESOLUTION
MAY 21, 1980

My name is Luella Kenny.... My husband and I with our two surviving sons were forced to abandon this residence because of the presence of toxins that had migrated from the Love Canal. Since that time we have lived a vagabond existence.... An old stream bed, which intersected with Love Canal, runs through our property. This stream bed is now filled and is part of our yard. In addition, at the back edge of our property is Black Creek which has been found to be contaminated with chemicals.... Also located on this property is a storm sewer which drains the area north of the Love Canal. Large amounts of Dioxin were found where this storm sewer empties into Black Creek. My sons spent many hours playing in the creek by this storm sewer. Our seven year old son died October 4th, 1978 from complications that resulted from nephrosis. This spring EPA erected a six foot fence in our yard and along Black Creek because of the hazard.

Jon became ill on June 6th, 1978. Initially his illness was diagnosed as an allergy, however on July 1st, ... he was diagnosed as having nephrosis ... [which] in its early stages is often masked by symptoms resembling allergies.... Jon had three relapses in two and half months and then he developed convulsions, visual hallucinations, and eventually a massive pulmonary embolism. Jon's death was caused by a cardiac arrest brought on by the exertion of trying to breathe.

At the time of Jon's death we had no idea that it could be linked to chemical toxicity. We requested an autopsy because we wanted to know why our son had died when we had been told all along that nephrosis was nothing to worry about.... [My] husband and I began to learn more about the disease. We began delving into medical journals, and corresponding with leading research groups in the field of nephrosis. We were shocked to find that during the past ten years there have been countless reports of people developing nephrosis when they were exposed to chemicals. We also did some research into dioxin toxicity and discovered that many of Jon's autopsy findings were related to dioxin poisoning. . . . Since we left our home in September our two sons have shown a remarkable improvement. . . .

Source: University of Buffalo Library On Line Collection of Love Canal Documents, http://ublib.buffalo.edu/libraries/projects/lovecanal/science_gif/records/paige1.html.

SENATE SUBCOMMITTEE ON TOXIC SUBSTANCES AND CHEMICAL WASTES
TESTIMONY OF MARIE POZNIAK
MAY 3, 1979

. . . I would like to express the necessity to identify, monitor and clean up all dump sites both open and festering and those buried and forgotten ticking away as public health time bombs. . . .

We need to immediately pass laws and form agencies who can and will take on the responsibilities of finding and cleaning up these dump sites.

From my own experience living in the Love Canal area I have watched the New York State Health Department as well as some federal agencies avoid issues so that they would not have to take responsibility or set any precedents.

Example: New York Governor Hugh Carey, at a public meeting made the statement that if people in the houses not immediately evacuated had health problems and air tests showed contamination they would be relocated immediately. The State Health Department air test did in fact show chemicals to [be] present in my home. On the advice of two different doctors I submitted the record so my nine year old daughter, who has an asthmatic condition, to the Health Department for review. They said it would take a week. . . . Then for nine weeks the State Health Department kept saying a few more days would be needed and then a few more. I then received a certified letter . . . as did 54 other families who had requested relocation, that the remedial construction would not hurt her. . . . I had to ask myself, had they even looked at her records? If they had, they would have had to agree with her two doctors who treat her . . . that further exposure would be harmful to her well being. . . .

Industry has been getting away with too much, for too long. We can no longer as citizens afford to pay the price of their doing business. The health and safety of our friends, ourselves and our families is too high a price to pay. . . . Implement laws NOW to stop negligent polluters, fine them, take the profit out of polluting and protect our health and environment before it is completely destroyed. . . .

We will long be remembered for our fight for clean air, water and most important clean and safe homes. . . . It started in our small community and has spread across the nation. We now have millions of people backing our struggle. . . .

Gentlemen, go back to Washington and tell your peers, the Love Canal people and our children, who are the future of America demand immediate action on our disaster. . . . Pass the needed laws and set a precedent and help the victims of the Love Canal.

Source: University of Buffalo Library On Line Collection of Love Canal Documents, http://ublib.buffalo.edu/libraries/projects/lovecanal/disaster_gif/records/pozni1.html (accessed July 27, 2004).

Document 14.7   U.S. Justice Department Announces Love Canal Settlement, Resists Changes to Superfund Law, 1995

> *Nearly two decades after the first lawsuits involving Hooker Chemical were filed, its parent company, Occidental Petroleum, finally reached a $129 million settlement with the U.S. government. Taxpayers were reimbursed for expenses incurred during the scientific assessment, evacuation, and remediation of the site. In announcing the settlement, the Clinton administration denounced proposed attempts by some corporate leaders and their congressional allies to weaken the corporate liability provisions of the Superfund law.*

OCCIDENTAL TO PAY $129 MILLION IN LOVE CANAL SETTLEMENT WASHINGTON, D.C.—In a successful end to a toxic dump disaster that became synonymous with the hazards of environmental pollution, and that gave birth to the nation's Superfund program to clean up the most hazardous toxic waste sites, the Justice Department and the Environmental Protection Agency announced today that the Occidental Chemical Corporation will pay the government $129 million to cover the costs of the Love Canal incident.... The agreement results from a Justice Department lawsuit filed 16 years ago after a toxic waste nightmare forced the evacuation of more than one thousand homes, an elementary school and an entire neighborhood in Niagara Falls, New York.

Attorney General Janet Reno said the settlement "should send a message of federal persistence and tenacity." "If Congress will give us the resources, we will work to get polluters to pay their share," said Reno. She noted that Congress is currently attempting to cut environmental enforcement.

EPA Administrator Carol M. Browner said "the Love Canal settlement underscores this Administration's firm commitment to ensuring that polluters—not the American people—pick up the tab for cleaning up toxic waste dumps. Strong enforcement of our nation's environmental laws is vital to protecting the health of the one in four Americans who still lives near toxic waste dumps.

Under the terms of today's settlement, the federal government would get back all of the $101 million it spent on cleanup and $28 million in interest. Occidental will pay $102 million to the EPA Superfund and $27 million to the United States on behalf of the Federal Emergency Management Agency. FEMA funded early cleanup and relocation activities, prior to the enactment of the Superfund law in December 1980....

The Federal District Court in Buffalo had already ruled that Occidental was a "responsible party" under the Superfund law.... In the lawsuit, Occidental had charged that the United States was also a responsible party and should contribute toward the cleanup costs based on regulatory actions or alleged dumping by several federal agencies. The United States denied Occidental's charges....

Assistant Attorney General Lois J. Schiffer, in charge of the Justice Department's Environment and Natural Resources Division, criticized current Superfund proposals which might give Occidental a $64.5 million tax credit for its

Love Canal payment. Schiffer said, "This would destroy the fundamental principle that a polluter should pay to clean up its own mess." Schiffer noted that one of the reasons the case was not settled earlier was that Occidental pursued extensive litigation to test the limits of the Superfund law. Administrator Browner added, "elimination of the 'retroactive liability' provisions in the Superfund law—as some in Congress have proposed—would have let this polluter off the hook, because Hooker dumped the toxic waste that polluted Love Canal in the 1940's and 1950's." . . .

Source: United States Justice Department, http://www.usdoj.gov/opa/pr/Pre_96/December95/638.txt.html (accessed July 29, 2004).

Document 14.8   Conservative Critic Michael Fumento Assails Love Canal Settlement, Superfund

---

Not everyone, of course, was pleased with the legacy of Love Canal. Fierce criticism came from some in the business community, as well as from defenders of an ideology of laissez faire economics and corporate capitalism. One such critic, Michael Fumento, argues that faulty science and the emotionally charged atmosphere surrounding the episode led to the Occidental settlement with the Justice Department, as well as the original relocation of residents.

It closes a chapter in what has been called "the nation's most notorious toxic dumping case." The Occidental Chemical Corporation has agreed to pay $129 million to cover the federal government's cleanup costs at Love Canal, New York. The problem is that the federal officials, who like all victors are the ones who write the history, have written a history that has little connection with reality.

Under the settlement, the EPA Superfund will receive $102 and the Federal Emergency Management Agency . . . will receive $27 million. . . . "Today we celebrate a transformation of an environmental disaster called Love Canal into a success story," Attorney General Janet Reno said at a press conference. . . .

Nobody questions that Occidental, or rather its predecessor, Hooker Chemicals & Plastics Corp., buried 22,000 tons of chemical waste in a half-dug canal from 1942 to 1953. Rarely mentioned, however is that Hooker tried desperately to convince the city of Niagara Falls (where Love Canal is located) not to build on the site.

. . . [The] city school board applied massive pressure to obtain the land despite Hooker's repeated warnings of potential health hazards. Finally Hooker gave in and sold the land for a symbolic dollar bill. It insisted, though, that the land was to be used for a school or parking lot or playground but was under no circumstances to be excavated.

Instead, the city decided to build a housing development on the site, digging into the protective clay covering and laying sewer lines through the waste. Then it sold the plots to unsuspecting home buyers.

Hooker had no choice but to dump its toxic waste somewhere. It was the city's choice to bring people to that somewhere. The bad guy wasn't the big faceless corporation, It was your friendly city government.

The second part of the Love Canal myth is that residents began suffering a health disaster in the late 1970s. As I documented in my book *Science Under Siege*, nobody at Love Canal complained of any exceptional illnesses until a muckraking environmentalist reporter for the local paper began a series of articles telling the people that they were sitting on a toxic waste site. Lo and behold, from then on every illness in the town was blamed on the ingredients brewing beneath the surface. It even made national news when one family's dog began inexplicably vomiting.

The media descended upon the town and relayed to the outside world every sneeze, every cough, and every ache and pain experienced by Love Canal residents, making it clear that they could only be caused by toxic waste, which included the dreaded dioxin.

The EPA and the governor of New York swaggered around, condemning the chemical company and promising to make everything better, no matter the cost. Ultimately tens of millions of dollars were spent evacuating the residents.

Only later did the truth begin to seep out. Study after study conducted by the federal government and the State of New York Department of Health found that Love Canal residents had no more illness than would be expected in any other area of similar size. Believe it or not, dogs who don't live on top of toxic waste dumps also vomit.

A New York Times editorial predicted correctly in 1981 when it said, "it may well turn out that the public suffered less from the chemicals there than from the hysteria generated by flimsy research irresponsibly handled." . . .

EPA Administrator Carol Browner used the myths of Love Canal to blast congressional Republican efforts to cut back on enforcement of environmental laws. Love Canal led to the creation of the Superfund for the cleanup of environmental hazards.

In seeking to reduce environmental spending by $25 million, she said, "Congress is attempting to roll back the environmental health protections that Superfund brought to Love Canal." Since there was never any health threat at the Love Canal, obviously Superfund brought no protections there. In any case, it's too bad Browner didn't go farther to point out that Superfund, . . . could soak up an amazing $500 billion over the next few decades. While a few of these toxic waste sites may pose a real hazard to persons living nearby, most have posed no demonstrated threat as large even as making dogs upchuck.

Source: Michael Fumento, "Footnotes in the Love Canal," *Washington Times*, January 3, 1996. Copyright © 1996 News World Communications, Inc. Reprinted with permission of The Washington Times. This reprint does not constitute or imply any endorsement or sponsorship of any product, service, company, or organization.

NOTES

1. Lois Marie Gibbs, "Learning from Love Canal: A 20th Anniversary Retrospective," *Orion Afield* v. 2, n. 2 (Spring 1998): 3–4.

2. Eric Zuesse, "Love Canal: The Truth Seeps Out," *Reason* 4 (February 1981). http://reason.com/8102/fe.ez.the.shtml (accessed August 3, 2004).

ANNOTATED BIBLIOGRAPHY

Bullard, Robert. *Dumping in Dixie: Race, Class, and Environmental Quality*. Boulder, CO: Westview Press, 2000. Well-researched social justice narrative of five black communities in Texas, West Virginia, Louisiana, and Alabama fighting to protect themselves from industrial pollution.

Colten, Craig E., and Peter N. Skinner. *The Road to Love Canal: Managing Industrial Waste before EPA*. Austin: University of Texas Press, 1996. Important book examining what waste managers knew about the dangers of hazardous waste prior to the 1970s, the technical and engineering capabilities that existed for treating such wastes, and the question of what guided the decisions about hazardous waste management.

Freeze, R. Allan. *The Environmental Pendulum: A Quest for the Truth about Toxic Chemicals, Human Health, and Environmental Protection*. Berkeley: University of California Press, 2000. Critical analysis of Superfund and the problems facing the management and cleanup of the nation's toxic waste sites.

Gibbs, Lois Marie. *Dying from Dioxin: A Citizen's Guide to Reclaiming Our Health and Rebuilding Democracy*. Cambridge, MA: South End Press, 1995. The Love Canal hero surveys the history of dioxin, the most toxic substance ever manufactured and one of the elements of the toxic stew buried in Love Canal. Serves as a "how-to" guide for citizens' grassroots organizing around the issue of dioxin contamination in and near communities.

———. *Love Canal: The Story Continues*. 1982. Rev. ed. Stony Creek, CT: New Society, 1998. The definitive, first-person chronicle of the community's struggle to bring an end to their nightmare and achieve some measure of justice, written by the leader of Love Canal Home Owners Association.

Hofrichter, Richard, ed. *Toxic Struggles: The Theory and Practice of Environmental Justice*. Salt Lake City: University of Utah Press, 2002. Documents confirm the movement for environmental justice across the country, involving farm and industrial workers, communities of color, poor people, civil rights groups, and local community activists.

Mazur, Allan. *A Hazardous Inquiry: The Rashomon Effect at Love Canal*. Cambridge, MA: Harvard University Press, 1998. The Love Canal story from contesting points of view, including the Love Canal Home Owners Association, the Hooker Chemical Company, and the New York State Department of Health. A reasonably successful effort to reconcile conflicting claims about what happened and did not happen at Love Canal.

Szasz, Andrew. *Ecopopulism: Toxic Waste and the Movement for Environmental Justice*. Minneapolis: University of Minnesota Press, 1994. Tracks the rise of the antitoxics movement that began at Love Canal.

15

The Endangered Species Act:
The Rights of Nature?

Nothing is more priceless and more worthy of preservation than the rich array of animal life with which our country has been blessed. It is a many faceted treasure, of value to scholars, scientists, and nature lovers alike, and it forms a vital part of the heritage we all share as Americans.
—President Richard M. Nixon, upon signing the
Endangered Species Act, December 28, 1973

The Endangered Species Act has become a most effective tool in the hands of the preservationist and those intent on destroying the livelihoods of millions of Americans.
—Abundant Wildlife Society, 2004

Signed into law by President Richard M. Nixon in 1973, the Endangered Species Act (ESA) has from its inception been one of the nation's most popular and effective environmental laws. It also has been the most vehemently resisted. The hope here is that a brief look at the purposes and history of the law will melt away this apparent paradox. The historical forces of environmental degradation and the resultant rising tide of popular environmentalism in the late 1960s and early 1970s brought the ESA into being with overwhelming support—including that of a business-minded, conservative president. Noble intent and images of majestic but beleaguered bald eagles engendered broad popular enthusiasm for the legislation, a level of support that has remained nearly constant. Most Americans, however, have had little appreciation for the law's complexity, or for the fundamental challenges that the ESA has posed to powerful economic forces that have been working assiduously to undermine it since the 1980s. Although anti-ESA crusaders have long conveyed their fight as a populist struggle of small landowners against the invasive power of an overbearing federal government, in truth, the persistent effort to derail or weaken the ESA has mostly been waged by large corporate interests.

Understanding the deeply polarizing nature of the ESA requires recognition that the law pierced two overarching American myths: that natural resources were endlessly abundant, and that humans were inherently superior to the rest of the natural world. That philosophical challenge of the ESA to ideas several centuries in the making made it, from the outset, the most fundamentally radical environmental statute ever devised. Since the 1960s these core American mythologies have been challenged by the grim facts of environmental degradation. Americans have generally become more knowledgeable and respectful toward the environment, and the ESA, more than any other law, epitomized those shifting attitudes. In addition, enforcement of the law compels, as one would expect, not only federal agencies, but also and more importantly, states, local municipalities, businesses, and private landowners to consider the impact of land use and development decisions upon the survival of endangered or threatened animal populations. The goal of preserving the nation's natural heritage must be achieved on both public and private land, affecting, on occasion, both the corporate profit margin and the small landowner's livelihood. This narrowing of private property interests to serve the public good—defined by anti-ESA forces as the sinister agenda of environmentalists—has been met with tenacious, increasingly rabid resistance. This has been especially so in the West and in rural sections of the country, where critical habitat for threatened or endangered species is most prevalent, and where, equally important, the idea of unregulated self-interest regarding the use of one's land is held most sacred.

Interest in preserving wildlife did not begin with the passage of the ESA. Statutory restrictions on the ability of settlers to take certain quantities of deer and other game and only at particular times of the year extend back to the seventeenth century. These were local laws, however, intended solely to ensure there would be plenty of said species to hunt the following year. And they coexisted alongside other statutes that paid hefty bounties to men who killed wolves, coyotes, and other predators. Established early on in American culture was the taxonomic bifurcation that separated the "good" or "noble" species—ungulates like elk and deer, songbirds, and others that provided pleasure or sustenance to humans—and the "evil" predatory types that threatened brave frontiersmen, their livestock, and families. The crusade to save the last remaining bison (Chapter 6) came during an era when it was still permissible to stone a bald eagle to death in Yellowstone Park.

The first truly national effort to conserve wildlife came, oddly enough, in response to changing tastes in women's fashion. In the 1890s, women who adorned their heads with hats topped with herons, egrets, and other diminishing species of exotic wild birds came under popular attack. Just as upperclass sportsmen deemed unseemly the hunting practices of immigrants and settlers who shot "for the pot" or the market, similarly it became a mark of bad taste to festoon one's head with a dead gull. Led by women's clubs, Audubon Societies, and similar organizations, the national campaign to stem the market for birds on hats ultimately translated into the first wildlife conservation law, the Lacey Act of 1900 (not to be confused with the 1894 law aimed at bison poaching in Yellowstone). The Lacey Act prohibited interstate trafficking of wildlife killed in violation of state laws and established the first national wildlife refuge.[1]

Despite success in achieving its limited goals, the Lacey Act failed to stop the continuing extinction of hundreds of animal and plant species. Most notable was the demise early in the century of the passenger pigeon, which once darkened the skies of portions of the country with flocks numbering in the millions. Few imagined it possible that an animal whose numbers once seemed irritatingly limitless could disappear. Except for a few biologists, few people in the early decades of the twentieth century were noticing that species were disappearing from the planet at an unprecedented and increasingly catastrophic rate, variously estimated at between one and ten thousand times the natural rate of extinction.

The boom economy of the post–World War II era brought more severe threats to greater numbers of species than ever before, ultimately prompting the Congress to pass the ESA. Suburban tract housing, shopping centers, and other secondary development that followed accelerated destruction of animal habitat. At its peak, the suburban boom consumed more than 3,000 acres a day. Compounding that development was the menace of ubiquitous chemicals about which Rachel Carson wrote so eloquently. Public outcry over the plight of such heralded species as the American bald eagle, the brown pelican, and the peregrine falcon led to the banning of dichloro-diphenyl-trichloroethane (DDT) and regulation of chemicals. Those sympathies also advanced passage of the Endangered Species Preservation Act of 1966, relatively weak legislation that paved the way for the ESA seven years later.

Though rightly regarded as an environmental milestone, even a revolutionary turning point in humanity's relationship with nature, the ESA was fundamentally anthropocentric legislation. In many ways it was established for the same reasons we build zoos: in President Nixon's words, for the "value" that the "treasure" of diminishing species hold for us. It was motivated by the human desire, increasingly acute in the modern age, to maintain contact with the natural world, animals in particular. As with zoos, national parks, and wildlife refuges, we have been most keen on saving and seeing those animals that seem to embody the highest, most noble traits that we want to see in ourselves. Indeed, the very act of preserving animals tells us what we most want to believe: that even we frenetically industrious, materially fixated Americans have not lost touch with the beauty and sentiment embodied in the animal world, that we are wise and prudent and romantic enough to care for all of creation. It can be argued that as the first law to defend in any way and for any reason the intrinsic value of all living things, the ESA ascribed "rights" to nature. This is the very reason why it has provoked such extreme animosity from those who hold absolutely inviolable and sacrosanct the property rights of man and the obligation of economic development that ESA seemed to threaten.

And yet at bottom the motivation behind the ESA, as Nixon's signing declaration reveals, was and is about us: the scientific, scholarly, and nature-loving value that the ever-shrinking natural world has for us moderns. Perhaps this is not surprising, given the equally anthropocentric rationale and "worthless lands" justification for America's other preservation jewels; designation of national parks, national monuments, and wilderness areas was and is generally contingent upon those lands being proven useless for extractive development.

This is not to dismiss the considerable achievements of ESA protection, which on the occasion of its thirtieth anniversary in 2003 extended to more than 1,250 species, including hugely popular success stories like that of the bald eagle rescued from the brink of extinction. Equally or more important, citizens groups and landowners, in cooperation with federal and state agencies, have protected millions of acres of public and private land, what the law defines as "critical habitat," to ensure the survival of threatened and endangered species. Moreover, the ESA, like those earlier American preservation statutes, has served as a global model for other nations' species-protection statutes. Relatively rigorous provisions mandating the listing of species and establishment of recovery plans have brought the ESA a remarkable record of success. Still it remains that the ESA was not born out of a cultural or political consensus that the life of, say, microscopic larvae is as important and worthy of protection as human life. This is the philosophy that came to be known by the 1970s as *deep ecology*. The value of threatened and endangered species had risen but remained narrowly delineated by the culture and politics of the nation, as well as the law itself. A thirtieth anniversary compendium of the achievements of the ESA, issued by a coalition of environmental organizations in 2003, seemed to affirm that, relying as much on the monetary value of protected wildlife to the tourist and recreational economies as any intrinsic biological or spiritual worth to defend the law.[2]

The legalistic strengths and circumscribed limitations of the ESA are called into relief in the two episodes highlighted in several documents in this chapter. The first tale concerns a three-inch long minnow called a snail darter that almost halted a nearly completed hydroelectric dam on the Little Tennessee River costing $116 million. For ESA supporters, the story tellingly illustrates both the power of the law and the immaturity of the nation's ecological sensibility. In the view of ESA critics, the Tellico Dam episode lays bare the failure of ESA supporters—including the U.S. Fish and Wildlife Service most responsible for enforcing the law—to use what ESA critics universally describe as "common sense" in applying it.

Yet interestingly, common sense was exactly the argument most of the people actually living in the region used in trying desperately to stop the flooding of their valley. By the time the Tennessee Valley Authority (TVA) proposed building the Tellico Dam on the "Little T," it had already built some sixty-eight dams in the state, impounding 2,500 miles of river. The dammed reservoirs had created more shoreline than all of the Great Lakes combined. Originating in the New Deal era, the TVA vision to bring hydroelectric power, flood control, and regional economic development through the engineering of the region's waters had been realized, though not without mounting social, economic, and environmental costs that had become increasingly severe since the 1950s. The ecological facts of the proposal, most importantly that the stretch of river to be dammed was the last remaining thirty-three miles of undammed flowing stream left on the Tennessee, was not the central argument of dam opponents. Nor was the fact that ancient and sacred Native American sites would be lost forever. Dam opponents (who included farmers, environmentalists, and the

Cherokees) built their case on firm utilitarian grounds. First and foremost was their well-documented case that the TVA grossly overstated the alleged economic benefits to accrue to the valley from the dam. They further challenged the TVA on the amount of land seized by eminent domain for the project: 38,000 acres were to be taken from 300 farmers, yet only 12,000 of those acres were going under water; the rest were to be sold at a large profit to the Boeing Corporation, which would build (through a generous federal subsidy for infrastructure) a model industrial city. This fantastic scenario served as the economic justification of the whole project. By the late 1960s farmers and other residents of the Tennessee Valley had plenty of reason to cast a wary eye on TVA promises.

Plaintiffs brought suit under the National Environmental Policy Act (NEPA), correctly alleging that the TVA had not prepared the required Environmental Impact Statement (EIS). The cornerstone of the 1969 law, the EIS compelled the TVA to acknowledge fully the benefits and the costs, as well as possible alternatives for the project. Forced to complete the EIS, the TVA had to delay the project, but it summarily dismissed alternative proposals that would have promoted development while sparing the valley. Attorney Zygmunt Plater's chronicle of the remainder of the story (Document 15.2) makes clear that the ESA served as the vehicle of last resort.

Whether dam opponents cynically used the law and the poor snail darter (who, it turned out, still thrived in the upper reaches of the Tennessee River) to stop a project they had otherwise failed to halt is in the eye of the reader. For community people, however, as well as for environmentalists, Cherokees, and many fiscal conservatives who worried about wasteful federal spending, the ESA mandated that the project be halted. The coalition to stop the Tellico Dam applied what supporters have argued is the most essential ingredient of the law (and what opponents have claimed to be its most dangerous element): the right of citizens without means to file suit against the federal government and compel an agency to explain in detail and justify a project that will sweep a species into extinction. A majority of the Supreme Court agreed, though Justice Lewis F. Powell's query regarding the "good" of the fish is revealing of the caricatured representation of the case put forth in the media: a useful dam blocked by a stupid little fish and its foolish defenders. In this view, those who would apply the ESA to cases such as these made a mockery of the law. Echoing Tennessee politicians, popular wisdom held that the ESA was intended to save grizzly bears and whales, not useless minnows swimming in the way of hydroelectric power.

The congressional end-run around the Supreme Court that ultimately brought construction of the Tellico Dam did more than bring hydropower to the valley and flood farmers from their homes; it would allow the process of listing endangered species to be undermined by countervailing economic factors. In the midst of the Tellico debacle, the contrivance of a cabinet-level endangered species committee known as the "God Squad," which had the power to waive or weaken ESA protection when economic benefits of a project demanded it, was incorporated as a permanent provision into the 1978 reauthorization of the law. That the Tellico controversy unfolded in the context of a worsening economic climate in the country suggests a political reality of the environmental age: that when conflicts are popularly understood as jobs versus the environment—even if the facts belie what may well be a distorted depiction—nature invariably loses.

Economic factors lie at the center of the second ESA cause celebre included here, the reintroduction of wolves into their historic range in the northern Rocky Mountains. Mandated by the ESA, the Recovery Plan for the Gray Wolf designated what the law calls "critical habitat," those areas with biological or physical features essential to the survival of species which necessitated special management for its recovery. Although the vast majority of the designated area in this case was on federal land—federal ownership itself being a matter of deep historical resentment in much of the West—many Idahoans fiercely resisted the program. Arguing further that wolf recovery constituted an unconstitutional threat to private property and would damage their economic interests, an alliance of corporate interests and citizens' organizations tried in vain to stop the recovery plan. Claiming that the ESA placed onerous and unconstitutional restrictions on private land designated as critical habitat for an endangered species, opponents hyperbolically declared the wolf, among other things, the "Saddam Hussein of the animal world." They fought wolf recovery in the courts, in Congress, and in the press. Resistance in the West to wolf reintroduction was met by an overwhelmingly favorable response from Americans across the country.

Following reintroduction in the mid-1990s, a few fought the wolf in the wild, following the time-honored tradition of shooting and poisoning wolves. Wolf defenders generally attributed ranchers' fears to the historic tendency of rural frontiersmen to blame wolves for any and all threats—real and imagined. In this case, ranchers faced real economic threats from large corporate interests who were coming to dominate the cattle industry, but it was much simpler and more effective to blame the wolf and the ESA. Despite the fears and warnings of wolf depredations of livestock, very few such incidents have occurred, and all have been compensated by environmental organizations. Recognizing the limitations of the "rights of nature" argument (particularly when it comes to this most loathed of all creatures), wolf advocates fell back on the monetary value of live wolves, citing far greater economic benefits to the entire region through increased tourism.

Lost in the great din of these debates are the law's actual provisions regarding private landowners and the protection of a listed species' critical habitat. Great flexibility characterizes the law in this respect. Most importantly, landowners are permitted to "take" a threatened or endangered species from their land if the action is "incidental to and not the purpose of carrying out otherwise lawful activities," and if the landowner demonstrates a plan for otherwise protecting the species on the property. And in the overwhelming majority of cases, a cooperative partnership between federal managers and private citizens has, as the law intended, resolved potential disputes. National numbers in the aggregate are telling: of more than 120,000 private development projects reviewed nationally from 1979–1999 for their potential adverse impacts on a listed species, fewer than 1 percent of them were determined to have a negative impact on the species, and less than three-tenths of 1 percent of *them*—that is to say, 34 total—were stopped as a result of the ESA.[3]

At the beginning of the new century, arguments over wolves and about the wisdom and efficacy of the ESA continued to rage. Resistance in the Congress throughout the 1990s to repeated attempts to weaken the law demonstrated that most Americans found the law, for all its failings, a reassuring emblem of national environmental wisdom. Reflecting much of Western popular opinion (though perhaps no longer a majority) and responding to corporate interests, President George W. Bush promised to sign a reauthorized and "reformed" ESA that "restored common sense" to wildlife policy. Environmental organizations confronted and largely defused claims from property rights groups that landowners' property values had been damaged due to species protection efforts. A telling sign of a privatizing culture that saw little value any longer in things belonging to "the people," ESA defenders contested the issue of animal protection largely on economic grounds. Few bothered to speak about the larger national goal of "shared heritage," certainly not of the wolf's right to live unmolested in its prehistoric environment.

DOCUMENTS

Document 15.1   Excerpts from the Endangered Species Act, 1973

Passage of the Endangered Species Act (ESA) of 1973 represented the culmination of an effort to protect and conserve American wildlife that dated to the Lacey Act. From the point of view of biologists and preservationists, the law's inclusion of "critical habitat" protection was essential. For proponents of unregulated economic development and the strict protection of private property rights, those sections of the law that seemed to place endangered or threatened animals and their habitat above the economic interests of Americans appeared threatening.

SEC. 2.

(a) FINDINGS.—The Congress finds and declares that—

   (1) various species of fish, wildlife, and plants in the United States have been rendered extinct as a consequence of economic growth and development untempered by adequate concern and conservation;

   (2) other species of fish, wildlife, and plants have been so depleted in numbers that they are in danger of or threatened with extinction;

   (3) these species of fish, wildlife, and plants are of aesthetic, ecological, educational, historical, recreational, and scientific value to the Nation and its people;

   (4) the United States has pledged itself as a sovereign state in the international community to conserve to the extent practicable the various species of fish or wildlife and plants facing extinction, . . .

(b) PURPOSES.—The purposes of this Act are to provide a means whereby the ecosystems upon which endangered species and threatened species depend may be conserved, to provide a program for the conservation of such endangered species and threatened species, and to take such steps as may be appropriate to achieve the purposes of the treaties and conventions set forth in subsection (a) of this section.

(c) POLICY.—

   (1) It is further declared to be the policy of Congress that all Federal departments and agencies shall seek to conserve endangered species and threatened species and shall utilize their authorities in furtherance of the purposes of this Act. . . .

   SEC. 3. For the purposes of this Act—. . .

   (5) (A) The term "critical habitat" for a threatened or endangered species means—

   (i) the specific areas within the geographical area occupied by the species, at the time it is listed in accordance with the provisions of section 4 of this Act, on which are found those physical or biological features (I) essential to the conservation of the species and (II) which may require special management considerations or protection;...

(B) Critical habitat may be established for those species now listed as threatened or endangered species for which no critical habitat has heretofore been established....

DETERMINATION OF ENDANGERED SPECIES
AND THREATENED SPECIES

SEC. 4.

(a) GENERAL.— (1) The Secretary shall by regulation promulgated in accordance with subsection (b) determine whether any species is an endangered species or a threatened species because of any of the following factors:

(A) the present or threatened destruction, modification, or curtailment of its habitat or range;

(B) overutilization for commercial, recreational, scientific, or educational purposes;

(C) disease or predation;

(D) the inadequacy of existing regulatory mechanisms;

(E) other natural or manmade factors affecting its continued existence....

(b) BASIS FOR DETERMINATIONS.—...

(2) The Secretary shall designate critical habitat, and make revisions thereto, under subsection (a)(3) on the basis of the best scientific data available and after taking into consideration the economic impact, and any other relevant impact, of specifying any particular area as critical habitat. The Secretary may exclude any area from critical habitat if he determines that the benefits of such exclusion outweigh the benefits of specifying such area as part of the critical habitat, unless he determines, based on the best scientific and commercial data available, that the failure to designate such area as critical habitat will result in the extinction of the species concerned....

(8) The publication in the Federal Register of any...regulation which is necessary...to carry out the purposes of this Act shall include a summary...of the data on which such regulation is based and shall show the relationship of such data to such regulation; and if such regulation designates or revises critical habitat, such summary shall, to the maximum extent practicable, also include a brief description and evaluation of those activities (whether public or private) which,...if undertaken may adversely modify such habitat,...

(d) PROTECTIVE REGULATIONS—Whenever any species is listed as a threatened species pursuant to subsection (c) of this section, the Secretary shall issue such regulations as he deems necessary and advisable to provide for the conservation of such species....

Source: Endangered Species Act of 1973 (P.L. 93-205; 87 Statute 884). Effective December 28, 1973.

Document 15.2   **Zygmunt Plater Recalls the 1970s Saga
of the Tellico Dam, 2000**

> *The Endangered Species Act was severely tested soon after its passage
> when a coalition of farmers, Cherokee Indians, and environmentalists
> used the law to try to halt construction of the Tellico Dam on the Little
> Tennessee River. In this excerpt from a 2000 lecture, environmental
> attorney Zygmunt Plater recalls his application of the Endangered
> Species Act in arguing before the U.S. Supreme Court for the saving of
> the three-inch Snail Darter and a halt to the construction of the dam.*

... The Endangered Species aspect of this case comes across, depending on
your perspective, as a fortuitous, rational ecological phenomenon that ultimately serves to make a case that good ecology is good government, or on the
other hand it can be seen as a hypocritical crypto-communist threat, pulled out
at the last moment by a bunch of no-good scientists and pinko enviros to stop
progress in its tracks.

In the summer of 1973, toward the end of the [failed] NEPA injunction,
Professor David Etnier...was doing a final census of the river's biology,
thinking that it was going to die. He was swimming along with goggles on—he
sees this little perch darting among the pebbles on the floor of the river—he
catches it in his fingers and stands up, holding it out to his students.... And
Professor Etnier says, "...this is an endangered species." Etnier later that day is
talking with a local farmer and says, "I think we've got a little fish that may
save your farm." Soon enough the citizens were accused of hypocritically using
the little fish to serve their own ends...

So we took a look at...Section 7 of the [Endangered Species] Act, and it
raises the question of whether we were hypocrites in using the ESA against the
Tellico Dam. Let us admit from the start that we knew that most people in
Congress, when they voted for the ESA, were thinking only about Bald Eagles,
Whooping Cranes, and things like that, and had no inkling that it could be used
to stop pork barrel projects.... Section 7... says "Interagency Cooperation,"
and if you're skimming the bill superficially, that looks like nothing. But if you
are an attorney, you take your pencil and start underlining operative words.
"All federal agencies **shall**...insure that actions authorized, funded, or carried
out by them **do not jeopardize the continued existence of such endangered
species and threatened species or result in the destruction or modification of
habitat** of such species...." Read this way, the words create two causes of
action, the legal formulas used by lawyers that define the legal requirements for
getting a judge to give them remedies they seek.... These two causes of action
fit the facts of Tellico, and so we filed the lawsuit....

With facts of Tellico and the words of ESA Section 7, we had all the elements
necessary ultimately for winning the injunction in the Supreme Court.... It
didn't take a great lawyer to win it. Basically we knew because of David Etnier's
testimony that this fish was in jeopardy, and also that its prime critical habitat
was being destroyed. What's the primary cause of species endangerment?... loss

or degradation of *habitat*, which is why so many resource exploitation industries and real estate developers are on a collision course with endangered species. It turns out that this little fish probably had lived throughout the upper Tennessee River systems. And one by one by one its populations were destroyed by—guess what?—dams. . . . But what about the common sense of it? Justice Powell leaned over the bench and asked, "What are these fish good for, anyway? Can you eat them? Are they good for bait?" And isn't that the question that everybody would want to ask? Why stop a humongous hydroelectric dam for a stupid little minnow? And I smiled gamely and said, "well, your Honor, . . . this fish is specifically adapted to shallow, cool, clear, highly oxygenated flowing water, and that its last best place for survival is on the shoals of the Little Tennessee River shows that those habitat qualities there are unique and endangered for human uses as well." It was an amateurish attempt to make the utilitarian argument for species protection.

Ultimately the Court decided for the darter, the river, and the citizens, but in the most parsimonious of terms. The Court wrote:

"We have no expert knowledge on the subject of endangered. Much less do we have a mandate from the people to strike a balance in favor of TVA. Congress has spoken in the plainest of words [*sic*] making it abundantly clear that the balance has been struck in favor of affording endangered species the highest of priorities . . . ," thereby adopting a policy which the Court described as 'institutionalized caution.' " Extinction is forever. . . .

After the Supreme Court, Tellico was sent into a special economic review process—the God Squad, created as an amendment to the ESA in response to this case by the pork lobby led by Senator Howard Baker, ... As Baker once said, "We didn't intend this Act to protect cold slimy things, but rather warm fuzzy things like eagles and polar bears." He insisted that a God Squad should be able to order extinctions, based on human economics. . . . The God Squad meets for the first time in history on January 23rd, 1979. We'd been trying for ten years to get the rational alternatives for the valley publicly considered. Now, for two hours, the committee's investigators lay out a deep and probing analysis of the dam and its alternatives. Then there was a silence. And then [Charles] Schultz, the economist, started speaking. . . . ". . . here is a project that is 95% finished, and [to] do it properly, *it still doesn't pay*. Which says something about the original design!"

The whole project was not worth—would not pay back—even 5% of its own cost! . . . because TVA had pushed for an override to the ESA, the embarrassing truth had finally been revealed in a public forum. . . .

Then four months later, in June of 1979, in 42 seconds, the TVA lawyers got Rep. John Duncan of Maryville (TN) to sneak a rider into the public works appropriations bill. . . . "Notwithstanding any provision of law to the contrary, the following project shall be completed: Tellico Dam." . . .

David Scates tells a sad story of watching as the water came up. . . . There was a budding rosebush at the edge of the river as the impoundment backed up, and as the sunlight filtered down through two feet of cold clear water that had drowned it, for the last time its flowers blossomed, staying there for a few days, under water. He told us, "I cried, seeing the blossoms open under the water as it came up."

Source: Zygmunt J. B. Plater, "The Snail Darter, the Tellico Dam, and Sustainable Democracy—Lessons for the Next President from a Classic Environmental Law Controversy" (February 12, 2000). *Boston College Law School. Boston College Law School Lectures and Presentations.* Working Paper 4. http://lsr.nellco.org/bc/bclslp/papers/4 (retrieved July 7, 2004). Reprinted with permission.

**Document 15.3   Central Idaho Wolf Coalition Protests the
                     Reintroduction of Wolves, 2001**

> *Mandated by the Endangered Species Act, reintroduction of the wolves
> into parts of their historic former range in the northern Rocky Mountains
> provoked fierce opposition from business interests and citizens' groups,
> in particular sheep and cattle ranchers, who feared the depredation
> of their animals by wolves. In addition to the constitutional arguments
> against wolf reintroduction made here by the Central Idaho Wolf Coa-
> lition, the historic visceral fear and loathing of wolves among rural
> Americans is also well expressed.*

January 29, 2001
State of Idaho
Dirk Kempthorne, Governor
Dear Governor Kempthorne:

When the Canadian Gray Wolf was **dumped** on the national forest lands of
Idaho, lands which are administered by the federal government within Idaho's
sovereign boundaries, a terrible miscarriage of justice was dealt to the people of
Idaho. . . .

In order to deal realistically with the current Canadian Gray wolf problem in
Idaho, a person has to face a basic truth about the wolf, that he is a **killer**, not only of
domestic livestock and wild game, but of **people** as well. The Canadian Gray Wolf
hunts 365 days a year and only eats red meat! Historically, people have feared the
wolf, and rightfully so. In certain places in the world today, such as Northern India
where people live with wolves on a daily basis, it has been documented and aired
on public television of the devastation on the human populations of that country.
Wolves kill and eat people: that is a truth! And as the United States Fish and
Wildlife Services has documented, wolves kill sheep and cattle, which are the
private property of the citizens of Idaho. They also decimate big game herds which
are the property of the State of Idaho, protected by Idaho Code #36-103(a). When
you accept these facts as the truth, as the people who live in the "wolf recovery
impact zone" do, then it elevates the wolf introduction issue to a civil rights issue
where the citizens of Idaho can request the State of Idaho to defend our constitutional rights. That is the right to protect our lives and our property from the **most
vicious predator in North America!**

When the federal government dumped Canadian Gray wolves into the national
forests contained within the boundaries of the sovereign State of Idaho, it was

implemented through the Endangered Species Act and through the rules and regulations promulgated in the Federal Register by the United States Fish and Wildlife Service, and completed with a management agreement/contract with the Nez Perce Indian Tribe of Idaho. Written into this legal mantle is the explicitly clear message that the citizens of Idaho cannot kill or harass a wolf unless it is attacking them or is in the process of attacking their livestock. If you own livestock then you can "grovel" and "beg" for a lethal take permit which gives you the "legal right" to kill a wolf if it comes onto your property and is in the process of attacking your livestock. **Since when do the citizens of the United States and the citizens of Idaho need a special permit to protect their lives or their property? We already have a permit: it is called the Constitution of the United States of America, and the Constitution of the State of Idaho.** . . .

With the federal government's **dumping** of the Canadian Gray Wolf into the national forest contained within the boundaries of the State of Idaho, it has overstepped its Constitutional authority and has consequently **deprived the citizens of Idaho of their 1) right to due process of law, 2) the right to equal protection under the law which is guaranteed by the 14th Amendment to the Constitution, and 3) deprives Idaho's legislators from carrying out their constitutionally required duties to protect the rights of Idaho's citizens to state jurisdiction and regulatory authority.**

The 14th Amendment gave us all dual citizenship. We are national citizens and we are citizens of the state in which we reside and we are entitled to judicial review under both. The Constitution recognized sovereignty in the federal government, the various state governments, and in the individual citizen, with all powers of government flowing from the people, not the government. **An individual state cannot cede its sovereignty to the federal government, which Idaho has done in the wolf introduction issue.** . . . **The deprivation of state processes is a deprivation of state citizenship, and all persons are entitled to separate state and federal processes as a part of the privileges and immunities, equal protection and due process of law as guaranteed by the 14th Amendment to the Constitution of the United States.**

We . . . live in fear of the excessive fines and the immediate retribution from the federal government if we kill a wolf to protect our **lives** and **our property**. We are intimidated and threatened by the federal government, and they pit neighbor against neighbor by offering rewards for information leading to a conviction when a wolf has been killed. **These acts of the government are a denial of our basic and fundamental constitutional rights, and have been upheld in federal courts!** But in truth, "it deprives persons of state processes on the federal lands of the United States without recourse in any judicial forum. If a wolf is killed, which is a documented man killer, are we prosecuted by state and local authorities, tried by a local jury, a jury of our peers? **No, we are denied that right!** Enforcement of specific federal rights, rights afforded to the federal government's wolves, actually deprives the constitutional rights of all persons on public lands, . . .

Idaho has large tracts of federal public domain land which remains in territorial status, and includes all federal public domain land and lands which were reserved by Executive Action, such as National Forests and National Monuments. When the federal government exercises territorial authority on federal lands with a sovereign state, it is acting as both the federal and state government, and is as capable of discriminating against the rights of individuals just as is a state government exercising its normal functions. **In the issue with the wolves, Idaho's authority over its citizens has been denied, . . . This denial of our Constitutional rights then elevates the wolf issue to that of a denial of our civil rights.**

In 1992, the United States Supreme Court applied the principle of federalism for the first time, to require that laws passed by Congress are unconstitutional if Congress renders itself or the states politically unaccountable to their constituents, by compelling or coercing a state to perform a federally mandated requirement, such as "wolf recovery in Idaho" as enforced by the Endangered Species Act and regulated by the United States Fish and Wildlife Service. . . . Congressman Mike Simpson, Idaho, stated clearly at a public meeting in Challis . . . that legislatively there was nothing he could do for Idaho concerning the wolf recovery issue, . . . **Through the manipulation of the federal government's wolf recovery program, it is obvious that the citizens of Idaho are being denied their right to constitutional accountability, not only at the state level, but at the federal level as well.** Our United States Congressmen . . . have **lost their ability to be accountable to the people of Idaho, which in turn denies the people of Idaho their constitutional rights.**

This issue of the loss of constitutional accountability by our United States Congressmen . . . and the **denial of Idaho's citizen's civil rights,** is the issue we wish to bring to the attention of the Office of the Governor. The Central Idaho Wolf Coalition is **strongly urging you,** . . . to address the issue of the **dumping** of the Canadian Gray Wolf into Idaho and its **serious unconstitutional** implications. We are urgently requesting you as the Chief Executive Constitutional Officer of the State of Idaho, **who has taken an oath to uphold and protect the Constitution, to take the leadership in this fight to defend the constitutional rights of the citizens of the Sovereign State of Idaho.**

Sincerely,
Marilyn Brower
Central Idaho Wolf Coalition
Steering Committee

Source: Natures [*sic*] Wolves: www.natureswolves.com/fighting_back/constitution.htm (retrieved July 16, 2004). Reprinted with permission.

Document 15.4   Defenders of Wildlife Argue for the Reintroduction of Wolves, 2004

Defenders of Wildlife was one of many environmental organizations that championed the issue of wolf reintroduction, a cause that long predated the Endangered Species Act. That wolf advocacy generally speaking did not directly address the issue of Fourteenth Amendment property rights that so incensed many westerners suggests that *proponents believed it necessary that the human economy had to reconcile itself to the ecological wisdom of wolf reintroduction. As we see here, however, wolf defenders (like Zygmunt Plater before Justice Powell on the snail darter) fell back on the utilitarian economic argument that wolf reintroduction was doing far more for regional economic interests than any possible losses suffered by cattle ranchers. Further, acknowledging the possibility of cattle depredation, this and other groups raised funds for that purpose to compensate ranchers. Defenders of Wildlife alone has paid more than $150,000 in the first decade of wolf reintroduction and established a large research effort to study ways to minimize wolf predation of livestock.*

WHY RESTORE WOLVES

Wolves—being large predators—are essential components of the ecosystems they inhabit. The reason why deer are so fast, moose so powerful, and bighorn sheep so agile is the continuous pressure of predators upon their prey. The wolf is the primary predator of animals such as elk and bison, both extremely abundant in Yellowstone National Park. Wolves are having a positive effect on these animals in Yellowstone by keeping their numbers in balance. In fact, the return of wolves has had a ripple effect that has touched almost all organisms in the Yellowstone ecosystem. Coyotes, which had become overabundant, are being displaced from their former territories by the reintroduced wolves. Coyote numbers have dropped and allowed small predators, such as foxes, to flourish once again. The reduction in elk and bison numbers has allowed willow and aspen trees to regenerate and regain their place in an ecosystem which had been overgrazed.

In addition, wolf restoration has benefited local economies by bringing in more tourist dollars. Since wolves returned to Yellowstone National Park in 1995, the region has seen a $10 million increase in economic activity, indicating that wolves are clearly having a positive impact on the economy of the greater Yellowstone area. Moreover, US Fish and Wildlife Service studies project that the wolf reintroduction program will continue to attract more park visitors, eventually bringing $23 million annually to Yellowstone.

Successful wolf recovery in Yellowstone has introduced a new source of revenue into the area. Visitors to the park now rank the wolf as the number one animal they come to see, thereby creating new demand for near-by lodging, guided wolf-watching tours and a variety of wolf-related merchandise. Merchants in the Lamar Valley reported that stuffed wolves, books on wolves, wolf T-shirts and wolf stationery have been selling briskly since the reintroductions. In tiny Cooke City, Montana, adjacent to the northeast entrance to Yellowstone, 22 percent more tourists passed through the town in the summer of 1995 than just one year prior. That figure rose again in the summer of 1996 with another record breaking tourist season. In a recent survey of Cooke City business owners, 71 percent thought wolf recovery was responsible for the increased tourist traffic.

WHERE'S THE BEEF?

The livestock industry has consistently been the most vocal and active opponent of wolf recovery. But FWS studies...demonstrate that wolves prefer native prey and kill livestock infrequently—at a fraction of one percent of the total number of livestock. Moreover, Defenders of Wildlife and most conservation organizations accept the prompt control of wolves that prey on livestock. Since the reintroduction in 1995, wolves in Yellowstone and Idaho have rarely clashed with ranching interests and predation on livestock has been low. . . .

Source: "Restoring Wolves to the Northern Rockies," from Web site of Defenders of Wildlife: http://www.defenders.org/wildlife/wolf/ynpfact.html (accessed July 15, 2004).

Document 15.5   **National Endangered Species Act Reform Coalition Demands Changes in ESA, 2004**

From the outset, the Endangered Species Act has received popular support from the overwhelming majority of Americans at the same time that it has provoked vehement opposition from a loosely formed but potent coalition of large corporate interests and small private landowners. Since the early 1990s, the largest organized entity has been the National Endangered Species Act Reform Coalition, self-described as "dedicated to achieving legislative improvements to the Endangered Species Act." Though it claims a "broad," "diverse," and "grassroots" membership, the leadership of the organization represents development interests largely located throughout the West, typical of the many groups that have arisen since the corporate-funded "Sagebrush Rebellion" of the late 1970s. Still, NESARC professes to seek "open debate" and reasonable modification so that "the ESA will work better both for the species it was designed to protect and the communities that have to live and work with the law."

WHAT NESARC IS FIGHTING FOR

Incentives to Conserve Habitat

ESA restrictions apply when land or water serves as habitat for threatened or endangered species. To avoid ESA regulation, some property owners have destroyed habitat to discourage the entry of protected species. The Act should be amended to provide incentives for property owners to conserve, rather than destroy, habitat and to provide regulatory certainty to property owners who voluntarily participate in conservation plans.

Citizen Participation

Private citizens, businesses and communities, especially those directly affected by conservation decisions, should have a prominent role in the ESA decision making processes. The Act should provide for earlier and more meaningful opportunities for citizens to participate, more citizen involvement in recovery plans, and a more prominent role in the consultation process for applicants for federal licenses and permits.

Fairness to Property Owners

Some ESA mandates have severely restricted the use and value of privately owned property. When severe restrictions occur without compensation by the federal government, the Act shifts costs and burdens to individual businesses and citizens that should be shared by **all** citizens. The ESA must be modified to prevent these inequities and encourage landowners to welcome protected species on their property. Specifically, when private property is preserved in a habitat conservation plan, the landowner must be compensated in a timely fashion.

Cost Effective Recovery Plans

Recovery plans are expensive to implement. Many of the costs are the direct expenses and lost opportunities of private parties and state and local governments. Costs to non-federal parties should be minimized by requiring implementation of the least costly recovery plan that would achieve the recovery of the species.

Good Science

The law requires that every ESA action must be based on scientific information on a species or its habitat. To ensure fair and sensible decision making, this information must be as accurate and thorough as possible. Scientific information can be improved by requiring minimum scientific standards and fair and impartial scientific peer review.

Shared Burdens

The ESA itself calls for "encouraging" states and private parties through a system of incentives to implement a program to conserve fish, wildlife and plants "for the benefit of all citizens." Contrary to this statement, however, ESA implementation often has been heavy-handed and inflexible, and the burdens of conservation have been placed disproportionately on private land owners, small and rural communities, and the employees of resource-based industries. If all citizens benefit from species conservation, then all citizens should bear the costs even handedly.

Primacy of State Water Law

The water law of the various states is a complex matrix that often establishes property rights to water. The ESA must be clarified to ensure that the Act is in harmony with, and recognizes the primacy of, state water law.

Source: National Endangered Species Act Reform Coalition Web site: http://www. nesarc.org/fighting.htm (accessed July 20, 2004).

Document 15.6   **Endangered Species Coalition Denounces Proposed**
                       Weakening of ESA, 2000

> *From the perspective of environmentalists, attempts to "reform" the ESA*
> *are little more than stealth efforts to weaken the most important*
> *protective provisions of the law. Here a broad coalition of environmen-*
> *tal organizations deconstructs one such legislative proposal to modify,*
> *and in their view, eviscerate the Endangered Species Act. Among its*
> *other provisions, HR 3160 would have turned much of the authority for*
> *implementation of ESA to the state and restricted the capacity of federal*
> *agencies to preserve endangered or threatened species. Recall Zygmunt*
> *Plater's reading of the ESA and note the proposed linguistic shift from*
> *"shall" to "may." Environmentalists certainly did.*

Representative Don Young (R-AK) and Representative Pombo (R-CA) recently introduced H.R. 3160, the "Common Sense Protections for Endangered
Species Act"—or what we like to call the "Nonsense Protections Act." With 32
cosponsors, the bill may gain legislative momentum....

H.R. 3160 essentially repeals the meaningful sections of the Endangered
Species Act. The low points include:

• **Listing:** The Young/Pombo bill would allow Governors to block additions to
the endangered species list. Under the Young/Pombo bill, Maine Governor
Angus King could make his wish come true and tie up the government's
recent decision to finally list Atlantic Salmon. And for species endemic to a
state, such as a plant in Hawaii that is found no where else, federal protection
will no longer apply if the state has some semblance of a state ESA—even if
it's like most state ESAs, unfunded and unenforced.

• **Critical Habitat:** The Young/Pombo bill eliminates critical habitat designation. The bill...substitutes the mandatory "shall" with the voluntary "may."
Under current law, Babbitt's Fish and Wildlife Service balks at the mandatory
critical habitat designation already (there are only court-ordered critical
habitat designations). Can you imagine what a voluntary program would
look like?

• **Federal Projects:** The Army Corps of Engineers and U.S. Forest Service could
find many ways to duck endangered species protections under the Young/
Pombo bill. By allowing agency core "missions" (such as damming rivers, or
maximizing forest harvest) to trump the ESA, the bill would make most
mitigation programs extinct. And the Fish and Wildlife Service would be hog-
tied because it could only step in if it could prove that significant numbers of
animals or plants would be lost—more of an extinction goal than a recovery
one. If that wasn't enough, biologists would be hampered by strict requirements to keep economic costs to a minimum. With additional loopholes for
"routine maintenance and operations" as well as speculative emergencies, the
Young/Pombo bill would let federal projects run amok.

• **Development permits:** Habitat Conservation Plans (HCPs) cover millions
of acres of endangered species habitat in this country. HCPs authorize

development and other habitat destruction and the Young/Pombo bill would make getting them a lot easier. Public review would be discouraged, mitigation requirements would be whatever the developer or timber company thinks is reasonable, and the permits would be locked in—with no changes under **ANY** circumstances, including no adaptive management—for unlimited amounts of time.

- **Recovery plans:** Recovery Plans are supposed to set out the fastest, most reliable plan to achieve endangered species recovery. But not under the Young/Pombo bill. The least cost is the bottom line, and a group of economists, wise use lawyers, and property owners with direct economic conflicts would make up the recovery planning team. Recovery plans could be replaced by "functional equivalents" (such as giant HCPs) or could be taken over by hostile state governors.
- **Appropriations:** To cap it all off, the bill authorizes dismal funding levels. Right now the agencies receive about $200 million each year for endangered species protection, far below what is needed to implement the current Act. The Young/Pombo bill would authorize less money to cover more endangered species and more bureaucratic requirements. On second thought—since the bill repeals most of the law's oars and leaves nothing but a ghost ship behind, maybe this is the only part of the Nonsense Protections Act that makes any sense.

Source: Endangered Species Coalition: http://www.defenders.org/esa-8.html (accessed October 1, 2004).

NOTES

1. See Jennifer Price, *Flight Maps: Adventures with Nature in Modern America* (New York: Basic Books, 2000), pp. 57–110.

2. Sarah Matsumo et al., *The Citizens' Guide to the Endangered Species Act* (Washington, DC: Earth Justice, 2003), p. 9.

3. Kenneth A. Bridle, Ph.D., "Endangered Species and Piedmont North Carolina Landowners," p. 3. Document prepared for Piedmont Land Conservancy in North Carolina. Accessed December 21, 2005 at http://www.wsi.nrcs.usda.gov/products/piedmont/app-c.pdf.

ANNOTATED BIBLIOGRAPHY

Barker, Rocky. *Saving All the Parts: Reconciling Economics and the Endangered Species Act.* Washington, DC: Island Press, 1993. A thoughtful and balanced account of the conflicts over species protection that afflict resource-dependent communities. The book's hopeful spirit points to a more sustainable future for communities whose economies have historically centered around activities such as logging and mining.

Burgess, Bonnie B. *Fate of the Wild: The Endangered Species Act and the Future of Biodiversity.* Athens: University of Georgia Press, 2001. Honest, balanced, and highly readable history of the Endangered Species Act, including a healthy discussion of the law's problems and a vision for a new way of thinking about species protection.

Clark, Tim W., Richard P. Reading, and Alice L. Clarke, eds. *Endangered Species Recovery: Finding the Lessons, Improving the Process.* Washington, DC: Island Press, 1994. The first effort to bring together biologists and sociologists to assess the effectiveness and shortcomings of the endangered species policy process. A number of case studies are featured, including the bitterly divisive northern spotted owl.

Czech, Brian, and Paul R. Krausman. *The Endangered Species Act: History, Conservation Biology and Public Policy*. Baltimore: Johns Hopkins University Press, 2001. The authors unravel the historical, political, and socioeconomic context of species protection under the Endangered Species Act. Recognizing societal and political limitations of species protection, the authors' formula for assessing the ESA's effectiveness is coupled with a strategy for improving the law.

Dunlap, Thomas. *Saving America's Wildlife: Ecology and the American Mind, 1850–1990.* 1988. Reprint, Princeton: Princeton University Press, 1991. Focusing on wolves and coyotes, recounts how popularized natural history helped to bring about a shift in consciousness on the ecological value of predators in the environment. Places the previous war of extermination and subsequent efforts to preserve these animals in historical and cultural context.

Ehrlich, Paul, and Anne Elrlich. *Extinction: The Causes and Consequences of the Disappearance of Species*. New York: Ballantine Books, 1985. Good overview of the historical forces that led to the passage of the Endangered Species Act, and some of the consequences of species extinction.

Lopez, Barry. *Of Wolves and Men*. New York: Scribner, 1978. Incisive, eloquent, and haunting look at the mostly horrific history of men and wolves. A brilliant book that tells us as much about men as it does about wolves, shedding particular light on attitudes that helped lead to the Endangered Species Act.

McIntyre, Rick, ed. *War against the Wolf: America's Campaign to Exterminate the Wolf*. Stillwater, MN: Voyageur Press, 1995. Expansive anthology, includes documents ranging from Native American myths and legends about wolves to government documents and newspaper and magazine articles.

McNamee, Thomas. *The Return of the Wolf to Yellowstone*. New York: Owl Books, 1998. An excellent interdisciplinary chronicle of the wolf's reintroduction to Yellowstone National Park. Covers well the history, politics, biology, and fierce resistance of some residents in the region to wolf reintroduction.

Shogren Jason F., and John Tschirhart, eds. *Protecting Endangered Species in the United States: Biological Needs, Political Realities, Economic Choices*. New York: Cambridge University Press, 2001. Moves beyond Clark, Reading, and Clarke's collection by including economists and the hard economic choices that society must face in protecting endangered species. The politics of protection, including useful discussions of cost-benefit analysis and the pressures applied by particular interest groups, are especially valuable.

Tobin, Richard J. *The Expendable Future: U.S. Politics and the Protection of Biological Diversity*. Durham, NC: Duke University Press, 1990. Tobin goes to the heart of the decision making process that underlies the political debate over endangered species. He explores the central question of how endangered animals are perceived within the political process and the related limitations of that system in addressing biological needs.

Wilcove, David S. *The Condor's Shadow: The Loss and Recovery of Wildlife in America*. New York: Freeman, 1999. A chilling tour of America's fractured habitat, wherein, the author argues, more than one-third of the nation's flora and fauna are endangered.

Yaffee, Steven Lewis. *Prohibitive Policy: Implementing the Federal Endangered Species Act*. Cambridge, MA: MIT Press, 1982. Although somewhat dated, examines one of the key arguments made by early opponents of the Endangered Species Act that the policy is rigid and ineffective in prohibiting negotiation between conflicting societal objectives.

16

Three Mile Island and the Search for a National Energy Policy

> To cherish what remains of the Earth and to foster its renewal is our only legitimate hope of survival.
>
> —Wendell Berry

> Those who preside over the worst energy shortage in our history tell us to use less, so that we will run out of oil, gasoline, and natural gas a little more slowly. Conservation is desirable, ... [but] ... America must get to work producing more energy.
>
> —Ronald Reagan, 1980

Like no other event in the last quarter of the twentieth century, the energy crisis of the 1970s left behind a tangled legacy of unresolved environmental issues and unsettling national security concerns. The national failure to confront honestly a voracious appetite for energy and address the long-term need for environmentally responsible energy independence continues to haunt policymakers in both areas. That the energy crisis erupted following the zenith of rising environmental consciousness of the late 1960s, when environmental concerns were already being overwhelmed by other anxieties—the collapse of faith in government, weakened confidence in American military power, economic growth in retreat— helps to account for what was essentially a national postponement of the energy challenge.

That is not to say that we have done nothing, but rather that we have done more of the same, increasing rather than reducing foreign oil dependency and generally ignoring the deleterious ecological effects and national security ramifications of our dependency on increasingly foreign, nonrenewable fuels. Only a relatively few scientists in the mid-1970s were warning of the potentially catastrophic dangers of global warming that might result (or was already) from the long-term burning of fossil fuels. They were easily dismissed. Within a generation there was an international scientific consensus on that issue, yet Americans had done little to reduce their disproportionate share of greenhouse gas emissions believed to be responsible for accelerating global climate change.

When the energy crisis began in 1973, many Americans placed high hopes in nuclear energy as one important element of a national energy policy. When the crisis returned a quarter-century later, that belief was reasserted, as was the conviction that nuclear power could help the U.S. address the global warming issue. Critics of nuclear power were (and are) generally dismissed as fear-mongers who irrationally resisted what appeared to be a clean and safe source that could help the United States control its own energy fate. Unlike coal and oil, nuclear power offered no hazardous air pollutants; the Atomic Energy Commission (whose chairman in the halcyon days of the 1950s had once promised energy "too cheap to meter") seemed to have all public health concerns, including the disposal of nuclear waste, well under control. Those reassuring promises were shattered in March 1979 with the worst accident in the history of the American nuclear power industry at the Three Mile Island plant near Harrisburg, Pennsylvania. Nuclear anxieties were compounded by the far worse nuclear accident at Chernobyl in 1986. The industry has never recovered. Nor has the problem of waste disposal been solved, at least not adequately enough to silence industry critics. They argue that the industry's safety record is suspect and that neither the technology nor the government agency responsible for regulating the industry can be trusted to safeguard the environment and public health.

Finally and perhaps most urgently, despite the clear warning that the Organization of Petroleum Exporting Countries (OPEC) oil embargo that initially triggered the crisis seemed to send about the need for the United States to alter its policy in the Middle East, little has changed. In the wake of the terrorist attacks of September 11, 2001, environmentalists, renewable energy experts, and public officials looked back on the failure in the 1970s and 1980s to wean the nation from its growing dependency on Middle Eastern oil as one root of the scourge of terrorism. Thus beyond its manifold environmental implications (the protection of energy-bearing wilderness areas also among these), the failure to develop a national strategy that both addressed environmental protection and prepared the United States for a post-fossil fuel era of world history was, in the post-9/11 era, understood as a national security threat. At bottom, because energy policy is attached to so many other issues, it is, many argued, the central environmental issue of the new century.

It began when the United States and western European nations rallied to the defense of Israel during the Yom Kippur War of October 1973. In retaliation, OPEC, a cartel of largely Arab oil-producing states, shut off the flow of oil to the United States and its allies. The OPEC Oil Embargo of 1973–1974 triggered the energy crisis, shattering the myth of endlessly abundant, cheap oil. With domestic peak oil production having already passed a couple years before, American producers were unable to increase their production and thus could not control soaring prices. The cost of gasoline nearly doubled; when it did flow again, the price of OPEC oil shot up 500 percent. And there didn't seem to be anything Americans could or were willing to do about it. Context is crucial: the embargo unfolded simultaneously with the final withdrawal of American forces from Vietnam, further weakening cold war assumptions about America's ability to dictate world events, and making Americans reluctant to commit troops abroad. And with the United States having reached peak oil at home (maximum historic rates of oil production), it had lost the ability—at least for the moment—to manipulate world energy markets.

Worse still were the severe economic repercussions wrought by the embargo. Herein lies the key to understanding the national failure to come to terms with what is an ecological problem, but was mainly conveyed (and is still) by politicians and understood by Americans in the familiar language of supply and demand. American automakers, still producing fleets of large, gas-hungry vehicles, were caught flat-footed. Consumers seeking more fuel-efficient vehicles looked to Japanese and German models while the industry quickly tried to retool. Already beset with the larger challenge of foreign competition, the industry tumbled into recession and sent shock waves throughout the American economy. Soaring prices of energy also damaged steel, plastics, textiles, trucking—essentially any product or service that depended upon cheap energy. Energy was not the lone (or even the biggest) problem afflicting the American economy; the demise of the manufacturing sector, imperceptibly emerging until then, had now assumed major, painful proportions. Still, the capacity of foreign energy suppliers to deepen the recession produced personal economic misery and bitter frustration for millions of Americans.

For most citizens, the crisis also naturally produced a desire for a quick painless fix and a return to the economic status quo. For nearly a decade environmentalists, scientists, and other academics had been warning grimly about a plethora of environmental ills that derived not only from the robust economic growth the nation enjoyed, but also, they rudely declared, from the nation's disproportionate take of the planet's resources. Books with such titles as *Limits to Growth* and *Diet for a Small Planet* had indicted the western industrialized world, in particular the postwar American middle-class lifestyle, as recklessly indifferent to the needs of the rest of the world and the environment. Their recommendations for more environmentally responsible energy technologies such as wind, solar, and geothermal had attracted popular interest in such forums as the best-selling *Whole Earth Catalog*. Still, corporate and government experts in the energy field labeled them "exotic" and too closely associated with the anti-institutional elements of the hippie counter culture. Practically speaking, the fact remained that without government subsidies for research and development, the price of high-performance, "green" renewable technologies left them noncompetitive in the energy market.

That situation would change little over the next thirty years. Despite the hopes and rhetoric of President Jimmy Carter and the modest government support he and the Congress pledged later in the decade, renewable sources seemed too futuristic to help resolve the immediate crisis. Despite the pleadings of environmentalists and academics, the energy crisis would continue to be seen not as a global concern requiring international cooperation and sacrifice from the western industrialized world; nor, despite occasional rhetorical flourish from

Presidents Nixon and especially Carter, was it perceived ecologically as a sign of diminishing natural resources and a globally degraded environment. Rather, American politicians were accountable to their own constituents and consistently cast the issue in largely economic terms. The mission was to keep the supply coming. This explains why, a generation later, Americans are *twice as dependent* on foreign oil as they were when the 1973 embargo hit. Most of that oil supply comes from volatile regions of the world, led by the Middle East. The 56 percent of oil imported from the region in 2004 is projected to soar to 65 percent by 2020. Among the Arab and Muslim population, the perception is very strong that the large American military presence in the Middle East, including the 2003 invasion of Iraq, derives solely from America's material interest in the region's oil. This, many observed following the September 11 attacks, has fueled the cycle of terrorism and invites the further American counter-response of additional military action. At a minimum, critics say, the enormous cost of U.S. military presence in the region—estimated at more than one-third of the $400 billion dollar U.S. defense budget—is a well-disguised, but significant hidden cost of continued access to cheap oil and gasoline. Beginning with Nixon's allusion to "increasing costs of foreign dependency," every president since 1973 has floated the attractive rhetoric of energy independence. And, failed—not only to achieve it, but even to move the United States in that direction.

The nation did achieve some success in the late 1970s toward improving its woefully inefficient use of energy. Tax credits for individuals and business, research and development funding, and other forms of government subsidy allowed millions of Americans to better insulate their homes, replace oil with coal and natural gas, invest in more efficient heating, cooling, and lighting systems, and even pilot solar panels and geothermal wells to more efficiently and cheaply go about their lives—without, as many feared, diminishing the quality of that life. Although Americans grew tired and increasingly skeptical of President Carter's repeated calls for sacrifice and conservation, particularly in 1979 when the collapse of the U.S.-supported dictatorship in Iran sent shock waves through the energy markets again and prices soared, energy efficiency proved to be a cost-effective investment. Between 1979 and 1986, at a time when Gross Domestic Product (GDP) grew by 20 percent, Americans reduced their "energy intensity"—the standard measure of the efficiency of energy consumption—by 21 percent and saved more than $100 billion on the national energy bill. Stimulated by modest government spending and regulation, energy efficiency had proven to be a quick and sound investment to which Americans and the financial markets naturally gravitated.[1]

Greater efficiency was not the dominant energy story in these years, however. Despite President Nixon's call for immediate and fairly drastic reductions in the use of energy to meet the urgent crisis of 1973–1974, his "Project Independence" urged greater domestic production. From the energy crisis forward through the rest of the decade, the Bureau of Land Management, the National Forest Service, and other federal agencies responsible for the stewardship of the nation's public lands shifted the emphasis on land management toward exploration and drilling of coal, oil, and natural gas. The nation held the world's greatest supply of coal, but the cheapest means of getting it—strip mining—had proven environmentally problematic. Further, the Clean Air Act had made burning coal in the nation's power plants, many of them employing antiquated and polluting technology, less appealing and more expensive. From Alaska to the offshore continental shelf, oil exploration and drilling became another focus. That too, faced opposition from Native Americans, environmentalists, and local and state officials; the latter argued for protecting fragile and pristine natural areas whose greatest economic value lay in tourism, not energy production.

Nuclear energy seemed to many to provide the most environmentally sound option for advancing America's energy independence. Unlike coal- or oil-fired power plants, nuclear reactors generated no polluting emissions or greenhouse gases that increasingly posed a threat to the stability of global climate. With a twenty-year track record of successful electric power generation, and at least as far as the public could tell, a flawless safety record, the nuclear industry seized the opportunity provided by the energy crisis to advocate the construction of new nuclear plants. They argued for the emergency streamlining of what they argued was a burdensome licensing process to bring a new plant on-line. President Nixon responded favorably, as did the Congress, and in 1973 utility companies ordered forty-one new nuclear plants, a one-year record. With persistent, latent anxiety among Americans over atom-splitting and a rising anti-nuclear power movement, President Carter did not pronounce nuclear as a central element of his energy policy; conservation, he proudly declared, was the "cornerstone." With strong reassurances regarding the safety of the technology, however, Carter did advocate the continued expansion of nuclear power. That momentum placed the industry on track to overtake both oil and natural gas by the early 1980s in the share of electricity generated nationally. By the 1990s nuclear power had become (behind coal), the second largest source of electricity in the country.

The industry's share of the electricity pie would undoubtedly be greater if not for the event that began on March 28, 1979, inside Unit 2 of the Three Mile Island nuclear plant outside Harrisburg, Pennsylvania. Although accounts of the Nuclear Regulatory Commission (NRC) and Three Mile Island Alert (TMIA), the leading citizens' watchdog organization in the region, still differ as to exactly what occurred inside the plant that morning and in the weeks leading up to the event, they do agree that a valve critical to the plant's cooling system malfunctioned and triggered a series of further technical and human errors that led to the worst nuclear accident in U.S. history. Through its own independent expert research, including testimony from inside whistleblowers, TMIA argued that the "pilot-operated relief valve" had been chronically malfunctioning and that the owner-operator of the facility, Metropolitan-Edison, covered that fact up with the complicity of NRC officials. When the valve remained stuck open that morning, hundreds of thousands of gallons of highly radioactive water ended up on the floor of the reactor containment building. This presented the possible worst-case scenario long feared by critics of nuclear power: the intense heat caused by the loss of coolant could have melted the plutonium fuel rods that are the fuel source for the plant. Such a meltdown could cause what is known as the "China Syndrome," carrying a huge radioactive mass through the floor of the reactor and into the surrounding environment.

The second and even more threatening stage of the accident occurred when the reactor's emergency cooling system, designed to be activated in just such a situation, was apparently shut off too soon. Some of the fuel rods overheated, creating a hydrogen bubble at the top of the reactor that ultimately came within ninety minutes of catastrophically exploding. In short, the nation came within less than two hours of a radioactive explosion the effects of which would have exceeded that of several small hydrogen bombs, extending far beyond central Pennsylvania. Technicians worked desperately and successfully to reduce the size of the bubble, thereby ending the crisis.

While these events unfolded over a period of two or three days, widespread confusion reigned throughout central Pennsylvania as to exactly what had happened and what danger the accident posed to the public. Conflicting and often confused information tumbled forth at news conferences from officials at all levels: Metropolitan-Edison, Pennsylvania governor Richard Thornburgh and his top officials, and federal officials from the NRC and eventually from the Carter White House. Here is a sampling of the twisted and seemingly contradictory statements that emerged over the first forty-eight hours:

> March 29, 1 p.m.—Metropolitan Edison President Walter Creitz: "Immediately when it happened we sent teams out.... We could detect nothing above natural background radiation. There was a small release, but you know, this couldn't detect it.... the exact amount, I'll be honest, I don't know."
>
> 2 p.m.—Jack Herbein, an official from Metropolitan-Edison: "Some workers may have been contaminated. It's nothing we can't take care of."
>
> 4 p.m.—Lieutenant Governor William Scranton: "This situation is more complex than the company first led us to believe. Metropolitan Edison has given you and us conflicting information (regarding radiation levels and exposure dangers)."
>
> The Nuclear Regulatory Commission: "The accident sent radiation through the plant's 4-foot thick walls and sent low-level radiation as far as a mile from the plant site.... Radioactivity inside the reactor dome was measured at 6,000 Roentgens. The normal level in the dome is 5 to 6 Roentgens. A damn lot of radiation."
>
> March 30, 11 a.m.—Met Ed official: "The vapor that is now going into the atmosphere (a deliberate release, designed to alleviate the buildup inside the reactor)... is only mildly radioactive within accepted limits. We concede that it's not just a little thing... There is presently no danger to the public health or safety. We didn't injure anybody, we didn't over-expose anybody and we certainly didn't kill anybody."[2]

Throughout the crisis, Governor Thornburgh expressed the kind of confounded frustration one would expect. Watching all of this unfold on television, many Americans had their long-standing fears of nuclear power confirmed, anxieties that had also been affirmed on the big screen that very month: in an uncanny moment of art anticipating reality, *The China Syndrome*, the Hollywood version of this nightmare, had premiered that month. Investors trembled at the future prospects of nuclear energy, and rightfully so. Confidence in the industry collapsed, and not a single nuclear plant has been built since in the United States.

Questions about the safety of nuclear power derived from the well-earned perception that Met Ed and NRC officials had obfuscated what had really happened and what danger to public health the incident had posed. In the years after the accident, TMIA and the Union of Concerned Scientists published independent findings documenting severe health effects (including radiation-linked cancer deaths) that seemed to belie official pronouncements from utility and NRC executives. The larger context is important here: since the 1960s Americans, because of Vietnam and Watergate primarily, had grown suspicious of governmental authorities at all levels. Rachel Carson's successful challenge of the chemical manufacturers and Ralph Nader's exposure of the falsification of safety assurances by the auto industry led to other questions about the truthfulness of previously unassailable voices of corporate authority, technological confidence, and government expertise. With genetic engineering, cloning, supersonic airplanes, and more, the very idea that science and technology always brought social good came to be challenged. That broader picture helps account for the automatic and deep suspicion that those living in central Pennsylvania and indeed many Americans had about the nuclear industry following TMI.

Despite enthusiastic support from President Ronald Reagan and both presidents Bush, other environmental issues plagued the industry's attempts to revive itself. Leading the list was the disposal of mountains of nuclear waste that lie scattered at nuclear power plants and weapons production facilities across the country. Transporting that waste to designated sites in remote sections of Nevada and New Mexico became, in the eyes of opponents, far more dangerous after September 11. Further out of sight of most Americans lay the problem of uranium mine waste. A uranium boom in Utah that fed the nuclear power industry back in the 1950s had left behind two generations of radiation-poisoned workers (many of them Navajo) who contracted leukemia and other radiological diseases. Add to that contaminated soil and water in vast sections of rural Utah. The worst site is just outside Moab, where by the 1980s 10,000 tons of radioactive soil were leaching into the Colorado River. And in an incident largely unknown to most Americans, in July 1979, 94 million gallons of radioactive effluent from uranium mining operations spilled into the Rio Puerco near Church Rock, New Mexico, permanently (at least for the 80,000-year half-life of the material) damaging the water supply of the Navajo population in the area.

Unfolding simultaneously with these nuclear accidents was a furious conflict that raged over energy development in the West among environmentalists, federal land managers, and a phenomenon known as the Sagebrush Rebellion. The latter represented a loosely allied coalition of ranchers and citizens funded largely by corporate interests determined to eviscerate the power of the federal government to regulate activities on public lands. Energy companies stood anxious to reap a whirlwind of profits by supplying increasing shares of the nation's energy needs; along with figures such as Joseph Coors who had long fought environmental regulations, energy executives became avid supporters and helped fund the Sagebrush Rebellion. Environmentalists and many westerners concerned about preserving the scenic beauty and integrity of their region (which many noticed actually generated far greater dollars and jobs than the energy industry) feared the West would become a "national sacrifice area." Just as the federal government had adopted a policy to intensify exploration and development of western energy resources, it also had committed itself to studying and protecting potential wilderness areas in the same region. The Federal Land Policy Management Act of 1976 became the major point of contention between environmentalists and Sagebrush Rebels. Its most important provision was the requirement that the Bureau of Land Management (BLM) complete a wilderness inventory for the vast acreages under its control; until such inventories were completed and potential wilderness areas identified, all development was halted. For several months, open confrontations ensued between BLM officials and county and state officials in the West, particularly in Utah. Death and bomb threats were issued to BLM officials, and county bulldozers carved out roads across wilderness study areas.

A self-declared sagebrush rebel, President Ronald Reagan buoyantly declared that the nation could solve its energy woes, not by conservation and sacrifice, but through greater production. Calling for a relaxing of environmental regulations that had been imposed in the previous decade, he signaled that his administration's energy policy would abandon the Carter administration's emphasis on renewable sources and conservation and focus on greater production. Production, not conservation, is the dominant chromosome in America's DNA. Despite continued quiet improvements in energy efficiency driven by the market tendency to go where investments can be made to pay most quickly, the Reagan years saw a recommitment to massive federal subsidies to fossil fuels industries and desperate attempts to revive the nuclear industry.

Clinging to the past in the form of nineteenth-century energy technologies, the Reagan policy also proved to be a harbinger of things to come. In 2001 Vice President Dick Cheney, one of many former energy executives dominating the administration of President George W. Bush, led the first serious effort in nearly twenty years to formulate a national energy strategy. Not surprisingly, the plan emphasized intensified domestic extraction, a return to nuclear energy, and a muscular foreign and military policy to secure foreign supplies of oil and natural gas for the United States. "Conservation," Cheney declared, "may be a virtue, but it is not the basis for a sound national energy policy." Critics of the Bush administration pointed out that the significant advances in energy efficiency achieved in the late 1970s and early 1980s belied that statement. Moreover, many energy and foreign policy experts wondered how continued reliance on the very strategies that had gotten America into its energy fix would be sufficient to advance the longstanding goal of energy independence.

DOCUMENTS

Document 16.1   **Scientists Offer Warning on Unsustainable Current Global Energy and Economic Development Patterns, 1972**

More than a year before most Americans confronted the energy crisis that was triggered by the OPEC Oil Embargo, an international conference of scientists and engineers, organized by the Society for Social Responsibility in Science (SSRS) met in London to address the interrelated issues of energy supply and consumption, environmental degradation, and global human development. The conferees generally shared the premise that the era of cheap, abundant energy sources was ending. Further, they warned of the global ecological and social consequences of not charting a new course for global energy development and reversing current consumption patterns. These excerpts address the particular issue of the global disparity in energy consumption and, perhaps prophetically, warn of global tension arising out of a world of energy haves and have-nots. American politicians eschewed the idea of a global energy policy. Conventional thinking held that such a global vision for solving energy problems bore potentially sobering implications for economic growth and alteration in the "middle-class lifestyle."

It is becoming increasingly more possible to foresee the consequences of our present highly technological way of life. The outcome of our failure to exercise restraint in any one of a number of important areas can now be predicted, and the effect that this will have on the future of mankind is a cause for concern.

The future of life as we know it on the Earth is subject to many interconnected constraints, such as in mineral resource depletion, food production, tolerable pollution levels, energy production and population growth. . . .

The global distribution of wealth (measured by the standard of living or energy consumption) and population are not coincident, 80% of the world's energy being consumed by the 30% of the population living in the industrialized countries. The USA (with 6% of the world's population) consumes 35% of the world's energy; while the world average annual consumption is about 2 tons coal equivalent per capita, the figure for the USA is nearer 12 tce. . .

To raise the whole world's per capita consumption of energy to the same value as that in the USA today would involve a sixfold increase. Additionally the USA is expected to consume as much energy in the last 30 years of this century as it has done all-told to date.

Clearly it is not possible for the world's resources to sustain a standard of living for all of us equal to that enjoyed now . . . in the "over-developed" countries. We are all aware that the Earth is finite, that resources are limited, and therefore we must see that, of course such growth cannot be sustained indefinitely. . . .

How do we tackle the problem of meeting the increasing demand for energy? Should we strive to fill the "energy gap" at any cost to the environment, by ever increasing exploitation and devastation and with the inevitable accompaniment of the generation of more and more atmospheric pollution? Should we, on the other hand, change our values and attack the demand by striving for a reasoned, global approach to economic usage of energy and conservation of fuel? . . .

—R. J. Crookes

THE VITAL NEED FOR A WORLD ENERGY POLICY

. . . It follows inevitably that the present free-for-all in the use of the world's energy cannot go on much longer. The rich countries have grown used to the idea that they can use as much energy as they like for any purpose that they can afford financially, while the poor countries can only look on in envy. Such a situation is leading inevitably to a steady increase in world tension, and eventually, will cause a disastrous situation in the rich countries when they can no longer base their civilization on an over liberal use of energy (both because of energy shortage and because of thermal pollution). Thus it is vitally important to prepare a world policy for fuel and energy, taking into account the needs of the less developed countries. . . .

—Prof. M. W. Thring

Source: Meredith W. Thring and Roy J. Crookes, eds., *Energy and Humanity.* PPL Series on Mankind and the Engineer, vol. 2 (Stevenage, England: Peter Peregrinus, Ltd., 1974); Crookes, p. v; Thring, pp. 184–85. Copyright © PPL. Reproduced with permission of IEE.

Document 16.2   President Nixon Announces "Project Independence," 1973

The national energy debate originated with what many historians argue is the defining event of the decade: the OPEC Oil Embargo that followed U.S. Support of Israel in the Yom Kippur War. The embargo prompted President Nixon to propose "Project Independence," a plan to wean the United States from its dependency on foreign oil. Nixon candidly recognizes that America's growing reliance on foreign sources had ominous implications for national security. His call to the U.S. Congress for solutions to the nation's energy needs says little, however, about the environmental impact of fossil fuel consumption, nor about any systemic changes in Americans' attitudes toward energy use. The focus here is on ameliorating the immediate crisis with temporary sacrifice and shoring up production for the long term.

November 8, 1973

To the Congress of the United States:

... Unfortunately, the energy crisis that once seemed a distant threat to many people is now closing upon us quickly.... Largely because of the [Yom Kippur] war, we must face up to the stark fact that we are heading toward the most acute shortage of energy since the Second World War. Of the 17 million barrels of oil a day that we would ordinarily consume this winter, more than two million barrels a day will no longer be available to us....

ADMINISTRATIVE ACTIONS TO MEET THIS EMERGENCY

... *First*, industries and utilities which use coal—our most abundant resource—will be prevented from converting to oil. Efforts will also be made to convert power plants from the use of oil to the use of coal.

Second, reduced quantities of fuel will be allocated to aircraft. This ... should not seriously disrupt air travel nor cause serious damage to the airline industry.

Third, there will be reductions of approximately 15 percent in the supply of heating oil for homes, offices and other establishments. This is a precautionary measure....

Fourth, there will be additional reductions in the consumption of energy by the Federal Government, cutting even deeper than the 7 percent reduction that I ordered earlier this year....

Fifth, I have asked the Atomic Energy Commission to speed up the licensing and construction of nuclear plants, seeking to reduce the time required to bring nuclear plants on line....

Legislation authorizing construction of the Alaskan pipeline must be the first order of business as we tackle our long-range energy problems....

This new effort to achieve self-sufficiency in energy, to be known as Project Independence, is absolutely critical to the maintenance of our ability to play our independent role in international affairs. In addition, we must recognize that a substantial part of our success in building a strong and vigorous economy in this century is attributable to the fact that we have always had access to almost unlimited amounts of cheap energy. If this growth is to continue, we must develop our capacity to provide enormous amounts of clean energy at the lowest possible cost. Thus, irrespective of the implications for our foreign policy and with the implicit understanding that our intentions are not remotely isolationist, the increasing costs of foreign energy further contribute to the necessity of our achieving self-sufficiency in energy.

Source: Richard M. Nixon, "Special Message to the Congress Proposing Emergency Energy Legislation," November 8, 1973. *Public Papers of the Presidents of the United States* (Washington, DC: United States Government Printing Office, 1973). Excerpted from The American Presidency Project Web site: http://www.presidency.ucsb.edu/ws/index .php?pid=4035&st=&st1 (accessed August 2, 2004).

Document 16.3   President Carter Announces National Energy Plan, 1977

Four years later, with the immediate crisis sparked by the OPEC embargo well over but the long-term challenge far from solved, President Jimmy Carter launched a new initiative aimed at galvanizing public support for a national energy policy. Though he believed this to be "the moral equivalent of war" around which the nation could rally, in the end Carter's more grim predictions and repeated calls for national sacrifice and changes in lifestyle wore thin with a public grown skeptical about energy shortages and cynical about government in general.

Tonight I want to have an unpleasant talk with you about a problem unprecedented in our history. With the exception of preventing war, this is the greatest challenge our country will face during our lifetimes. The energy crisis has not yet overwhelmed us, but it will if we do not act quickly.

It is a problem we will not solve in the next few years, and it is likely to get progressively worse through the rest of this century....

We simply must balance our demand for energy with our rapidly shrinking resources. By acting now, we can control our future instead of letting the future control us....

This difficult effort will be the "moral equivalent of war"—except that we will be uniting our efforts to build and not destroy....

But our energy problem is worse tonight than it was in 1973...because more waste has occurred, and more time has passed by without our planning for the future. And it will get worse every day until we act.

The oil and natural gas we rely on for 75 percent of our energy are running out. In spite of increased effort, domestic production has been dropping steadily at about six percent a year. Imports have doubled in the last five years....

The world has not prepared for the future. During the 1950s, people used twice as much oil as during the 1940s. During the 1960s, we used twice as much as during the 1950s. And in each of those decades, more oil was consumed than in all of mankind's previous history....

I know that many of you have suspected that some supplies of oil and gas are being withheld. You may be right, but suspicions about oil companies cannot change the fact that we are running out of petroleum....

Each new inventory of world oil reserves has been more disturbing than the last. World oil production can probably keep going up for another six or eight years. But some time in the 1980s it can't go up much more. Demand will overtake production. We have no choice about that....

Each American uses the energy equivalent of 60 barrels of oil per person each year. Ours is the most wasteful nation on earth.... With about the same standard of living, we use twice as much energy per person as do other countries like Germany, Japan and Sweden....

If we do not act, then by 1985 we will be using 33 percent more energy than we do today. We can't substantially increase our domestic production, so we would need to import twice as much oil as we do now....

Now we have a choice. But if we wait, we will live in fear of embargoes. We could endanger our freedom as a sovereign nation to act in foreign affairs....Within ten years we would not be able to import enough oil—from any country, at any acceptable price....

We will feel mounting pressure to plunder the environment. We will have a crash program to build more nuclear plants, strip-mine and burn more coal, and drill more offshore wells than we will need if we begin to conserve now. Inflation will soar, production will go down, people will lose their jobs. Intense competition will build up among nations and among the different regions within our own country....

But we still have another choice. We can begin to prepare right now....

Our national energy plan is based on ten fundamental principles.

The first principle is that we can have an effective and comprehensive energy policy only if the government takes responsibility for it and if the people understand the seriousness of the challenge and are willing to make sacrifices.

The second principle is that healthy economic growth must continue. Only by saving energy can we maintain our standard of living and keep our people at work. An effective conservation program will create hundreds of thousands of new jobs.

The third principle is that we must protect the environment. Our energy problems have the same cause as our environmental problems—wasteful use of resources. Conservation helps us solve both at once.

The fourth principle is that we must reduce our vulnerability to potentially devastating embargoes. We can protect ourselves from uncertain supplies by reducing our demand for oil, making the most of our abundant resources such as coal, and developing a strategic petroleum reserve....

The sixth principle, and the cornerstone of our policy, is to reduce the demand through conservation. Our emphasis on conservation is a clear difference between this plan and others which merely encouraged crash production efforts. Conservation is the quickest, cheapest, most practical source of energy....

The seventh principle is that prices should generally reflect the true replacement costs of energy. We are only cheating ourselves if we make energy artificially cheap and use more than we can really afford....

The ninth principle is that we must conserve the fuels that are scarcest and make the most of those that are more plentiful....We need to shift to plentiful coal while taking care to protect the environment, and to apply stricter safety standards to nuclear energy....

I can't tell you that these measures will be easy, nor will they be popular. But I think most of you realize that a policy which does not ask for changes or sacrifices would not be an effective policy.

This plan is essential to protect our jobs, our environment, our standard of living, and our future....

We have been proud of our leadership in the world. Now we have a chance again to give the world a positive example.

And we have been proud of our vision of the future. We have always wanted to give our children and grandchildren a world richer in possibilities than we've had. They are the ones we must provide for now. They are the ones who will suffer most if we don't act. . . .

I am sure each of you will find something you don't like about the specifics of our proposal. It will demand that we make sacrifices and changes in our lives. . . . It will lead to some higher costs, and to some greater inconveniences for everyone.

But the sacrifices will be gradual, realistic and necessary. Above all, they will be fair. . . . The citizens who insist on driving large, unnecessarily powerful cars must expect to pay more for that luxury. . . .

There should be only one test for this program: whether it will help our country.

Other generations of Americans have faced and mastered great challenges. I have faith that meeting this challenge will make our own lives even richer. If you will join me so that we can work together with patriotism and courage, we will again prove that our great nation can lead the world into an age of peace, independence and freedom.

Source: Jimmy Carter, "The President's Proposed Energy Policy." April 18, 1977. *Vital Speeches of the Day*, Vol. 43, No. 14, May 1, 1977, pp. 418–20.

Document 16.4   G. Hoyt Whipple Pronounces the Virtues of Nuclear Energy, 1971

With the energy crisis already looming in the form of rising prices, in 1972 the Atomic Energy Commission sponsored a forum to discuss the merits of nuclear power generation versus conventional fuels. In this excerpt from his presentation at that forum, nuclear industry veteran and radiological health expert G. Hoyt Whipple dismisses as "irrational" the growing fears of nuclear power and asserts the safety and cost-effectiveness of the industry. He speaks with the calculated reasoning of an erudite scientist and engineer and predictably derisively finds the rising protests against nuclear power to be stoked by emotional fear. At the time of the AEC forum, nuclear energy was emerging as an important element of the debate and would be promoted by both presidents Nixon and Carter as one means to national energy independence.

You must wonder . . . whether there is anything to be said for or against nuclear power that has not already been said. . . . The reflexes have all been well conditioned. . . . If I am able to trick a few of you into rational thought on the subject of nuclear power, this evening will be successful beyond my wildest expectations. . . .

Why is nuclear power the best thing that has happened to us since prohibition was repealed? . . .

1. The fissioning of uranium offers a large, new source of energy that has become practical at a time when traditional sources of energy are beginning to become scarce, difficult to obtain, and expensive.

2. The safety standards under which nuclear power has developed are the best ever seen by any industry, even in its worst nightmares. The nuclear safety standards incorporate more scientific knowledge and more cautious judgment than do any other standards we have.

3. Nuclear power plants are intrinsically clean and safe. Were this not so, no sane engineer would consider building and operating one under the limitations imposed by the Atomic Energy Commission.

These things are true. Why then, the uproar? Why the loud cries to prohibit nuclear power? I do not understand the reasons for the protests, but . . . I have come to believe that the reasons may have come after the conclusions rather than before. . . .

What . . . are the consequences of subjecting the world population to 1.3 man-rem [of radioactive tritium he has estimated emanates from a nuclear power plant] spread over many decades? . . . You add up all the years of life lost because of the tritium produced by the nuclear plant in one year, and you arrive at the figure of 12/10 of a man-year. In other words, the production of 1,000 [megawatts] for one year with a nuclear plant will . . . have the ultimate effect of shortening one life by about one month. . . . [By contrast] the estimate that producing 1,000 Megawatts for one year with 3% sulfur coal will have the ultimate overall effects of reducing life expectancy in the world population by about 10,000 man-years. . . .

It is said that the AEC has been placed in an impossible position, having, as it does, the responsibility for both promoting and regulating nuclear power. Howsoever this may be, . . . the AEC has never licensed a plant to operate anywhere near the limits set by these [safety] standards. . . . Now, in further retreat from the best energy source we have ever had, comes "as low as practicable." In other words, let us reduce nothing by a factor of 10 or 100 and become even holier than the holiest opponent of nuclear power.

This flight from common sense, lead by a frightened AEC and largely unopposed by timid, short-sighted electric utilities, will lead to increased costs of electricity. The high costs of building and operating safer-than-safe nuclear plants, or comparable coal plants, will be passed on to the customers in their light bills. And then, after a few years, when these customers rise and ask why their bills are so high, the answer will have to be: this was the price of peace, timidity, and fear in the early 1970s.

Source: G. Hoyt Whipple, "Nuclear Power: You Never Had It So Good," in *The Environmental and Ecological Forum 1970–1971* (Washington, DC: Atomic Energy Commission, 1972), pp. 157–60.

**Document 16.5   Barry Commoner Criticizes Emphasis of Nuclear
                       Power in National Energy Act, 1979**

Well known for his landmark publication, The Closing Circle, *environmental scientist and author Barry Commoner assailed President Carter's ultimate failure of leadership on the energy issue. In particular, he charges here that Carter and the Congress allowed the final version of the energy bill to contain too great an emphasis on nuclear power as opposed to alternative forms of renewable energy. Along with millions of other Americans, Commoner had long been skeptical of the promises and feared the dangers of nuclear power. Their criticisms held far greater weight in the wake of the accident at Three Mile Island in March 1979.*

[The] Carter administration has made a strong effort to revive the dying industry by proposing legislation that would limit environmental challenges to new plants. The administration's intense interest in expanding the role of nuclear power comes as a surprise to those citizens who remember Mr. Carter's declaration, during the election campaign, that nuclear power is a "last resort," a position he has reiterated in subsequent public statements. . . . [Energy Secretary] Dr. Schlesinger has been more forthright and has proclaimed that nuclear power is "enshrined in the president's program." . . .

For many Americans the Plan's emphasis on nuclear power elicits the terrifying prospect of a nuclear catastrophe. . . .

A good deal of this opposition . . . was based on concern over the hazards of their intensely radioactive wastes. In the absence of a "disposal" procedure that can isolate them from people and the environment over the 100,00-to-200,000-year period in which they will remain dangerous, the wastes have been stored in temporary places. The federal government's effort to find long-term storage sites has met considerable resistance from local populations and state governments. . . .

The accident at the Three Mile Island Nuclear Power Plant in March 1979 is certain to intensify this opposition, and not only in the United States. . . . Even from the sketchy information that was available about the accident shortly after it happened, it was clear that the event confirmed the view that because of its very design nuclear power is an *inherently* dangerous technology. The high and growing cost of nuclear power plants is due . . . to its unique feature, the use of fission to supply the heat needed to produce steam [that is turned into electricity]. The accident at Harrisburg showed that a failure in the steam-to-electricity section of the plant that would have caused very little trouble in a conventional power plant came close to producing a catastrophic disaster in the nuclear one. . . .

Like the horseshoe nail that lost a kingdom, the failure of a pump at . . . Three Mile Island . . . may have lost the entire industry. It dramatized the vulnerability of the complex system that is embodied in the elaborate technology of nuclear power. In that design, the normally benign and easily controlled process of producing steam to drive an electric generator turned into a trigger for a radioactive catastrophe.

Even if it is ever possible to resolve these troubles, the nuclear power industry...cannot support the transition to a renewable energy system. Present...reactors are fueled with natural uranium, and can operate only as long as this fuel is available at some reasonable cost. But natural uranium is a nonrenewable fuel and...would be exhausted...in about twenty-five to thirty years. Nuclear power can sustain a renewable energy system...only if it is based on breeder reactors, in which the nuclear reaction is so arranged as to produce new fuel as the reactor generates power....But before that can happen, nuclear power will need to survive the growing challenge to both its economic and its political viability.

Source: From *The Politics of Energy* by Barry Commoner, copyright © 1979 by Barry Commoner. Used by permission of Alfred A. Knopf, a division of Random House, Inc.

Document 16.6 **Citizens' Group Challenges the Nuclear Regulatory Commission's Fact Sheet on the Accident at Three Mile Island, 2004**

Within hours of the accident at the Three Mile Island Nuclear Power Plant near Harrisburg, Pennsylvania, debate began over exactly what happened inside the plant and the danger to public health. The most contentious argument was that between officials of the Nuclear Regulatory Commission (NRC, formerly the Atomic Energy Commission) and Three Mile Island Alert (TMIA), a citizens' group that had organized in the mid-1970s to monitor the safety of the plant and possible dangers to public health. The debate continues more than a quarter-century later. Here are excerpts of the NRC Fact Sheet, interspersed with the response from TMIA.

SUMMARY OF EVENTS

NRC: The accident began about 4:00 a.m. on March 28, 1979, when the plant experienced a failure in the secondary, non-nuclear section of the plant. The main feedwater pumps stopped running, caused by either a mechanical or electrical failure, which prevented the steam generators from removing heat.

TMIA: The problems did not start with the feedwater pumps, trouble began in the condensate polisher system....No one knows why the accident began to this day.

NRC: Signals available to the operator failed to show that the valve was still open. As a result, cooling water poured out of the stuck-open valve and caused the core of the reactor to overheat.

TMIA: Because TMI had been falsifying reactor leak rates to the NRC in the weeks leading to the accident, operators had learned to ignore the most obvious sign that the [valve] had stuck open and that coolant was being lost through this pathway....operators

had become accustomed to this anomaly because of the criminal falsification which al-
lowed this condition to exist for several weeks. **It should be noted that if the company**
had operated lawfully, the plant would have been shut down for repairs and
there would have been no accident on March 28ᵗʰ 1979 *(emphasis TMIA's).*

It is also noteworthy that NRC inspectors at TMI during the weeks before the
accident failed to find or note the reactor coolant leak. Later, the company pleaded "no
contest" to federal charges of criminal falsifications. On May 22, 1979, former control
room operator Harold W. Hartman, Jr. tells the NRC investigators that Metropolitan
Edison-General Public Utilities had been falsifying primary-coolant, leak rate data for
months prior to the accident.

NRC: In a worst-case accident, the melting of nuclear fuel would lead to a
breach of the walls of the containment building and release massive quantities
of radiation to the environment. But this did not occur as a result of the Three
Mile Island accident.

TMIA: It was only by luck that the reactor walls were not breached. The industry
conjectured that voids in the coolant prevented molten fuel from burning through the
reactor walls. It is not known if these voids will form to prevent a total meltdown in
future accidents. Fifteen million curies of radiation is a "massive quantity."

NRC: In an atmosphere of growing uncertainty about the condition of the
plant, the governor of Pennsylvania, Richard L. Thornburgh, consulted with the
NRC about evacuating the population near the plant. Eventually, he and NRC
Chairman Joseph Hendrie agreed that it would be prudent for those members
of society most vulnerable to radiation to evacuate the area. Thornburgh announced that he was advising pregnant women and pre-school-age children
within a 5-mile radius of the plant to leave the area.

TMIA: The NRC's agreed upon conditions of a reactor, which would require
evacuation of nearby communities had already been met two days earlier on Wednesday
the 28ᵗʰ. Governor Thornburgh complained about the conflicting and confusing data
coming from the plant and the NRC.

NRC: In the months following the accident, although questions were raised
about possible adverse effects from radiation on human, animal, and plant life
in the TMI area, none could be directly correlated to the accident. Thousands of
environmental samples of air, water, milk, vegetation, soil, and foodstuffs were
collected by various groups monitoring the area. Very low levels of radionu-
clides could be attributed to releases from the accident. However, comprehensive investigations and assessments by several well-respected organizations
have concluded that in spite of serious damage to the reactor, most of the
radiation was contained and that the actual release had negligible effects on the
physical health of individuals or the environment.

TMIA: In August 1996, a study by the University of North Carolina-Chapel Hill,
authored by Dr. Steven Wing, reviewed the Susser-hatch Study (Columbia University,
1991). Dr. Wing reported that ". . . there were reports of erythema, hair loss, vomiting,
and pet death near TMI at the time of the accident. . . . Accident doses were positively
associated with cancer incidence. Associations were largest for leukemia, intermediate for
lung cancer, and smallest for all cancers combined. . . . Inhaled radionuclide contamina-
tion could differentially impact lung cancers, which show a clear dose-related increase.

Findings from the re-analysis of cancer incidence around Three Mile Island is
consistent with the theory that radiation from the accident increased cancer in areas

that were in the path of radioactive plumes. "This cancer increase would not be expected to occur over a short time in the general population unless doses were far higher than estimated by industry and government authorities," Wing said. "Rather, our findings support the allegation that the people who reported rashes, hair loss, vomiting, and pet deaths after the accident were exposed to high level radiation and not only suffering from emotional stress."

NRC: The accident was caused by a combination of personnel error, design deficiencies, and component failures.

TMIA: Also add to the list: criminal activity, the NRC's failure to disseminate safety data, NRC inspection and enforcement failures, failure to fix problems noted by control room operators, sloppy control room housekeeping and economic gain placed above safety.

Source: Three Mile Island Alert (TMIA) (Harrisburg, PA, 2004) http://www.tmia.com/accident/whatswrong.html. TMIA refers to the United States Nuclear Regulatory Commission Fact Sheet, available at http://www.tmia.com/accident/NRCFactSheet.pdf (retrieved August 5, 2004).

Document 16.7   President Reagan Celebrates Deregulated Energy Production

---

President Ronald Reagan delivered the following speech at the opening ceremonies for the International Energy Exposition in Knoxville, Tennessee, May 1, 1982. With renewed energy supplies and falling prices, the issue had faded from the public agenda. Despite a failure to revive the nuclear industry following the TMI accident, two years into his presidency, Reagan could speak of the triumph of bullish energy production at home and abroad. Although he trumpeted the virtues of American technological genius, more prominent and featured in this excerpt is the old-fashioned production of fossil fuels and laissez faire deregulation of industry (as he notes)—the twin pillars of his energy policy.

The theme of this fair, "Energy Turns the World," is appropriate for this decade, as our nation and many of our allies struggle to produce and use energy efficiently—to provide for our energy security....

Here in America, in this administration, our national energy policy dictates that one of the government's chief energy roles is to guard against sudden interruptions of energy supplies. In the past, we tried to manage a shortage by interfering with the market process. The results were gas lines, bottlenecks, and bureaucracy. A newly created Department of Energy passed more regulations, hired more bureaucrats, raised taxes, and spent much more money, and it didn't produce a single drop of oil. In fact, American oil production continued to decline....

Already we have dramatically increased our Strategic Petroleum Reserve. Instead of managing scarcity, we'll help ensure continued supplies from a strategic stockpile, alleviating shortages while permitting the private market to work.

Our stockpile . . . is now one of the largest in the world—more than a quarter billion barrels. . . . Last year, this reserve has been stocked with more than twice as much oil as was accumulated in the preceding 4 years. We will increase it to nearly three times our current supply as a symbol to our allies of our resolve to reduce our vulnerability. We will ensure that our people and our economy are never again held hostage by the whim of any country or cartel. . . .

But we can't afford to be complacent. Our energy appetite means our energy production must be allowed to keep pace.

In the last year, our oil production in the lower 48 States ended its decades-long decline. . . . What caused this turnaround? The same principle responsible for most of the prosperity, production, and progress in the world today: free enterprise.

Our economic and energy problems were in large part caused by government excesses and quick fixes, not by a basic scarcity of supply. . . . But if America is to provide for her energy security, if we're to continue growing more self-reliant, . . . we must press toward the ultimate solution to our energy problems: the decontrol of all of our energy sources. . . .

Within our boundaries and just off our shores, experts estimate that compared to our current reserves, three times as much oil and gas are yet to be discovered. We're also blessed with a quarter of the free world's coal and uranium resources. . . .

We still have to depend on practical sources available today, such as nuclear power, which now produces more of America's electricity than oil. The Clinch River reactor, which will use new breeder technology, and the Oak Ridge National Laboratory, not far from here, symbolize our commitment to developing safe nuclear energy and technology to secure our energy future.

Our Secretary of Energy . . . tells the story about the time in his home State of South Carolina he spotted a car bearing a bumper sticker, "Split wood, not atoms." Well, he said he didn't think the fellow driving the car had ever split much wood . . . because it isn't very easy. I can testify to that. But Jim said he wanted to tell him that America must split both atoms and wood. It'll take the use of many technologies to satisfy our future energy demands.

Source: President Ronald Wilson Reagan, "Remarks at the Opening Ceremonies for the Knoxville International Energy Exposition (World's Fair) in Tennessee," May 1, 1982. Available at the Ronald Reagan Presidential Library Web site: http://www.reagan .utexas.edu/archives/speeches/1982/50182d.htm (accessed August 9, 2004).

NOTES

1. For an incisive analysis of this history, see Amory B. Lovins and L. Huner Lovins, "Mobilizing Energy Solutions," *American Prospect* (January 28, 2002), www.prospect.org/print/V13/2/lovins-a.html (accessed July 22, 2004).

2. "Timeline of Official Statements," *Harrisburg Patriot-News*, March 30, 1979, p. 12.

ANNOTATED BIBLIOGRAPHY

Deffeyes, Kenneth S. *Hubbert's Peak: The Impending World Oil Shortage*. Princeton: Princeton University Press, 2003. Oil industry veteran and geologist Deffeyes predicts that global production of oil will peak between 2004 and 2008 (the historical moment of "peak oil"), after which point it will continue to slide downward toward the end of the petroleum era, with grave ramifications for those nations unprepared.

Gray, Mike, and Ira Rosen. *The Warning: Accident at Three Mile Island: A Nuclear Omen for the Age of Terror.* 1982. Reprint, New York: W. W. Norton, 2003. Based partly on interviews with key operating personnel, this book is still worth reading more than a generation after its initial publication. Reprint illuminates the significance of TMI in a post–9/11 context, offering insightful discussion of nuclear energy, the environment, and renewable energy technologies in the context of the threat of terrorism.

Heinberg, Richard. *The Party's Over: Oil, War and the Fate of Industrial Societies.* Gabriola Island, BC: New Society, 2003. Places the energy crises of the past thirty years in historical and geopolitical context. Argues that competition for diminishing supplies of energy in the twenty-first century is already fomenting resource wars around the world and makes the case that as the most voracious and inefficient consumer of oil, the U.S. must accelerate development of renewable energy technologies.

Horowitz, Daniel, ed. *Jimmy Carter and the Energy Crisis of the 1970s: The "Crisis of Confidence" Speech of July 15, 1979.* New York: Bedford/St. Martin's Press, 2005. A wide range of documents deftly edited reveals much about administration decision-making, the broader national debate over energy in the 1970s, as well as the links between American economic and foreign policy that are very much still with us.

Leggett, Jeremy. *Carbon War: Global Warming and the End of the Oil Era.* New York: Routledge Press, 2001. Leggett adds the additional urgency of meeting the challenge of global warming as one more reason to accelerate development of renewable energy technologies.

Nye, David. *Consuming Power: A Social History of American Energies.* Cambridge, MA: MIT Press, 1999. An ambitious and generally successful attempt to demonstrate how the United States became the world's largest consumer of energy. His analysis unravels the ways in which culture and technology unwittingly conspired to entangle Americans in a voraciously energy-dependent, consumer-driven lifestyle.

Osif, Bonnie A., Anthony J. Baratta, and Thomas W. Conkling. *TMI 25 Years Later: The Three Mile Island Nuclear Power Plant Accident and Its Impact.* University Park: Pennsylvania State University Press, 2004. More independent and objective view of the event than Walker's NRC history. Comprehensive, well-documented, and multi-angled view that addresses a number of issues related to the accident, including health effects, the role of the media, impacts upon industry, regulatory agencies, and the environment. It also discusses the broader role of nuclear power in meeting national energy needs.

Roberts, Paul. *The End of Oil: On the Edge of a Perilous New World.* New York: Houghton Mifflin, 2004. An alarming and thoroughly convincing analysis of the political and economic ramifications of the historical moment known as "peak oil" reached early in the twenty-first century.

Smil, Vaclav. *Energy at the Crossroads: Global Perspectives and Uncertainties.* Cambridge, MA: MIT Press, 2003. A thorough but generally optimistic overview of long-term trends in energy production, includes extensive discussions of the profound impact of energy—its supply, pricing, and production—on the U.S. and global economy and on the environment.

Walker, Samuel J. *Three Mile Island: A Nuclear Crisis in Historical Perspective.* Berkeley: University of California Press, 2004. A solid administrative, albeit defensive history of the Three Mile Island accident written by the official historian of the Nuclear Regulatory Commission.

Selected Bibliography

Abelson, Philip H., ed. *Food: Politics, Economics, Nutrition, and Research*. Washington, DC: American Association for the Advancement of Science, 1975.

Aduddell, Robert, and Louis P. Cain. "Location and Collusion in the Meat Packing Industry." In *Business Enterprise and Economic Change*, edited by Louis P. Cain and Paul J. Uselding. Kent, OH: Kent State University Press, 1973.

Andrews, Richard N. L. *Managing the Environment, Managing Ourselves: A History of American Environmental Policy*. New Haven: Yale University Press, 1999.

Armstrong, Ellis L., Michael C. Robinson, and Suellen Hoy, eds. *History of Public Works in the United States, 1776–1976*. Chicago: American Public Works Association, 1976.

Arnould, Richard J. "Changing Patterns of Concentration in American Meat Packing, 1880–1963." *Business History Review* 45 (Spring 1971): 18–34.

Ashworth, William. *The Carson Factor*. New York: Hawthorn Books, 1979.

———. *The Late, Great Lakes: An Environmental History*. New York: Alfred A. Knopf, 1986.

Barsness, Larry. *Heads, Hides & Horns: The Compleat Buffalo Book*. Fort Worth: Texas Christian University Press, 1985.

Belue, Ted Franklin. *The Long Hunt: Death of the Buffalo East of the Mississippi*. Mechanicsburg, PA: Stackpole Books, 1996.

Bernstein, Steven. "The Rise of Air Pollution as a National Political Issue: A Study of Issue Development." Ph.D. diss., Auburn University, 1984.

Blumberg, Louis, and Robert Gottlieb. *War on Waste: Can America Win Its Battle with Garbage?* Washington, DC: Island Press, 1989.

Bogue, Margaret Beattie. *Fishing the Great Lakes: An Environmental History, 1783–1933*. Madison: University of Wisconsin Press, 2000.

Bonnifield, Paul. *The Dust Bowl: Men, Dirt, and Depression*. Albuquerque: University of New Mexico Press, 1979.

Boubel, Richard W., Donald L. Fox, D. Bruce Turner, and Arthur C. Stern. *Fundamentals of Air Pollution*. 3rd ed. London: Academic Press, 1994.

Box, Thadis. "Range Deterioration in West Texas." *Southwestern Historical Quarterly* 71 (1967–1968): 37–45.

Brant, Irving. *Adventures in Conservation with Franklin D. Roosevelt*. Flagstaff, AZ: Northland, 1989.

Brasch, Walter M. *Forerunners of Revolution: Muckrakers and the American Social Conscience*. Lanham, MD: University Press of America, 1990.

Brechin, Gary A. *Imperial San Francisco: Urban Power, Earthly Ruin*. Berkeley: University of California Press, 2001.

Breen, T. H. *Tobacco Culture: The Mentality of the Great Tidewater Planters on the Eve of Revolution*. Princeton: Princeton University Press, 1985.

Brimblecombe, Peter. *The Big Smoke: A History of Air Pollution*. New York: Taylor and Francis Group, 1989.

Brown, Alan S. "Caroline Bartlett Crane and Urban Reform," In *Michigan Perspectives: People, Events, and Issues*, edited by Alan S. Brown, John T. Houdek, and John H. Yzenbaard. Dubuque, IA: Kendall/Hunt, 1974, pp. 167–78.

Buell, Lawrence. *The Environmental Imagination: Thoreau, Nature Writing, and the Formation of American Culture*. Cambridge, MA: Harvard University Press, 1995.

Bullard, Robert. *Dumping in Dixie: Race, Class, and Environmental Quality*. Boulder, CO: Westview Press, 2000.

———, ed. *Unequal Protection: Environmental Justice and Communities of Color*. San Francisco: Sierra Club Books, 1994.

Burgess, Bonnie B. *Fate of the Wild: The Endangered Species Act and the Future of Biodiversity*. Athens: University of Georgia Press, 2001.

Burns, John F. *Taming the Elephant: Politics, Government, and Law in Pioneer California*. San Francisco: University of California Press, 2003.

Callenbach, Ernest. *Bring Back the Buffalo! A Sustainable Future for America's Great Plains*. Washington, DC: Island Press, 1996.

Calloway, Colin G. *New Worlds for All: Indians, Europeans, and the Remaking of Early America*. Baltimore: Johns Hopkins University Press, 1997.

Camacho, David E., ed. *Environmental Injustices, Political Struggles: Race, Class, and the Environment*. Durham, NC: Duke University Press, 1998.

Carr, Donald E. *The Breath of Life*. New York: W. W. Norton, 1965.

Carson, Rachel. *Silent Spring*. 1962. Reprint, Boston: Houghton Mifflin, 1987.

Caudill, Harry M. *My Land Is Dying*. New York: E. P. Dutton, 1971.

———. *Night Comes to the Cumberlands*. Boston: Atlantic Monthly Press, 1962.

Chase, Alston. *In a Dark Wood: The Fight over Forests and the Rising Tyranny of Ecology*. Boston: Houghton Mifflin, 1995.

Clark, Christopher. *The Roots of Rural Capitalism: Western Massachusetts, 1780–1860*. Ithaca, NY: Cornell University Press, 1990.

Clark, Tim W., Richard P. Reading, and Alice L. Clarke, eds. *Endangered Species Recovery: Finding the Lessons, Improving the Process*. Washington, DC: Island Press, 1994.

Clarke, Robert. *Ellen Swallow: The Woman Who Founded Ecology*. Chicago: Follett, 1973.

Clements, Kendrick A. *Hoover, Conservation, and Consumerism: Engineering the Good Life*. Lawrence: University Press of Kansas, 2000.

———. "Politics and the Park: San Francisco's Fight for Hetch Hetchy, 1908–1913." *Pacific Historical Review* 48 (1979): 184–215.

Cockburn, Alexander. "A Short, Meat-Oriented History of the World. From Eden to the Mattole." *New Left Review* 215 (January/February 1996): 16–42.

Cohen, Michael P. *The History of the Sierra Club, 1892–1977*. San Francisco: Sierra Club Books, 1988.

———. *The Pathless Way: John Muir and the American Wilderness*. Madison: University of Wisconsin Press, 1984.

Colburn, Theo, Dianne Dumanoski, and John P. Meyers. *Our Stolen Future: How We Are Threatening Our Fertility, Intelligence and Survival—A Scientific Detective Story*. New York: Plume Books, 1997.

Colten, Craig E., and Peter N. Skinner. *The Road to Love Canal: Managing Industrial Waste before EPA*. Austin: University of Texas Press, 1996.

Commoner, Barry. *The Closing Circle: Nature, Man and Technology*. New York: Alfred A. Knopf, 1971.

Corn, Jacqueline K. *Responses to Occupational Health Hazards: A Historical Perspective*. New York: Van Nostrand Rienhold, 1992.

Cowdrey, Albert E. *This Land, This South: An Environmental History*. Rev. ed. Lexington: University Press of Kentucky, 1996.

Cox, Thomas R., Robert S. Maxwell, Phillip D. Thomas, and Joseph J. Malone. *This Well-Wooded Land: Americans and Their Forests from Colonial Times to the Present*. Lincoln: University of Nebraska Press, 1985.

Crane, Caroline Bartlett. *Everyman's House*. Garden City, NY: Doubleday, Page, 1925.

Cronon, William. *Changes in the Land: Indians, Colonists, and the Ecology of New England*. New York: Hill and Wang, 1983; reprinted 2003.

———. *Nature's Metropolis: Chicago and the Great West*. New York: W. W. Norton, 1992.

———, ed. *Uncommon Ground: Rethinking the Human Place in Nature*. New York: W. W. Norton, 1996.

Crosby, Alfred W., Jr. *The Columbian Exchange: Biological and Cultural Consequences of 1492*. Westport, CT: Greenwood Press, 1972.

———. *Ecological Imperialism: The Biological Expansion of Europe, 900–1900*. New York: Cambridge University Press, 1986.

Cumbler, John T. "The Early Making of an Environmental Consciousness: Fish, Fisheries Commissions, and the Connecticut River." *Environmental History Review* 15 (Winter 1991): 73–91.

———. *Reasonable Use: The People, the Environment, and the State, New England 1790–1930*. New York: Oxford University Press, 2001.

Czech, Brian, and Paul R. Krausman. *The Endangered Species Act: History, Conservation Biology, and Public Policy*. Baltimore: Johns Hopkins University Press, 2001.

D'Antonio, Michael. *Atomic Harvest: Hanford and the Lethal Toll of America's Nuclear Arsenal*. New York: Crown, 1993.

Dary, David. *The Buffalo Book: The Full Saga of the American Animal*. Athens, OH: Swallow Press, 1990.

Dasmann, Raymond. *The Destruction of California*. New York: Macmillan, 1965.

Davis, Devra. *When Smoke Ran like Water: Tales of Environmental Deception and the Battle against Pollution*. New York: Basic Books, 2002.

Davis, Donald Edward. *Where There Are Mountains: An Environmental History of the Southern Appalachians*. Athens: University of Georgia Press, 2000.

Davis, Richard C., ed. *Encyclopedia of American Forest and Conservation History*. 2 vols. New York: Macmillan, 1983.

Dawson, Robert, and Gary Brechin. *Farewell, Promised Land: Waking from the California Dream*. Berkeley: University of California Press, 1999.

DeBuys, William. *Salt Dreams: Land and Water in Low-Down California*. Albuquerque: University of New Mexico Press, 1999.

———. *Seeing Things Whole: The Essential John Wesley Powell*. Washington, DC: Shearwater Books/Island Press, 2001.

Deffeyes, Kenneth S. *Hubbert's Peak: The Impending World Oil Shortage*. Princeton: Princeton University Press, 2003.

Dewey, Scott H. *Don't Breathe the Air: Air Pollution and U.S. Environmental Politics, 1945–1970*. College Station: Texas A & M University Press, 2000.

Diamond, Jared. *Collapse: How Societies Choose to Fail or Succeed*. New York: Viking Press, 2004.

———. *Guns, Germs, and Steel: The Fate of Human Societies*. New York: W. W. Norton, 1997.

Dietrich, William. *The Final Forest: The Battle for the Last Great Trees of the Pacific Northwest*. New York: Simon and Schuster, 1992.

Donahue, Brian. "'Dammed at Both Ends and Cursed in the Middle': The 'Flowage' of the Concord River Meadows, 1798–1862." *Environmental Review* 13 (Fall/Winter 1989): 47–67.

———. *The Great Meadow: Farmers and the Land in Colonial Concord*. New Haven: Yale University Press, 2004.

———. "Plowland, Pastureland, Woodland and Meadow: Husbandry in Concord, Massachusetts, 1635–1771." Ph.D. diss., Brandeis University, 1995.

Dowie, Mark. *Losing Ground: American Environmentalism at the Close of the Twentieth Century*. Cambridge, MA: MIT Press, 1995.

Dunlap, Thomas. *DDT: Scientists, Citizens, and Public Policy*. Princeton: Princeton University Press, 1983.

———. *Saving America's Wildlife: Ecology and the American Mind, 1850–1990*. 1988. Reprint, Princeton: Princeton University Press, 1991.

———. "Wildlife, Science, and the National Parks, 1920–1940." *Pacific Historical Review* 59 (May 1990): 187–202.

Dyal, Donald H. "Mormon Pursuit of the Agrarian Ideal." *Agricultural History* 63 (Fall 1989): 19–35.

Earle, Carville. *Geographical Inquiry and American Historical Problems*. Stanford, CA: Stanford University Press, 1992.

Easterbrook, Gregg. *A Moment on the Earth: The Coming Age of Environmental Optimism*. New York: Viking Press, 1995.

Echeverria, John, and Raymond Booth Eby. *Let the People Judge: Wise Use and the Private Property Rights Movement*. Washington, DC: Island Press, 1995.

Ehrlich, Paul, and Anne Ehrlich. *Extinction: The Causes and Consequences of the Disappearance of Species*. New York: Ballantine Books, 1985.

Ekirch, Arthur A. *Man and Nature in America*. New York: Columbia University Press, 1963.

Ely, S. B. "Air Pollution in Pittsburgh." *AMA Archives of Industrial Hygiene and Occupational Medicine* 3 (January 1951): 44–47.

Evenden, Matthew D. *Fish Versus Power: An Environmental History of the Fraser River*. New York: Cambridge University Press, 2004.

Fausold, Martin L. *Gifford Pinchot: Bull Moose Progressive*. Syracuse, NY: Syracuse University Press, 1961.

Ferriss, Susan, and Ricardo Sandoval. *The Fight in the Fields: Cesar Chavez and the Farmworkers Movement*. San Diego, CA: Harvest/HBJ Books, 1998.

Flader, Susan L. *Thinking like a Mountain: Aldo Leopold and the Evolution of an Ecological Attitude toward Deer, Wolves, and Forests*. Columbia: University of Missouri Press, 1974.

Flagg, Samuel B. *1912 City Smoke Ordinances and Smoke Abatement*, Bulletin 49. U.S. Bureau of Mines. Washington, DC: Government Printing Office, 1912.

Flannery, Tim. *The Eternal Frontier: An Ecological History of North America and Its Peoples*. New York: Atlantic Monthly Press, 2001.

Flippen, J. Brooks. *Nixon and the Environment*. Albuquerque: University of New Mexico Press, 2000.

Fox, Stephen. *The American Conservation Movement: John Muir and His Legacy*. Madison: University of Wisconsin Press, 1986.

Fradkin, Philip L. *A River No More: The Colorado River and the West*. Tucson: University of Arizona Press, 1984.

Frankel, Noralee, and Nancy S. Dye, eds. *Gender, Class, Race, and Reform in the Progressive Era*. Lexington: University Press of Kentucky, 1995.

Frazier, Ian. *Great Plains*. New York: Farrar, Straus, and Giroux, 1989.

Freeze, R. Allan. *The Environmental Pendulum: A Quest for the Truth about Toxic Chemicals, Human Health, and Environmental Protection*. Berkeley: University of California Press, 2000.

Freund, Peter, and George Martin. *The Ecology of the Automobile*. Montreal: Black Rose, 1993.

Geist, Valerius. *Buffalo Nation: History and Legend of the North American Bison*. Stillwater, MN: Voyageur Press, 1998.

Gelbspan, Ross. *The Heat Is On: The High Stakes Battle over Earth's Threatened Climate*. Reading, MA: Addison-Wesley, 1997.

Gibbs, Lois Marie. *Dying from Dioxin: A Citizen's Guide to Reclaiming Our Health and Rebuilding Democracy*. Cambridge, MA: South End Press, 1995.

———. *Love Canal: The Story Continues*. 1982. Rev. ed. Stony Creek, CT: New Society, 1998.

Gilbert, Bil. *God Gave Us This Country: Tekamthi and the First American Civil War*. New York: Scribner, 1989.

Gordon, Deborah. *Steering a New Course: Transportation, Energy, and the Environment*. Washington, DC: Island Press, 1991.

Gottlieb, Robert. *Forcing the Spring: The Transformation of the American Environmental Movement*. Rev. ed. Washington, DC: Island Press, 2005.

Gray, Mike, and Ira Rosen. *The Warning: Accident at Three Mile Island: A Nuclear Omen for the Age of Terror*. 1982. Reprint, New York: W. W. Norton, 2003.

Griffen, Keith. *The Political Economy of Agrarian Change: An Essay on the Green Revolution*. London: Macmillan, 1974.

Griffiths, Tom, and Libby Robin. *Ecology and Empire: Environmental History of Settler Societies*. Seattle: University of Washington Press, 1998.

Grinde, Donald A. *Ecocide of Native America: Environmental Destruction of Indian Lands and Peoples*. Santa Fe, NM: Clear Light Books, 1998.

Gutierrez, Ramon A. *Contested Eden: California before the Gold Rush*. San Francisco: California Historical Society, 1998.

———. *When Jesus Came, the Corn Mothers Went Away*. Stanford, CA: Stanford University Press, 1991.

Hahn, Steven. "Hunting, Fishing, and Foraging: Common Rights and Class Relations in the Post-Bellum South." *Radical History Review* 26 (October 1982): 37–64.

———. *The Roots of Southern Populism: Yeoman Farmers and the Transformation of the Georgia Up-Country, 1850–1890*. New York: Oxford University Press, 1983.

Hahn, Steven, and Jonathan Prude, eds. *The Countryside in the Age of Capitalist Transformation*. Chapel Hill: University of North Carolina Press, 1985.

Haines, Frances. *The Buffalo*. Norman: University of Oklahoma Press, 1995.

Halliday, E. C. *An Historical Review of Atmospheric Pollution*. New York: World Health Organization, 1961.

Hallock, Thomas. *From the Fallen Tree: Frontier Narratives, Environmental Politics, and the Roots of a National Pastoral, 1749–1826*. Chapel Hill: University of North Carolina Press, 2003.

Hamilton, Alice. *Exploring the Dangerous Trades: The Autobiography of Alice Hamilton*. 1943. Reprinted with an introduction by Jean Spencer Felton. Boston: Northeastern University Press, 1985.

Hardy, Charles. "Fish or Foul: A History of the Delaware River Basin through the Perspective of the American Shad, 1682 to the Present." *Pennsylvania History* 66 (Autumn 1999): 506–34.

Harvey, Mark W. T. *A Symbol of Wilderness: Echo Park and the American Conservation Movement.* Albuquerque: University of New Mexico Press, 1994.

Hays, Samuel P. *Beauty, Health, and Permanence: Environmental Politics in the United States, 1955–1985.* New York: Cambridge University Press, 1989.

———. *Conservation and the Gospel of Efficiency: The Progressive Conservation Movement, 1890–1920.* Cambridge, MA: Harvard University Press, 1959.

———. *A History of Environmental Politics since 1945.* Pittsburgh, PA: University of Pittsburgh Press, 2000.

Heinberg, Richard. *The Party's Over: Oil, War and the Fate of Industrial Societies.* Gabriola Island, BC: New Society, 2003.

Heizer, Robert Fleming. *The Destruction of California Indians: A Collection of Documents from the Period 1847 to 1865 in which Are Described Some of the Things that Happened.* Lincoln: University of Nebraska Press, 1993.

Helms, Douglas. "Conserving the Plains: The Soil Conservation Service in the Great Plains." *Agricultural History* 64 (Spring 1990): 58–73.

Helvarg, David. *The War against the Greens: The "Wise-Use" Movement, the New Right, and Anti-Environmental Violence.* San Francisco: Sierra Club Books, 1997.

Hill, Mary. *Gold: The California Story.* Berkeley: University of California Press, 1999.

Hirt, Paul W. *A Conspiracy of Optimism: Management of the National Forests since World War II.* Lincoln: University of Nebraska Press, 1994.

Hofrichter, Richard, ed. *Toxic Struggles: The Theory and Practice of Environmental Justice.* Salt Lake City: University of Utah Press, 2002.

Holliday, James S. *Rush for Riches: Gold Fever and the Making of California.* Berkeley: University of California Press, 1999.

Hornaday, William T. *Our Vanishing Wildlife: Its Extermination and Preservation.* New York: Charles Scribner's Sons, 1913.

Horowitz, Daniel, ed. *Jimmy Carter and the Energy Crisis of the 1970s: The "Crisis of Confidence" Speech of July 15, 1979.* New York: Bedford/St. Martin's Press, 2005.

Hoy, Suellen. *Chasing Dirt: The American Pursuit of Cleanliness.* New York: Oxford University Press, 1996.

Hundley, Norris, Jr. *The Great Thirst: Californians and Water—A History.* Rev. ed. Berkeley: University of California Press, 2001.

Hurley, Andrew, ed. *Common Fields: An Environmental History of St. Louis.* St. Louis: Missouri Historical Society, 1997.

Hurt, R. Douglas. *The Dust Bowl: An Agricultural and Social History.* Chicago: Nelson-Hall, 1981.

Huth, Hans. *Nature and the American: Three Centuries of Changing Attitudes.* Rev. ed. Lincoln: University of Nebraska Press, 1991.

Isenberg, Andrew C. *The Destruction of the Bison: An Environmental History, 1750–1920.* New York: Cambridge University Press, 2000.

———. *Mining California: An Ecological History.* New York: Hill and Wang, 2005.

Iverson, Peter. *When Indians Became Cowboys: Native Peoples and Cattle Ranching in the American West.* Norman: University of Oklahoma Press, 1994.

Jackson, Kenneth T. *Crabgrass Frontier: The Suburbanization of the United States.* New York: Oxford University Press, 1985.

Jacoby, Karl. *Crimes against Nature: Squatters, Poachers, Thieves, and the Hidden History of American Conservation.* Berkeley: University of California Press, 2001.

Jenkins, Virginia. *The Lawn: A History of an American Obsession.* Washington, DC: Smithsonian Institution Press, 1994.

Jennings, Francis. *The Invasion of America: Indians, Colonialism, and the Cant of Conquest*. New York: W. W. Norton, 1976.

Johnson, Hildegard Binder. *Order upon the Land: The U.S. Rectangular Land Survey and the Upper Mississippi Country*. New York: Oxford University Press, 1976.

Johnson, Stephen, Robert Dawson, and Gerald Haslam. *The Great Central Valley: California's Heartland*. Berkeley: University of California Press, 1993.

Jones, Holway. *John Muir and the Sierra Club: The Battle for Yosemite*. San Francisco: Sierra Club Books, 1965.

Judd, Richard W. *Common Lands, Common People: The Origins of Conservation in Northern New England*. Cambridge: Harvard University Press, 2000.

Keiter, Robert B., and Mark S. Boyce. *The Greater Yellowstone Ecosystem: Redefining America's Wilderness Heritage*. New Haven: Yale University Press, 1991.

Kelley, Robert. *Gold vs. Grain: The Hydraulic Mining Controversy in California's Sacramento Valley*. Glendale, CA: Arthur H. Clark, 1959.

Kovarik, William Joseph. "The Ethyl Controversy: The News Media and the Public Health Debate over Leaded Gasoline, 1924–1926." Ph.D. diss., University of Maryland, College Park, 1993.

Krech, Shepard, III. *The Ecological Indian: Myth and History*. New York: W. W. Norton, 1999.

Kuletz, Valerie L. *The Tainted Desert: Environmental and Social Ruin in the American West*. New York: Routledge, 1998.

Kutzler, Charles A. "American Myth: Can Forests Bring Rain to the Plains?" *Journal of Forest History* 15 (October 1971): 14–21.

Langston, Nancy. *Forest Dreams, Forest Nightmares: The Paradox of Old Growth in the Inland West*. Seattle: University of Washington Press, 1995.

Lappe, Marc, and Britt Bailey. *Against the Grain: Biotechnology and the Corporate Takeover of Your Food*. Monroe, ME: Common Courage Press, 1998.

Lear, Linda. *Rachel Carson: Witness for Nature*. New York: Henry Holt, 1998.

Leavitt, Judith Walzer, ed. *Women and Health in America: Historical Readings*. Madison: University of Wisconsin Press, 1999.

Leggett, Jeremy. *Carbon War: Global Warming and the End of the Oil Era*. New York: Routledge Press, 2001.

Levy, Jacques. *Cesar Chavez: Autobiography of La Causa*. 1969. Reprint, New York: W. W. Norton, 1975.

Lewis, David L., and Laurence Goldstein, eds. *The Automobile and American Culture*. Ann Arbor: University of Michigan Press, 1983.

Limerick, Patricia. *The Legacy of Conquest: The Unbroken Past of the American West*. NewYork: W. W. Norton, 1987.

Linklater, Andro. *Measuring America: How an Untamed Wilderness Shaped the United States and Fulfilled the Promise of Democracy*. New York: Walker, 2002.

Lomborg, Bjorn. *The Skeptical Environmentalist: Measuring the Real State of the World*. Cambridge: Cambridge University Press, 2001.

Lookingbill, Brad D. *Dust Bowl, USA: Depression America and the Ecological Imagination, 1929–1941*. Athens: Ohio University Press, 2001.

Lopez, Barry. *Of Wolves and Men*. New York: Scribner, 1979.

Low, Ann Marie. *Dust Bowl Diary*. Lincoln: University of Nebraska Press, 1984.

Lowenthal, David. *George Perkins Marsh: Prophet of Conservation*. Seattle: University of Washington Press, 2000.

MacGillivray, Alex. *Rachel Carson's Silent Spring: Words that Changed the World*. Hauppauge, NY: Barron's Education Series, 2004.

Magdoff, Fred, John B. Foster, and Frederick H. Buttel. *Hungry for Profit: The Agribusiness Threat to Farmers, Food, and the Environment*. New York: Monthly Review Press, 2000.

Magoc, Chris J., ed. *So Glorious a Landscape: Nature and the Environment in American History and Culture*. Wilmington, DE: Scholarly Resources, 2001.

———. *Yellowstone: The Creation and Selling of an American Landscape, 1870–1903*. Albuquerque: University of New Mexico Press, 1999.

Malin, James C. *The Grasslands of North America: Prolegomena to Its History*. 1947. Reprint, Gloucester, MA: Peter Smith, 1967.

———. *History and Ecology: Studies of the Grassland*. Edited by Robert P. Swierenga. Lincoln: University of Nebraska Press, 1984.

Manning, Richard. *Grassland: The History, Biology, Politics, and Promise of the American Prairie*. New York: Penguin, 1995.

Markowitz, Gerald, and David Rosner. *Deceit and Denial: The Deadly Politics of Industrial Pollution*. Berkeley: University of California Press, 2002.

Marsh, George Perkins. *Man and Nature*. 1864. Reprinted with a foreword by William Cronon and edited by David Lowenthal. Seattle: University of Washington Press, 2003.

Marshall, Suzanne. *"Lord We're Just Trying to Save Your Water": Environmental Activism and Dissent in the Appalachian South*. Gainesville: University Press of Florida, 2002.

Marston, Ed, ed. *Reopening the Western Frontier*. Washington, DC: Island Press, 1989.

Martin, Calvin. *Keepers of the Game: Indian-Animal Relationships and the Fur Trade*. Berkeley: University of California Press, 1978.

Martin, Russell. *A Story that Stands like a Dam: Glen Canyon and the Struggle for the Soul of the West*. 1989. Reprint, Salt Lake City: University of Utah Press, 1999.

Matthews, Anne. *Where the Buffalo Roam: Restoring America's Great Plains*. 2nd ed. Chicago: University of Chicago Press, 2002.

Matthiessen, Peter. *Sal Si Puedes: Cesar Chavez and the New American Revolution*. 1969. Reprint, Berkeley: University of California Press, 2000.

———. *Wildlife in America*. Rev. ed. New York: Penguin Books, 1984.

Mazur, Allan. *A Hazardous Inquiry: The Rashomon Effect at Love Canal*. Cambridge, MA: Harvard University Press, 1998.

McClelland, Peter D. *Sowing Modernity: America's First Agricultural Revolution*. Ithaca, NY: Cornell University Press, 1997.

McEvoy, Arthur F. *The Fisherman's Problem: Ecology and Law in the California Fisheries, 1850–1980*. New York: Cambridge University Press, 1986.

McHugh, Tom. *The Time of the Buffalo*. 1972. Reprint, Victoria, BC: Castle Books, 2004.

McIntyre, Rick, ed. *War against the Wolf: America's Campaign to Exterminate the Wolf*. Stillwater, MN: Voyageur Press, 1995.

McNamee, Thomas. *The Return of the Wolf to Yellowstone*. New York: Owl Books, 1998.

McNeill, John R. *Something New under the Sun: An Environmental History of the Twentieth-Century World*. New York: W. W. Norton, 2000.

Melosi, Martin V. *Coping with Abundance: Energy and Environment in Industrial America, 1820–1980*. Philadelphia: Temple University Press, 1985.

———. *Garbage in the Cities: Refuse, Reform, and the Environment, 1880–1980*. College Station: Texas A & M University Press, 1981.

———. *The Sanitary City: Urban Infrastructure in America from Colonial Times to the Present*. Baltimore: Johns Hopkins University Press, 2000.

———, ed. *Pollution and Reform in American Cities, 1870–1930*. Austin: University of Texas Press, 1980.

Merchant, Carolyn. *The Columbia Guide to American Environmental History*. New York: Columbia University Press, 2002.

———. *The Death of Nature: Women, Ecology, and the Scientific Revolution*. 1980. Reprint, San Francisco: Harper and Row, 1990.

————. *Ecological Revolutions: Nature, Gender, and Science in New England*. Chapel Hill: University of North Carolina Press, 1989.

————, ed. *Major Problems in American Environmental History: Documents and Essays*. Lexington, MA: D. C. Heath, 1993.

Mighetto, Lisa. *Wild Animals and American Environmental Ethics*. Tucson: University of Arizona Press, 1991.

Miller, Char. *Gifford Pinchot and the Making of Modern Environmentalism*. Washington, DC: Shearwater Books/Island Press, 2004.

Mitchell, Don. *The Lie of the Land: Migrant Workers and the California Landscape*. Minneapolis: University of Minnesota Press, 1996.

Morris, Edmund. *The Rise of Theodore Roosevelt*. New York: Coward, McCann, and Geoghegan, 1979.

Moses, Marion. *Harvest of Sorrow: Farm Workers and Pesticides*. San Francisco: Pesticide Education Center, 1992.

Muir, Diana. *Reflections in Bullough's Pond: Economy and Ecosystem in New England*. Hanover, NH: University Press of New England, 2000.

Muncy, Robyn. *Creating a Female Dominion in American Reform 1890–1935*. New York: Oxford University Press, 1994.

Murphy, Priscilla Coit. *What a Book Can Do: The Publication and Reception of Silent Spring*. Amherst: University of Massachusetts Press, 2005.

Nash, Roderick. *The Rights of Nature: A History of Environmental Ethics*. Madison: University of Wisconsin Press, 1989.

————. *Wilderness and the American Mind*. 4th ed. New Haven: Yale University Press, 2001.

Norwood, Vera. *Made from This Earth: American Women and Nature*. Chapel Hill: University of North Carolina Press, 1993.

Nye, David. *Consuming Power: A Social History of American Energies*. Cambridge, MA: MIT Press, 1999.

Onuf, Peter S. *Jefferson's Empire: The Language of American Nationhood*. Charlottesville: University of Virginia Press, 2000.

Opie, John. "100 Years of Climate Risk Assessment on the High Plains: Which Farm Paradigm Does Irrigation Serve?" *Agricultural History* 63 (Spring 1989): 243–69.

————. *The Law of the Land: Two Hundred Years of American Farmland Policy*. Lincoln: University of Nebraska Press, 1987.

————. *Nature's Nation: An Environmental History of the United States*. Fort Worth, TX: Harcourt Brace, 1998.

————. *Ogallala: Water for a Dry Land*. Lincoln: University of Nebraska Press, 1993.

Osif, Bonnie A., Anthony J. Baratta, and Thomas W. Conkling. *TMI 25 Years Later: The Three Mile Island Nuclear Power Plant Accident and Its Impact*. University Park: Pennsylvania State University Press, 2004.

Penick, James, Jr. *Progressive Politics and Conservation: The Ballinger-Pinchot Affair*. Chicago: University of Chicago Press, 1968.

Peterson, Shannon. "The Modern Ark: A History of the Endangered Species Act." Ph.D. diss., University of Wisconsin, Madison, 2000.

Petulla, Joseph M. *American Environmental History: The Exploitation and Conservation of Natural Resources*. Boston: Boyd and Fraser, 1988.

Pinchot, Gifford. *Breaking New Ground*. 1947. Commemorative edition. Washington, DC: Island Press, 1998. First published 1947 by Harcourt, Brace.

————. *The Fight for Conservation*. New York: Doubleday, Page, 1910.

Pisani, Donald J. *From the Family Farm to Agribusiness: The Irrigation Crusade in California, 1850–1931*. Berkeley: University of California Press, 1984.

————. *To Reclaim a Divided West: Water, Law, and Public Policy, 1848–1902*. Albuquerque: University of New Mexico Press, 1992.

———. *Water and American Government: The Reclamation Bureau, National Water Policy, and the West, 1902–1935*. Berkeley: University of California Press, 2002.

Powell, John Wesley. *The Arid Lands*. Rev. ed. With a foreword by Wallace Stegner. Lincoln, NE: Bison Books, 2004.

Pratt, Joseph A. "Letting the Grandchildren Do It: Environmental Planning during the Ascent of Oil as the Major Energy Source." *Public Historian* 2 (Fall 1980): 28–61.

Price, Jennifer. *Flight Maps: Adventures with Nature in Modern America*. New York: Basic Books, 2000.

Prude, Jonathan. *The Coming of Industrial Order: Town and Factory Life in Rural Massachusetts, 1810–1860*. Amherst: University of Massachusetts Press, 1985.

Rappaport, Roy. "The Flow of Energy in an Agricultural Society." In *Energy and Power*, edited by Dennis Flanagan et al. San Francisco: Freeman, 1971.

Rawls, James J. *A Golden State: Mining and Economic Development in Gold Rush California*. San Francisco: California Historical Society, 1999.

Reiger, John F. *American Sportsmen and the Origins of Conservation*. New York: Winchester Press, 1975.

Reisner, Marc. *Cadillac Desert: The American West and Its Disappearing Water*. 1986. Rev. ed. New York: Penguin Books, 1993.

Richardson, Elmo R. "The Struggle for the Valley: California's Hetch Hetchy Controversy, 1905–1913." *California Historical Society Quarterly* 38 (Autumn 1959): 249–58.

Richter, Daniel K. *Facing East from Indian Country: A Native History of Early America*. Cambridge, MA: Harvard University Press, 2003.

Rickard, O'Ryan. *A Just Verdict: The Life of Caroline Bartlett Crane*. Kalamazoo: Western Michigan University Press, 1994.

Riebsame, William E. "The Dust Bowl: Historical Image, Psychological Anchor, and Ecological Taboo." *Great Plains Quarterly* 6 (Spring 1986): 127–36.

Rifkin, Jeremy. *Beyond Beef: The Rise and Fall of the Cattle Culture*. New York: Plume Books, 1993.

Righter, Robert W. *The Battle over Hetch Hetchy: America's Most Controversial Dam and the Birth of Modern Environmentalism*. New York: Oxford University Press, 2005.

Roberts, Paul. *The End of Oil: On the Edge of a Perilous New World*. New York: Houghton Mifflin, 2004.

Robinson, Michael. *The Buffalo Hunters*. Abilene, TX: State House Press, 1995.

Rogin, Michael Paul. *Fathers and Children: Andrew Jackson and the Subjugation of the American Indian*. New York: Vintage Books, 1975.

Rohrbough, Malcolm J. *Days of Gold: The California Gold Rush and the American Nation*. Berkeley: University of California Press, 1997.

Rome, Adam. *The Bulldozer in the Countryside: Suburban Sprawl and the Rise of American Environmentalism*. New York: Cambridge University Press, 2001.

———. "Coming to Terms with Pollution: The Language of Environmental Reform, 1865–1915." *Geographical Review* 88 (April 1998): 259–74.

Rosenberg, Norman J. "Adaptations to Adversity: Agriculture, Climate and the Great Plains of North America." *Great Plains Quarterly* 6 (Summer 1986): 202–17.

Rosenkranz, Barbara Gutmann. *Public Health and the State: Changing Views in Massachusetts, 1842–1936*. Cambridge, MA: Harvard University Press, 1972.

Ross, Andrew. *Strange Weather: Culture, Science and Technology in the Age of Limits*. London: Verso, 1991.

Rothman, Hal K. *Devil's Bargains: Tourism in the Twentieth-Century American West*. Lawrence: University Press of Kansas, 1998.

Runte, Alfred. *Yosemite: The Embattled Wilderness*. 3rd ed. Lincoln, NE: Bison Books, 1997.

Russell, Edmund. *War and Nature: Fighting Humans and Insects with Chemicals from World War I to "Silent Spring."* New York: Cambridge University Press, 2001.

Rynbrandt, Linda J. *Caroline Bartlett Crane and Progressive Reform: Social Housekeeping as Sociology*. New York: Garland, 1998.

Sale, Kirkpatrick. *The Green Revolution: The American Environmental Movement, 1962–1992*. New York: Hill and Wang, 1993.

Sample, Michael. *Bison: Symbol of the American West*. Billings, MT: Falcon Press, 1987.

Sandweiss, Stephen. "The Social Construction of Environmental Justice." In *Environmental Injustices, Political Struggles: Race, Class, and the Environment*, edited by David E. Camacho. Durham, NC: Duke University Press, 1998.

Saunt, Claudio. *A New Order of Things: Property, Power, and the Transformation of the Creek Indians, 1733–1816*. New York: Cambridge University Press, 1999.

Schlosser, Eric. *Fast Food Nation: The Dark Side of the All-American Meal*. Boston: Houghton Mifflin, 2001.

Schnaiberg, Allan. *The Environment: From Surplus to Scarcity*. New York: Oxford University Press, 1980.

Schuyler, Michael W. *The Dread of Plenty: Agricultural Relief Activities of the Federal Government in the Middle West, 1933–1939*. Manhattan, KS: Sunflower University Press, 1989.

Sears, Paul B. *Deserts on the March*. 1935. Reprint, Washington, DC: Island Press, 1989.

Sellars, Richard West. *Preserving Nature in the National Parks: A History*. New Haven: Yale University Press, 1997.

Shogren, Jason F., ed. *Private Property and the Endangered Species Act: Saving Habitats, Protecting Homes*. Austin: University of Texas Press, 1999.

Sicherman, Barbara, ed. *Alice Hamilton: A Life in Letters*. Cambridge, MA: Harvard University Press, 1984. Reprint. Urbana: University of Illinois Press, 2003.

Simmons, Ian G. *Changing the Face of the Earth: Culture, Environment, History*. Oxford: Basil Blackwell, 1989.

Skaggs, Jimmy M. *Prime Cut: Livestock Raising and Meatpacking in the United States, 1607–1983*. College Station: Texas A & M University Press, 1986.

Smil, Vaclav. *Energy at the Crossroads: Global Perspectives and Uncertainties*. Cambridge, MA: MIT Press, 2003.

Smith, Duane A. *Mining America: The Industry and the Environment, 1800–1980*. 1987. Reprint, Boulder: University Press of Colorado, 1993.

Smits, David D. "The Frontier Army and the Destruction of the Buffalo, 1865–1883." *Western Historical Quarterly* 25 (Autumn 1994): 313–38.

Snyder, Lynn P. "The Death-Dealing Smog over Donora, Pennsylvania: Industrial Air Pollution, Public Health Policy and the Politics of Expertise, 1948–1949." *Environmental History Review* 15 (Spring 1994): 117–38.

Spence, Mark David. *Dispossessing the Wilderness: Indian Removal and the Making of the National Parks*. New York: Oxford University Press, 1999.

Starr, Kevin. *Rooted in Barbarous Soil: People, Culture, and Community in Gold Rush California*. San Francisco: California Historical Society, 2000.

Steen, Harold K. *The U.S. Forest Service: A History*. 1976. Centennial edition. Seattle: University of Washington Press, 2004.

Stegner, Wallace. *Beyond the Hundredth Meridian: John Wesley Powell and the Second Opening of the West*. 1954. Reprint, New York: Penguin Books, 1992.

Steinberg, Theodore. *Down to Earth: Nature's Role in American History*. New York: Oxford University Press, 2002.

———. *Nature Incorporated: Industrialization and the Waters of New England*. New York: Oxford University Press, 1994.

Steingraber, Sandra. *Living Downstream: A Scientist's Personal Investigation of Cancer and the Environment*. 1997. Reprint, New York: Vintage Books, 1998.

Sternglass, Ernest. *Secret Fallout: Low-Level Radiation from Hiroshima to Three Mile Island.* New York: McGraw Hill, 1981.

Stone, Christopher. "Should Trees Have Standing? Toward Legal Rights for Natural Objects," *Southern California Law Review* 45 (1972): 450–52.

Stradling, David, ed. *Conservation in the Progressive Era: Classic Texts.* Seattle: University of Washington Press, 2004.

———. *Smokestacks and Progressives: Environmentalists, Engineers, and Air Quality in America, 1881–1951.* Baltimore: Johns Hopkins University Press, 2003.

Svobida, Lawrence. *Farming the Dust Bowl: A First-Hand Account from Kansas.* 1941. Reprint, Lawrence: University Press of Kansas, 1986.

Szasz, Andrew. *Ecopopulism: Toxic Waste and the Movement for Environmental Justice.* Minneapolis: University of Minnesota Press, 1994.

Tarr, Joel, ed. *Devastation and Renewal: An Environmental History of Pittsburgh and Its Region.* Pittsburgh, PA: University of Pittsburgh Press, 2003.

———. *The Search for the Ultimate Sink: Urban Pollution in Historical Perspective.* Akron, OH: University of Akron Press, 1996.

Taylor, Alan. "Unnatural Inequalities: Social and Environmental Histories." *Environmental History* 1 (October 1996): 6–19.

———. " 'Wasty Ways': Stories of American Settlement." *Environmental History* 3 (July 1998): 219–310.

Taylor, Ray W. *Hetch Hetchy: The Story of San Francisco's Struggle to Provide a Water Supply for Her Future Needs.* San Francisco: R. J. Orozco, 1926.

Terrie, Philip G. *Contested Terrain: A New History of Nature and People in the Adirondacks.* Syracuse, NY: Syracuse University Press, 1999.

———. *Forever Wild: Environmental Aesthetics and the Adirondack Forest Preserve.* Fleischmanns, NY: Harbor Hill Books, 1985.

Thoreau, Henry David. *A Week on the Concord and Merrimack Rivers.* Edited by Carl F. Hovde, William L. Howarth, and Elizabeth Hall Witherell, with a new introduction by John McPhee. Princeton: Princeton University Press, 2004.

Tober, James A. *Who Owns the Wildlife? The Political Economy of Conservation in Nineteenth-Century America.* Westport, CT: Greenwood Press, 1981.

Tobin, Richard J. *The Expendable Future: U.S. Politics and the Protection of Biological Diversity.* Durham, NC: Duke University Press, 1990.

Trafzer, Clifford E. and Joel R. Hyer, eds. *"Exterminate Them": Written Accounts of the Murder, Rape, and Slavery of Native Americans during the California Gold Rush, 1848–1868.* East Lansing: Michigan State University Press, 1999.

Tucker, Richard P. *The United States and the Ecological Degradation of the Tropical World.* Berkeley: University of California Press, 2000.

Turner, Frederick W. *Beyond Geography: The Western Spirit against the Wilderness.* New York: Viking Press, 1980.

U. S. Public Health Service. *National Conference on Air Pollution, November 18–20, 1958.* Washington, DC: U.S. Government Printing Office, 1959.

Walker, Samuel J. *Three Mile Island: A Nuclear Crisis in Historical Perspective.* Berkeley: University of California Press, 2004.

Wallace, Anthony F. C. *Jefferson and the Indians: The Tragic Fate of the First Americans.* Cambridge, MA: Belknap Press, 2001.

Warren, Louis S. *The Hunter's Game: Poachers and Conservationists in Twentieth-Century America.* New Haven: Yale University Press, 1997.

Warrick, Richard A. "Drought in the U.S. Great Plains: Shifting Social Consequences?" In *Interpretations of Calamity*, edited by K. Hewitt. Boston: Allen and Unwin, 1983.

Watson, Harry L. " 'The Common Rights of Mankind': Subsistence, Shad, and Commerce in the Early Republican South." *Journal of American History* 83 (June 1996): 13–43.

Webb, Walter Prescott. *The Great Plains*. Boston: Ginn, 1931.

Weir, David, and Mark Shapiro. *Circle of Poison: Pesticides and People in a Hungry World*. Oakland, CA: Institute for Food and Development Policy, 1981.

West, Elliott. *The Way to the West: Essays on the Central Plains*. Albuquerque: University of New Mexico Press, 1995.

Wheeler, David L. "The Blizzard of 1886 and Its Effect on the Range Cattle Industry in the Southern Plains." *Southwestern Historical Quarterly* 94 (1990–1991): 415–32.

White, Richard. *"It's Your Misfortune and None of My Own": A New History of the American West*. Norman: University of Oklahoma Press, 1991.

———. *Land Use, Environment, and Social Change: The Shaping of Island County, Washington*. Seattle: University of Washington Press, 1980.

———. *The Middle Ground: Indians, Empires, and Republics in the Great Lakes Region: 1650–1815*. New York: Cambridge University Press, 1991.

———. *The Organic Machine: The Remaking of the Columbia River*. New York: Hill and Wang, 1995.

———. *The Roots of Dependency: Subsistence, Environment, and Social Change among the Choctaws, Pawnees, and Navajos*. Lincoln: University of Nebraska Press, 1983.

Whorton, James W. *Before Silent Spring: Pesticides and Public Health in pre-DDT America*. Princeton: Princeton University Press, 1974.

Whyte, William. *The Last Landscape*. Garden City, NY: Doubleday, 1968.

Wilcove, David S. *The Condor's Shadow: The Loss and Recovery of Wildlife in America*. New York: Freeman, 1999.

Williams, Michael. *Americans and their Forests: A Historical Geography*. New York: Cambridge University Press, 1992.

Wilson, Alexander. *The Culture of Nature: North American Landscape from Disney to the Exxon Valdez*. Cambridge, MA: Blackwell, 1992.

Wirth, John D. *Smelter Smoke in North America: The Politics of Transborder Pollution*. Lawrence: University Press of Kansas, 2000.

Wolfe, Linnie Marsh. *Son of the Wilderness: The Life of John Muir*. 1945. Reprint, Madison: University of Wisconsin Press, 1978.

Worster, Donald. *Dust Bowl: The Southern Plains in the 1930s*. 1982. Reprint, New York: Oxford University Press, 1997.

———. *Nature's Economy: A History of Ecological Ideas*. 1977. Reprint, New York: Cambridge University Press, 1990.

———. *A River Running West: The Life of John Wesley Powell*. New York: Oxford University Press, 2002.

———. *Rivers of Empire: Water, Aridity, and the Growth of the American West*. New York: Oxford University Press, 1992.

———. "A Tapestry of Change: Nature and Culture on the Prairie." In *The Inhabited Prairie*. Photographed and compiled by Terry Evans. Lawrence: University Press of Kansas, 1998.

———. "Transformations of the Earth: Toward an Agroecological Perspective in History." *Journal of American History* 76 (March 1990): 1087–1106.

———, ed. *The Ends of the Earth: Perspectives on Modern Environmental History*. New York: Cambridge University Press, 1989.

Yaffee, Steven Lewis. *Prohibitive Policy: Implementing the Federal Endangered Species Act*. Cambridge, MA: MIT Press, 1982.

Young, Angela Nugent. "Interpreting the Dangerous Trades: Workers' Health in America and the Career of Alice Hamilton, 1910–1935." Ph.D. diss., Brown University, 1982.

Index

About the Author

CHRIS J. MAGOC is Associate Professor of History at Mercyhurst College. From his childhood in Tarentum, PA, to his work in the 1980s with conservation organizations in the West, to his current leadership of the Mercyhurst College "Green Team," Magoc has had a life-long passion for environmental issues. He is the author of *Yellowstone: The Creation and Selling of An American Landscape, 1870–1903* and *So Glorious a Landscape: Nature and the Environment in American History and Culture.*